Air Fryer Cookbook for Beginners 2020

800 Most Wanted, Easy and Healthy Recipes to Fry, Bake, Grill & Roast

By Andrea Leonard

Copyright ©2019 By Andrea Leonard

All rights reserved.

No part of this guide may be reproduced in any form without permission in writing from the publisher except in the case of brief quotations embodied in critical articles or reviews.

Legal & Disclaimer

The information contained in this book and its contents is not designed to replace or take the place of any form of medical or professional advice; and is not meant to replace the need for independent medical, financial, legal or other professional advice or services, as may be required. The content and information in this book has been provided for educational and entertainment purposes only.

The content and information contained in this book has been compiled from sources deemed reliable, and it is accurate to the best of the Author's knowledge, information and belief. However, the Author cannot guarantee its accuracy and validity and cannot be held liable for any errors and/or omissions. Further, changes are periodically made to this book as and when needed. Where appropriate and/or necessary, you must consult a professional (including but not limited to your doctor, attorney, financial advisor or such other professional advisor) before using any of the suggested remedies, techniques, or information in this book.

Table of Content

Air Fryer Basics 1
   What is an Air Fryer? 1
   Using Your Air Fryer 1
   Tips for Using an Air Fryer 2
   Cleaning Your Air Fryer 2
   Cooking Keto with an Air Fryer 2

Breakfast 3
   Mushroom Spinach Fritatta 3
   Veggie Omelet 3
   Three Cheese Omelet 4
   Bacon and Cheese Fritatta 4
   Hard Boiled Eggs 4
   Spinach Parmesan Baked Eggs 5
   Avocado Baked Eggs 5
   Easy Baked Eggs 5
   Bacon and Eggs for One 6
   Keto Chocolate Chip Muffins 6
   Keto Blueberry Muffins 6
   Raspberry Muffins 7
   Strawberry Muffins 7
   Sausage and Cheese Omelet 7
   Sausage and Spinach Omelet 8
   Meat Lovers Omelet 8
   Bacon and Brie Frittata 9
   Bacon and Kale Fritatta 9
   Zucchini and Sausage Bake 9
   Cheesy Zucchini Bake 10
   Zucchini and Bacon Egg Bread 10
   Veggie Egg Bread 11
   Almond Flour Pancake 11
   Raspberry Almond Pancake 11
   Blueberry Pancake 12
   Strawberry Pancake 12
   Chocolate Pancake 13
   Cinnamon Almond Pancake 13
   Pumpkin Pancake 13
   Coconut Pancake 14
   Coconut Rum Pancake 14
   Coconut Chocolate Pancake 15
   Curried Omelet 15
   French Herb Omelet 15

   Indian Masala Omelet 16
   Za'atar Eggs 16
   Spicy Cheesy Omelet 17
   Pesto Omelet 17
   Gremolata Eggs 17
   Roasted Garlic Eggs 18
   Prosciutto Omelet 18
   Prosciutto Parmesan Omelet 19
   Kimchi Breakfast 19
   Chocolate Muffins 19
   Mocha Muffins 20
   Espresso Muffins 20
   Cheddar Jalapeno Muffins 20
   Nutty Granola 21
   Fruit and Nut Keto Granola 21
   Strawberry and Nut Cereal 21
   Seedy Breakfast Granola 22
   Pepper Stuffed Spinach Parmesan Baked Eggs .. 22
   Pepper Stuffed Spinach and Feta Eggs 23
   Egg Stuffed Peppers and Cheese 23
   Bacon and Egg Stuffed Peppers 23
   Peppers and Eggs 24
   Pepper Stuffed Spinach Parmesan Baked Eggs .. 24
   Brussels Hash 24
   Zucchini Hash 25
   Vegetable Hash 25
   Ham, Cheese and Mushroom Melt 25
   Ham and Pepper Melt 26
   Veggie Melt 26
   Blueberry Breakfast Cake 26
   Red Pepper Breakfast Cake 27
   Zucchini Breakfast Cake 27
   Strawberry Breakfast Bread 27
   Raspberry Breakfast Cake 28
   Cheesy Bacon Pancake 28
   Cheesy Pancake 29
   Strawberry Feta Pancake 29
   Pepper Pancake 29
   Sausage Omelette 30
   Ham and Cheese Omelet 30

Snacks 31

Turkey Pepper Nachos	31
Spicy Hot Pepper Nachos	31
Veggie Pepper Nachos	31
Chicken Pepper Nachos	32
Cranberry Dark Chocolate Granola Bars	32
Double Dark Chocolate Granola Bars	33
Blueberry Dark Chocolate Granola Bars	33
Coconut Dark Chocolate Granola Bars	34
Seedy Chocolate Granola Bars	34
Nut and Dark Chocolate Granola Bars	35
Chicharrones	35
Spicy Chicharrones	35
Herbed Chicharrones	36
Cocoa Chicharrones	36
Cheesy Chicharrones	36
Cajun Chicharrones	37
Cheesy Garlic Bread Muffins	37
Parmesan Garlic Bread Muffins	38
Spicy Garlic Bread Muffins	38
Herby Cheesy Muffins	38
Beef Muffins Snack	39
Bacon Muffin Bites	39
Smoky Muffins	40
BBQ Muffin Snack	40
Brussel Sprout Chips	41
Cayenne Brussels Sprout Chips	41
Black Pepper Brussels Sprout Chips	41
Asian Style Brussel Sprout Chips	42
Balsamic Brussel Sprout Chips	42
Bacon Brussel Sprout Chips	42
Maple Brussel Sprout Chips	43
Garlic Brussel Sprout Chips	43
Herbed Parmesan Crackers	43
Super Seed Parmesan Crackers	44
Cheddar Crackers	44
Chipotle Cheddar Crackers	45
Pizza Crackers	45
Bacon Cheddar Crackers	46
Black Pepper Parmesan Crackers	46
Cauliflower Crunch	47
Spicy Cauliflower Crunch	47
Broccoli Crunch	47
Red Hot Broccoli Crunch	48
Lemon Pepper Broccoli Crunch	48
Sweet Broccoli Crunch	48
Maple Broccoli Crunch	49
Veggie Crunch	49
Chili Lime Broccoli Crunch	50
Zucchini Chips	50
Cayenne Zucchini Chips	50
Salt and Vinegar Zucchini Chips	51
Smoked Zucchini Chips	51
Yellow Zucchini Chips	51
Cajun Cauliflower Crunch	51
Soft Pretzels	52
Soft Garlic Parmesan Pretzels	52
Soft Cinnamon Pretzels	53
Soft Pecan Pretzels	53
Soft Cheesy Pretzels	54
Sweet Zucchini Chips	54
Cucumber Chips	54
Dill and Onion Cucumber Chips	55
Smokey Cucumber Chips	55
Garlic Parmesan Cucumber Chips	55
Sea Salt and Black Pepper Cucumber Chips	56
Taco Cucumber Chips	56
Dilly Almonds	56
Garlic Almonds	57
Sweet and Salty Almonds	57
Cayenne Almonds	57
Black Pepper Almonds	58
Sweet Candied Pecans	58
Garlicky Cauliflower Crunch	58
Desserts	**59**
Peanut Butter Cookies	59
Peanut Butter Chocolate Chip Cookies	59
Peanut Butter Flaxseed Cookies	59
Peanut Butter and Jelly Cookies	60
Chocolate Walnuts	60
Spicy Chocolate Walnuts	60
Mexican Chocolate Walnuts	61
Chocolate Almonds	61
Sweet and Spicy Walnuts	62
Chocolate Peanut Butter Walnuts	62
Vanilla Cake	63
Vanilla Raspberry Cake	63
Blueberry Cake	64
Cinnamon Cake	64
Spice Cake	65
Caramel Cake	65
Chocolate Chip Cake	66
Strawberry Vanilla Cake	66

Espresso Cake	67
Almond Cake	67
Chocolate Cake	68
Peanut Butter Cake	68
Hazelnut Cake	69
Walnut Cake	69
NY Keto Cheesecake	70
Strawberry Cheesecake	70
Blueberry Cheesecake	71
Raspberry Cheesecake	71
Cinnamon Cheesecake	72
Chocolate Keto Cheesecake	72
Chocolate Chip Cheesecake	73
Pumpkin Spice Cheesecake	73
Lemon Cheesecake	74
Gingerbread Cheesecake	74
Mascarpone Cheesecake	75
Coconut Cheesecake	75
Fudge Brownies	76
Double Chocolate Brownies	76
Chocolate Walnuts Brownies	77
Peanut Butter Brownies	77
Almond Brownies	77
Chocolate Coconut Brownies	78
Chocolate Mint Brownies	78
Hazelnut Brownies	79
Espresso Brownies	79
Caramel Fudge Brownies	79
Raspberry Brownies	80
Strawberry Fudge Brownies	80
Cheesecake Fudge Brownies	81
Chocolate Chip Cookies	81
Butter Cookies	82
Walnut Cookies	82
Coconut Cookies	82
Almond Cookies	83
Chocolate Chip Almond Cookies	83
Peanut Butter Cookies	84
Peanut Butter Chocolate Chip Cookies	84
Hazelnut Cookies	85
Hazelnut Chocolate Chip Cookies	85
Seedy Cookies	85
Raspberry Cookies	86
Cocoa Cookies	86
Double Chocolate Cookies	87
Peanut Butter Chocolate Cookies	87
Cinnamon Chocolate Chip Cookies	88
Pumpkin Spice Cookies	88
Pumpkin Chocolate Chip Cookies	88
Cream Cheese Cookies	89
Keto Shortbread	89
Lemon Shortbread	90
Almond Shortbread	90
Lime Shortbread	90
Chocolate Shortbread	91
Chocolate Chip Shortbread	91
Peanut Butter Shortbread	92
Walnut Shortbread	92
Coconut Shortbread	92
Fish and Seafood	**93**
Crispy Salmon	93
Spicy Crunchy Salmon	93
Crunchy Garlic Salmon	93
Cajun Salmon	94
Black Pepper Parmesan Salmon	94
Spicy Crunchy Garlic Salmon	94
Asian Style Crunchy Salmon	95
Tuna Stuffed Mushrooms	95
Crispy Flounder	96
Tuna Cakes	96
Salmon Cakes	96
Red Hot Tuna Cakes	97
Cajun Tuna Cakes	97
Lemon Tuna Cakes	98
Cod Fish Sticks	98
Tuna Sticks	98
Maple Walnut Salmon	99
Almond Crusted Salmon	99
Maple Walnut Flounder	100
Sesame Walnut Tuna	100
Spicy Cod Fish Sticks	100
Italian Fish Sticks	101
Lemon Pepper Fish Sticks	101
Salmon Fish Sticks	102
Cajun Salmon Fish Sticks	102
Bacon Wrapped Fish Sticks	102
Keto Tuna Melt Cups	103
Garlic Shrimp Bacon Bake	103
Gruyere Shrimp Bacon Bake	104
Cajun Shrimp Bacon Bake	104
Garlic Shrimp Prosciutto Bake	104
Garlic Shrimp Tuna Bake	105

Jalapeno Tuna Melt Cups	105
Herbed Tuna Melt Cups	105
Cajun Tuna Melt Cups	106
Cheddar Tuna Melt Cups	106
Sesame Tuna Melt Cups	106
Asian Style Crunchy Flounder	107
Prosciutto Wrapped Cod	107
Prosciutto Wrapped Salmon	108
Fast Seared Scallops	108
Lemon Scallops	108
Dijon Baked Salmon	109
Garlic Dijon Baked Salmon	109
Maple Dijon Baked Salmon	109
Creamy Baked Scallops	110
Cajun Seared Scallops	110
Crispy Scallops	110
Bacon Scallops	110
Scallops and Spinach	111
Salmon and Asparagus	111
Cod and Asparagus	111
Parmesan Salmon and Asparagus	112
Parmesan Flounder and Asparagus	112
Crispy Shrimp	112
Parmesan Salmon and Brussel Sprouts	113
Parmesan Tuna and Brussel Sprouts	113
Lemon Dill Wrapped Cod	113
Mediterranean Salmon	114
Lemon Dill Parchment Salmon	114
Mediterranean Flounder	115
Tomato Parchment Cod	115
Italian Style Flounder	115
Lemon Parchment Salmon	116
Prosciutto Wrapped Ahi Ahi	116
Prosciutto Wrapped Tuna Bites	116
Crab Stuffed Mushrooms	117
Bacon and Crab Stuffed Mushrooms	117
Crab and Spinach Mushrooms	117
Garlicy and Crab Stuffed Mushrooms	118
Black Pepper Flounder	118
Parmesan Butter Flounder	119
Herbed Butter Flounder	119
Garlic Butter Shrimp	119
Cajun Butter Shrimp	120
Parmesan Shrimp	120
Salmon Egg Salad	120
Poultry	**121**
Keto Fried Chicken	121
Buffalo Chicken Pizza	121
Spicy Fried Chicken	122
Dijon Baked Chicken Breast	122
Maple Dijon Baked Chicken Breast	122
Sweet and Spicy Dijon Baked Chicken Breast	123
Herbed Fried Chicken	123
BBQ Fried Chicken	123
Chicken Nuggets	124
Greek Garlic Chicken	124
Creamy Garlic Chicken Thighs	125
Lemon Garlic Chicken Thighs	125
Brussels and Garlic Chicken	125
Creamy Brussels and Garlic Chicken	126
Bacon Chicken Thighs	126
Maple Chicken Thighs with Brussels	127
Maple Bacon Chicken Thighs	127
Lemon Feta Garlic Chicken	128
Garlic Parmesan Chicken Thighs	128
Black Pepper Chicken Thighs	128
Garlic Chicken and Spinach	129
Rotisserie Style Chicken Thighs	129
Spicy Chicken Nuggets	130
Italian Seasoned Chicken Nuggets	130
Sweet and Spicy Chicken Nuggets	130
Creamy Tuscan Chicken	131
Creamy Tomato Chicken	131
Marinara Chicken	132
Creamy Tomato Turkey	132
Creamy Tomato Chicken	132
Creamy Garlic Ground Chicken	133
Creamy Garlic Ground Turkey	133
Creamy Olive Chicken	134
Cream Cheese and Spinach Stuffed Chicken	134
Cream Cheese and Kale Stuffed Chicken	135
Cream Cheese and Asparagus Stuffed Chicken	135
Buffalo Fried Chicken	136
Chicken Melt Cups	136
Spicy Chicken Melt Cups	136
Jalapeno Chicken Melt Cups	137
Cheddar Chicken Melt Cups	137
BBQ Chicken Melt Cups	138
Teriyaki Chicken Melt Cups	138
Buffalo Chicken Melt Cups	138
Chicken Patties	139
BBQ Chicken Patties	139

Lemon Pepper Chicken Patties.......................... 140
Garlic Chicken Patties............................140
Prosciutto Wrapped Chicken.......................... 140
Pepper and Prosciutto Chicken.......................... 141
Roasted Chicken Thighs.......................... 141
Dijon Roasted Chicken Thighs.......................... 142
Cajun Roasted Chicken Thighs..........................142
Lemon Roasted Chicken Thighs.......................... 142
Roasted Chicken Thighs and Brussels.............. 143
Maple Roasted Chicken Thighs........................ 143
Prosciutto and Lemon Chicken........................ 144
Blackened Chicken Patties............................. 144
Garlic Chicken Bacon Bake............................ 144
Garlic Chicken Bake.................................. 145
Spicy Chicken Bacon Bake............................. 145
Chicken Zucchini Boats............................... 145
Chicken Stuffed Mushrooms........................... 146
Bacon Chicken Stuffed Mushrooms................. 146
Turkey Stuffed Mushrooms............................ 147
Turkey Garlic Mushrooms............................. 147
Mediterranean Chicken................................ 147
Lemon Parchment Chicken............................ 148
Maple Walnut Chicken Breast........................ 148
Maple Sesame Chicken Breast........................149
Maple Walnut Chicken Breast with Spinach.... 149
Tomato Parchment Chicken........................... 149
Fajita Chicken... 150
Sweet and Salty Chicken...............................150
Chicken and Egg Salad................................. 151
Pesto Fried Chicken.................................... 151

Vegan and Vegetarian..152
Egg Salad...152
Cream of Asparagus Soup..............................152
Roasted Mushrooms and Grits........................152
Roasted Pepper Grits................................... 153
Loaded Baked Zucchini................................ 153
Butternut Squash Soup................................. 154
Spinach and Artichoke Casserole.................... 154
Spinach Parmesan Egg Casserole.................... 154
Garlic, Spinach and Artichoke Casserole......... 155
Spinach and Sundried Tomato Casserole......... 155
Brussels Sprout Casserole............................. 156
Asparagus and Tomato Casserole.................... 156
Asparagus Egg White Casserole..................... 156
Cheesy Egg Casserole.................................. 157
Broccoli Cheese Soup.................................. 157

Pepper Stuffed Mushrooms...............................158
Spinach Stuffed Mushrooms..............................158
Cauliflower Soup... 158
Roasted Veggie Soup.. 159
Loaded Veggie Pizza...159
Strawberry Arugula Pizza................................. 160
Green Power Soup..160
Pumpkin Soup... 160
Broccoli Cheese Fritters....................................161
Carrot Cheese Fritters...................................... 161
Broccoli and Mushroom Fritters.......................162
Broccoli Parmesan Fritters................................162
Spicy Broccoli Cheese Fritters..........................162
Broccoli Red Pepper Fritters.............................163
Veggie Baked Zucchini Boats........................... 163
Warmed Nuts and Grits....................................164
Keto Pizza.. 164
Extra Cheese Pizza...165
Roasted Squash Grits....................................... 165
Broccoli and Grits.. 165
Mug Lasagna... 166
Mushroom Lunch Lasagna................................166
Eggplant Caprese Rollups.................................167
Eggplant Parmesan Rollups.............................. 167
Eggplant Zucchini Rollups................................167
Zucchini Caprese Rollups................................. 168
Spicy Eggplant Rollups.................................... 168
Eggplant Tahini Rollups................................... 168
Lemon Eggplant Rollups.................................. 169
Tomato Lasagna.. 169
Spicy Egg Salad... 169
Roasted Brussels Sprout Salad..........................170
Spicy Pepper Lasagna...................................... 170
Onion Lasagna.. 170
Cheesey Stromboli... 171
Maple Brussels Sprout Salad............................ 171
Avocado Egg Salad.. 171
Deviled Egg Salad..172
Spicy Sriracha Egg Salad..................................172
Cheesy Brussels Sprout Salad...........................172
Roasted Broccoli Salad.................................... 173
Asian Broccoli Salad.. 173
Fall Broccoli Salad... 173

Beef, Lamb and Pork.. 174
Cheesy Italian Meatloaf................................... 174
Pepper and Cheese Meatloaf.............................174

Garlic Meatloaf 175	Brussels, Tomatoes and Pork Chops 188
Asian Style Meatloaf 175	Veggies Roasted Pork Chops 188
Classic Meatballs 175	Dijon Roasted Pork Chops 189
Asian Style Meatballs 176	Maple Roasted Pork Chops and Veggies 189
Bacon Wrapped Meatballs 176	Brussels and Roasted Pork Chops 189
Spicy Meatballs 176	Sweet Veggies Roasted Pork Chops 190
Egg Cobb Salad 177	Spinach and Bacon Casserole 190
Beef Stuffed Mushrooms 177	Asparagus and Bacon Casserole 191
Mexican Stuffed Mushrooms 177	Spinach and Maple Bacon Casserole 191
Bacon Stuffed Mushrooms 178	Bacon and Cheese Casserole 191
Bacon and Mushroom Baked Zucchini 178	Bacon Veggie Casserole 192
Bacon Pizza 179	Broccoli and Bacon Fritters 192
Bacon and Cheese Egg Salad 179	Cauliflower and Bacon Fritters 193
Bacon and Mushroom Baked Zucchini 179	Mushroom and Bacon Fritters 193
Prosciutto and Parmesan Pizza 180	Cheesy Bacon Fritters 193
BBQ Pork Pizza 180	Eggplant Bacon Caprese Rollups 194
Bacon Lasagna 181	Cheesy Bacon Rollups 194
Italian Lunch Lasagna 181	Zucchini Bacon Rollups 195
Bacon and Cheese Stromboli 181	Eggplant Bacon Hummus Rollups 195
Pepperoni Mozzarella Stromboli 182	Red Pepper Meatballs 195
Ham and Cheese Stromboli 182	Spicy Meatballs 196
Dijon Baked Pork Chops 183	Extra Juicy Meatballs 196
Maple Dijon Baked Pork Chops 183	Lamb Meatballs 196
Sweet and Spicy Dijon Baked Pork Chops 183	Indian Style Lamb Meatballs 197
Creamy Tuscan Pork Chops 184	Baharat Lamb Meatballs 197
Greek Garlic Pork Chops 184	Curried Lamb Meatballs 197
Lemon Garlic Pork Chops 185	Lemon Garlic Lamb Chops 197
Creamy Garlic Pork Chops 185	Minty Lamb Chops 198
Lemon Pepper Pork Chops 186	Curry Brussels and Lamb Chops 198
Brussels and Pork Chops 186	**Appendix 1: 28 Days Keto Meal Plan with Air Fryer 199**
Maple Brussels and Pork Chops 187	
Bacon Brussels and Pork Chops 187	**Appendix 2: Recipes Index 201**

Air Fryer Basics

The air fryer is a fairly new household kitchen appliance that may have you pretty excited regarding the possibilities of the machine. You should be excited! The air fryer can do some amazing things! It really is an appliance that you want to keep on your counter year-round- it will get a lot of use! So, what exactly is an air fryer and how does it work? Let's take a look!

What is an Air Fryer?

An air fryer is a small kitchen appliance that imitates the results of deep-frying foods without all the extra grease. Rather than submerge food in oil in order to fry it, the food is placed inside the air fryer along with a very small amount of oil. The food is then "fried" using only hot air.

When turned, the appliance heats up to a high temperature, like an oven. Fans inside the oven circulate the hot air and push it around the food you are cooking. Food is cooked quickly thanks to the high heat and, due to the small amount of oil on the outside of the food, the exterior will be crispy, as if it were fried!

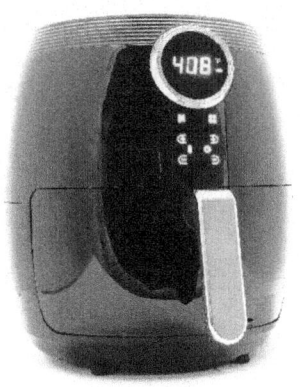

Using Your Air Fryer

Every air fryer on the market will work a little differently, however, the general idea for every machine is the same. To begin, you will need to plug the air fryer in and then turn the dial (or use the buttons) to set the temperature.

The air fryer will need to heat up just like any oven or fryer which may take a few minutes. Most air fryers have a digital display that will let you know when the appliance is ready.

The food that you are cooking is then loaded into the fryer basket and inserted back into the air fryer.

The food is cooked for the appropriate amount of time, according to your recipe, and then enjoyed- simple as that!

Your air fryer may come with various accessories that you can use such as a grill rack, a muffin tin or even finer, mesh baskets for cooking small food. However, the general idea is the same no matter what you are making- turn the machine on, let it heat, add the food and cook!

Tips for Using an Air Fryer

As with any kitchen appliance, there are a few tips and tricks that you can use to get the most out of your air fryer. Read over these little techniques that will improve your air frying abilities.

1. Shake the basket- Just as if you were deep frying food, it can help to remove the basket from the air fryer about half-way through the cooking process and give it a little shake. This will help cook the food more evenly and ensure that you get that all-around crispy food you are craving.
2. Use a healthy oil- Adding oil to the food you will be cooking is the only way to get the crispy outside that you want. Choose a keto-friendly oil like avocado oil, olive oil or coconut oil. If you are baking in the air fryer, you can skip the oil exterior but the recipes should guide you on what to do!
3. Don't add too much food- You want to avoid overcrowding the basket of the air fryer to help foods cook evenly and thoroughly. The air fryer relies on air circulating correctly and this requires space. Cook your food in batches, if needed, rather than packing it into the air fryer.
4. Don't just fry!- The air fryer has many uses, not just creating crispy, fried foods. Luckily, this cookbook is full of ideas and recipes that you can make in the air fryer that utilize the machine in different ways.

The more you use your air fryer, the more comfortable you will become with the appliance. It is not a hard kitchen tool to master and, after one or two recipes, you are sure to have a good grasp on the quirks and variances of the machine.

Cleaning Your Air Fryer

One of the hardest things about cooking at home is cleaning up afterward! However, the air fryer is quite easy to clean. Follow these easy steps to clean your air fryer after every use. The more frequently you clean it, the better it will work and the newer it will look!

1. Allow the air fryer to cool down and then unplug it from the wall.
2. To clean the outside of the machine, simply wipe the air fryer down with a damp sponge or towel and then let it air dry or dry it off with a new, clean towel.
3. Wash the pan or basket of the air fryer by hand, using a gentle dish soap or detergent. Many air fryer components (including most baskets and racks) are dishwasher safe. Check your brand of air fryer and see if your accessories can be placed directly in the air fryer. This makes clean up even easier!
4. Wipe the inside of the air fryer with hot water and a clean sponge. Get any small food particles out of the machine that may have blown around during the cooking process. Remember to wipe off the heating element on the top of the machine, above where the basket is inserted.
5. Make sure the appliance is completely dry before plugging it back in. It is now ready to use once again!

Cooking Keto with an Air Fryer

Thanks to the many abilities that the air fryer has, you can cook practically anything inside the machine. That includes delicious keto-friendly foods! It really is the only appliance that you need to begin on your keto cooking journey. Using the air fryer, you will be able to make keto breakfast, keto lunches, keto snacks and also keto dinners. You will cook everything from low carb muffins to perfect omelets. It really is amazing!

You are likely very ready to start making some tasty keto dishes using your new favorite kitchen appliance. So, why wait any longer! Time to start cooking! Open up this keto air fryer cookbook and get ready to be amazed. Happy cooking!

Breakfast

Mushroom Spinach Fritatta

Prep time: 10 minutes , Cook time:15 minutes , Serves 2

Ingredients:
4 eggs
3 Tbsp heavy whipping cream
¼ cup cheddar cheese, grated
1 cup sliced mushrooms
1 cup baby spinach
½ tsp salt
¼ tsp ground black pepper

Instructions
1. Preheat your air fryer to 350 degrees F and line a baking pan with parchment paper. Be sure the pan will fit in your air fryer- typically a seven inch round pan will work perfectly.
2. In a small bowl, whisk together the eggs, cream, salt and pepper
3. Stir in the mushrooms, cheese and spinach to the bowl.
4. Pour the mix into the prepared baking pan and then place the pan in your preheated air fryer.
5. Cook for about 15 minutes or until the eggs are completely set.
6. Slice into wedges and serve while hot.

Nutrition Facts Per Serving
Calories 147, Total Fat 11g, Saturated Fat 6g, Total Carbs 3g, Net Carbs 2g, Protein 9g, Sugar 1g, Fiber 1g, Sodium 133mg, Potassium 237g

Veggie Omelet

Prep time: 10 minutes , Cook time:15 minutes , Serves 2

Ingredients:
4 eggs
3 Tbsp heavy whipping cream
½ cup cheddar cheese, grated
¼ cup sliced mushrooms
½ cup baby spinach
¼ cup diced tomato
½ tsp salt
¼ tsp ground black pepper

Instructions
1. Preheat your air fryer to 350 degrees F and line a baking pan with parchment paper. Be sure the pan will fit in your air fryer- typically a seven inch round pan will work perfectly.
2. In a small bowl, whisk together the eggs, cream, salt and pepper
3. Stir in the mushrooms, spinach and tomato to the bowl.
4. Pour the mix into the prepared baking pan and then place the pan in your preheated air fryer.
5. Cook for about 15 minutes or until the eggs are completely set.
6. Sprinkle the cheese over half of the omelet then fold the omelet in half, over the cheese. Let sit for 5 minutes to allow the cheese time to melt.
7. Slice into wedges and serve while hot.

Nutrition Facts Per Serving
Calories 153, Total Fat 14g, Saturated Fat 7g, Total Carbs 2g, Net Carbs 1g, Protein 10g, Sugar 1g, Fiber 1g, Sodium 133mg, Potassium 147g

Three Cheese Omelet

Prep time: 5 minutes , Cook time: 11 minutes , Serves 4

Ingredients:
4 eggs
3 Tbsp heavy whipping cream
¼ cup cheddar cheese, grated
¼ cup feta cheese
¼ cup provolone cheese
½ tsp salt
¼ tsp ground black pepper

Instructions
1. Preheat your air fryer to 350 degrees F and line a baking pan with parchment paper. Be sure the pan will fit in your air fryer- typically a seven inch round pan will work perfectly.
2. In a small bowl, whisk together the eggs, cream, salt and pepper
3. Pour the mix into the prepared baking pan and then place the pan in your preheated air fryer.
4. Cook for about 10 minutes or until the eggs are completely set.
5. Sprinkle the cheeses across the cooked eggs and return the pan to the air fryer for another minute to melt the cheese.
6. Fold the omelet in half.
7. Slice into wedges and serve while hot.

Nutrition Facts Per Serving
Calories 189, Total Fat 16g, Saturated Fat 8g, Total Carbs 3g, Net Carbs 2g, Protein 7g, Sugar 1g, Fiber 1g, Sodium 133mg, Potassium 65g

Bacon and Cheese Fritatta

Prep time: 10 minutes , Cook time: 10 minutes , Serves 2

Ingredients:
4 eggs
3 Tbsp heavy whipping cream
½ cup chopped, cooked bacon
½ cup cheddar cheese, grated
½ tsp salt
¼ tsp ground black pepper

Instructions
1. Preheat your air fryer to 350 degrees F and line a baking pan with parchment paper. Be sure the pan will fit in your air fryer- typically a seven inch round pan will work perfectly.
2. In a small bowl, whisk together the eggs, cream, salt and pepper
3. Stir in the bacon and cheese to the bowl.
4. Pour the mix into the prepared baking pan and then place the pan in your preheated air fryer.
5. Cook for about 15 minutes or until the eggs are completely set.
6. Slice into wedges and serve while hot.

Nutrition Facts Per Serving
Calories 284, Total Fat 18g, Saturated Fat 8g, Total Carbs 2g, Net Carbs 1g, Protein 13g, Sugar 1g, Fiber 1g, Sodium 368mg, Potassium 54g

Hard Boiled Eggs

Prep time: 1 minutes , Cook time: 16 minutes , Serves 2

Ingredients:
4 eggs

Instructions
1. Preheat your air fryer to 250 degrees F.
2. Place a wire rack in the air fryer and place the eggs on top of the rack.
3. Cook for 16 minutes then remove the eggs and place them directly into an ice water bath to cool and stop the cooking process.
4. Peel the eggs and enjoy!

Nutrition Facts Per Serving
Calories 125, Total Fat 8g, Saturated Fat 2g, Total Carbs 1g, Net Carbs 1g, Protein 12g, Sugar 0g, Fiber 0g, Sodium 124mg, Potassium 138g

Spinach Parmesan Baked Eggs

Prep time: 5 minutes , Cook time: 7 minutes , Serves 1

Ingredients:
2 eggs
1 Tbsp heavy cream
1 Tbsp frozen, chopped spinach, thawed
1 Tbsp grated parmesan cheese
¼ tsp salt
1/8 tsp ground black pepper

Instructions
1. Preheat your air fryer to 330 degrees F.
2. Spray a silicone muffin cup or a small ramekin with cooking spray.
3. In a small bowl, whisk together all the ingredients
4. Pour the eggs into the prepared ramekin and bake for 7 minutes.
5. Enjoy straight out of the baking cup!

Nutrition Facts Per Serving
Calories 162, Total Fat 11g, Saturated Fat 4g, Total Carbs 3g, Net Carbs 3g, Protein 14g, Sugar 1g, Fiber 1g, Sodium 134mg, Potassium 148g

Avocado Baked Eggs

Prep time: 5 minutes , Cook time: 7 minutes , Serves 1

Ingredients:
2 eggs
1 Tbsp heavy cream
¼ avocado, diced
1 Tbsp grated cheddar cheese
¼ tsp salt
1/8 tsp ground black pepper

Instructions
1. Preheat your air fryer to 330 degrees F.
2. Spray a silicone muffin cup or a small ramekin with cooking spray.
3. In a small bowl, whisk together the eggs, cream, cheddar cheese, salt, pepper.
4. Stir in the avocado.
5. Pour the eggs into the prepared ramekin and bake for 7 minutes.
6. Enjoy straight out of the baking cup!

Nutrition Facts Per Serving
Calories 199, Total Fat 14g, Saturated Fat 7g, Total Carbs 4g, Net Carbs 3g, Protein 14g, Sugar 1g, Fiber 1g, Sodium 168mg, Potassium 192g

Easy Baked Eggs

Prep time: 5 minutes , Cook time: 6 minutes , Serves 1

Ingredients:
2 eggs
1 Tbsp heavy cream
¼ tsp salt
1/8 tsp ground black pepper

Instructions
1. Preheat your air fryer to 330 degrees F.
2. Spray a silicone muffin cup or a small ramekin with cooking spray.
3. In a small bowl, whisk together all the ingredients
4. Pour the eggs into the prepared ramekin and bake for 6 minutes.
5. Enjoy straight out of the baking cup!

Nutrition Facts Per Serving
Calories 142, Total Fat 10g, Saturated Fat 3g, Total Carbs 2g, Net Carbs 2g, Protein 13g, Sugar 0g, Fiber 0g, Sodium 135mg, Potassium 143g

Bacon and Eggs for One

Prep time: 5 minutes , Cook time: 8 minutes , Serves 1

Ingredients:
2 eggs
1 Tbsp heavy cream
2 Tbsp cooked, crumbled bacon
¼ tsp salt
1/8 tsp ground black pepper

Instructions
1. Preheat your air fryer to 330 degrees F.
2. Spray a silicone muffin cup or a small ramekin with cooking spray.
3. In a small bowl, whisk together all the ingredients
4. Pour the eggs into the prepared ramekin and bake for 8 minutes.
5. Enjoy straight out of the baking cup!

Nutrition Facts Per Serving
Calories 192, Total Fat 15g, Saturated Fat 8g, Total Carbs 4g, Net Carbs 3g, Protein 14g, Sugar 2g, Fiber 1g, Sodium 215mg, Potassium 156g

Keto Chocolate Chip Muffins

Prep time: 10 minutes , Cook time: 14 minutes , Serves 12

Ingredients:
1 cup almond flour
1 Tbsp powdered stevia
¼ cup whole milk
1 egg
¼ tsp salt
1 ½ tsp baking powder
½ cup mini dark chocolate chips (sugar free)

Instructions
1. Preheat your air fryer to 350 degrees F.
2. Spray 12 silicone muffin cups lightly with cooking spray.
3. In a large bowl, stir together the almond flour, stevia, salt, cinnamon, and baking powder.
4. Add the eggs and milk and stir well.
5. Fold in the chocolate chips
6. Divide the muffin batter between each muffin cup, filling about ¾ of the way full.
7. Place the muffins into the air fryer basket and cook for 14 minutes or until a toothpick comes out cleanly when inserted into the center.
8. Remove from the air fryer and let cool.
9. Serve and enjoy!

Nutrition Facts Per Serving
Calories 45, Total Fat 4g, Saturated Fat 1g, Total Carbs 2g, Net Carbs 1g, Protein 2g, Sugar 0g, Fiber 1g, Sodium 39mg, Potassium 68g

Keto Blueberry Muffins

Prep time: 10 minutes , Cook time: 14 minutes , Serves 12

Ingredients:
1 cup almond flour
1 Tbsp powdered stevia
¼ cup whole milk
1 egg
¼ tsp salt
¼ tsp ground cinnamon
1 ½ tsp baking powder
½ cup frozen or fresh blueberries

Instructions
1. Preheat your air fryer to 350 degrees F.
2. Spray 12 silicone muffin cups lightly with cooking spray.
3. In a large bowl, stir together the almond flour, stevia, salt, cinnamon, and baking powder.
4. Add the eggs and milk and stir well.
5. Fold in the blueberries.
6. Divide the muffin batter between each muffin cup, filling about ¾ of the way full.
7. Place the muffins into the air fryer basket and cook for 14 minutes or until a toothpick comes out cleanly when inserted into the center.
8. Remove from the air fryer and let cool.
9. Serve and enjoy!

Nutrition Facts Per Serving
Calories 42, Total Fat 3g, Saturated Fat 1g, Total Carbs 3g, Net Carbs 2g, Protein 2g, Sugar 0g, Fiber 1g, Sodium 36mg, Potassium 68g

Raspberry Muffins

Prep time: 10 minutes , Cook time: 15 minutes , Serves 12

Ingredients:
- 1 cup almond flour
- 1 Tbsp powdered stevia
- ¼ cup whole milk
- 1 egg
- ¼ tsp salt
- ¼ tsp ground cinnamon
- 1 ½ tsp baking powder
- ½ cup frozen or fresh raspberries

Instructions
1. Preheat your air fryer to 350 degrees F.
2. Spray 12 silicone muffin cups lightly with cooking spray.
3. In a large bowl, stir together the almond flour, stevia, salt, cinnamon, and baking powder.
4. Add the eggs and milk and stir well.
5. Fold in the raspberries.
6. Divide the muffin batter between each muffin cup, filling about ¾ of the way full.
7. Place the muffins into the air fryer basket and cook for 14 minutes or until a toothpick comes out cleanly when inserted into the center.
8. Remove from the air fryer and let cool.
9. Serve and enjoy!

Nutrition Facts Per Serving
Calories 42, Total Fat 3g, Saturated Fat 1g, Total Carbs 7g, Net Carbs 4g, Protein 2g, Sugar 4g, Fiber 3g, Sodium 36mg, Potassium 68g

Strawberry Muffins

Prep time: 10 minutes , Cook time: 15 minutes , Serves 12

Ingredients:
- 1 cup almond flour
- 1 Tbsp powdered stevia
- ¼ cup whole milk
- 1 egg
- ¼ tsp salt
- ¼ tsp ground cinnamon
- 1 ½ tsp baking powder
- ½ cup chopped strawberries

Instructions
1. Preheat your air fryer to 350 degrees F.
2. Spray 12 silicone muffin cups lightly with cooking spray.
3. In a large bowl, stir together the almond flour, stevia, salt, cinnamon, and baking powder.
4. Add the eggs and milk and stir well.
5. Fold in the strawberries.
6. Divide the muffin batter between each muffin cup, filling about ¾ of the way full.
7. Place the muffins into the air fryer basket and cook for 14 minutes or until a toothpick comes out cleanly when inserted into the center.
8. Remove from the air fryer and let cool.
9. Serve and enjoy!

Nutrition Facts Per Serving
Calories 42, Total Fat 3g, Saturated Fat 1g, Total Carbs 8g, Net Carbs 6g, Protein 2g, Sugar 4g, Fiber 2g, Sodium 36mg, Potassium 68g

Sausage and Cheese Omelet

Prep time: 5 minutes , Cook time: 12 minutes , Serves 4

Ingredients:
- 4 eggs
- 3 Tbsp heavy whipping cream
- ¼ cup cheddar cheese, grated
- ½ cup cooked, crumbled sausage
- ½ tsp salt
- ¼ tsp ground black pepper

Instructions
1. Preheat your air fryer to 350 degrees F and line a baking pan with parchment paper. Be sure the pan will fit in your air fryer- typically a seven inch round pan will work perfectly.
2. In a small bowl, whisk together the eggs, cream, salt and pepper.
3. Fold in the cooked sausage.
4. Pour the mix into the prepared baking pan and then place the pan in your preheated air fryer.
5. Cook for about 10 minutes or until the eggs are completely set.

6. Sprinkle the cheeses across the cooked eggs and return the pan to the air fryer for another 2 minutes to melt the cheese.
7. Fold the omelet in half.
8. Slice into wedges and serve while hot.

Nutrition Facts Per Serving
Calories 218, Total Fat 14g, Saturated Fat 8g, Total Carbs 4g, Net Carbs 2g, Protein 7g, Sugar 1g, Fiber 2g, Sodium 128mg, Potassium 65g

Sausage and Spinach Omelet

Prep time: 5 minutes , Cook time: 12 minutes , Serves 4

Ingredients:
4 eggs
3 Tbsp heavy whipping cream
¼ cup cheddar cheese, grated
½ cup cooked, crumbled sausage
½ cup baby spinach
½ tsp salt
¼ tsp ground black pepper

Instructions
1. Preheat your air fryer to 350 degrees F and line a baking pan with parchment paper. Be sure the pan will fit in your air fryer- typically a seven inch round pan will work perfectly.
2. In a small bowl, whisk together the eggs, cream, salt and pepper.
3. Fold in the cooked sausage and baby spinach
4. Pour the mix into the prepared baking pan and then place the pan in your preheated air fryer.
5. Cook for about 10 minutes or until the eggs are completely set.
6. Sprinkle the cheeses across the cooked eggs and return the pan to the air fryer for another 2 minutes to melt the cheese.
7. Fold the omelet in half.
8. Slice into wedges and serve while hot.

Nutrition Facts Per Serving
Calories 222, Total Fat 14g, Saturated Fat 8g, Total Carbs 6g, Net Carbs 4g, Protein 7g, Sugar 2g, Fiber 2g, Sodium 128mg, Potassium 84g

Meat Lovers Omelet

Prep time: 5 minutes , Cook time: 12 minutes , Serves 4

Ingredients:
4 eggs
3 Tbsp heavy whipping cream
¼ cup cheddar cheese, grated
¼ cup cooked, crumbled sausage
¼ cup cooked, crumbled bacon
½ tsp salt
¼ tsp ground black pepper

Instructions
1. Preheat your air fryer to 350 degrees F and line a baking pan with parchment paper. Be sure the pan will fit in your air fryer- typically a seven inch round pan will work perfectly.
2. In a small bowl, whisk together the eggs, cream, salt and pepper.
3. Fold in the cooked sausage and bacon.
4. Pour the mix into the prepared baking pan and then place the pan in your preheated air fryer.
5. Cook for about 10 minutes or until the eggs are completely set.
6. Sprinkle the cheeses across the cooked eggs and return the pan to the air fryer for another 2 minutes to melt the cheese.
7. Fold the omelet in half.
8. Slice into wedges and serve while hot.

Nutrition Facts Per Serving
Calories 224, Total Fat 14g, Saturated Fat 8g, Total Carbs 4g, Net Carbs 2g, Protein 7g, Sugar 1g, Fiber 2g, Sodium 128mg, Potassium 65g

Bacon and Brie Frittata

Prep time: 10 minutes , Cook time: 10 minutes , Serves 2

Ingredients:
4 eggs
3 Tbsp heavy whipping cream
½ cup chopped, cooked bacon
½ cup brie, sliced
½ tsp salt
¼ tsp ground black pepper

Instructions
1. Preheat your air fryer to 350 degrees F and line a baking pan with parchment paper. Be sure the pan will fit in your air fryer- typically a seven inch round pan will work perfectly.
2. In a small bowl, whisk together the eggs, cream, salt and pepper
3. Stir in the bacon and brie pieces to the bowl.
4. Pour the mix into the prepared baking pan and then place the pan in your preheated air fryer.
5. Cook for about 15 minutes or until the eggs are completely set.
6. Slice into wedges and serve while hot.

Nutrition Facts Per Serving
Calories 281, Total Fat 16g, Saturated Fat 7g, Total Carbs 2g, Net Carbs 1g, Protein 13g, Sugar 1g, Fiber 1g, Sodium 368mg, Potassium 54g

Bacon and Kale Fritatta

Prep time: 10 minutes , Cook time: 10 minutes , Serves 2

Ingredients:
4 eggs
3 Tbsp heavy whipping cream
½ cup chopped, cooked bacon
½ cup chopped kale, stem removed
½ tsp salt
¼ tsp ground black pepper

Instructions
1. Preheat your air fryer to 350 degrees F and line a baking pan with parchment paper. Be sure the pan will fit in your air fryer- typically a seven inch round pan will work perfectly.
2. In a small bowl, whisk together the eggs, cream, salt and pepper
3. Stir in the bacon and kale to the bowl.
4. Pour the mix into the prepared baking pan and then place the pan in your preheated air fryer.
5. Cook for about 15 minutes or until the eggs are completely set.
6. Slice into wedges and serve while hot.

Nutrition Facts Per Serving
Calories 253, Total Fat 13g, Saturated Fat 6g, Total Carbs 5g, Net Carbs 3g, Protein 8g, Sugar 1g, Fiber 2g, Sodium 333mg, Potassium 132g

Zucchini and Sausage Bake

Prep time: 15 minutes , Cook time: 45 minutes , Serves 12

Ingredients:
1 pound Italian sausage, casing removed, cooked and crumbled
½ cup almond flour
2 tsp baking powder
½ tsp ground black pepper
1 tsp salt
½ pound cream cheese
10 eggs
4 cups grated zucchini
1 cup grated cheddar cheese

Instructions
1. Preheat your air fryer to 350 degrees F and line a baking pan with parchment paper. Be sure the pan will fit in your air fryer- typically a seven inch round pan will work perfectly.
2. Whisk together the almond flour, salt, pepper and baking powder.
3. In a separate bowl, beat the cream cheese until it is nice and smooth then add the eggs. Beat until well combined.
4. Add the zucchini to the cream cheese mix and stir until incorporated.

5. Add the dry mixture to the cream cheese bowl and stir well.
6. Fold in the cheese and the sausage.
7. Pour into the prepared pan and cook in the air fryer for 45 minutes.
8. Let cool slightly before slicing and serving.

Nutrition Facts Per Serving
Calories 344, Total Fat 27g, Saturated Fat 8g, Total Carbs 10g, Net Carbs 6g, Protein 16g, Sugar 3g, Fiber 4g, Sodium 736mg, Potassium 342g

Cheesy Zucchini Bake

Prep time: 15 minutes , Cook time: 45 minutes , Serves 12

Ingredients:
½ cup almond flour
2 tsp baking powder
½ tsp ground black pepper
1 tsp salt
½ pound cream cheese
10 eggs
4 cups grated zucchini
1 cup grated cheddar cheese

Instructions
1. Preheat your air fryer to 350 degrees F and line a baking pan with parchment paper. Be sure the pan will fit in your air fryer- typically a seven inch round pan will work perfectly. If you can fit a larger pan, do so!
2. Whisk together the almond flour, salt, pepper and baking powder.
3. In a separate bowl, beat the cream cheese until it is nice and smooth then add the eggs. Beat until well combined.
4. Add the zucchini to the cream cheese mix and stir until incorporated.
5. Add the dry mixture to the cream cheese bowl and stir well.
6. Fold in the cheddar cheese.
7. Pour into the prepared pan and cook in the air fryer for 45 minutes.
8. Let cool slightly before slicing and serving.

Nutrition Facts Per Serving
Calories 278, Total Fat 18g, Saturated Fat 4g, Total Carbs 9g, Net Carbs 6g, Protein 8g, Sugar 3g, Fiber 4g, Sodium 434mg, Potassium 289g

Zucchini and Bacon Egg Bread

Prep time: 15 minutes , Cook time: 45 minutes , Serves 12

Ingredients:
1 pound bacon cooked and crumbled
½ cup almond flour
2 tsp baking powder
½ tsp ground black pepper
1 tsp salt
½ pound cream cheese
10 eggs
4 cups grated zucchini
1 cup grated cheddar cheese

Instructions
1. Preheat your air fryer to 350 degrees F and line a baking pan with parchment paper. Be sure the pan will fit in your air fryer- typically a seven inch round pan will work perfectly.
2. Whisk together the almond flour, salt, pepper and baking powder.
3. In a separate bowl, beat the cream cheese until it is nice and smooth then add the eggs. Beat until well combined.
4. Add the zucchini to the cream cheese mix and stir until incorporated.
5. Add the dry mixture to the cream cheese bowl and stir well.
6. Fold in the cheddar cheese and the bacon.
7. Pour into the prepared pan and cook in the air fryer for 45 minutes.
8. Let cool slightly before slicing and serving.

Nutrition Facts Per Serving
Calories 344, Total Fat 27g, Saturated Fat 8g, Total Carbs 10g, Net Carbs 6g, Protein 16g, Sugar 3g, Fiber 4g, Sodium 736mg, Potassium 342g

Veggie Egg Bread

Prep time: 15 minutes , Cook time: 45 minutes , Serves 12

Ingredients:
- ½ cup chopped tomatoes
- ½ cup sliced mushrooms, cooked
- ½ cup almond flour
- 2 tsp baking powder
- ½ tsp ground black pepper
- 1 tsp salt
- ½ pound cream cheese
- 10 eggs
- 4 cups grated zucchini
- 1 cup grated cheddar cheese

Instructions
1. Preheat your air fryer to 350 degrees F and line a baking pan with parchment paper. Be sure the pan will fit in your air fryer- typically a seven inch round pan will work perfectly.
2. Whisk together the almond flour, salt, pepper and baking powder.
3. In a separate bowl, beat the cream cheese until it is nice and smooth then add the eggs. Beat until well combined.
4. Add the zucchini to the cream cheese mix and stir until incorporated.
5. Add the dry mixture to the cream cheese bowl and stir well.
6. Fold in the cheddar cheese, tomatoes and cooked mushrooms.
7. Pour into the prepared pan and cook in the air fryer for 45 minutes.
8. Let cool slightly before slicing and serving.

Nutrition Facts Per Serving
Calories 252, Total Fat 16g, Saturated Fat 4g, Total Carbs 12g, Net Carbs 8g, Protein 6g, Sugar 3g, Fiber 4g, Sodium 177mg, Potassium 215g

Almond Flour Pancake

Prep time: 10 minutes , Cook time: 8 minutes , Serves 2

Ingredients:
- 2 eggs
- ½ cup whole milk
- 2 Tbsp butter, melted
- 1 tsp vanilla extract
- 1 ¼ cup almond flour
- 2 Tbsp granulated erythritol
- 1 tsp baking powder
- 1/8 tsp salt

Instructions
1. Preheat your air fryer to 400 degrees F and line a baking pan with parchment paper. Be sure the pan will fit in your air fryer- typically a seven inch round pan will work perfectly.
2. Place the eggs, milk, butter and vanilla extract in a blender and puree for about thirty seconds.
3. Add the remaining ingredients to the blender and puree until smooth.
4. Pour the pancake batter into the prepared pan and place in the air fryer.
5. Cook for 7 minutes or until the pancake is puffed and the top is golden brown.
6. Slice and serve with keto, sugar free syrup!

Nutrition Facts Per Serving
Calories 219, Total Fat 22g, Saturated Fat 12g, Total Carbs 7g, Net Carbs 4g, Protein 9g, Sugar 3g, Fiber 3g, Sodium 125mg, Potassium 111g

Raspberry Almond Pancake

Prep time: 10 minutes , Cook time: 9 minutes , Serves 2

Ingredients:
- 2 eggs
- ½ cup whole milk
- 2 Tbsp butter, melted
- 1 tsp almond extract
- 1 ¼ cup almond flour
- 2 Tbsp granulated erythritol
- 1 tsp baking powder
- 1/8 tsp salt
- ¼ cup fresh or frozen raspberries

Instructions
1. Preheat your air fryer to 400 degrees F and line a baking pan with parchment paper. Be

sure the pan will fit in your air fryer- typically a seven inch round pan will work perfectly.
2. Place the eggs, milk, butter and almond extract in a blender and puree for about thirty seconds.
3. Add the remaining ingredients to the blender and puree until smooth.
4. Pour the pancake batter into the prepared pan and stir in the raspberries gently.
5. Place in the air fryer.
6. Cook for 9 minutes or until the pancake is puffed and the top is golden brown.
7. Slice and serve with keto, sugar free syrup!

Nutrition Facts Per Serving
Calories 225, Total Fat 22g, Saturated Fat 12g, Total Carbs 13g, Net Carbs 8g, Protein 9g, Sugar 3g, Fiber 5g, Sodium 125mg, Potassium 111g

Blueberry Pancake

Prep time: 10 minutes , Cook time: 9 minutes , Serves 2

Ingredients:
2 eggs
½ cup whole milk
2 Tbsp butter, melted
1 tsp vanilla extract
1 ¼ cup almond flour
2 Tbsp granulated erythritol
1 tsp baking powder
1/8 tsp salt
¼ cup fresh or frozen blueberries

Instructions
1. Preheat your air fryer to 400 degrees F and line a baking pan with parchment paper. Be sure the pan will fit in your air fryer- typically a seven inch round pan will work perfectly.
2. Place the eggs, milk, butter and vanilla extract in a blender and puree for about thirty seconds.
3. Add the remaining ingredients to the blender and puree until smooth.
4. Pour the pancake batter into the prepared pan and stir in the blueberries gently.
5. Place in the air fryer.
6. Cook for 9 minutes or until the pancake is puffed and the top is golden brown.
7. Slice and serve with keto, sugar free syrup!

Nutrition Facts Per Serving
Calories 232, Total Fat 22g, Saturated Fat 12g, Total Carbs 15g, Net Carbs 10g, Protein 9g, Sugar 3g, Fiber 5g, Sodium 125mg, Potassium 111g

Strawberry Pancake

Prep time: 10 minutes , Cook time: 9 minutes , Serves 2

Ingredients:
2 eggs
½ cup whole milk
2 Tbsp butter, melted
1 tsp vanilla extract
1 ¼ cup almond flour
2 Tbsp granulated erythritol
1 tsp baking powder
1/8 tsp salt
¼ cup fresh chopped strawberries

Instructions
1. Preheat your air fryer to 400 degrees F and line a baking pan with parchment paper. Be sure the pan will fit in your air fryer- typically a seven inch round pan will work perfectly.
2. Place the eggs, milk, butter and vanilla extract in a blender and puree for about thirty seconds.
3. Add the remaining ingredients to the blender and puree until smooth.
4. Pour the pancake batter into the prepared pan and stir in the strawberries gently.
5. Place in the air fryer.
6. Cook for 9 minutes or until the pancake is puffed and the top is golden brown.
7. Slice and serve with keto, sugar free syrup!

Nutrition Facts Per Serving
Calories 232, Total Fat 22g, Saturated Fat 12g, Total Carbs 11g, Net Carbs 9g, Protein 9g, Sugar 3g, Fiber 2g, Sodium 125mg, Potassium 111g

Chocolate Pancake

Prep time: 10 minutes , Cook time: 9 minutes , Serves 2

Ingredients:
2 eggs
½ cup whole milk
2 Tbsp butter, melted
1 tsp vanilla extract
1 ¼ cup almond flour
2 Tbsp cocoa powder
3 Tbsp granulated erythritol
1 tsp baking powder
1/8 tsp salt

Instructions
1. Preheat your air fryer to 400 degrees F and line a baking pan with parchment paper. Be sure the pan will fit in your air fryer- typically a seven inch round pan will work perfectly.
2. Place the eggs, milk, butter and vanilla extract in a blender and puree for about thirty seconds.
3. Add the remaining ingredients to the blender and puree until smooth.
4. Pour the pancake batter into the prepared pan.
5. Place in the air fryer.
6. Cook for 9 minutes or until the pancake is puffed and the top is golden brown.
7. Slice and serve with keto, sugar free syrup!

Nutrition Facts Per Serving
Calories 245, Total Fat 28g, Saturated Fat 14g, Total Carbs 9g, Net Carbs 5g, Protein 9g, Sugar 2g, Fiber 4g, Sodium 125mg, Potassium 111g

Cinnamon Almond Pancake

Prep time: 10 minutes , Cook time: 9 minutes , Serves 2

Ingredients:
2 eggs
½ cup whole milk
2 Tbsp butter, melted
1 tsp almond extract
1 ¼ cup almond flour
2 Tbsp granulated erythritol
1 tsp baking powder
1/8 tsp salt
½ tsp cinnamon

Instructions
1. Preheat your air fryer to 400 degrees F and line a baking pan with parchment paper. Be sure the pan will fit in your air fryer- typically a seven inch round pan will work perfectly.
2. Place the eggs, milk, butter and almond extract in a blender and puree for about thirty seconds.
3. Add the remaining ingredients to the blender and puree until smooth.
4. Pour the pancake batter into the prepared pan.
5. Place in the air fryer.
6. Cook for 9 minutes or until the pancake is puffed and the top is golden brown.
7. Slice and serve with keto, sugar free syrup!

Nutrition Facts Per Serving
Calories 210, Total Fat 20g, Saturated Fat 12g, Total Carbs 9g, Net Carbs 5g, Protein 9g, Sugar 3g, Fiber 4g, Sodium 125mg, Potassium 111g

Pumpkin Pancake

Prep time: 10 minutes , Cook time: 9 minutes , Serves 2

Ingredients:
2 eggs
½ cup whole milk
2 Tbsp butter, melted
1 tsp vanilla extract
2 Tbsps pumpkin puree
1 ¼ cup almond flour
2 Tbsp granulated erythritol
1 tsp baking powder
1/8 tsp salt
½ tsp pumpkin spice

Instructions
1. Preheat your air fryer to 400 degrees F and line a baking pan with parchment paper. Be sure the pan will fit in your air fryer- typically a seven inch round pan will work perfectly.

2. Place the eggs, milk, butter, pumpkin puree and vanilla extract in a blender and puree for about thirty seconds.
3. Add the remaining ingredients to the blender and puree until smooth.
4. Pour the pancake batter into the prepared pan and stir in the raspberries gently.
5. Place in the air fryer.
6. Cook for 9 minutes or until the pancake is puffed and the top is golden brown.
7. Slice and serve with keto, sugar free syrup!

Nutrition Facts Per Serving
Calories 210, Total Fat 22g, Saturated Fat 12g, Total Carbs 9g, Net Carbs 7g, Protein 9g, Sugar 3g, Fiber 2g, Sodium 125mg, Potassium 111g

Coconut Pancake

Prep time: 10 minutes, Cook time: 9 minutes, Serves 2

Ingredients:
2 eggs
½ cup whole milk
2 Tbsp butter, melted
1 tsp vanilla extract
1 ¼ cup coconut flour
2 Tbsp granulated erythritol
1 tsp baking powder
1/8 tsp salt
¼ cup shredded, unsweetened coconut

Instructions
1. Preheat your air fryer to 400 degrees F and line a baking pan with parchment paper. Be sure the pan will fit in your air fryer- typically a seven inch round pan will work perfectly.
2. Place the eggs, milk, butter and vanilla extract in a blender and puree for about thirty seconds.
3. Add the remaining ingredients to the blender and puree until smooth.
4. Pour the pancake batter into the prepared pan and stir in the shredded coconut.
5. Place in the air fryer.
6. Cook for 9 minutes or until the pancake is puffed and the top is golden brown.
7. Slice and serve with keto, sugar free syrup!

Nutrition Facts Per Serving
Calories 210, Total Fat 24g, Saturated Fat 14g, Total Carbs 8g, Net Carbs 4g, Protein 9g, Sugar 3g, Fiber 4g, Sodium 125mg, Potassium 111g

Coconut Rum Pancake

Prep time: 10 minutes, Cook time: 9 minutes, Serves 2

Ingredients:
2 eggs
½ cup whole milk
2 Tbsp butter, melted
1 tsp rum extract
1 ¼ cup coconut flour
2 Tbsp granulated erythritol
1 tsp baking powder
1/8 tsp salt
¼ cup shredded, unsweetened coconut

Instructions
1. Preheat your air fryer to 400 degrees F and line a baking pan with parchment paper. Be sure the pan will fit in your air fryer- typically a seven inch round pan will work perfectly.
2. Place the eggs, milk, butter and rum extract in a blender and puree for about thirty seconds.
3. Add the remaining ingredients to the blender and puree until smooth.
4. Pour the pancake batter into the prepared pan and stir in the shredded coconut.
5. Place in the air fryer.
6. Cook for 9 minutes or until the pancake is puffed and the top is golden brown.
7. Slice and serve with keto, sugar free syrup!

Nutrition Facts Per Serving
Calories 210, Total Fat 24g, Saturated Fat 14g, Total Carbs 8g, Net Carbs 4g, Protein 9g, Sugar 3g, Fiber 4g, Sodium 125mg, Potassium 111g

Coconut Chocolate Pancake

Prep time: 10 minutes, Cook time: 9 minutes, Serves 2

Ingredients:
2 eggs
½ cup whole milk
2 Tbsp butter, melted
1 tsp vanilla extract
1 ¼ cup coconut flour
2 Tbsp cocoa powder
3 Tbsp granulated erythritol
1 tsp baking powder
1/8 tsp salt
¼ cup shredded, unsweetened coconut

Instructions
1. Preheat your air fryer to 400 degrees F and line a baking pan with parchment paper. Be sure the pan will fit in your air fryer- typically a seven inch round pan will work perfectly.
2. Place the eggs, milk, butter and vanilla extract in a blender and puree for about thirty seconds.
3. Add the remaining ingredients to the blender and puree until smooth.
4. Pour the pancake batter into the prepared pan and stir in the shredded coconut.
5. Place in the air fryer.
6. Cook for 9 minutes or until the pancake is puffed and the top is golden brown.
7. Slice and serve with keto, sugar free syrup!

Nutrition Facts Per Serving
Calories 223, Total Fat 24g, Saturated Fat 14g, Total Carbs 8g, Net Carbs 4g, Protein 9g, Sugar 3g, Fiber 4g, Sodium 125mg, Potassium 111g

Curried Omelet

Prep time: 5 minutes, Cook time:11 minutes, Serves 4

Ingredients:
4 eggs
3 Tbsp heavy whipping cream
¼ cup feta cheese
½ tsp salt
¼ tsp ground black pepper
1 tsp curry powder

Instructions
1. Preheat your air fryer to 350 degrees F and line a baking pan with parchment paper. Be sure the pan will fit in your air fryer- typically a seven inch round pan will work perfectly.
2. In a small bowl, whisk together the eggs, cream, salt, curry powder and pepper
3. Pour the mix into the prepared baking pan and then place the pan in your preheated air fryer.
4. Cook for about 10 minutes or until the eggs are completely set.
5. Sprinkle the cheeses across the cooked eggs and return the pan to the air fryer for another minute to melt the cheese.
6. Fold the omelet in half.
7. Slice into wedges and serve while hot.

Nutrition Facts Per Serving
Calories 189, Total Fat 16g, Saturated Fat 8g, Total Carbs 3g, Net Carbs 2g, Protein 7g, Sugar 1g, Fiber 1g, Sodium 133mg, Potassium 65g

French Herb Omelet

Prep time: 5 minutes, Cook time: 10 minutes, Serves 4

Ingredients:
4 eggs
3 Tbsp heavy whipping cream
½ tsp salt
¼ tsp ground black pepper
2 tsp fresh chopped fines herbs

Instructions
1. Preheat your air fryer to 350 degrees F and line a baking pan with parchment paper. Be sure the pan will fit in your air fryer- typically a seven inch round pan will work perfectly.
2. In a small bowl, whisk together the eggs, cream, salt, fines herbs and pepper
3. Pour the mix into the prepared baking pan and then place the pan in your preheated air fryer.

4. Cook for about 10 minutes or until the eggs are completely set.
5. Fold the omelet in half.
6. Slice into wedges and serve while hot.

Nutrition Facts Per Serving
Calories 162, Total Fat 11g, Saturated Fat 4g, Total Carbs 3g, Net Carbs 2g, Protein 7g, Sugar 1g, Fiber 1g, Sodium 133mg, Potassium 65g

Indian Masala Omelet

Prep time: 5 minutes , Cook time:10 minutes , Serves 4

Ingredients:
4 eggs
3 Tbsp heavy whipping cream
½ tsp salt
¼ tsp ground black pepper
1 tsp curry powder
¼ tsp garam masala
1 Tbsp chopped green onions

Instructions
1. Preheat your air fryer to 350 degrees F and line a baking pan with parchment paper. Be sure the pan will fit in your air fryer- typically a seven inch round pan will work perfectly.
2. In a small bowl, whisk together the eggs, cream, salt, curry powder, garam masala, onions and pepper
3. Pour the mix into the prepared baking pan and then place the pan in your preheated air fryer.
4. Cook for about 10 minutes or until the eggs are completely set.
5. Fold the omelet in half.
6. Slice into wedges and serve while hot.

Nutrition Facts Per Serving
Calories 164, Total Fat 10g, Saturated Fat 5g, Total Carbs 2g, Net Carbs 1g, Protein 7g, Sugar 1g, Fiber 1g, Sodium 133mg, Potassium 65g

Za'atar Eggs

Prep time: 5 minutes , Cook time: 10 minutes , Serves 4

Ingredients:
4 eggs
3 Tbsp heavy whipping cream
¼ cup cheddar cheese, grated
¼ cup feta cheese
1 tsp za'atar spice
½ tsp salt
¼ tsp ground black pepper

Instructions
1. Preheat your air fryer to 350 degrees F and line a baking pan with parchment paper. Be sure the pan will fit in your air fryer- typically a seven inch round pan will work perfectly.
2. In a small bowl, whisk together the eggs, cream, salt, za'atar spice and pepper
3. Pour the mix into the prepared baking pan and then place the pan in your preheated air fryer.
4. Cook for about 10 minutes or until the eggs are completely set.
5. Sprinkle the cheeses across the cooked eggs and return the pan to the air fryer for another minute to melt the cheese.
6. Fold the omelet in half.
7. Slice into wedges and serve while hot.

Nutrition Facts Per Serving
Calories 189, Total Fat 16g, Saturated Fat 8g, Total Carbs 3g, Net Carbs 2g, Protein 7g, Sugar 1g, Fiber 1g, Sodium 133mg, Potassium 65g

Spicy Cheesy Omelet

Prep time: 5 minutes , Cook time: 11 minutes , Serves 4

Ingredients:
4 eggs
3 Tbsp heavy whipping cream
¼ cup pepper jack cheese, grated
1 tsp sriracha sauce
½ tsp salt
¼ tsp ground black pepper

Instructions
1. Preheat your air fryer to 350 degrees F and line a baking pan with parchment paper. Be sure the pan will fit in your air fryer- typically a seven inch round pan will work perfectly.
2. In a small bowl, whisk together the eggs, cream, salt, sriracha sauce and pepper
3. Pour the mix into the prepared baking pan and then place the pan in your preheated air fryer.
4. Cook for about 10 minutes or until the eggs are completely set.
5. Sprinkle the cheeses across the cooked eggs and return the pan to the air fryer for another minute to melt the cheese.
6. Fold the omelet in half.
7. Slice into wedges and serve while hot.

Nutrition Facts Per Serving
Calories 174, Total Fat 14g, Saturated Fat 7g, Total Carbs 3g, Net Carbs 2g, Protein 7g, Sugar 1g, Fiber 1g, Sodium 213mg, Potassium 65g

Pesto Omelet

Prep time: 5 minutes , Cook time: 11 minutes , Serves 4

Ingredients:
4 eggs
3 Tbsp heavy whipping cream
2 Tbsp keto Pesto
¼ cup parmesan
½ tsp salt
¼ tsp ground black pepper

Instructions
1. Preheat your air fryer to 350 degrees F and line a baking pan with parchment paper. Be sure the pan will fit in your air fryer- typically a seven inch round pan will work perfectly.
2. In a small bowl, whisk together the eggs, cream, pesto, salt and pepper
3. Pour the mix into the prepared baking pan and then place the pan in your preheated air fryer.
4. Cook for about 10 minutes or until the eggs are completely set.
5. Sprinkle the cheeses across the cooked eggs and return the pan to the air fryer for another minute to melt the cheese.
6. Fold the omelet in half.
7. Slice into wedges and serve while hot.

Nutrition Facts Per Serving
Calories 196, Total Fat 13g, Saturated Fat 7g, Total Carbs 2g, Net Carbs 1g, Protein 7g, Sugar 1g, Fiber 1g, Sodium 189mg, Potassium 65g

Gremolata Eggs

Prep time: 5 minutes , Cook time: 10 minutes , Serves 4

Ingredients:
4 eggs
3 Tbsp heavy whipping cream
½ tsp salt
¼ tsp ground black pepper
¼ cup keto gremolata spread

Instructions
1. Preheat your air fryer to 350 degrees F and line a baking pan with parchment paper. Be sure the pan will fit in your air fryer- typically a seven inch round pan will work perfectly.
2. In a small bowl, whisk together the eggs, cream, salt and pepper
3. Pour the mix into the prepared baking pan and then place the pan in your preheated air fryer.
4. Cook for about 10 minutes or until the eggs are completely set.

5. Spread the gremolata across the top of the eggs.
6. Fold the omelet in half.
7. Slice into wedges and serve while hot.

Nutrition Facts Per Serving
Calories 154, Total Fat 10g, Saturated Fat 5g, Total Carbs 3g, Net Carbs 2g, Protein 7g, Sugar 1g, Fiber 1g, Sodium 210mg, Potassium 115g

Roasted Garlic Eggs

Prep time: 5 minutes , Cook time: 10 minutes , Serves 4

Ingredients:
- 4 eggs
- 3 Tbsp heavy whipping cream
- ¼ cup parmesan cheese
- ½ tsp salt
- ¼ tsp ground black pepper
- 2 cloves roasted garlic, smashed

Instructions
1. Preheat your air fryer to 350 degrees F and line a baking pan with parchment paper. Be sure the pan will fit in your air fryer- typically a seven inch round pan will work perfectly.
2. In a small bowl, whisk together the eggs, cream, salt and pepper.
3. Stir in the roasted garlic cloves
4. Pour the mix into the prepared baking pan and then place the pan in your preheated air fryer.
5. Cook for about 10 minutes or until the eggs are completely set.
6. Sprinkle the cheeses across the cooked eggs and return the pan to the air fryer for another minute to melt the cheese.
7. Fold the omelet in half.
8. Slice into wedges and serve while hot.

Nutrition Facts Per Serving
Calories 193, Total Fat 14g, Saturated Fat 5g, Total Carbs 5g, Net Carbs 2g, Protein 7g, Sugar 2g, Fiber 3g, Sodium 133mg, Potassium 85g

Prosciutto Omelet

Prep time: 5 minutes , Cook time:11 minutes , Serves 4

Ingredients:
- 4 eggs
- 3 Tbsp heavy whipping cream
- 1 oz thin sliced prosciutto
- ½ tsp salt
- ¼ tsp ground black pepper

Instructions
1. Preheat your air fryer to 350 degrees F and line a baking pan with parchment paper. Be sure the pan will fit in your air fryer- typically a seven inch round pan will work perfectly.
2. In a small bowl, whisk together the eggs, cream, salt and pepper
3. Pour the mix into the prepared baking pan and then place the pan in your preheated air fryer.
4. Cook for about 10 minutes or until the eggs are completely set.
5. Place the prosciutto over the top of the cooked eggs.
6. Fold the omelet in half.
7. Slice into wedges and serve while hot.

Nutrition Facts Per Serving
Calories 215, Total Fat 18g, Saturated Fat 10g, Total Carbs 3g, Net Carbs 2g, Protein 11g, Sugar 2g, Fiber 1g, Sodium 382mg, Potassium 85g

Prosciutto Parmesan Omelet

Prep time: 5 minutes , Cook time: 11 minutes , Serves 4

Ingredients:
- 4 eggs
- 3 Tbsp heavy whipping cream
- 1 oz thin sliced prosciutto
- ¼ cup grated parmesan
- ½ tsp salt
- ¼ tsp ground black pepper

Instructions
1. Preheat your air fryer to 350 degrees F and line a baking pan with parchment paper. Be sure the pan will fit in your air fryer- typically a seven inch round pan will work perfectly.
2. In a small bowl, whisk together the eggs, cream, salt and pepper
3. Pour the mix into the prepared baking pan and then place the pan in your preheated air fryer.
4. Cook for about 10 minutes or until the eggs are completely set.
5. Place the prosciutto over the top of the cooked eggs and sprinkle the parmesan over the top.
6. Fold the omelet in half.
7. Slice into wedges and serve while hot.

Nutrition Facts Per Serving Calories 235, Total Fat 22g, Saturated Fat 13g, Total Carbs 5g, Net Carbs 4g, Protein 11g, Sugar 3g, Fiber 1g, Sodium 394mg, Potassium 95g

Kimchi Breakfast

Prep time: 5 minutes , Cook time: 10 minutes , Serves 4

Ingredients:
- 4 eggs
- 3 Tbsp heavy whipping cream
- ½ tsp salt
- ¼ tsp ground black pepper
- ¼ cup kimchi

Instructions
1. Preheat your air fryer to 350 degrees F and line a baking pan with parchment paper. Be sure the pan will fit in your air fryer- typically a seven inch round pan will work perfectly.
2. In a small bowl, whisk together the eggs, cream, salt and pepper
3. Pour the mix into the prepared baking pan and then place the pan in your preheated air fryer.
4. Cook for about 10 minutes or until the eggs are completely set.
5. Spread the kimchi across the top of the eggs.
6. Fold the omelet in half.
7. Slice into wedges and serve while hot.

Nutrition Facts Per Serving
Calories 164, Total Fat 8g, Saturated Fat 4g, Total Carbs 4g, Net Carbs 3g, Protein 7g, Sugar 1g, Fiber 1g, Sodium 210mg, Potassium 115g

Chocolate Muffins

Prep time: 10 minutes , Cook time: 14 minutes , Serves 12

Ingredients:
- 1 cup almond flour
- 2 Tbsp powdered stevia
- ¼ cup whole milk
- 1 egg
- ¼ tsp salt
- 1 ½ tsp baking powder
- ¼ cup cocoa powder

Instructions
1. Preheat your air fryer to 350 degrees F.
2. Spray 12 silicone muffin cups lightly with cooking spray.
3. In a large bowl, stir together the almond flour, stevia, salt, cocoa powder, and baking powder.
4. Add the eggs and milk and stir well.
5. Divide the muffin batter between each muffin cup, filling about ¾ of the way full.
6. Place the muffins into the air fryer basket and cook for 14 minutes or until a toothpick comes out cleanly when inserted into the center.
7. Remove from the air fryer and let cool.

Nutrition Facts Per Serving
Calories 55, Total Fat 5, Saturated Fat 2g, Total Carbs 2g, Net Carbs 1g, Protein 2g, Sugar 1g, Fiber 1g, Sodium 39mg, Potassium 68g

Mocha Muffins

Prep time: 10 minutes , Cook time: 14 minutes , Serves 12

Ingredients:
1 cup almond flour
2 Tbsp powdered stevia
1 Tbsp espresso powder
¼ cup whole milk
1 egg
¼ tsp salt
1 ½ tsp baking powder
¼ cup cocoa powder

Instructions
1. Preheat your air fryer to 350 degrees F.
2. Spray 12 silicone muffin cups lightly with cooking spray.
3. In a large bowl, stir together the almond flour, espresso powder, stevia, salt, cocoa powder, and baking powder.
4. Add the eggs and milk and stir well.
5. Divide the muffin batter between each muffin cup, filling about ¾ of the way full.
6. Place the muffins into the air fryer basket and cook for 14 minutes or until a toothpick comes out cleanly when inserted into the center.
7. Remove from the air fryer and let cool.
8. Serve and enjoy!

Nutrition Facts Per Serving
Calories 59, Total Fat 5, Saturated Fat 2g, Total Carbs 2g, Net Carbs 1g, Protein 2g, Sugar 1g, Fiber 1g, Sodium 39mg, Potassium 68g

Espresso Muffins

Prep time: 10 minutes , Cook time: 14 minutes , Serves 12

Ingredients:
1 cup almond flour
2 Tbsp powdered stevia
¼ cup whole milk
1 egg
¼ tsp salt
1 ½ tsp baking powder
1 Tbsp espresso powder

Instructions
1. Preheat your air fryer to 350 degrees F.
2. Spray 12 silicone muffin cups lightly with cooking spray.
3. In a large bowl, stir together the almond flour, stevia, salt, espresso, and baking powder.
4. Add the eggs and milk and stir well.
5. Divide the muffin batter between each muffin cup, filling about ¾ of the way full.
6. Place the muffins into the air fryer basket and cook for 14 minutes or until a toothpick comes out cleanly when inserted into the center.
7. Remove from the air fryer and let cool.
8. Serve and enjoy!

Nutrition Facts Per Serving
Calories 58, Total Fat 5, Saturated Fat 2g, Total Carbs 2g, Net Carbs 1g, Protein 2g, Sugar 1g, Fiber 1g, Sodium 39mg, Potassium 68g

Cheddar Jalapeno Muffins

Prep time: 10 minutes , Cook time: 14 minutes , Serves 12

Ingredients:
1 cup almond flour
2 Tbsp powdered stevia
¼ cup whole milk
1 egg
¼ tsp salt
1 ½ tsp baking powder
¼ cup grated cheddar cheese
¼ cup chopped jalapeno

Instructions
1. Preheat your air fryer to 350 degrees F.
2. Spray 12 silicone muffin cups lightly with cooking spray.
3. In a large bowl, stir together the almond flour, stevia, salt, cocoa powder, and baking powder.
4. Add the eggs and milk and stir well.
5. Fold in the grated cheddar cheese and jalapenos.
6. Divide the muffin batter between each muffin cup, filling about ¾ of the way full.

7. Place the muffins into the air fryer basket and cook for 14 minutes or until a toothpick comes out cleanly when inserted into the center.
8. Remove from the air fryer and let cool.
9. Serve and enjoy!

Nutrition Facts Per Serving
Calories 83, Total Fat 8, Saturated Fat 4g, Total Carbs 5g, Net Carbs 4g, Protein 5g, Sugar 1g, Fiber 1g, Sodium 54mg, Potassium 78g

Nutty Granola

Prep time: 10 minutes , Cook time: 18 minutes , Serves 12

Ingredients:
- 1 cup almonds, chopped finely
- ½ cup walnuts, chopped finely
- ½ cup hazelnuts, peeled, chopped finely
- 1 cup pecans, chopped finely
- 1/3 cup pumpkin seeds
- 1/3 cup hemp seeds
- ½ cup ground flaxseeds
- 1 tsp vanilla
- 1 egg white, whisked
- ¼ cup butter, melted

Instructions
1. Preheat your air fryer to 325 degrees F.
2. Line your air fryer basket with parchment.
3. Place the chopped nuts in a large bowl and then add the pumpkin seeds, hemp seeds and flaxseed. Toss well.
4. Add the remaining ingredients and toss well.
5. Pour the nut mix into the air fryer basket and bake for 18 minutes, tossing halfway through to bake evenly.
6. Empty the granola onto a try and let cool completely. Enjoy with milk or own its own.

Nutrition Facts Per Serving
Calories 278, Total Fat 26, Saturated Fat 18g, Total Carbs 7g, Net Carbs 2g, Protein 7g, Sugar 1g, Fiber 5g, Sodium 187mg, Potassium 54g

Fruit and Nut Keto Granola

Prep time: 10 minutes , Cook time: 18 minutes , Serves 12

Ingredients:
- 1 cup almonds, chopped finely
- ½ cup walnuts, chopped finely
- ½ cup hazelnuts, peeled, chopped finely
- ½ cup dried blueberries
- 1/3 cup pumpkin seeds
- 1/3 cup hemp seeds
- ½ cup ground flaxseeds
- 1 tsp vanilla
- 1 egg white, whisked
- ¼ cup butter, melted

Instructions
1. Preheat your air fryer to 325 degrees F.
2. Line your air fryer basket with parchment.
3. Place the chopped nuts in a large bowl and then add the pumpkin seeds, hemp seeds, dried blueberries and flaxseed. Toss well.
4. Add the remaining ingredients and toss well.
5. Pour the nut mix into the air fryer basket and bake for 18 minutes, tossing halfway through to bake evenly.
6. Empty the granola onto a try and let cool completely. Enjoy with milk or own its own.

Nutrition Facts Per Serving
Calories 328, Total Fat 26, Saturated Fat 18g, Total Carbs 13g, Net Carbs 8g, Protein 7g, Sugar 3g, Fiber 5g, Sodium 187mg, Potassium 54g

Strawberry and Nut Cereal

Prep time: 10 minutes , Cook time: 12 minutes , Serves 12

Ingredients:
- 1 cup almonds, chopped finely
- ½ cup walnuts, chopped finely
- ½ cup dried strawberries
- 1 cup pecans, chopped finely
- 1/3 cup pumpkin seeds
- 1/3 cup hemp seeds
- ½ cup ground flaxseeds
- 1 tsp vanilla
- 1 egg white, whisked
- ¼ cup butter, melted

Instructions
1. Preheat your air fryer to 325 degrees F.

2. Line your air fryer basket with parchment.
3. Place the chopped nuts in a large bowl and then add the pumpkin seeds, hemp seeds and flaxseed. Toss well.
4. Add the remaining ingredients and toss well.
5. Pour the nut mix into the air fryer basket and bake for 18 minutes, tossing halfway through to bake evenly.
6. Empty the granola onto a try and let cool completely. Enjoy with milk or own its own.

Nutrition Facts Per Serving
Calories 298, Total Fat 27, Saturated Fat 18g, Total Carbs 11g, Net Carbs 6g, Protein 7g, Sugar 3g, Fiber 5g, Sodium 187mg, Potassium 54g

Seedy Breakfast Granola

Prep time: 10 minutes , Cook time: 18 minutes , Serves 12

Ingredients:
1 cup almonds, chopped finely
½ cup walnuts, chopped finely
½ cup hazelnuts, peeled, chopped finely
1 cup pecans, chopped finely
1/3 cup pumpkin seeds
1/3 cup hemp seeds
1/3 cup chia seeds
½ cup ground flaxseeds
1 tsp vanilla
1 egg white, whisked
¼ cup butter, melted

Instructions
1. Preheat your air fryer to 325 degrees F.
2. Line your air fryer basket with parchment.
3. Place the chopped nuts in a large bowl and then add the pumpkin seeds, hemp seeds, chia seeds and flaxseed. Toss well.
4. Add the remaining ingredients and toss well.
5. Pour the nut mix into the air fryer basket and bake for 18 minutes, tossing halfway through to bake evenly.
6. Empty the granola onto a try and let cool completely. Enjoy with milk or own its own.

Nutrition Facts Per Serving
Calories 342, Total Fat 32, Saturated Fat 22g, Total Carbs 7g, Net Carbs 2g, Protein 9g, Sugar 1g, Fiber 5g, Sodium 187mg, Potassium 54g

Pepper Stuffed Spinach Parmesan Baked Eggs

Prep time: 5 minutes , Cook time: 14 minutes , Serves 2

Ingredients:
4 eggs
2 Tbsp heavy cream
2 Tbsp frozen, chopped spinach, thawed
2 Tbsp grated parmesan cheese
½ tsp salt
1/8 tsp ground black pepper
1 large red pepper, cut in half vertically, seeds removed

Instructions
1. Preheat your air fryer to 330 degrees F.
2. Place red pepper halves in the air fryer basket and cook for 5 minutes.
3. In a small bowl, whisk together all the ingredients
4. Pour the eggs into the partially cooked peppers and bake for 7 minutes.
5. Enjoy straight out of the baking cup!

Nutrition Facts Per Serving
Calories 189, Total Fat 11g, Saturated Fat 4g, Total Carbs 5g, Net Carbs 3g, Protein 14g, Sugar 2g, Fiber 2g, Sodium 134mg, Potassium 148g

Pepper Stuffed Spinach and Feta Eggs

Prep time: 5 minutes , Cook time: 14 minutes , Serves 2

Ingredients:
4 eggs
2 Tbsp heavy cream
2 Tbsp frozen, chopped spinach, thawed
¼ cup feta crumbles
½ tsp salt
1/8 tsp ground black pepper
1 large red pepper, cut in half vertically, seeds removed

Instructions
1. Preheat your air fryer to 330 degrees F.
2. Place red pepper halves in the air fryer basket and cook for 5 minutes.
3. In a small bowl, whisk together all the ingredients
4. Pour the eggs into the partially cooked peppers and bake for 7 minutes.
5. Enjoy straight out of the baking cup!

Nutrition Facts Per Serving
Calories 192, Total Fat 11g, Saturated Fat 6g, Total Carbs 5g, Net Carbs 3g, Protein 14g, Sugar 2g, Fiber 2g, Sodium 156mg, Potassium 148g

Egg Stuffed Peppers and Cheese

Prep time: 5 minutes , Cook time: 14 minutes , Serves 2

Ingredients:
4 eggs
2 Tbsp heavy cream
2 Tbsp grated cheddar cheese
2 Tbsp grated parmesan cheese
½ tsp salt
1/8 tsp ground black pepper
1 large red pepper, cut in half vertically, seeds removed

Instructions
1. Preheat your air fryer to 330 degrees F.
2. Place red pepper halves in the air fryer basket and cook for 5 minutes.
3. In a small bowl, whisk together all the ingredients
4. Pour the eggs into the partially cooked peppers and bake for 7 minutes.
5. Enjoy straight out of the baking cup!

Nutrition Facts Per Serving
Calories 178, Total Fat 16g, Saturated Fat 8g, Total Carbs 5g, Net Carbs 3g, Protein 10g, Sugar 2g, Fiber 2g, Sodium 134mg, Potassium 148g

Bacon and Egg Stuffed Peppers

Prep time: 5 minutes , Cook time: 14 minutes , Serves 2

Ingredients:
4 eggs
2 Tbsp heavy cream
2 Tbsp chopped cooked bacon
2 Tbsp grated cheddar cheese
½ tsp salt
1/8 tsp ground black pepper
1 large red pepper, cut in half vertically, seeds removed

Instructions
1. Preheat your air fryer to 330 degrees F.
2. Place red pepper halves in the air fryer basket and cook for 5 minutes.
3. In a small bowl, whisk together all the ingredients
4. Pour the eggs into the partially cooked peppers and bake for 7 minutes.
5. Enjoy straight out of the baking cup!

Nutrition Facts Per Serving
Calories 210, Total Fat 19g, Saturated Fat 9, Total Carbs 9g, Net Carbs 4g, Protein 14g, Sugar 2g, Fiber 5g, Sodium 198mg, Potassium 148g

Peppers and Eggs

Prep time: 5 minutes , Cook time: 14 minutes , Serves 2

Ingredients:
4 eggs
2 Tbsp heavy cream
1 jalapeno, sliced
2 Tbsp grated cheddar cheese
½ tsp salt
1/8 tsp ground black pepper
1 large red pepper, cut in half vertically, seeds removed

Instructions
1. Preheat your air fryer to 330 degrees F.
2. Place red pepper halves in the air fryer basket and cook for 5 minutes.
3. In a small bowl, whisk together all the ingredients
4. Pour the eggs into the partially cooked peppers and bake for 7 minutes.
5. Enjoy straight out of the baking cup!

Nutrition Facts Per Serving
Calories 154, Total Fat 11g, Saturated Fat 4g, Total Carbs 5g, Net Carbs 3g, Protein 9g, Sugar 2g, Fiber 2g, Sodium 126mg, Potassium 154g

Pepper Stuffed Spinach Parmesan Baked Eggs

Prep time: 5 minutes , Cook time: 14 minutes , Serves 2

Ingredients:
4 eggs
2 Tbsp heavy cream
¼ zucchini, sliced and chopped thinly
2 Tbsp grated parmesan cheese
½ tsp salt
1/8 tsp ground black pepper
1 large red pepper, cut in half vertically, seeds removed

Instructions
1. Preheat your air fryer to 330 degrees F.
2. Place red pepper halves in the air fryer basket and cook for 5 minutes.
3. In a small bowl, whisk together all the ingredients
4. Pour the eggs into the partially cooked peppers and bake for 7 minutes.
5. Enjoy straight out of the baking cup!

Nutrition Facts Per Serving
Calories 172, Total Fat 7g, Saturated Fat 3g, Total Carbs 8g, Net Carbs 4g, Protein 14g, Sugar 2g, Fiber 4g, Sodium 117mg, Potassium 154g

Brussels Hash

Prep time: 10 minutes , Cook time: 25 minutes , Serves 4

Ingredients:
6 slices bacon, chopped, cooked
½ cup chopped white onion
1 pound Brussel sprouts, sliced in quarters
½ tsp salt
½ tsp ground black pepper
2 cloves garlic, minced
4 eggs, whisked

Instructions
1. Preheat your air fryer to 350 degrees F.
2. Toss the bacon, onion, Brussels, salt, pepper and garlic together in a large bowl.
3. Pour the mix into a seven inch pan that will fit in your air fryer basket.
4. Place in the air fryer and cook for 15 minutes.
5. Pour the whisked eggs in the basket and return the pan to the air fryer to cook for 10 more minutes.
6. Mix well to break up the hash and enjoy while hot.

Nutrition Facts Per Serving
Calories 238, Total Fat 12g, Saturated Fat 7g, Total Carbs 6g, Net Carbs 3g, Protein 12g, Sugar 1g, Fiber 3g, Sodium 189mg, Potassium 217g

Zucchini Hash

Prep time: 10 minutes, Cook time: 25 minutes, Serves 4

Ingredients:
6 slices bacon, chopped, cooked
½ cup chopped white onion
1 pound shredded zucchini, water squeezed out
½ tsp salt
½ tsp ground black pepper
2 cloves garlic, minced
4 eggs, whisked

Instructions
1. Preheat your air fryer to 350 degrees F.
2. Toss the bacon, onion, zucchini, salt, pepper and garlic together in a large bowl.
3. Pour the mix into a seven inch pan that will fit in your air fryer basket.
4. Place in the air fryer and cook for 15 minutes.
5. Pour the whisked eggs in the basket and return the pan to the air fryer to cook for 10 more minutes.
6. Mix well to break up the hash and enjoy while hot.

Nutrition Facts Per Serving Calories 215, Total Fat 11g, Saturated Fat 7g, Total Carbs 8g, Net Carbs 5g, Protein 10g, Sugar 3g, Fiber 3g, Sodium 189mg, Potassium 211g

Vegetable Hash

Prep time: 10 minutes, Cook time: 25 minutes, Serves 4

Ingredients:
6 slices bacon, chopped, cooked
½ cup chopped white onion
2 cups Brussel sprouts, sliced in quarters
2 cups diced green bell peppers
½ tsp salt
½ tsp ground black pepper
2 cloves garlic, minced
4 eggs, whisked

Instructions
1. Preheat your air fryer to 350 degrees F.
2. Toss the bacon, onion, Brussels, bell peppers, salt, pepper and garlic together in a large bowl.
3. Pour the mix into a seven inch pan that will fit in your air fryer basket.
4. Place in the air fryer and cook for 15 minutes.
5. Pour the whisked eggs in the basket and return the pan to the air fryer to cook for 10 more minutes.
6. Mix well to break up the hash and enjoy while hot.

Nutrition Facts Per Serving
Calories 238, Total Fat 12g, Saturated Fat 7g, Total Carbs 6g, Net Carbs 3g, Protein 12g, Sugar 1g, Fiber 3g, Sodium 189mg, Potassium 217g

Ham, Cheese and Mushroom Melt

Prep time: 12 minutes, Cook time: 18 minutes, Serves 4

Ingredients:
2 Tbsp butter
½ pound sliced mushrooms
1 clove garlic, minced
¼ cup white onion, diced
1-16 oz ham steak, cooked
¼ cup cooked, crumbled bacon
1 Tbsp fresh parsley, chopped
1 cup grated gruyere cheese

Instructions
1. Preheat your air fryer to 350 degrees F.
2. In a pan that will fit inside your air fryer, combine the butter and diced onion. Place in the preheated air fryer and cook for 5 minutes.
3. Remove the pan from the air fryer and stir in the garlic and mushrooms. Return to the air fryer for another 5 minutes.
4. Remove the pan again and add the ham steak, pushing it toward the bottom of the pan. Top with the bacon and grated cheese and place in the air fryer for another 8 minutes.
5. Move the ham steak and pan contents to a plate, garnish with the parsley and serve while hot.

Nutrition Facts Per Serving Calories 352, Total Fat 22g, Saturated Fat 11g, Total Carbs 5g, Net Carbs 4g, Protein 34g, Sugar 2g, Fiber 1g, Sodium 1576mg, Potassium 387g

Ham and Pepper Melt

Prep time: 10 minutes, Cook time: 18 minutes, Serves 4

Ingredients:
2 Tbsp butter
1 cup diced red peppers
1 clove garlic, minced
¼ cup white onion, diced
1-16 oz ham steak, cooked
¼ cup cooked, crumbled bacon
1 Tbsp fresh parsley, chopped
1 cup blue cheese

Instructions
1. Preheat your air fryer to 350 degrees F.
2. In a pan that will fit inside your air fryer, combine the butter, bell peppers and diced onion. Place in the preheated air fryer and cook for 5 minutes.
3. Remove the pan from the air fryer and stir in the garlic and mushrooms. Return to the air fryer for another 5 minutes.
4. Remove the pan again and add the ham steak, pushing it toward the bottom of the pan. Top with the bacon and blue cheese and place in the air fryer for another 8 minutes.
5. Move the ham steak and pan contents to a plate, garnish with the parsley and serve while hot.

Nutrition Facts Per Serving
Calories 382, Total Fat 25g, Saturated Fat 13g, Total Carbs 5g, Net Carbs 4g, Protein 35g, Sugar 2g, Fiber 1g, Sodium 1576mg, Potassium 387g

Veggie Melt

Prep time: 10 minutes, Cook time: 14 minutes, Serves 4

Ingredients:
2 Tbsp butter
½ pound sliced mushrooms
1 clove garlic, minced
¼ cup white onion, diced
1 cup diced green bell peppers
1 cup diced zucchini
1 cup chopped baby spinach
1 Tbsp fresh parsley, chopped
1 cup grated gruyere cheese

Instructions
1. Preheat your air fryer to 350 degrees F.
2. In a pan that will fit inside your air fryer, combine the butter, bell pepper and diced onion. Place in the preheated air fryer and cook for 5 minutes.
3. Remove the pan from the air fryer and stir in the garlic, zucchini and mushrooms. Return to the air fryer for another 5 minutes.
4. Remove the pan again and add the baby spinach and grated cheese and place in the air fryer for another 4 minutes.
5. Move the ham steak and pan contents to a plate, garnish with the parsley and serve while hot.

Nutrition Facts Per Serving
Calories 268, Total Fat 11g, Saturated Fat 7g, Total Carbs 8g, Net Carbs 5g, Protein 34g, Sugar 2g, Fiber 3g, Sodium 452mg, Potassium 254g

Blueberry Breakfast Cake

Prep time: 10 minutes, Cook time: 24 minutes, Serves 12

Ingredients:
1 cup almond flour
1 Tbsp powdered stevia
¼ cup whole milk
1 egg
¼ tsp salt
¼ tsp ground cinnamon
2 tsp baking powder
½ cup frozen or fresh blueberries

Instructions
1. Preheat your air fryer to 350 degrees F.
2. Spray a cake pan lightly with cooking spray. A seven inch pan will fit in most air fryers.
3. In a large bowl, stir together the almond flour, stevia, salt, cinnamon, and baking powder.
4. Add the eggs and milk and stir well.
5. Fold in the blueberries.
6. Pour the batter into the prepared pan and place into the air fryer basket and cook for 24

minutes or until a toothpick comes out cleanly when inserted into the center.
7. Remove from the air fryer and let cool.
8. Serve and enjoy!

Nutrition Facts Per Serving
Calories 42, Total Fat 3g, Saturated Fat 1g, Total Carbs 3g, Net Carbs 2g, Protein 2g, Sugar 0g, Fiber 1g, Sodium 36mg, Potassium 68g

Red Pepper Breakfast Cake

Prep time: 10 minutes , Cook time: 24 minutes , Serves 12

Ingredients:
1 cup almond flour
1 Tbsp powdered stevia
¼ cup whole milk
1 egg
¼ tsp salt
¼ tsp ground cayenne
2 tsp baking powder
½ cup sauted red peppers, diced

Instructions
1. Preheat your air fryer to 350 degrees F.
2. Spray a cake pan lightly with cooking spray. A seven inch pan will fit in most air fryers.
3. In a large bowl, stir together the almond flour, stevia, salt, cayenne, and baking powder.
4. Add the eggs and milk and stir well.
5. Fold in the red peppers.
6. Pour the batter into the prepared pan and place into the air fryer basket and cook for 24 minutes or until a toothpick comes out cleanly when inserted into the center.
7. Remove from the air fryer and let cool.
8. Serve and enjoy!

Nutrition Facts Per Serving
Calories 32, Total Fat 3g, Saturated Fat 1g, Total Carbs 2g, Net Carbs 2g, Protein 2g, Sugar 0g, Fiber 1g, Sodium 36mg, Potassium 68g

Zucchini Breakfast Cake

Prep time: 10 minutes , Cook time: 28 minutes , Serves 12

Ingredients:
1 cup almond flour
1 Tbsp powdered stevia
¼ cup whole milk
1 egg
¼ tsp salt
¼ tsp ground cinnamon
2 tsp baking powder
½ cup shredded zucchini, water squeezed out

Instructions
1. Preheat your air fryer to 350 degrees F.
2. Spray a cake pan lightly with cooking spray. A seven inch pan will fit in most air fryers.
3. In a large bowl, stir together the almond flour, stevia, salt, cinnamon, and baking powder.
4. Add the eggs and milk and stir well.
5. Fold in the zucchini.
6. Pour the batter into the prepared pan and place into the air fryer basket and cook for 24 minutes or until a toothpick comes out cleanly when inserted into the center.
7. Remove from the air fryer and let cool.
8. Serve and enjoy!

Nutrition Facts Per Serving
Calories 42, Total Fat 3g, Saturated Fat 1g, Total Carbs 3g, Net Carbs 2g, Protein 2g, Sugar 0g, Fiber 1g, Sodium 36mg, Potassium 68g

Strawberry Breakfast Bread

Prep time: 10 minutes , Cook time: 24 minutes , Serves 12

Ingredients:
1 cup almond flour
1 Tbsp powdered stevia
¼ cup whole milk
1 egg
¼ tsp salt
¼ tsp ground cinnamon
2 tsp baking powder
½ cup chopped fresh strawberries

Instructions
1. Preheat your air fryer to 350 degrees F.

2. Spray a cake pan lightly with cooking spray. A seven inch pan will fit in most air fryers.
3. In a large bowl, stir together the almond flour, stevia, salt, cinnamon, and baking powder.
4. Add the eggs and milk and stir well.
5. Fold in the strawberries.
6. Pour the batter into the prepared pan and place into the air fryer basket and cook for 24 minutes or until a toothpick comes out cleanly when inserted into the center.
7. Remove from the air fryer and let cool.
8. Serve and enjoy!

Nutrition Facts Per Serving
Calories 42, Total Fat 3g, Saturated Fat 1g, Total Carbs 3g, Net Carbs 2g, Protein 2g, Sugar 0g, Fiber 1g, Sodium 36mg, Potassium 68g

Raspberry Breakfast Cake

Prep time: 10 minutes , Cook time: 24 minutes , Serves 12

Ingredients:
1 cup almond flour
1 Tbsp powdered stevia
¼ cup whole milk
1 egg
¼ tsp salt
¼ tsp ground cinnamon
2 tsp baking powder
½ cup frozen or fresh raspberries

Instructions
1. Preheat your air fryer to 350 degrees F.
2. Spray a cake pan lightly with cooking spray. A seven inch pan will fit in most air fryers.
3. In a large bowl, stir together the almond flour, stevia, salt, cinnamon, and baking powder.
4. Add the eggs and milk and stir well.
5. Fold in the raspberries.
6. Pour the batter into the prepared pan and place into the air fryer basket and cook for 24 minutes or until a toothpick comes out cleanly when inserted into the center.
7. Remove from the air fryer and let cool.
8. Serve and enjoy!

Nutrition Facts Per Serving
Calories 42, Total Fat 3g, Saturated Fat 1g, Total Carbs 7g, Net Carbs 4g, Protein 2g, Sugar 4g, Fiber 3g, Sodium 36mg, Potassium 68g

Cheesy Bacon Pancake

Prep time: 10 minutes , Cook time: 9 minutes , Serves 2

Ingredients:
2 eggs
½ cup whole milk
2 Tbsp butter, melted
1 tsp vanilla extract
1 ¼ cup almond flour
2 Tbsp granulated erythritol
1 tsp baking powder
1/8 tsp salt
½ cup crumbled, cooked bacon
¼ cup grated cheddar cheese

Instructions
1. Preheat your air fryer to 400 degrees F and line a baking pan with parchment paper. Be sure the pan will fit in your air fryer- typically a seven inch round pan will work perfectly.
2. Place the eggs, milk, butter and vanilla extract in a blender and puree for about thirty seconds.
3. Add the remaining ingredients to the blender and puree until smooth.
4. Pour the pancake batter into the prepared pan and stir in the cheese and bacon.
5. Place in the air fryer.
6. Cook for 9 minutes or until the pancake is puffed and the top is golden brown.
7. Slice and serve with keto, sugar free syrup!

Nutrition Facts Per Serving
Calories 278, Total Fat 28g, Saturated Fat 12g, Total Carbs 15g, Net Carbs 10g, Protein 15g, Sugar 3g, Fiber 5g, Sodium 125mg, Potassium 111g

Cheesy Pancake

Prep time: 10 minutes, Cook time: 9 minutes, Serves 2

Ingredients:
- 2 eggs
- ½ cup whole milk
- 2 Tbsp butter, melted
- 1 tsp vanilla extract
- 1 ¼ cup almond flour
- 2 Tbsp granulated erythritol
- 1 tsp baking powder
- 1/8 tsp salt
- ½ cup grated cheddar cheese

Instructions
1. Preheat your air fryer to 400 degrees F and line a baking pan with parchment paper. Be sure the pan will fit in your air fryer- typically a seven inch round pan will work perfectly.
2. Place the eggs, milk, butter and vanilla extract in a blender and puree for about thirty seconds.
3. Add the remaining ingredients to the blender and puree until smooth.
4. Pour the pancake batter into the prepared pan and stir in the cheese.
5. Place in the air fryer.
6. Cook for 9 minutes or until the pancake is puffed and the top is golden brown.
7. Slice and serve with keto, sugar free syrup!

Nutrition Facts Per Serving
Calories 261, Total Fat 28g, Saturated Fat 12g, Total Carbs 12g, Net Carbs 9g, Protein 9g, Sugar 3g, Fiber 5g, Sodium 125mg, Potassium 111g

Strawberry Feta Pancake

Prep time: 10 minutes, Cook time: 9 minutes, Serves 2

Ingredients:
- 2 eggs
- ½ cup whole milk
- 2 Tbsp butter, melted
- 1 tsp vanilla extract
- 1 ¼ cup almond flour
- 2 Tbsp granulated erythritol
- 1 tsp baking powder
- 1/8 tsp salt
- ¼ cup chopped strawberries
- ¼ cup feta cheese

Instructions
1. Preheat your air fryer to 400 degrees F and line a baking pan with parchment paper. Be sure the pan will fit in your air fryer- typically a seven inch round pan will work perfectly.
2. Place the eggs, milk, butter and vanilla extract in a blender and puree for about thirty seconds.
3. Add the remaining ingredients to the blender and puree until smooth.
4. Pour the pancake batter into the prepared pan and stir in the feta and strawberries.
5. Place in the air fryer.
6. Cook for 9 minutes or until the pancake is puffed and the top is golden brown.
7. Slice and serve with keto, sugar free syrup!

Nutrition Facts Per Serving
Calories 262, Total Fat 22g, Saturated Fat 10g, Total Carbs 15g, Net Carbs 10g, Protein 15g, Sugar 3g, Fiber 5g, Sodium 145mg, Potassium 109g

Pepper Pancake

Prep time: 10 minutes, Cook time: 9 minutes, Serves 2

Ingredients:
- 2 eggs
- ½ cup whole milk
- 2 Tbsp butter, melted
- 1 tsp vanilla extract
- 1 ¼ cup almond flour
- 2 Tbsp granulated erythritol
- 1 tsp baking powder
- 1/8 tsp salt
- ½ cup diced bell pepper

Instructions
1. Preheat your air fryer to 400 degrees F and line a baking pan with parchment paper. Be sure the pan will fit in your air fryer-

typically a seven inch round pan will work perfectly.
2. Place the eggs, milk, butter and vanilla extract in a blender and puree for about thirty seconds.
3. Add the remaining ingredients to the blender and puree until smooth.
4. Pour the pancake batter into the prepared pan and stir in the bell pepper.
5. Place in the air fryer.
6. Cook for 9 minutes or until the pancake is puffed and the top is golden brown.
7. Slice and serve with keto, sugar free syrup!

Nutrition Facts Per Serving
Calories 189, Total Fat 16g, Saturated Fat 8g, Total Carbs 12g, Net Carbs 7g, Protein 9g, Sugar 3g, Fiber 5g, Sodium 125mg, Potassium 111g

Sausage Omelette

Prep time: 5 minutes , Cook time:11 minutes , Serves 4

Ingredients:
4 eggs
3 Tbsp heavy whipping cream
¼ cup cheddar cheese, grated
½ cup cooked, chopped sausage
½ tsp salt
¼ tsp ground black pepper

Instructions
1. Preheat your air fryer to 350 degrees F and line a baking pan with parchment paper. Be sure the pan will fit in your air fryer- typically a seven inch round pan will work perfectly.
2. In a small bowl, whisk together the eggs, cream, salt and pepper. Stir in the sausage.
3. Pour the mix into the prepared baking pan and then place the pan in your preheated air fryer.
4. Cook for about 10 minutes or until the eggs are completely set.
5. Sprinkle the cheese across the cooked eggs and return the pan to the air fryer for another minute to melt the cheese.
6. Fold the omelet in half.
7. Slice into wedges and serve while hot.

Nutrition Facts Per Serving
Calories 210, Total Fat 22g, Saturated Fat 14g, Total Carbs 6g, Net Carbs 3g, Protein 7g, Sugar 1g, Fiber 3g, Sodium 863mg, Potassium 125g

Ham and Cheese Omelet

Prep time: 5 minutes , Cook time:11 minutes , Serves 4

Ingredients:
4 eggs
3 Tbsp heavy whipping cream
¼ cup cheddar cheese, grated
½ cup chopped, cooked ham
½ tsp salt
¼ tsp ground black pepper

Instructions
1. Preheat your air fryer to 350 degrees F and line a baking pan with parchment paper. Be sure the pan will fit in your air fryer- typically a seven inch round pan will work perfectly.
2. In a small bowl, whisk together the eggs, cream, salt and pepper. Stir in the ham.
3. Pour the mix into the prepared baking pan and then place the pan in your preheated air fryer.
4. Cook for about 10 minutes or until the eggs are completely set.
5. Sprinkle the cheese across the cooked eggs and return the pan to the air fryer for another minute to melt the cheese.
6. Fold the omelet in half.
7. Slice into wedges and serve while hot.

Nutrition Facts Per Serving
Calories 218, Total Fat 19g, Saturated Fat 9g, Total Carbs 6g, Net Carbs 2g, Protein 7g, Sugar 1g, Fiber 4g, Sodium 890mg, Potassium 343g

Snacks

Turkey Pepper Nachos

Prep time: 10 minutes , Cook time: 7 minutes , Serves 6

Ingredients:
- 1 Tbsp chili powder
- 1 tsp ground cumin
- 1 tsp salt
- ½ tsp ground black pepper
- 1 tsp garlic powder
- ½ tsp fresh chopped cilantro
- 1 pound ground turkey
- 1 pound red bell peppers, cut into strips
- 1 ½ cups grated cheddar cheese

Instructions
1. Preheat your air fryer to 400 degrees F.
2. Mix the spices together in a small bowl.
3. Add the turkey to a large skillet and cook until browned. Stir in the spice mix.
4. Place the bell pepper strips in a lightly greased baking pan and top with the cooked turkey and cheese.
5. Place the pan in the air fryer and cook for 8 minutes to melt and lightly brown the cheese. Serve hot!

Nutrition Facts Per Serving
Calories 351, Total Fat 22g, Saturated Fat 9g, Total Carbs 7g, Net Carbs 4g, Protein 7g, Sugar 2g, Fiber 3g, Sodium 245mg, Potassium 98g

Spicy Hot Pepper Nachos

Prep time: 10 minutes , Cook time: 7 minutes , Serves 6

Ingredients:
- 1 Tbsp chili powder
- 1 tsp ground cumin
- 1 tsp salt
- ½ tsp ground black pepper
- 1 tsp garlic powder
- ½ tsp fresh chopped cilantro
- 1 pound ground turkey
- 1 pound red bell peppers, cut into strips
- 1 jalapeno, sliced
- 1 tsp sriracha sauce
- 1 ½ cups grated cheddar cheese

Instructions
1. Preheat your air fryer to 400 degrees F.
2. Mix the spices together in a small bowl.
3. Add the turkey to a large skillet and cook until browned. Stir in the spice mix.
4. Place the bell pepper strips in a lightly greased baking pan and top with the cooked turkey, jalapeno and cheese.
5. Place the pan in the air fryer and cook for 8 minutes to melt and lightly brown the cheese. Drizzle sriracha over the top and serve hot!

Nutrition Facts Per Serving
Calories 377, Total Fat 22g, Saturated Fat 9g, Total Carbs 9g, Net Carbs 5g, Protein 7g, Sugar 2g, Fiber 4g, Sodium 266mg, Potassium 189g

Veggie Pepper Nachos

Prep time: 10 minutes , Cook time: 7 minutes , Serves 6

Ingredients:
- 1 Tbsp chili powder
- 1 tsp ground cumin
- 1 tsp salt
- ½ tsp ground black pepper
- 1 tsp garlic powder
- ½ cup minces mushrooms
- ½ cup minced tomatoes
- ½ tsp fresh chopped cilantro
- 1 pound ground turkey
- 1 pound red bell peppers, cut into strips
- 1 ½ cups grated cheddar cheese
- 1 avocado, diced

Instructions
1. Preheat your air fryer to 400 degrees F.
2. Mix the spices together in a small bowl.
3. Add the mushrooms to a large skillet and cook until browned. Stir in the spice mix and tomatoes.

4. Place the bell pepper strips in a lightly greased baking pan and top with the cooked veggies and cheese.
5. Place the pan in the air fryer and cook for 8 minutes to melt and lightly brown the cheese. Sprinkle with the cilantro and the avocado. Serve hot!

Nutrition Facts Per Serving
Calories 422, Total Fat 32g, Saturated Fat 15g, Total Carbs 12g, Net Carbs 9g, Protein 7g, Sugar 4g, Fiber 3g, Sodium 211mg, Potassium 110g

Chicken Pepper Nachos

Prep time: 10 minutes , Cook time: 7 minutes , Serves 6

Ingredients:
1 Tbsp chili powder
1 tsp ground cumin
1 tsp salt
½ tsp ground black pepper
1 tsp garlic powder
½ tsp fresh chopped cilantro
1 pound ground chicken
1 pound red bell peppers, cut into strips
1 ½ cups grated cheddar cheese

Instructions
1. Preheat your air fryer to 400 degrees F.
2. Mix the spices together in a small bowl.
3. Add the turkey to a large skillet and cook until browned. Stir in the spice mix.
4. Place the bell pepper strips in a lightly greased baking pan and top with the cooked chicken and cheese.
5. Place the pan in the air fryer and cook for 8 minutes to melt and lightly brown the cheese. Serve hot!

Nutrition Facts Per Serving
Calories 362, Total Fat 22g, Saturated Fat 8g, Total Carbs 8g, Net Carbs 4g, Protein 7g, Sugar 3g, Fiber 3g, Sodium 245mg, Potassium 98g

Cranberry Dark Chocolate Granola Bars

Prep time: 10 minutes , Cook time: 25 minutes , Serves 16 bars

Ingredients:
1 cup unsweetened shredded coconut
1 cup sliced almonds
½ cup chopped pecans
1/3 cup dried cranberries
1/3 cup unsweetened, dark chocolate chips
½ cup hemp seeds
½ tsp salt
½ cup butter
2 tsp keto maple syrup
½ cup powdered erythritol
½ tsp vanilla

Instructions
1. Preheat your air fryer to 300 degrees F and line the air fryer tray with parchment paper.
2. Add the coconut, nuts and hemp seeds to a food processor and pulse until well mixed and crumbly.
3. Place the mix in a large bowl along with the cranberries, dark chocolate chips and salt.
4. In a small pot, melt the butter and maple syrup over low heat.
5. Whisk in the erythritol and stir until melted. Turn off the heat and add the vanilla extract.
6. Pour the butter mix over the nut mix and stir quickly to coat evenly.
7. Pour the mix onto the prepared sheet tray and press down so the mix is flat and even. Try to compact it as much as possible so the bars hold together well.
8. Place the tray in the oven and bake for 20 minutes. The edges should turn slightly brown.
9. Cool the bars completely and then slice and serve!

Nutrition Facts Per Serving
Calories 179, Total Fat 16g, Saturated Fat 8g, Total Carbs 6g, Net Carbs 3g, Protein 3g, Sugar 2g, Fiber 3g, Sodium 189mg, Potassium 72g

Double Dark Chocolate Granola Bars

Prep time: 10 minutes , Cook time: 25 minutes , Serves 16 bars

Ingredients:
- 1 cup unsweetened shredded coconut
- 1 cup sliced almonds
- ½ cup chopped pecans
- 1/3 cup unsweetened, dark chocolate chips
- ½ cup hemp seeds
- ½ tsp salt
- ½ cup butter
- 2 tsp keto maple syrup
- ½ cup powdered erythritol
- ½ tsp vanilla
- 2 Tbsp cocoa powder, unsweetened

Instructions
1. Preheat your air fryer to 300 degrees F and line the air fryer tray with parchment paper.
2. Add the coconut, nuts and hemp seeds to a food processor and pulse until well mixed and crumbly.
3. Place the mix in a large bowl along with the dark chocolate chips and salt.
4. In a small pot, melt the butter and maple syrup over low heat.
5. Whisk in the erythritol and stir until melted. Turn off the heat and add the vanilla extract and cocoa powder and stir.
6. Pour the butter mix over the nut mix and stir quickly to coat evenly.
7. Pour the mix onto the prepared sheet tray and press down so the mix is flat and even. Try to compact it as much as possible so the bars hold together well.
8. Place the tray in the oven and bake for 20 minutes. The edges should turn slightly brown.
9. Cool the bars completely and then slice and serve!

Nutrition Facts Per Serving
Calories 145, Total Fat 16g, Saturated Fat 8g, Total Carbs 4g, Net Carbs 2g, Protein 3g, Sugar 2g, Fiber 2g, Sodium 189mg, Potassium 72g

Blueberry Dark Chocolate Granola Bars

Prep time: 10 minutes , Cook time: 25 minutes , Serves 16 bars

Ingredients:
- 1 cup unsweetened shredded coconut
- 1 cup sliced almonds
- ½ cup chopped pecans
- 1/3 cup dried blueberries
- 1/3 cup unsweetened, dark chocolate chips
- ½ cup hemp seeds
- ½ tsp salt
- ½ cup butter
- 2 tsp keto maple syrup
- ½ cup powdered erythritol
- ½ tsp vanilla

Instructions
1. Preheat your air fryer to 300 degrees F and line the air fryer tray with parchment paper.
2. Add the coconut, nuts and hemp seeds to a food processor and pulse until well mixed and crumbly.
3. Place the mix in a large bowl along with the blueberries, dark chocolate chips and salt.
4. In a small pot, melt the butter and maple syrup over low heat.
5. Whisk in the erythritol and stir until melted. Turn off the heat and add the vanilla extract.
6. Pour the butter mix over the nut mix and stir quickly to coat evenly.
7. Pour the mix onto the prepared sheet tray and press down so the mix is flat and even. Try to compact it as much as possible so the bars hold together well.
8. Place the tray in the oven and bake for 20 minutes. The edges should turn slightly brown.
9. Cool the bars completely and then slice and serve!

Nutrition Facts Per Serving
Calories 179, Total Fat 16g, Saturated Fat 8g, Total Carbs 6g, Net Carbs 3g, Protein 3g, Sugar 2g, Fiber 3g, Sodium 189mg, Potassium 72g

Coconut Dark Chocolate Granola Bars

Prep time: 10 minutes , Cook time: 25 minutes , Serves 16 bars

Ingredients:
- 1 cup unsweetened shredded coconut
- 1 cup sliced almonds
- ½ cup chopped pecans
- 1/3 cup unsweetened, dark chocolate chips
- ½ cup hemp seeds
- ½ tsp salt
- ½ cup butter
- 2 tsp keto maple syrup
- ½ cup powdered erythritol
- ½ tsp coconut extract

Instructions
1. Preheat your air fryer to 300 degrees F and line the air fryer tray with parchment paper.
2. Add the coconut, nuts and hemp seeds to a food processor and pulse until well mixed and crumbly.
3. Place the mix in a large bowl along with the dark chocolate chips and salt.
4. In a small pot, melt the butter and maple syrup over low heat.
5. Whisk in the erythritol and stir until melted. Turn off the heat and add the coconut extract.
6. Pour the butter mix over the nut mix and stir quickly to coat evenly.
7. Pour the mix onto the prepared sheet tray and press down so the mix is flat and even. Try to compact it as much as possible so the bars hold together well.
8. Place the tray in the oven and bake for 20 minutes. The edges should turn slightly brown.
9. Cool the bars completely and then slice and serve!

Nutrition Facts Per Serving
Calories 149, Total Fat 16g, Saturated Fat 8g, Total Carbs 3g, Net Carbs 1g, Protein 3g, Sugar 2g, Fiber 2g, Sodium 189mg, Potassium 72g

Seedy Chocolate Granola Bars

Prep time: 10 minutes , Cook time: 25 minutes , Serves 16 bars

Ingredients:
- 1 cup unsweetened shredded coconut
- 1 cup sliced almonds
- ½ cup chopped pecans
- 1/3 cup sunflower seeds
- ¼ cup chia seeds
- 1/3 cup unsweetened, dark chocolate chips
- ½ cup hemp seeds
- ½ tsp salt
- ½ cup butter
- 2 tsp keto maple syrup
- ½ cup powdered erythritol
- ½ tsp vanilla

Instructions
1. Preheat your air fryer to 300 degrees F and line the air fryer tray with parchment paper.
2. Add the coconut, nuts, sunflower seeds and hemp seeds to a food processor and pulse until well mixed and crumbly.
3. Place the mix in a large bowl along with the chia seeds, dark chocolate chips and salt.
4. In a small pot, melt the butter and maple syrup over low heat.
5. Whisk in the erythritol and stir until melted. Turn off the heat and add the vanilla extract.
6. Pour the butter mix over the nut mix and stir quickly to coat evenly.
7. Pour the mix onto the prepared sheet tray and press down so the mix is flat and even. Try to compact it as much as possible so the bars hold together well.
8. Place the tray in the oven and bake for 20 minutes. The edges should turn slightly brown.
9. Cool the bars completely and then slice and serve!

Nutrition Facts Per Serving
Calories 192, Total Fat 18g, Saturated Fat 8g, Total Carbs 6g, Net Carbs 2g, Protein 8g, Sugar 2g, Fiber 4g, Sodium 182mg, Potassium 93g

Nut and Dark Chocolate Granola Bars

Prep time: 10 minutes , Cook time: 25 minutes , Serves 16 bars

Ingredients:
- 1 cup unsweetened shredded coconut
- 1 cup sliced almonds
- ½ cup chopped pecans
- 1/3 cup chopped walnuts
- 1/3 cup unsweetened, dark chocolate chips
- ½ cup hemp seeds
- ½ tsp salt
- ½ cup butter
- 2 tsp keto maple syrup
- ½ cup powdered erythritol
- ½ tsp vanilla

Instructions
1. Preheat your air fryer to 300 degrees F and line the air fryer tray with parchment paper.
2. Add the coconut, nuts and hemp seeds to a food processor and pulse until well mixed and crumbly.
3. Place the mix in a large bowl along with the dark chocolate chips and salt.
4. In a small pot, melt the butter and maple syrup over low heat.
5. Whisk in the erythritol and stir until melted. Turn off the heat and add the vanilla extract.
6. Pour the butter mix over the nut mix and stir quickly to coat evenly.
7. Pour the mix onto the prepared sheet tray and press down so the mix is flat and even. Try to compact it as much as possible so the bars hold together well.
8. Place the tray in the oven and bake for 20 minutes. The edges should turn slightly brown.
9. Cool the bars completely and then slice and serve!

Nutrition Facts Per Serving
Calories 177, Total Fat 18g, Saturated Fat 9g, Total Carbs 7g, Net Carbs 3g, Protein 3g, Sugar 2g, Fiber 4g, Sodium 189mg, Potassium 72g

Chicharrones

Prep time: 30 minutes , Cook time: 3 hours , Serves 10

Ingredients:
- 4 pounds pork back fat with skin
- 2 Tbsp olive oil
- 1 tsp salt
- ½ tsp ground black pepper

Instructions
1. Preheat your air fryer to 225 degrees F and line the air fryer tray with parchment paper.
2. Cut the pork fat into one inch by two inch strips and remove as much of the fat from the skin as possible.
3. Place the chopped skins on the prepared sheet tray and place the fat in a large pot.
4. Drizzle with the olive oil.
5. Bake for 3 hours to dry out the skins.
6. Heat the pork fat pot over medium heat.
7. Place the dried skins into the hot pork oil and fry until the Chicharrones bubble up, about 2-3 minutes.
8. Place in a large bowl and toss with the salt and pepper. Enjoy warm

Nutrition Facts Per Serving
Calories 152, Total Fat 9g, Saturated Fat 7g, Total Carbs 1g, Net Carbs 1g, Protein 8g, Sugar 0g, Fiber 0g, Sodium 867mg, Potassium 89g

Spicy Chicharrones

Prep time: 30 minutes , Cook time: 3 hours , Serves 10

Ingredients:
- 4 pounds pork back fat with skin
- 2 Tbsp olive oil
- 1 tsp salt
- ½ tsp ground black pepper
- 1 tsp cayenne pepper

Instructions
1. Preheat your air fryer to 225 degrees F and line the air fryer tray with parchment paper.
2. Cut the pork fat into one inch by two inch strips and remove as much of the fat from the skin as possible.
3. Place the chopped skins on the prepared sheet tray and place the fat in a large pot.

4. Drizzle with the olive oil.
5. Bake for 3 hours to dry out the skins.
6. Heat the pork fat pot over medium heat.
7. Place the dried skins into the hot pork oil and fry until the Chicharrones bubble up, about 2-3 minutes.
8. Place in a large bowl and toss with the salt, cayenne and pepper. Enjoy warm

Nutrition Facts Per Serving
Calories 152, Total Fat 9g, Saturated Fat 7g, Total Carbs 1g, Net Carbs 1g, Protein 8g, Sugar 0g, Fiber 0g, Sodium 867mg, Potassium 89g

Herbed Chicharrones

Prep time: 30 minutes , Cook time: 3 hours , Serves 10

Ingredients:
4 pounds pork back fat with skin
2 Tbsp olive oil
1 tsp salt
½ tsp ground black pepper
1 tsp Italian seasoning

Instructions
1. Preheat your air fryer to 225 degrees F and line the air fryer tray with parchment paper.
2. Cut the pork fat into one inch by two inch strips and remove as much of the fat from the skin as possible.
3. Place the chopped skins on the prepared sheet tray and place the fat in a large pot.
4. Drizzle with the olive oil.
5. Bake for 3 hours to dry out the skins.
6. Heat the pork fat pot over medium heat.
7. Place the dried skins into the hot pork oil and fry until the Chicharrones bubble up, about 2-3 minutes.
8. Place in a large bowl and toss with the salt, Italian seasoning and pepper. Enjoy warm

Nutrition Facts Per Serving
Calories 152, Total Fat 9g, Saturated Fat 7g, Total Carbs 1g, Net Carbs 1g, Protein 8g, Sugar 0g, Fiber 0g, Sodium 867mg, Potassium 89g

Cocoa Chicharrones

Prep time: 30 minutes , Cook time: 3 hours , Serves 10

Ingredients:
4 pounds pork back fat with skin
2 Tbsp olive oil
1 tsp salt
½ tsp ground black pepper
1 Tbsp unsweetened cocoa powder

Instructions
1. Preheat your air fryer to 225 degrees F and line the air fryer tray with parchment paper.
2. Cut the pork fat into one inch by two inch strips and remove as much of the fat from the skin as possible.
3. Place the chopped skins on the prepared sheet tray and place the fat in a large pot.
4. Drizzle with the olive oil.
5. Bake for 3 hours to dry out the skins.
6. Heat the pork fat pot over medium heat.
7. Place the dried skins into the hot pork oil and fry until the Chicharrones bubble up, about 2-3 minutes.
8. Place in a large bowl and toss with the salt, cocoa powder and pepper. Enjoy warm

Nutrition Facts Per Serving
Calories 164, Total Fat 10g, Saturated Fat 7g, Total Carbs 1g, Net Carbs 1g, Protein 8g, Sugar 0g, Fiber 0g, Sodium 867mg, Potassium 89g

Cheesy Chicharrones

Prep time: 30 minutes , Cook time: 3 hours , Serves 10

Ingredients:
4 pounds pork back fat with skin
2 Tbsp olive oil
1 tsp salt
½ tsp ground black pepper
2 Tbsp dried grated parmesan cheese

Instructions
1. Preheat your air fryer to 225 degrees F and line the air fryer tray with parchment paper.

2. Cut the pork fat into one inch by two inch strips and remove as much of the fat from the skin as possible.
3. Place the chopped skins on the prepared sheet tray and place the fat in a large pot.
4. Drizzle with the olive oil.
5. Bake for 3 hours to dry out the skins.
6. Heat the pork fat pot over medium heat.
7. Place the dried skins into the hot pork oil and fry until the Chicharrones bubble up, about 2-3 minutes.
8. Place in a large bowl and toss with the salt, cheese and pepper. Enjoy warm

Nutrition Facts Per Serving
Calories 162, Total Fat 10g, Saturated Fat 8g, Total Carbs 1g, Net Carbs 1g, Protein 9g, Sugar 0g, Fiber 0g, Sodium 867mg, Potassium 89g

Cajun Chicharrones

Prep time: 30 minutes , Cook time: 3 hours , Serves 10

Ingredients:
4 pounds pork back fat with skin
2 Tbsp olive oil
1 tsp Cajun seasoning
½ tsp ground black pepper

Instructions
1. Preheat your air fryer to 225 degrees F and line the air fryer tray with parchment paper.
2. Cut the pork fat into one inch by two inch strips and remove as much of the fat from the skin as possible.
3. Place the chopped skins on the prepared sheet tray and place the fat in a large pot.
4. Drizzle with the olive oil.
5. Bake for 3 hours to dry out the skins.
6. Heat the pork fat pot over medium heat.
7. Place the dried skins into the hot pork oil and fry until the Chicharrones bubble up, about 2-3 minutes.
8. Place in a large bowl and toss with the Cajun and pepper. Enjoy warm

Nutrition Facts Per Serving
Calories 152, Total Fat 9g, Saturated Fat 7g, Total Carbs 1g, Net Carbs 1g, Protein 8g, Sugar 0g, Fiber 0g, Sodium 867mg, Potassium 89g

Cheesy Garlic Bread Muffins

Prep time: 20 minutes , Cook time: 25 minutes , Serves 12

Ingredients:
6 Tbsp melted butter
¼ cup minced garlic
½ cup sour cream
4 eggs
2 cups almond flour
1 cup coconut flour
2 tsp baking powder
1 cup shredded cheddar cheese
¼ cup chopped parsley
¼ cup fresh chopped mozzarella

Instructions
1. Preheat your air fryer to 325 degrees F and spray a muffin tin or individual muffin cups with cooking spray.
2. Place the sour cream, 1 Tbsp garlic, eggs and salt in a food processor and puree until smooth.
3. Add the flours, cheddar cheese, and parsley to the food processor and pulse until a smooth dough forms.
4. Scoop half of the batter into the muffin cups then divide the chopped mozzarella between the cups. Top with the remaining batter, covering the mozzarella completely.
5. Combine the melted butter and the remaining garlic and then brush the tops of each muffin with the butter mix.
6. Place the muffins in the air fryer and bake for 25 minutes or until the tops are golden brown.
7. Cool before serving then enjoy!

Nutrition Facts Per Serving
Calories 322, Total Fat 27g, Saturated Fat 9g, Total Carbs 7g, Net Carbs 4g, Protein 13g, Sugar 0g, Fiber 3g, Sodium 321mg, Potassium 116g

Parmesan Garlic Bread Muffins

Prep time: 20 minutes , Cook time: 25 minutes , Serves 12

Ingredients:
6 Tbsp melted butter
¼ cup minced garlic
½ cup sour cream
4 eggs
2 cups almond flour
1 cup coconut flour
2 tsp baking powder
1 cup shredded cheddar cheese
¼ cup chopped parsley
¼ cup fresh grated parmesan

Instructions
1. Preheat your air fryer to 325 degrees F and spray a muffin tin or individual muffin cups with cooking spray.
2. Place the sour cream, 1 Tbsp garlic, eggs and salt in a food processor and puree until smooth.
3. Add the flours, cheddar cheese, and parsley to the food processor and pulse until a smooth dough forms.
4. Scoop half of the batter into the muffin cups then divide the grated parmesan between the cups. Top with the remaining batter, covering the parmesan completely.
5. Combine the melted butter and the remaining garlic and then brush the tops of each muffin with the butter mix.
6. Place the muffins in the air fryer and bake for 25 minutes or until the tops are golden brown.
7. Cool before serving then enjoy!

Nutrition Facts Per Serving
Calories 312, Total Fat 27g, Saturated Fat 9g, Total Carbs 7g, Net Carbs 4g, Protein 13g, Sugar 0g, Fiber 3g, Sodium 342mg, Potassium 116g

Spicy Garlic Bread Muffins

Prep time: 20 minutes , Cook time: 25 minutes , Serves 12

Ingredients:
6 Tbsp melted butter
¼ cup minced garlic
½ cup sour cream
4 eggs
2 cups almond flour
1 cup coconut flour
2 tsp baking powder
1 tsp red pepper flakes
1 cup shredded cheddar cheese
¼ cup chopped parsley

Instructions
1. Preheat your air fryer to 325 degrees F and spray a muffin tin or individual muffin cups with cooking spray.
2. Place the sour cream, 1 Tbsp garlic, eggs and salt in a food processor and puree until smooth.
3. Add the flours, baking powder, red pepper flakes, cheddar cheese, and parsley to the food processor and pulse until a smooth dough forms.
4. Scoop the batter into the muffin cups.
5. Combine the melted butter and the remaining garlic and then brush the tops of each muffin with the butter mix.
6. Place the muffins in the air fryer and bake for 25 minutes or until the tops are golden brown.
7. Cool before serving then enjoy!

Nutrition Facts Per Serving
Calories 283, Total Fat 19g, Saturated Fat 6g, Total Carbs 6g, Net Carbs 3g, Protein 11g, Sugar 0g, Fiber 3g, Sodium 218mg, Potassium 94g

Herby Cheesy Muffins

Prep time: 20 minutes , Cook time: 25 minutes , Serves 12

Ingredients:
6 Tbsp melted butter
¼ cup minced garlic
½ cup sour cream
4 eggs
2 cups almond flour
1 cup coconut flour
2 tsp baking powder
1 cup shredded cheddar cheese

¼ cup chopped parsley
½ tsp dried basil
½ tsp dried, chopped rosemary

Instructions
1. Preheat your air fryer to 325 degrees F and spray a muffin tin or individual muffin cups with cooking spray.
2. Place the sour cream, 1 Tbsp garlic, eggs and salt in a food processor and puree until smooth.
3. Add the flours, cheddar cheese, and herbs to the food processor and pulse until a smooth dough forms.
4. Scoop the batter into the muffin cups.
5. Combine the melted butter and the remaining garlic and then brush the tops of each muffin with the butter mix.
6. Place the muffins in the air fryer and bake for 25 minutes or until the tops are golden brown.
7. Cool before serving then enjoy!

Nutrition Facts Per Serving
Calories 322, Total Fat 27g, Saturated Fat 9g, Total Carbs 7g, Net Carbs 4g, Protein 13g, Sugar 0g, Fiber 3g, Sodium 321mg, Potassium 116g

Beef Muffins Snack

Prep time: 20 minutes , Cook time: 25 minutes , Serves 12

Ingredients:
6 Tbsp melted butter
¼ cup minced garlic
½ cup sour cream
4 eggs
2 cups almond flour
1 cup coconut flour
2 tsp baking powder
1 cup shredded cheddar cheese
¼ cup chopped parsley
¼ cup cooked, ground beef

Instructions
1. Preheat your air fryer to 325 degrees F and spray a muffin tin or individual muffin cups with cooking spray.
2. Place the sour cream, 1 Tbsp garlic, eggs and salt in a food processor and puree until smooth.
3. Add the flours, cheddar cheese, and parsley to the food processor and pulse until a smooth dough forms.
4. Scoop half of the batter into the muffin cups then divide the ground beef between the cups. Top with the remaining batter, covering the ground beef completely.
5. Combine the melted butter and the remaining garlic and then brush the tops of each muffin with the butter mix.
6. Place the muffins in the air fryer and bake for 25 minutes or until the tops are golden brown.
7. Cool before serving then enjoy!

Nutrition Facts Per Serving
Calories 389, Total Fat 32g, Saturated Fat 15g, Total Carbs 7g, Net Carbs 4g, Protein 19g, Sugar 1g, Fiber 3g, Sodium 300mg, Potassium 216g

Bacon Muffin Bites

Prep time: 20 minutes , Cook time: 25 minutes , Serves 24 mini muffins

Ingredients:
6 Tbsp melted butter
¼ cup minced garlic
½ cup sour cream
4 eggs
2 cups almond flour
1 cup coconut flour
2 tsp baking powder
1 cup shredded cheddar cheese
¼ cup chopped parsley
½ cup cooked, crumbled bacon

Instructions
1. Preheat your air fryer to 325 degrees F and spray a mini muffin tin or individual mini muffin cups with cooking spray.
2. Place the sour cream, 1 Tbsp garlic, eggs and salt in a food processor and puree until smooth.
3. Add the flours, cheddar cheese, and parsley to the food processor and pulse until a smooth dough forms.
4. Fold in the bacon crumbles.
5. Scoop the batter into the muffin cups.

6. Combine the melted butter and the remaining garlic and then brush the tops of each muffin with the butter mix.
7. Place the muffins in the air fryer and bake for 18 minutes or until the tops are golden brown.
8. Cool before serving then enjoy!

Nutrition Facts Per Serving
Calories 198, Total Fat 19g, Saturated Fat 12g, Total Carbs 5g, Net Carbs 1g, Protein 12g, Sugar 1g, Fiber 4g, Sodium 122mg, Potassium 109g

Smoky Muffins

Prep time: 20 minutes , Cook time: 25 minutes , Serves 12

Ingredients:
6 Tbsp melted butter
¼ cup minced garlic
½ cup sour cream
4 eggs
2 cups almond flour
1 cup coconut flour
2 tsp baking powder
1 cup shredded cheddar cheese
1 tsp smoked paprika

Instructions
1. Preheat your air fryer to 325 degrees F and spray a muffin tin or individual muffin cups with cooking spray.
2. Place the sour cream, 1 Tbsp garlic, eggs and salt in a food processor and puree until smooth.
3. Add the flours, smoked paprika, cheddar cheese, and parsley to the food processor and pulse until a smooth dough forms.
4. Scoop the batter into the muffin cups.
5. Combine the melted butter and the remaining garlic and then brush the tops of each muffin with the butter mix.
6. Place the muffins in the air fryer and bake for 25 minutes or until the tops are golden brown.
7. Cool before serving then enjoy!

Nutrition Facts Per Serving
Calories 275, Total Fat 19g, Saturated Fat 9g, Total Carbs 6g, Net Carbs 3g, Protein 12g, Sugar 1g, Fiber 3g, Sodium 109mg, Potassium 97g

BBQ Muffin Snack

Prep time: 20 minutes , Cook time: 25 minutes , Serves 12

Ingredients:
6 Tbsp melted butter
¼ cup minced garlic
½ cup sour cream
4 eggs
2 cups almond flour
1 cup coconut flour
2 tsp baking powder
1 cup shredded cheddar cheese
¼ cup chopped parsley
¼ cup cooked, shredded chicken
2 Tbsp keto BBQ sauce

Instructions
1. Preheat your air fryer to 325 degrees F and spray a muffin tin or individual muffin cups with cooking spray.
2. Toss the cooked chicken with the BBQ sauce and set aside.
3. Place the sour cream, 1 Tbsp garlic, eggs and salt in a food processor and puree until smooth.
4. Add the flours, cheddar cheese, and parsley to the food processor and pulse until a smooth dough forms.
5. Scoop half of the batter into the muffin cups then divide the BBQ chicken between the cups. Top with the remaining batter, covering the chicken completely.
6. Combine the melted butter and the remaining garlic and then brush the tops of each muffin with the butter mix.
7. Place the muffins in the air fryer and bake for 25 minutes or until the tops are golden brown.
8. Cool before serving then enjoy!

Nutrition Facts Per Serving
Calories 389, Total Fat 32g, Saturated Fat 15g, Total Carbs 7g, Net Carbs 4g, Protein 19g, Sugar 1g, Fiber 3g, Sodium 300mg, Potassium 216g

Brussel Sprout Chips

Prep time: 10 minutes , Cook time: 15 minutes , Serves 4

Ingredients:
1 Pound Brussel Sprouts, ends removed
2 Tbsp olive oil
1 tsp sea salt

Instructions
1. Preheat your air fryer to 2400 degrees F and line the air fryer tray with parchment paper.
2. Peel the Brussels sprouts one leaf at a time, placing the leaves in a large bowl as you peel them.
3. Toss the leaves with the olive oil and salt and then spread on the prepared tray.
4. Bake for 15 minutes in the air fryer, tossing halfway through to cook evenly.
5. Serve hot or wrap in an air tight container once cooled.

Nutrition Facts Per Serving
Calories 104, Total Fat 7g, Saturated Fat 4g, Total Carbs 9g, Net Carbs 5g, Protein 3g, Sugar 0g, Fiber 4g, Sodium 496mg, Potassium 211g

Cayenne Brussels Sprout Chips

Prep time: 10 minutes , Cook time: 15 minutes , Serves 4

Ingredients:
1 Pound Brussel Sprouts, ends removed
2 Tbsp olive oil
1 tsp sea salt
1 tsp cayenne pepper

Instructions
1. Preheat your air fryer to 2400 degrees F and line the air fryer tray with parchment paper.
2. Peel the Brussels sprouts one leaf at a time, placing the leaves in a large bowl as you peel them.
3. Toss the leaves with the olive oil, cayenne and salt and then spread on the prepared tray.
4. Bake for 15 minutes in the air fryer, tossing halfway through to cook evenly.
5. Serve hot or wrap in an air tight container once cooled.

Nutrition Facts Per Serving
Calories 110, Total Fat 7g, Saturated Fat 4g, Total Carbs 9g, Net Carbs 5g, Protein 3g, Sugar 0g, Fiber 4g, Sodium 498mg, Potassium 215g

Black Pepper Brussels Sprout Chips

Prep time: 10 minutes , Cook time: 15 minutes , Serves 4

Ingredients:
1 Pound Brussel Sprouts, ends removed
2 Tbsp olive oil
1 tsp sea salt
1 tsp fresh ground pepper

Instructions
1. Preheat your air fryer to 2400 degrees F and line the air fryer tray with parchment paper.
2. Peel the Brussels sprouts one leaf at a time, placing the leaves in a large bowl as you peel them.
3. Toss the leaves with the olive oil, fresh ground pepper and salt and then spread on the prepared tray.
4. Bake for 15 minutes in the air fryer, tossing halfway through to cook evenly.
5. Serve hot or wrap in an air tight container once cooled.

Nutrition Facts Per Serving
Calories 111, Total Fat 7g, Saturated Fat 4g, Total Carbs 9g, Net Carbs 5g, Protein 3g, Sugar 1g, Fiber 4g, Sodium 496mg, Potassium 211g

Asian Style Brussel Sprout Chips

Prep time: 10 minutes, Cook time: 15 minutes, Serves 4

Ingredients:
1 Pound Brussel Sprouts, ends removed
1 Tbsp olive oil
1 Tbsp coconut aminos
1 tsp sea salt

Instructions
1. Preheat your air fryer to 2400 degrees F and line the air fryer tray with parchment paper.
2. Peel the Brussels sprouts one leaf at a time, placing the leaves in a large bowl as you peel them.
3. Toss the leaves with the olive oil, coconut aminos and salt and then spread on the prepared tray.
4. Bake for 15 minutes in the air fryer, tossing halfway through to cook evenly.
5. Serve hot or wrap in an air tight container once cooled.

Nutrition Facts Per Serving
Calories 123, Total Fat 7g, Saturated Fat 4g, Total Carbs 11g, Net Carbs 7g, Protein 3g, Sugar 1g, Fiber 4g, Sodium 843mg, Potassium 271g

Balsamic Brussel Sprout Chips

Prep time: 10 minutes, Cook time: 15 minutes, Serves 4

Ingredients:
1 Pound Brussel Sprouts, ends removed
2 Tbsp olive oil
1 Tbsp balsamic vinegar
1 tsp sea salt

Instructions
1. Preheat your air fryer to 2400 degrees F and line the air fryer tray with parchment paper.
2. Peel the Brussels sprouts one leaf at a time, placing the leaves in a large bowl as you peel them.
3. Toss the leaves with the olive oil and salt and then spread on the prepared tray.
4. Bake for 15 minutes in the air fryer, tossing halfway through to cook evenly.
5. Remove tray from the air fryer and toss with the balsamic immediately.
6. Serve hot or wrap in an air tight container once cooled.

Nutrition Facts Per Serving
Calories 126, Total Fat 7g, Saturated Fat 4g, Total Carbs 11g, Net Carbs 5g, Protein 3g, Sugar 2g, Fiber 4g, Sodium 496mg, Potassium 211g

Bacon Brussel Sprout Chips

Prep time: 10 minutes, Cook time: 15 minutes, Serves 4

Ingredients:
1 Pound Brussel Sprouts, ends removed
1 Tbsp olive oil
1 tsp sea salt
½ cup minced bacon, uncooked

Instructions
1. Preheat your air fryer to 2400 degrees F and line the air fryer tray with parchment paper.
2. Peel the Brussels sprouts one leaf at a time, placing the leaves in a large bowl as you peel them.
3. Toss the leaves with the bacon, olive oil and salt and then spread on the prepared tray.
4. Bake for 15 minutes in the air fryer, tossing halfway through to cook evenly.
5. Serve hot or wrap in an air tight container once cooled.

Nutrition Facts Per Serving
Calories 192, Total Fat 12g, Saturated Fat 9g, Total Carbs 10g, Net Carbs 6g, Protein 5g, Sugar 1g, Fiber 4g, Sodium 873mg, Potassium 190g

Maple Brussel Sprout Chips

Prep time: 10 minutes , Cook time: 15 minutes , Serves 4

Ingredients:
1 Pound Brussel Sprouts, ends removed
2 Tbsp olive oil
1 tsp sea salt
1 tsp maple extract

Instructions
1. Preheat your air fryer to 2400 degrees F and line the air fryer tray with parchment paper.
2. Peel the Brussels sprouts one leaf at a time, placing the leaves in a large bowl as you peel them.
3. Toss the leaves with the olive oil, maple extract and salt and then spread on the prepared tray.
4. Bake for 15 minutes in the air fryer, tossing halfway through to cook evenly.
5. Serve hot or wrap in an air tight container once cooled.

Nutrition Facts Per Serving
Calories 110, Total Fat 7g, Saturated Fat 4g, Total Carbs 9g, Net Carbs 5g, Protein 3g, Sugar 1g, Fiber 4g, Sodium 496mg, Potassium 211g

Garlic Brussel Sprout Chips

Prep time: 10 minutes , Cook time: 15 minutes , Serves 4

Ingredients:
1 Pound Brussel Sprouts, ends removed
2 Tbsp olive oil
1 tsp sea salt
1 tsp garlic powder

Instructions
1. Preheat your air fryer to 2400 degrees F and line the air fryer tray with parchment paper.
2. Peel the Brussels sprouts one leaf at a time, placing the leaves in a large bowl as you peel them.
3. Toss the leaves with the olive oil, garlic powder and salt and then spread on the prepared tray.
4. Bake for 15 minutes in the air fryer, tossing halfway through to cook evenly.
5. Serve hot or wrap in an air tight container once cooled.

Nutrition Facts Per Serving
Calories 109, Total Fat 7g, Saturated Fat 4g, Total Carbs 9g, Net Carbs 5g, Protein 3g, Sugar 0g, Fiber 4g, Sodium 496mg, Potassium 211g

Herbed Parmesan Crackers

Prep time: 25 minutes , Cook time: 45 minutes, Serves 10

Ingredients:
1 ½ cups sunflower seeds
¾ cup parmesan cheese, grated
2 Tbsp Italian seasoning
½ cup chia seeds
½ tsp garlic powder
½ tsp baking powder
1 egg
2 Tbsp butter, melted
Salt

Instructions
1. Preheat your air fryer to 300 degrees F.
2. Place the sunflower seeds and chia seeds in a food processor until finely blended into a powder. Place in a large bowl.
3. Add the cheese, Italian seasoning, garlic powder and baking powder to the bowl and mix well.
4. Add in the melted butter and egg and stir until a nice dough forms.
5. Place the dough on a piece of parchment and then place another piece of parchment on top.
6. Roll the dough into a thin sheet about 1/8 inch thick.
7. Remove the top piece of parchment and lift the dough using the bottom parchment and place on a sheet tray that will fit in the air fryer.
8. Score the cracker dough into your desired shape and then bake for 40-45 minutes.
9. Break the crackers apart and enjoy!

Nutrition Facts Per Serving
Calories 223, Total Fat 18g, Saturated Fat 6g, Total Carbs 9g, Net Carbs 2g, Protein 9g, Sugar 1g, Fiber 7g, Sodium 563mg, Potassium 211g

Super Seed Parmesan Crackers

Prep time: 25 minutes , Cook time: 45 minutes, Serves 10

Ingredients:
- 1 cups sunflower seeds
- ½ cup hulled hemp seeds
- ¾ cup parmesan cheese, grated
- 2 Tbsp Italian seasoning
- ½ cup chia seeds
- ½ tsp garlic powder
- ½ tsp baking powder
- 1 egg
- 2 Tbsp butter, melted
- Salt

Instructions
1. Preheat your air fryer to 300 degrees F.
2. Place the sunflower seeds, hemp seeds and chia seeds in a food processor until finely blended into a powder. Place in a large bowl.
3. Add the cheese, Italian seasoning, garlic powder and baking powder to the bowl and mix well.
4. Add in the melted butter and egg and stir until a nice dough forms.
5. Place the dough on a piece of parchment and then place another piece of parchment on top.
6. Roll the dough into a thin sheet about 1/8 inch thick.
7. Remove the top piece of parchment and lift the dough using the bottom parchment and place on a sheet tray that will fit in the air fryer.
8. Score the cracker dough into your desired shape and then bake for 40-45 minutes.
9. Break the crackers apart and enjoy!

Nutrition Facts Per Serving
Calories 243, Total Fat 21g, Saturated Fat 8g, Total Carbs 9g, Net Carbs 2g, Protein 9g, Sugar 1g, Fiber 7g, Sodium 572mg, Potassium 215g

Cheddar Crackers

Prep time: 25 minutes , Cook time: 45 minutes, Serves 10

Ingredients:
- 1 ½ cups sunflower seeds
- ¾ cup cheddar cheese, grated
- 2 Tbsp Italian seasoning
- ½ cup chia seeds
- ½ tsp garlic powder
- ½ tsp baking powder
- 1 egg
- 2 Tbsp butter, melted
- Salt

Instructions
1. Preheat your air fryer to 300 degrees F.
2. Place the sunflower seeds and chia seeds in a food processor until finely blended into a powder. Place in a large bowl.
3. Add the cheese, Italian seasoning, garlic powder and baking powder to the bowl and mix well.
4. Add in the melted butter and egg and stir until a nice dough forms.
5. Place the dough on a piece of parchment and then place another piece of parchment on top.
6. Roll the dough into a thin sheet about 1/8 inch thick.
7. Remove the top piece of parchment and lift the dough using the bottom parchment and place on a sheet tray that will fit in the air fryer.
8. Score the cracker dough into your desired shape and then bake for 40-45 minutes.
9. Break the crackers apart and enjoy!

Nutrition Facts Per Serving
Calories 218, Total Fat 18g, Saturated Fat 6g, Total Carbs 9g, Net Carbs 2g, Protein 9g, Sugar 1g, Fiber 7g, Sodium 542mg, Potassium 198g

Chipotle Cheddar Crackers

Prep time: 25 minutes, Cook time: 45 minutes, Serves 10

Ingredients:
1 ½ cups sunflower seeds
¾ cup parmesan cheese, grated
2 tsp chipotle powder
½ cup chia seeds
½ tsp garlic powder
½ tsp baking powder
1 egg
2 Tbsp butter, melted
Salt

Instructions
1. Preheat your air fryer to 300 degrees F.
2. Place the sunflower seeds and chia seeds in a food processor until finely blended into a powder. Place in a large bowl.
3. Add the cheese, chipotle powder, garlic powder and baking powder to the bowl and mix well.
4. Add in the melted butter and egg and stir until a nice dough forms.
5. Place the dough on a piece of parchment and then place another piece of parchment on top.
6. Roll the dough into a thin sheet about 1/8 inch thick.
7. Remove the top piece of parchment and lift the dough using the bottom parchment and place on a sheet tray that will fit in the air fryer.
8. Score the cracker dough into your desired shape and then bake for 40-45 minutes.
9. Break the crackers apart and enjoy!

Nutrition Facts Per Serving
Calories 218, Total Fat 18g, Saturated Fat 6g, Total Carbs 9g, Net Carbs 2g, Protein 9g, Sugar 1g, Fiber 7g, Sodium 542mg, Potassium 207g

Pizza Crackers

Prep time: 25 minutes, Cook time: 45 minutes, Serves 10

Ingredients:
1 ¼ cups sunflower seeds
¼ cup chopped sundried tomatoes
½ cup parmesan cheese, grated
¼ cup grated mozzarella cheese
2 Tbsp Italian seasoning
½ cup chia seeds
½ tsp garlic powder
½ tsp baking powder
1 egg
2 Tbsp butter, melted
Salt

Instructions
1. Preheat your air fryer to 300 degrees F.
2. Place the sunflower seeds and chia seeds in a food processor until finely blended into a powder. Place in a large bowl.
3. Add the cheeses, sundried tomatoes, Italian seasoning, garlic powder and baking powder to the bowl and mix well.
4. Add in the melted butter and egg and stir until a nice dough forms.
5. Place the dough on a piece of parchment and then place another piece of parchment on top.
6. Roll the dough into a thin sheet about 1/8 inch thick.
7. Remove the top piece of parchment and lift the dough using the bottom parchment and place on a sheet tray that will fit in the air fryer.
8. Score the cracker dough into your desired shape and then bake for 40-45 minutes.
9. Break the crackers apart and enjoy!

Nutrition Facts Per Serving
Calories 252, Total Fat 22g, Saturated Fat 9g, Total Carbs 14g, Net Carbs 7g, Protein 10g, Sugar 3g, Fiber 7g, Sodium 589mg, Potassium 278g

Bacon Cheddar Crackers

Prep time: 25 minutes, Cook time: 45 minutes, Serves 10

Ingredients:
- 1 ½ cups sunflower seeds
- ¾ cup cheddar cheese, grated
- 2 Tbsp Italian seasoning
- ½ cup chia seeds
- ½ tsp garlic powder
- ½ tsp baking powder
- 1 egg
- ½ cup cooked, crumbled bacon
- 1 Tbsp butter, melted
- Salt

Instructions
1. Preheat your air fryer to 300 degrees F.
2. Place the sunflower seeds and chia seeds in a food processor until finely blended into a powder. Place in a large bowl.
3. Add the cheese, Italian seasoning, garlic powder and baking powder to the bowl and mix well.
4. Add in the melted butter bacon crumbles, and egg and stir until a nice dough forms.
5. Place the dough on a piece of parchment and then place another piece of parchment on top.
6. Roll the dough into a thin sheet about 1/8 inch thick.
7. Remove the top piece of parchment and lift the dough using the bottom parchment and place on a sheet tray that will fit in the air fryer.
8. Score the cracker dough into your desired shape and then bake for 40-45 minutes.
9. Break the crackers apart and enjoy!

Nutrition Facts Per Serving
Calories 312, Total Fat 26g, Saturated Fat 10g, Total Carbs 11g, Net Carbs 3g, Protein 12g, Sugar 2g, Fiber 8g, Sodium 769mg, Potassium 410g

Black Pepper Parmesan Crackers

Prep time: 25 minutes, Cook time: 45 minutes, Serves 10

Ingredients:
- 1 ½ cups sunflower seeds
- ¾ cup parmesan cheese, grated
- 1 Tbsp Italian seasoning
- 1 Tbsp ground black pepper
- ½ cup chia seeds
- ½ tsp garlic powder
- ½ tsp baking powder
- 1 egg
- 2 Tbsp butter, melted
- Salt

Instructions
1. Preheat your air fryer to 300 degrees F.
2. Place the sunflower seeds and chia seeds in a food processor until finely blended into a powder. Place in a large bowl.
3. Add the cheese, Italian seasoning, ground black pepper, garlic powder and baking powder to the bowl and mix well.
4. Add in the melted butter and egg and stir until a nice dough forms.
5. Place the dough on a piece of parchment and then place another piece of parchment on top.
6. Roll the dough into a thin sheet about 1/8 inch thick.
7. Remove the top piece of parchment and lift the dough using the bottom parchment and place on a sheet tray that will fit in the air fryer.
8. Score the cracker dough into your desired shape and then bake for 40-45 minutes.
9. Break the crackers apart and enjoy!

Nutrition Facts Per Serving
Calories 232, Total Fat 19g, Saturated Fat 6g, Total Carbs 9g, Net Carbs 2g, Protein 9g, Sugar 1g, Fiber 7g, Sodium 563mg, Potassium 211g

Cauliflower Crunch

Prep time: 5 minutes, Cook time: 6 Hours, Serves 4

Ingredients:
4 cups cauliflower florets, chopped into bite sized pieces
1 Tbsp olive oil
1 tsp sea salt

Instructions
1. Preheat your air fryer to 135 degrees F.
2. Wash and drain the cauliflower florets.
3. Place the cauliflower in a large bowl and toss with the olive oil and sea salt.
4. Add the cauliflower to the basket of your air fryer or spread them in a flat layer on the tray of your air fryer (either option will work!).
5. Cook in the air fryer for about 6 hours, tossing the cauliflower every hour or so to cook evenly. Essentially, you will be dehydrating the cauliflower.
6. Once the cauliflower is fully dried, remove it from the air fryer and then let cool. It will keep crisping as it cools.
7. Enjoy fresh or store in an airtight container for up to a month.

Nutrition Facts Per Serving
Calories 55, Total Fat 3g, Saturated Fat 0g, Total Carbs 4g, Net Carbs 3g, Protein 1g, Sugar 2g, Fiber 1g, Sodium 615mg, Potassium 320g

Spicy Cauliflower Crunch

Prep time: 5 minutes, Cook time: 6 Hours, Serves 4

Ingredients:
4 cups cauliflower florets, chopped into bite sized pieces
1 Tbsp olive oil
1 tsp sea salt
1 tsp cayenne pepper

Instructions
1. Preheat your air fryer to 135 degrees F.
2. Wash and drain the cauliflower florets.
3. Place the cauliflower in a large bowl and toss with the olive oil and sea salt.
4. Add the cauliflower to the basket of your air fryer or spread them in a flat layer on the tray of your air fryer (either option will work!).
5. Cook in the air fryer for about 6 hours, tossing the cauliflower every hour or so to cook evenly. Essentially, you will be dehydrating the cauliflower.
6. Once the cauliflower is fully dried, remove it from the air fryer, toss it with the cayenne pepper, and then let cool. It will keep crisping as it cools.
7. Enjoy fresh or store in an airtight container for up to a month.

Nutrition Facts Per Serving
Calories 61, Total Fat 3g, Saturated Fat 0g, Total Carbs 4g, Net Carbs 3g, Protein 1g, Sugar 2g, Fiber 1g, Sodium 632mg, Potassium 320g

Broccoli Crunch

Prep time: 5 minutes, Cook time: 6 Hours, Serves 4

Ingredients:
4 cups broccoli florets, chopped into bite sized pieces
1 Tbsp olive oil
1 tsp sea salt

Instructions
1. Preheat your air fryer to 135 degrees F.
2. Wash and drain the broccoli florets.
3. Place the broccoli in a large bowl and toss with the olive oil and sea salt.
4. Add the broccoli to the basket of your air fryer or spread them in a flat layer on the tray of your air fryer (either option will work!).
5. Cook in the air fryer for about 6 hours, tossing the broccoli every hour or so to cook evenly. Essentially, you will be dehydrating the broccoli.
6. Once the broccoli is fully dried, remove it from the air fryer and then let cool. It will keep crisping as it cools.

7. Enjoy fresh or store in an airtight container for up to a month.

Nutrition Facts Per Serving
Calories 50, Total Fat 3g, Saturated Fat 0g, Total Carbs 3g, Net Carbs 1g, Protein 2g, Sugar 0g, Fiber 2g, Sodium 610mg, Potassium 0g

Red Hot Broccoli Crunch

Prep time: 5 minutes , Cook time: 6 Hours, Serves 4

Ingredients:
4 cups broccoli florets, chopped into bite sized pieces
1 Tbsp olive oil
1 tsp sea salt
1 tsp red pepper flakes

Instructions
1. Preheat your air fryer to 135 degrees F.
2. Wash and drain the broccoli florets.
3. Place the broccoli in a large bowl and toss with the olive oil and sea salt.
4. Add the broccoli to the basket of your air fryer or spread them in a flat layer on the tray of your air fryer (either option will work!).
5. Cook in the air fryer for about 6 hours, tossing the broccoli every hour or so to cook evenly. Essentially, you will be dehydrating the broccoli.
6. Once the broccoli is fully dried, remove it from the air fryer, toss with the red pepper flakes, and then let cool. It will keep crisping as it cools.
7. Enjoy fresh or store in an airtight container for up to a month.

Nutrition Facts Per Serving
Calories 51, Total Fat 3g, Saturated Fat 0g, Total Carbs 3g, Net Carbs 1g, Protein 2g, Sugar 0g, Fiber 2g, Sodium 611mg, Potassium 0g

Lemon Pepper Broccoli Crunch

Prep time: 5 minutes , Cook time: 6 Hours, Serves 4

Ingredients:
4 cups broccoli florets, chopped into bite sized pieces
1 Tbsp olive oil
1 tsp sea salt
1 tsp lemon pepper seasoning

Instructions
1. Preheat your air fryer to 135 degrees F.
2. Wash and drain the broccoli florets.
3. Place the broccoli in a large bowl and toss with the olive oil and sea salt.
4. Add the broccoli to the basket of your air fryer or spread them in a flat layer on the tray of your air fryer (either option will work!).
5. Cook in the air fryer for about 6 hours, tossing the broccoli every hour or so to cook evenly. Essentially, you will be dehydrating the broccoli.
6. Once the broccoli is fully dried, remove it from the air fryer, toss with the lemon pepper seasoning, and then let cool. It will keep crisping as it cools.
7. Enjoy fresh or store in an airtight container for up to a month.

Nutrition Facts Per Serving
Calories 53, Total Fat 3g, Saturated Fat 0g, Total Carbs 3g, Net Carbs 1g, Protein 2g, Sugar 0g, Fiber 2g, Sodium 629mg, Potassium 0g

Sweet Broccoli Crunch

Prep time: 5 minutes , Cook time: 6 Hours, Serves 4

Ingredients:
4 cups broccoli florets, chopped into bite sized pieces
1 Tbsp olive oil
1 tsp sea salt
1 tsp granulated erythritol

Instructions
1. Preheat your air fryer to 135 degrees F.
2. Wash and drain the broccoli florets.
3. Place the broccoli in a large bowl and toss with the olive oil, erythritol, and sea salt.

4. Add the broccoli to the basket of your air fryer or spread them in a flat layer on the tray of your air fryer (either option will work!).
5. Cook in the air fryer for about 6 hours, tossing the broccoli every hour or so to cook evenly. Essentially, you will be dehydrating the broccoli.
6. Once the broccoli is fully dried, remove it from the air fryer and then let cool. It will keep crisping as it cools.
7. Enjoy fresh or store in an airtight container for up to a month.

Nutrition Facts Per Serving
Calories 62, Total Fat 3g, Saturated Fat 0g, Total Carbs 5g, Net Carbs 2g, Protein 2g, Sugar 0g, Fiber 3g, Sodium 610mg, Potassium 0g

Maple Broccoli Crunch

Prep time: 5 minutes , Cook time: 6 Hours, Serves 4

Ingredients:
4 cups broccoli florets, chopped into bite sized pieces
1 Tbsp olive oil
1 tsp sea salt
1 ½ tsp maple extract

Instructions
1. Preheat your air fryer to 135 degrees F.
2. Wash and drain the broccoli florets.
3. Place the broccoli in a large bowl and toss with the olive oil, maple extract, and sea salt.
4. Add the broccoli to the basket of your air fryer or spread them in a flat layer on the tray of your air fryer (either option will work!).
5. Cook in the air fryer for about 6 hours, tossing the broccoli every hour or so to cook evenly. Essentially, you will be dehydrating the broccoli.
6. Once the broccoli is fully dried, remove it from the air fryer and then let cool. It will keep crisping as it cools.
7. Enjoy fresh or store in an airtight container for up to a month.

Nutrition Facts Per Serving
Calories 54, Total Fat 3g, Saturated Fat 0g, Total Carbs 3g, Net Carbs 1g, Protein 2g, Sugar 1g, Fiber 2g, Sodium 610mg, Potassium 0g

Veggie Crunch

Prep time: 5 minutes , Cook time: 6 Hours, Serves 4

Ingredients:
2 cups broccoli florets, chopped into bite sized pieces
2 cups cauliflower florets, chopped into bite sized pieces
1 Tbsp olive oil
1 tsp sea salt

Instructions
1. Preheat your air fryer to 135 degrees F.
2. Wash and drain the florets.
3. Place the florets in a large bowl and toss with the olive oil and sea salt.
4. Add the florets to the basket of your air fryer or spread them in a flat layer on the tray of your air fryer (either option will work!).
5. Cook in the air fryer for about 6 hours, tossing the florets every hour or so to cook evenly. Essentially, you will be dehydrating the veggies.
6. Once the florets is fully dried, remove it from the air fryer and then let cool. It will keep crisping as it cools.
7. Enjoy fresh or store in an airtight container for up to a month.

Nutrition Facts Per Serving
Calories 53, Total Fat 3g, Saturated Fat 0g, Total Carbs 3g, Net Carbs 1g, Protein 2g, Sugar 0g, Fiber 2g, Sodium 610mg, Potassium 0g

Chili Lime Broccoli Crunch

Prep time: 5 minutes, Cook time: 6 Hours, Serves 4

Ingredients:
4 cups broccoli florets, chopped into bite sized pieces
1 Tbsp olive oil
1 tsp sea salt
1 tsp lime zest
1 Tbsp lime juice
1 tsp chili powder

Instructions
1. Preheat your air fryer to 135 degrees F.
2. Wash and drain the broccoli florets.
3. Place the broccoli in a large bowl and toss with the olive oil, lime juice, lime zest and sea salt.
4. Add the broccoli to the basket of your air fryer or spread them in a flat layer on the tray of your air fryer (either option will work!).
5. Cook in the air fryer for about 6 hours, tossing the broccoli every hour or so to cook evenly. Essentially, you will be dehydrating the broccoli.
6. Once the broccoli is fully dried, remove it from the air fryer, toss with the chili powder, and then let cool. It will keep crisping as it cools.
7. Enjoy fresh or store in an airtight container for up to a month.

Nutrition Facts Per Serving
Calories 62, Total Fat 3g, Saturated Fat 0g, Total Carbs 3g, Net Carbs 1g, Protein 2g, Sugar 1g, Fiber 2g, Sodium 647mg, Potassium 0g

Zucchini Chips

Prep time: 15 minutes, Cook time: 4 Hours, Serves 8

Ingredients:
4 cups very thin zucchini slices
2 Tbsp olive oil
2 tsp sea salt

Instructions
1. Preheat your air fryer to 135 degrees F.
2. Toss the thin zucchini slices with the oil and sea salt.
3. Place the zucchini on the air fryer tray or in the air fryer basket.
4. Cook for 4 hours, tossing the zucchini occasionally to allow it to dehydrate evenly.
5. Once crisp, remove the zucchini from the air fryer and enjoy!

Nutrition Facts Per Serving
Calories 40, Total Fat 4g, Saturated Fat 0g, Total Carbs 3g, Net Carbs 2g, Protein 1g, Sugar 2g, Fiber 1g, Sodium 570mg, Potassium 0g

Cayenne Zucchini Chips

Prep time: 15 minutes, Cook time: 4 Hours, Serves 8

Ingredients:
4 cups very thin zucchini slices
2 Tbsp olive oil
2 tsp sea salt
1 tsp cayenne pepper

Instructions
1. Preheat your air fryer to 135 degrees F.
2. Toss the thin zucchini slices with the oil, cayenne and sea salt.
3. Place the zucchini on the air fryer tray or in the air fryer basket.
4. Cook for 4 hours, tossing the zucchini occasionally to allow it to dehydrate evenly.
5. Once crisp, remove the zucchini from the air fryer and enjoy!

Nutrition Facts Per Serving
Calories 42, Total Fat 4g, Saturated Fat 0g, Total Carbs 3g, Net Carbs 2g, Protein 1g, Sugar 2g, Fiber 1g, Sodium 575mg, Potassium 0g

Salt and Vinegar Zucchini Chips

Prep time: 15 minutes , Cook time: 4 Hours, Serves 8

Ingredients:
4 cups very thin zucchini slices
2 Tbsp olive oil
2 tsp sea salt
1 Tbsp white balsamic vinegar

Instructions
1. Preheat your air fryer to 135 degrees F.
2. Toss the thin zucchini slices with the oil, vinegar and sea salt.
3. Place the zucchini on the air fryer tray or in the air fryer basket.
4. Cook for 4 hours, tossing the zucchini occasionally to allow it to dehydrate evenly.
5. Once crisp, remove the zucchini from the air fryer and enjoy!

Nutrition Facts Per Serving
Calories 42, Total Fat 4g, Saturated Fat 0g, Total Carbs 3g, Net Carbs 2g, Protein 1g, Sugar 2g, Fiber 1g, Sodium 570mg, Potassium 0g

Smoked Zucchini Chips

Prep time: 15 minutes , Cook time: 4 Hours, Serves 8

Ingredients:
4 cups very thin zucchini slices
2 Tbsp olive oil
2 tsp smoked sea salt

Instructions
1. Preheat your air fryer to 135 degrees F.
2. Toss the thin zucchini slices with the oil and smoked sea salt.
3. Place the zucchini on the air fryer tray or in the air fryer basket.
4. Cook for 4 hours, tossing the zucchini occasionally to allow it to dehydrate evenly.
5. Once crisp, remove the zucchini from the air fryer and enjoy!

Nutrition Facts Per Serving
Calories 40, Total Fat 4g, Saturated Fat 0g, Total Carbs 3g, Net Carbs 2g, Protein 1g, Sugar 2g, Fiber 1g, Sodium 570mg, Potassium 0g

Yellow Zucchini Chips

Prep time: 15 minutes , Cook time: 4 Hours, Serves 8

Ingredients:
4 cups very thin yellow zucchini slices
2 Tbsp olive oil
2 tsp sea salt

Instructions
1. Preheat your air fryer to 135 degrees F.
2. Toss the thin zucchini slices with the oil and sea salt.
3. Place the zucchini on the air fryer tray or in the air fryer basket.
4. Cook for 4 hours, tossing the zucchini occasionally to allow it to dehydrate evenly.
5. Once crisp, remove the zucchini from the air fryer and enjoy!

Nutrition Facts Per Serving
Calories 45, Total Fat 4g, Saturated Fat 0g, Total Carbs 3g, Net Carbs 2g, Protein 1g, Sugar 2g, Fiber 1g, Sodium 570mg, Potassium 0g

Cajun Cauliflower Crunch

Prep time: 5 minutes , Cook time: 6 Hours, Serves 4

Ingredients:
4 cups cauliflower florets, chopped into bite sized pieces
1 Tbsp olive oil
1 tsp sea salt
1 tsp Cajun seasoning

Instructions
1. Preheat your air fryer to 135 degrees F.
2. Wash and drain the cauliflower florets.
3. Place the cauliflower in a large bowl and toss with the olive oil and sea salt.
4. Add the cauliflower to the basket of your air fryer or spread them in a flat layer on the tray of your air fryer (either option will work!).
5. Cook in the air fryer for about 6 hours, tossing the cauliflower every hour or so to

6. cook evenly. Essentially, you will be dehydrating the cauliflower.
7. Once the cauliflower is fully dried, remove it from the air fryer, toss with the Cajun seasoning, and then let cool. It will keep crisping as it cools.
8. Enjoy fresh or store in an airtight container for up to a month.

Nutrition Facts Per Serving
Calories 59, Total Fat 3g, Saturated Fat 0g, Total Carbs 4g, Net Carbs 3g, Protein 1g, Sugar 2g, Fiber 1g, Sodium 621mg, Potassium 320g

Soft Pretzels

Prep time: 15 minutes, Cook time: 14 minutes, Serves 6

Ingredients:
- 2 cups almond flour
- 1 Tbsp baking powder
- 1 tsp garlic powder
- 1 tsp onion powder
- 3 eggs
- 5 Tbsp softened cream cheese
- 3 cups mozzarella cheese, grated
- 1 tsp sea salt

Instructions
1. Preheat your air fryer to 400 degrees F and prepare the air fryer tray with parchment paper.
2. Place the almond flour, onion powder, baking powder and garlic powder in a large bowl and stir well.
3. Combine the cream cheese and mozzarella in a separate bowl and melt in the microwave, heating slowly and stirring several times to ensure the cheese melts and does not burn.
4. Add two eggs to the almond flour mix along with the melted cheese. Stir well until a dough forms.
5. Divide the dough into six equal pieces and roll into your desired pretzel shape.
6. Place the pretzels on the prepared sheet tray.
7. Whisk the remaining eggs and brush over the pretzels then sprinkle them all with the sea salt.
8. Bake in the air fryer for 12 minutes or until the pretzels are golden brown.
9. Remove from the air fryer and enjoy while warm!

Nutrition Facts Per Serving
Calories 449, Total Fat 36g, Saturated Fat 7g, Total Carbs 10g, Net Carbs 6g, Protein 28, Sugar 3g, Fiber 4g, Sodium 234mg, Potassium 48g

Soft Garlic Parmesan Pretzels

Prep time: 15 minutes, Cook time: 14 minutes, Serves 6

Ingredients:
- 2 cups almond flour
- 1 Tbsp baking powder
- 1 tsp garlic powder
- 1 tsp onion powder
- 3 eggs
- 5 Tbsp softened cream cheese
- 3 cups mozzarella cheese, grated
- 1 tsp sea salt
- ½ tsp garlic powder
- ¼ cup parmesan cheese

Instructions
1. Preheat your air fryer to 400 degrees F and prepare the air fryer tray with parchment paper.
2. Place the almond flour, onion powder, baking powder and 1 tsp garlic powder in a large bowl and stir well.
3. Combine the cream cheese and mozzarella in a separate bowl and melt in the microwave, heating slowly and stirring several times to ensure the cheese melts and does not burn.
4. Add two eggs to the almond flour mix along with the melted cheese. Stir well until a dough forms.
5. Divide the dough into six equal pieces and roll into your desired pretzel shape.
6. Place the pretzels on the prepared sheet tray.
7. Whisk the remaining eggs and brush over the pretzels then sprinkle them all with the sea salt, parmesan, and ½ tsp garlic powder.
8. Bake in the air fryer for 12 minutes or until the pretzels are golden brown.
9. Remove from the air fryer and enjoy while warm!

Nutrition Facts Per Serving
Calories 493, Total Fat 39g, Saturated Fat 8g, Total Carbs 10g, Net Carbs 6g, Protein 28, Sugar 3g, Fiber 4g, Sodium 234mg, Potassium 48g

Soft Cinnamon Pretzels

Prep time: 15 minutes , Cook time: 14 minutes, Serves 6

Ingredients:
2 cups almond flour
1 Tbsp baking powder
1 tsp salt
3 eggs
5 Tbsp softened cream cheese
3 cups mozzarella cheese, grated
½ tsp ground cinnamon

Instructions
1. Preheat your air fryer to 400 degrees F and prepare the air fryer tray with parchment paper.
2. Place the almond flour, baking powder and salt in a large bowl and stir well.
3. Combine the cream cheese and mozzarella in a separate bowl and melt in the microwave, heating slowly and stirring several times to ensure the cheese melts and does not burn.
4. Add two eggs to the almond flour mix along with the melted cheese. Stir well until a dough forms.
5. Divide the dough into six equal pieces and roll into your desired pretzel shape.
6. Place the pretzels on the prepared sheet tray.
7. Whisk the remaining eggs and brush over the pretzels then sprinkle them all with the cinnamon.
8. Bake in the air fryer for 12 minutes or until the pretzels are golden brown.
9. Remove from the air fryer and enjoy while warm!

Nutrition Facts Per Serving
Calories 432, Total Fat 34g, Saturated Fat 7g, Total Carbs 10g, Net Carbs 6g, Protein 28, Sugar 3g, Fiber 4g, Sodium 212mg, Potassium 48g

Soft Pecan Pretzels

Prep time: 15 minutes , Cook time: 14 minutes, Serves 6

Ingredients:
2 cups almond flour
1 Tbsp baking powder
1 tsp garlic powder
1 tsp onion powder
3 eggs
5 Tbsp softened cream cheese
3 cups mozzarella cheese, grated
1 tsp sea salt
¼ cup chopped pecans

Instructions
1. Preheat your air fryer to 400 degrees F and prepare the air fryer tray with parchment paper.
2. Place the almond flour, onion powder, baking powder and garlic powder in a large bowl and stir well.
3. Combine the cream cheese and mozzarella in a separate bowl and melt in the microwave, heating slowly and stirring several times to ensure the cheese melts and does not burn.
4. Add two eggs to the almond flour mix along with the melted cheese. Stir well until a dough forms.
5. Divide the dough into six equal pieces and roll into your desired pretzel shape.
6. Place the pretzels on the prepared sheet tray.
7. Whisk the remaining eggs and brush over the pretzels then sprinkle them all with the sea salt and chopped pecans
8. Bake in the air fryer for 12 minutes or until the pretzels are golden brown.
9. Remove from the air fryer and enjoy while warm!

Nutrition Facts Per Serving
Calories 512, Total Fat 41g, Saturated Fat 10g, Total Carbs 10g, Net Carbs 6g, Protein 31g, Sugar 3g, Fiber 4g, Sodium 234mg, Potassium 48g

Soft Cheesy Pretzels

Prep time: 15 minutes , Cook time: 14 minutes, Serves 6

Ingredients:
2 cups almond flour
1 Tbsp baking powder
1 Tbsp grated parmesan cheese
1 tsp garlic powder
3 eggs
5 Tbsp softened cream cheese
3 cups mozzarella cheese, grated
1 tsp sea salt
½ grated cheddar cheese

Instructions
1. Preheat your air fryer to 400 degrees F and prepare the air fryer tray with parchment paper.
2. Place the almond flour, parmesan, baking powder and garlic powder in a large bowl and stir well.
3. Combine the cream cheese and mozzarella in a separate bowl and melt in the microwave, heating slowly and stirring several times to ensure the cheese melts and does not burn.
4. Add two eggs to the almond flour mix along with the melted cheese. Stir well until a dough forms.
5. Divide the dough into six equal pieces and roll into your desired pretzel shape.
6. Place the pretzels on the prepared sheet tray.
7. Whisk the remaining eggs and brush over the pretzels then sprinkle them all with the sea salt and the grated cheddar cheese.
8. Bake in the air fryer for 12 minutes or until the pretzels are golden brown.
9. Remove from the air fryer and enjoy while warm!

Nutrition Facts Per Serving Calories 513, Total Fat 40g, Saturated Fat 10g, Total Carbs 10g, Net Carbs 6g, Protein 28, Sugar 3g, Fiber 4g, Sodium 234mg, Potassium 48g

Sweet Zucchini Chips

Prep time: 15 minutes , Cook time: 4 Hours, Serves 8

Ingredients:
4 cups very thin zucchini slices
2 Tbsp olive oil
2 tsp sea salt
1 Tbsp granulated erythritol

Instructions
1. Preheat your air fryer to 135 degrees F.
2. Toss the thin zucchini slices with the oil, erythritol and sea salt.
3. Place the zucchini on the air fryer tray or in the air fryer basket.
4. Cook for 4 hours, tossing the zucchini occasionally to allow it to dehydrate evenly.
5. Once crisp, remove the zucchini from the air fryer and enjoy!

Nutrition Facts Per Serving
Calories 40, Total Fat 4g, Saturated Fat 0g, Total Carbs 6g, Net Carbs 5g, Protein 1g, Sugar 4g, Fiber 1g, Sodium 570mg, Potassium 0g

Cucumber Chips

Prep time: 15 minutes , Cook time: 3 Hours, Serves 4

Ingredients:
4 cups very thin cucumber slices
2 Tbsp apple cider vinegar
2 tsp sea salt

Instructions
1. Preheat your air fryer to 200 degrees F.
2. Place the cucumber slices on a paper towel and layer another paper towel on top to absorb the moisture in the cucumbers.
3. Place the dried slices in a large bowl and toss with the vinegar and salt.
4. Place the cucumber slices on a tray lined with parchment and then bake in the air fryer for 3 hours. The cucumbers will begin to curl and brown slightly.
5. Turn off the air fryer and let the cucumber slices cool inside the fryer (this will help them dry a little more).
6. Enjoy right away or store in an airtight container.

Nutrition Facts Per Serving Calories 15, Total Fat 0g, Saturated Fat 0g, Total Carbs 4g, Net Carbs 3g, Protein 1g, Sugar 2g, Fiber 1g, Sodium 34mg, Potassium 0g

Dill and Onion Cucumber Chips

Prep time: 15 minutes, Cook time: 3 Hours, Serves 4

Ingredients:
- 4 cups very thin cucumber slices
- 2 Tbsp apple cider vinegar
- 2 tsp sea salt
- 1 tsp dried dill
- 1 tsp ground onion powder

Instructions
1. Preheat your air fryer to 200 degrees F.
2. Place the cucumber slices on a paper towel and layer another paper towel on top to absorb the moisture in the cucumbers.
3. Place the dried slices in a large bowl and toss with the vinegar, dried dill, onion powder and salt.
4. Place the cucumber slices on a tray lined with parchment and then bake in the air fryer for 3 hours. The cucumbers will begin to curl and brown slightly.
5. Turn off the air fryer and let the cucumber slices cool inside the fryer (this will help them dry a little more).
6. Enjoy right away or store in an airtight container.

Nutrition Facts Per Serving
Calories 17, Total Fat 0g, Saturated Fat 0g, Total Carbs 4g, Net Carbs 3g, Protein 1g, Sugar 2g, Fiber 1g, Sodium 34mg, Potassium 0g

Smokey Cucumber Chips

Prep time: 15 minutes, Cook time: 3 Hours, Serves 4

Ingredients:
- 4 cups very thin cucumber slices
- 2 Tbsp apple cider vinegar
- 2 tsp smoked sea salt

Instructions
1. Preheat your air fryer to 200 degrees F.
2. Place the cucumber slices on a paper towel and layer another paper towel on top to absorb the moisture in the cucumbers.
3. Place the dried slices in a large bowl and toss with the vinegar and salt.
4. Place the cucumber slices on a tray lined with parchment and then bake in the air fryer for 3 hours. The cucumbers will begin to curl and brown slightly.
5. Turn off the air fryer and let the cucumber slices cool inside the fryer (this will help them dry a little more).
6. Enjoy right away or store in an airtight container.

Nutrition Facts Per Serving
Calories 18, Total Fat 0g, Saturated Fat 0g, Total Carbs 4g, Net Carbs 3g, Protein 1g, Sugar 2g, Fiber 1g, Sodium 34mg, Potassium 0g

Garlic Parmesan Cucumber Chips

Prep time: 15 minutes, Cook time: 3 Hours, Serves 4

Ingredients:
- 4 cups very thin cucumber slices
- 2 Tbsp apple cider vinegar
- 2 tsp sea salt
- 1 tsp garlic powder
- ¼ cup parmesan cheese

Instructions
1. Preheat your air fryer to 200 degrees F.
2. Place the cucumber slices on a paper towel and layer another paper towel on top to absorb the moisture in the cucumbers.
3. Place the dried slices in a large bowl and toss with the vinegar, garlic powder, parmesan, and salt.
4. Place the cucumber slices on a tray lined with parchment and then bake in the air fryer for 3 hours. The cucumbers will begin to curl and brown slightly.
5. Turn off the air fryer and let the cucumber slices cool inside the fryer (this will help them dry a little more).
6. Enjoy right away or store in an airtight container.

Nutrition Facts Per Serving
Calories 34, Total Fat 1g, Saturated Fat 0g, Total Carbs 5g, Net Carbs 4g, Protein 1g, Sugar 3g, Fiber 1g, Sodium 34mg, Potassium 0g

Sea Salt and Black Pepper Cucumber Chips

Prep time: 15 minutes, Cook time: 3 Hours, Serves 4

Ingredients:
4 cups very thin cucumber slices
2 Tbsp apple cider vinegar
2 tsp sea salt
1 Tsp ground black pepper

Instructions
1. Preheat your air fryer to 200 degrees F.
2. Place the cucumber slices on a paper towel and layer another paper towel on top to absorb the moisture in the cucumbers.
3. Place the dried slices in a large bowl and toss with the vinegar, ground black pepper, and salt.
4. Place the cucumber slices on a tray lined with parchment and then bake in the air fryer for 3 hours. The cucumbers will begin to curl and brown slightly.
5. Turn off the air fryer and let the cucumber slices cool inside the fryer (this will help them dry a little more).
6. Enjoy right away or store in an airtight container.

Nutrition Facts Per Serving
Calories 16, Total Fat 0g, Saturated Fat 0g, Total Carbs 4g, Net Carbs 3g, Protein 1g, Sugar 2g, Fiber 1g, Sodium 34mg, Potassium 0g

Taco Cucumber Chips

Prep time: 15 minutes, Cook time: 3 Hours, Serves 4

Ingredients:
4 cups very thin cucumber slices
2 Tbsp apple cider vinegar
2 tsp sea salt
2 tsp taco seasoning

Instructions
1. Preheat your air fryer to 200 degrees F.
2. Place the cucumber slices on a paper towel and layer another paper towel on top to absorb the moisture in the cucumbers.
3. Place the dried slices in a large bowl and toss with the vinegar, taco seasoning, and salt.
4. Place the cucumber slices on a tray lined with parchment and then bake in the air fryer for 3 hours. The cucumbers will begin to curl and brown slightly.
5. Turn off the air fryer and let the cucumber slices cool inside the fryer (this will help them dry a little more).
6. Enjoy right away or store in an airtight container.

Nutrition Facts Per Serving
Calories 23, Total Fat 0g, Saturated Fat 0g, Total Carbs 4g, Net Carbs 3g, Protein 1g, Sugar 2g, Fiber 1g, Sodium 38mg, Potassium 0g

Dilly Almonds

Prep time: 5 minutes, Cook time: 10 minutes, Serves 6

Ingredients:
1 egg white
3 cups whole almonds
2 tsp salt
2 tsp dried dill
½ tsp ground black pepper

Instructions
1. Preheat your air fryer to 325 degrees F and prepare the air fryer tray with parchment paper.
2. Place the egg whites in a large bowl and whip until stiff peaks form.
3. Add the almonds and toss to coat.
4. Sprinkle with the seasonings and then place the almonds on the tray, laying them out as evenly as possible on the tray.
5. Bake in the air fryer for 10 minutes. The almonds should be golden brown.
6. Remove from the air fryer and let cool.

Nutrition Facts Per Serving
Calories 414, Total Fat 34g, Saturated Fat 8g, Total Carbs 14g, Net Carbs 7g, Protein 14, Sugar 2g, Fiber 8g, Sodium 210mg, Potassium 0g

Garlic Almonds

Prep time: 5 minutes, Cook time: 10 minutes, Serves 6

Ingredients:
1 egg white
3 cups whole almonds
2 tsp salt
2 tsp garlic powder
½ tsp ground black pepper

Instructions
1. Preheat your air fryer to 325 degrees F and prepare the air fryer tray with parchment paper.
2. Place the egg whites in a large bowl and whip until stiff peaks form.
3. Add the almonds and toss to coat.
4. Sprinkle with the seasonings and then place the almonds on the tray, laying them out as evenly as possible on the tray.
5. Bake in the air fryer for 10 minutes. The almonds should be golden brown.
6. Remove from the air fryer and let cool.

Nutrition Facts Per Serving
Calories 412, Total Fat 34g, Saturated Fat 8g, Total Carbs 14g, Net Carbs 7g, Protein 14, Sugar 2g, Fiber 8g, Sodium 212mg, Potassium 0g

Sweet and Salty Almonds

Prep time: 5 minutes, Cook time: 10 minutes, Serves 6

Ingredients:
1 egg white
3 cups whole almonds
2 tsp salt
1 Tbsp swerve sweetener
½ tsp ground black pepper

Instructions
1. Preheat your air fryer to 325 degrees F and prepare the air fryer tray with parchment paper.
2. Place the egg whites in a large bowl and whip until stiff peaks form.
3. Add the almonds and toss to coat.
4. Sprinkle with the salt, swerve and ground black pepper, and then place the almonds on the tray, laying them out as evenly as possible on the tray.
5. Bake in the air fryer for 10 minutes. The almonds should be golden brown.
6. Remove from the air fryer and let cool.

Nutrition Facts Per Serving
Calories 409, Total Fat 34g, Saturated Fat 8g, Total Carbs 14g, Net Carbs 7g, Protein 14, Sugar 2g, Fiber 8g, Sodium 201mg, Potassium 0g

Cayenne Almonds

Prep time: 5 minutes, Cook time: 10 minutes, Serves 6

Ingredients:
1 egg white
3 cups whole almonds
2 tsp salt
2 tsp cayenne pepper
½ tsp ground black pepper

Instructions
1. Preheat your air fryer to 325 degrees F and prepare the air fryer tray with parchment paper.
2. Place the egg whites in a large bowl and whip until stiff peaks form.
3. Add the almonds and toss to coat.
4. Sprinkle with the seasonings and then place the almonds on the tray, laying them out as evenly as possible on the tray.
5. Bake in the air fryer for 10 minutes. The almonds should be golden brown.
6. Remove from the air fryer and let cool.

Nutrition Facts Per Serving
Calories 414, Total Fat 34g, Saturated Fat 8g, Total Carbs 14g, Net Carbs 7g, Protein 14, Sugar 2g, Fiber 8g, Sodium 210mg, Potassium 0g

Black Pepper Almonds

Prep time: 5 minutes, Cook time: 10 minutes, Serves 6

Ingredients:
1 egg white
3 cups whole almonds
2 tsp salt
1 tsp ground black pepper

Instructions
1. Preheat your air fryer to 325 degrees F and prepare the air fryer tray with parchment paper.
2. Place the egg whites in a large bowl and whip until stiff peaks form.
3. Add the almonds and toss to coat.
4. Sprinkle with the salt and pepper and then place the almonds on the tray, laying them out as evenly as possible on the tray.
5. Bake in the air fryer for 10 minutes. The almonds should be golden brown.
6. Remove from the air fryer and let cool.

Nutrition Facts Per Serving
Calories 414, Total Fat 34g, Saturated Fat 8g, Total Carbs 14g, Net Carbs 7g, Protein 14, Sugar 2g, Fiber 8g, Sodium 210mg, Potassium 0g

Sweet Candied Pecans

Prep time: 5 minutes, Cook time: 10 minutes, Serves 6

Ingredients:
1 egg white
3 cups whole pecans
2 tsp salt
1 Tbsp swerve

Instructions
1. Preheat your air fryer to 325 degrees F and prepare the air fryer tray with parchment paper.
2. Place the egg whites in a large bowl and whip until stiff peaks form.
3. Add the almonds and toss to coat.
4. Sprinkle with the swerve and salt and then place the almonds on the tray, laying them out as evenly as possible on the tray.
5. Bake in the air fryer for 10 minutes. The almonds should be golden brown.
6. Remove from the air fryer and let cool.

Nutrition Facts Per Serving
Calories 409, Total Fat 34g, Saturated Fat 8g, Total Carbs 14g, Net Carbs 7g, Protein 14, Sugar 2g, Fiber 8g, Sodium 201mg, Potassium 0g

Garlicky Cauliflower Crunch

Prep time: 5 minutes, Cook time: 6 Hours, Serves 4

Ingredients:
4 cups cauliflower florets, chopped into bite sized pieces
1 Tbsp olive oil
1 tsp sea salt
1 tsp garlic powder

Instructions
1. Preheat your air fryer to 135 degrees F.
2. Wash and drain the cauliflower florets.
3. Place the cauliflower in a large bowl and toss with the olive oil and sea salt.
4. Add the cauliflower to the basket of your air fryer or spread them in a flat layer on the tray of your air fryer (either option will work!).
5. Cook in the air fryer for about 6 hours, tossing the cauliflower every hour or so to cook evenly. Essentially, you will be dehydrating the cauliflower.
6. Once the cauliflower is fully dried, remove it from the air fryer, toss it with the garlic powder, and then let cool. It will keep crisping as it cools.
7. Enjoy fresh or store in an airtight container for up to a month.

Nutrition Facts Per Serving
Calories 57, Total Fat 3g, Saturated Fat 0g, Total Carbs 4g, Net Carbs 3g, Protein 1g, Sugar 2g, Fiber 1g, Sodium 619mg, Potassium 320g

Desserts

Peanut Butter Cookies

Prep time: 5 minutes , Cook time: 12 minutes, Serves 5

Ingredients:
½ cup peanut butter
¼ cup swerve sweetener
1 egg yolk
½ tsp vanilla extract
1/8 tsp sea salt

Instructions
1. Preheat your air fryer to 235 degrees F and prepare the air fryer tray with parchment paper.
2. Combine all the ingredients in a large bowl until a nice dough forms.
3. Scoop the dough onto the prepared sheet tray and use a fork to press them down, making the signature peanut butter cookie pattern on the top.
4. Bake in the air fryer for 12 minutes.
5. Allow to cool slightly before removing from the tray and serving.

Nutrition Facts Per Serving
Calories 133, Total Fat 12g, Saturated Fat 8g, Total Carbs 12g, Net Carbs 6g, Protein 6, Sugar 3g, Fiber 6g, Sodium 216mg, Potassium 148g

Peanut Butter Chocolate Chip Cookies

Prep time: 5 minutes , Cook time: 12 minutes, Serves 5

Ingredients:
½ cup peanut butter
¼ cup swerve sweetener
1 egg yolk
½ tsp vanilla extract
1/8 tsp sea salt
¼ cup Lily's dark chocolate chips

Instructions
1. Preheat your air fryer to 235 degrees F and prepare the air fryer tray with parchment paper.
2. Combine all the ingredients in a large bowl until a nice dough forms.
3. Scoop the dough onto the prepared sheet tray and use a fork to press them down, making the signature peanut butter cookie pattern on the top.
4. Bake in the air fryer for 12 minutes.
5. Allow to cool slightly before removing from the tray and serving.

Nutrition Facts Per Serving
Calories 185, Total Fat 16g, Saturated Fat 8g, Total Carbs 14g, Net Carbs 8g, Protein 6, Sugar 5g, Fiber 6g, Sodium 216mg, Potassium 148g

Peanut Butter Flaxseed Cookies

Prep time: 5 minutes , Cook time: 12 minutes, Serves 5

Ingredients:
½ cup peanut butter
¼ cup swerve sweetener
2 Tbsp ground flaxseeds
1 egg yolk
½ tsp vanilla extract
1/8 tsp sea salt

Instructions
1. Preheat your air fryer to 235 degrees F and prepare the air fryer tray with parchment paper.
2. Combine all the ingredients in a large bowl until a nice dough forms.
3. Scoop the dough onto the prepares sheet tray and use a fork to press them down, making the signature peanut butter cookie pattern on the top.
4. Bake in the air fryer for 12 minutes.
5. Allow to cool slightly before removing from the tray and serving.

Nutrition Facts Per Serving
Calories 169, Total Fat 12g, Saturated Fat 8g, Total Carbs 12g, Net Carbs 6g, Protein 8, Sugar 3g, Fiber 6g, Sodium 216mg, Potassium 169g

Peanut Butter and Jelly Cookies

Prep time: 5 minutes , Cook time: 12 minutes, Serves 5

Ingredients:
- ½ cup peanut butter
- ¼ cup swerve sweetener
- 10 fresh raspberries
- 1 egg yolk
- ½ tsp vanilla extract
- 1/8 tsp sea salt

Instructions
1. Preheat your air fryer to 235 degrees F and prepare the air fryer tray with parchment paper.
2. Combine all the ingredients in a large bowl until a nice dough forms. It is okay if the raspberries smash into the dough- you want them to be blended in too!
3. Scoop the dough onto the prepared sheet tray and use a fork to press them down, making the signature peanut butter cookie pattern on the top.
4. Bake in the air fryer for 12 minutes.
5. Allow to cool slightly before removing from the tray and serving.

Nutrition Facts Per Serving
Calories 189, Total Fat 12g, Saturated Fat 8g, Total Carbs 14g, Net Carbs 8g, Protein 6, Sugar 8g, Fiber 6g, Sodium 216mg, Potassium 148g

Chocolate Walnuts

Prep time: 10 minutes , Cook time: 10 minutes, Serves 5

Ingredients:
- 2 cups walnuts
- 1 cup unsweetened chocolate chips
- ¼ cup powdered swerve sweetener
- 2 Tbsp coconut oil
- 1 tsp vanilla extract
- 1 Tbsp unsweetened cocoa powder
- ½ tsp sea salt

Instructions
1. Preheat your air fryer to 300 degrees F and prepare the air fryer tray with parchment paper.
2. Place the walnuts on the tray and toast for 10 minutes or until the nuts begin to turn a slight golden brown.
3. Remove the nuts from the air fryer and let cool.
4. Mix the unsweetened chocolate chops, coconut oil and swerve sweetener in a small pot and heat over low heat, stirring constantly until the mixture is smooth.
5. Add the cocoa powder, salt, and vanilla to the chocolate mix and stir well.
6. Remove the pot from the heat and toss in the toasted walnuts.
7. Pour the nuts onto a piece of parchment paper and let cool until the chocolate has hardened. Enjoy!

Nutrition Facts Per Serving
Calories 240, Total Fat 8g, Saturated Fat 3g, Total Carbs 7g, Net Carbs 3g, Protein 4g, Sugar 3g, Fiber 4g, Sodium 418mg, Potassium 212g

Spicy Chocolate Walnuts

Prep time: 10 minutes , Cook time: 10 minutes, Serves 5

Ingredients:
- 2 cups walnuts
- 1 cup unsweetened chocolate chips
- ¼ cup powdered swerve sweetener
- 1 tsp cayenne pepper
- 2 Tbsp coconut oil
- 1 tsp vanilla extract
- 1 Tbsp unsweetened cocoa powder
- ½ tsp sea salt

Instructions
1. Preheat your air fryer to 300 degrees F and prepare the air fryer tray with parchment paper.
2. Place the walnuts on the tray and toast for 10 minutes or until the nuts begin to turn a slight golden brown.
3. Remove the nuts from the air fryer and let cool.

4. Mix the unsweetened chocolate chips, coconut oil and swerve sweetener in a small pot and heat over low heat, stirring constantly until the mixture is smooth.
5. Add the cocoa powder, salt, and vanilla to the chocolate mix and stir well.
6. Remove the pot from the heat and toss in the toasted walnuts.
7. Pour the nuts onto a piece of parchment paper and let cool until the chocolate has hardened. Enjoy!

Nutrition Facts Per Serving
Calories 241, Total Fat 8g, Saturated Fat 3g, Total Carbs 7g, Net Carbs 3g, Protein 4g, Sugar 3g, Fiber 4g, Sodium 418mg, Potassium 212g

Mexican Chocolate Walnuts

Prep time: 10 minutes , Cook time: 10 minutes, Serves 5

Ingredients:
2 cups walnuts
1 cup unsweetened chocolate chips
¼ cup powdered swerve sweetener
2 Tbsp coconut oil
1 tsp vanilla extract
1 Tbsp unsweetened cocoa powder
1 tsp ground cinnamon
½ tsp sea salt

Instructions
1. Preheat your air fryer to 300 degrees F and prepare the air fryer tray with parchment paper.
2. Place the walnuts on the tray and toast for 10 minutes or until the nuts begin to turn a slight golden brown.
3. Remove the nuts from the air fryer and let cool.
4. Mix the unsweetened chocolate chips, coconut oil and swerve sweetener in a small pot and heat over low heat, stirring constantly until the mixture is smooth.
5. Add the cocoa powder, cinnamon, salt, and vanilla to the chocolate mix and stir well.
6. Remove the pot from the heat and toss in the toasted walnuts.
7. Pour the nuts onto a piece of parchment paper and let cool until the chocolate has hardened. Enjoy!

Nutrition Facts Per Serving
Calories 244, Total Fat 8g, Saturated Fat 3g, Total Carbs 7g, Net Carbs 3g, Protein 4g, Sugar 3g, Fiber 4g, Sodium 418mg, Potassium 212g

Chocolate Almonds

Prep time: 10 minutes , Cook time: 10 minutes, Serves 5

Ingredients:
2 cups whole almonds
1 cup unsweetened chocolate chips
¼ cup powdered swerve sweetener
2 Tbsp coconut oil
1 tsp vanilla extract
1 Tbsp unsweetened cocoa powder
½ tsp sea salt

Instructions
1. Preheat your air fryer to 300 degrees F and prepare the air fryer tray with parchment paper.
2. Place the almonds on the tray and toast for 10 minutes or until the nuts begin to turn a slight golden brown.
3. Remove the nuts from the air fryer and let cool.
4. Mix the unsweetened chocolate chips, coconut oil and swerve sweetener in a small pot and heat over low heat, stirring constantly until the mixture is smooth.
5. Add the cocoa powder, salt, and vanilla to the chocolate mix and stir well.
6. Remove the pot from the heat and toss in the toasted almonds.
7. Pour the nuts onto a piece of parchment paper and let cool until the chocolate has hardened. Enjoy!

Nutrition Facts Per Serving
Calories 262, Total Fat 10g, Saturated Fat 4g, Total Carbs 8g, Net Carbs 3g, Protein 4g, Sugar 3g, Fiber 4g, Sodium 424mg, Potassium 243g

Sweet and Spicy Walnuts

Prep time: 10 minutes , Cook time: 10 minutes, Serves 5

Ingredients:
2 cups walnuts
1 cup unsweetened chocolate chips
¼ cup powdered swerve sweetener
2 Tbsp coconut oil
1 tsp vanilla extract
1 Tbsp unsweetened cocoa powder
½ tsp red pepper flakes
½ tsp sea salt

Instructions
1. Preheat your air fryer to 300 degrees F and prepare the air fryer tray with parchment paper.
2. Place the walnuts on the tray and toast for 10 minutes or until the nuts begin to turn a slight golden brown.
3. Remove the nuts from the air fryer and let cool.
4. Mix the unsweetened chocolate chips, coconut oil and swerve sweetener in a small pot and heat over low heat, stirring constantly until the mixture is smooth.
5. Add the cocoa powder, red pepper flakes, salt, and vanilla to the chocolate mix and stir well.
6. Remove the pot from the heat and toss in the toasted walnuts.
7. Pour the nuts onto a piece of parchment paper and let cool until the chocolate has hardened. Enjoy!

Nutrition Facts Per Serving
Calories 244, Total Fat 8g, Saturated Fat 3g, Total Carbs 7g, Net Carbs 3g, Protein 4g, Sugar 3g, Fiber 4g, Sodium 418mg, Potassium 212g

Chocolate Peanut Butter Walnuts

Prep time: 10 minutes , Cook time: 10 minutes, Serves 5

Ingredients:
2 cups walnuts
1 cup unsweetened chocolate chips
1 Tbsp unsweetened peanut butter
¼ cup powdered swerve sweetener
2 Tbsp coconut oil
1 tsp vanilla extract
1 Tbsp unsweetened cocoa powder
½ tsp sea salt

Instructions
1. Preheat your air fryer to 300 degrees F and prepare the air fryer tray with parchment paper.
2. Place the walnuts on the tray and toast for 10 minutes or until the nuts begin to turn a slight golden brown.
3. Remove the nuts from the air fryer and let cool.
4. Mix the unsweetened chocolate chips, peanut butter, coconut oil and swerve sweetener in a small pot and heat over low heat, stirring constantly until the mixture is smooth.
5. Add the cocoa powder, salt, and vanilla to the chocolate mix and stir well.
6. Remove the pot from the heat and toss in the toasted walnuts.
7. Pour the nuts onto a piece of parchment paper and let cool until the chocolate has hardened. Enjoy!

Nutrition Facts Per Serving
Calories 278, Total Fat 13g, Saturated Fat 6g, Total Carbs 7g, Net Carbs 3g, Protein 4g, Sugar 5g, Fiber 4g, Sodium 478mg, Potassium 259g

Vanilla Cake

Prep time: 30 minutes, Cook time: 30 minutes, Serves 12

Ingredients:
- 2 ½ cups almond flour
- ¼ cup coconut flour
- ¼ cup vanilla protein powder
- ½ tsp salt
- 1 Tbsp baking powder
- 2/3 cup granulated erythritol
- ½ cup butter
- ¾ cup whole milk
- 1 tsp vanilla
- 4 whole eggs

Instructions
1. Preheat your air fryer to 325 degrees F and grease and 8" cake pan.
2. Place the butter in a mixing bowl along with the erythritol and beat until fluffy.
3. In a separate bowl, mix the eggs, milk and vanilla together.
4. In a third bowl, combine the remaining dry ingredients.
5. Add half of the wet mixture to the bowl with the fluffy butter and beat together slowly.
6. Add half of the dry mix to the bowl and beat again until smooth.
7. Add the remaining wet ingredients, mix and add the remaining dry ingredients and blend until a smooth batter forms.
8. Pour the cake batter into the prepared pan and place in the air fryer to cook for 30 minutes. The cake will be golden brown and a toothpick will come out cleanly when inserted into the center of the cake.
9. Remove from the air fryer and cool in the pan for 20 minutes. Flip the cake out of the pan, slice and enjoy! You can also frost the cake however you'd like with a tasty keto frosting.

Nutrition Facts Per Serving
Calories 308, Total Fat 32g, Saturated Fat 12g, Total Carbs 8g, Net Carbs 4g, Protein 10g, Sugar 4g, Fiber 4g, Sodium 312mg, Potassium 45g

Vanilla Raspberry Cake

Prep time: 30 minutes, Cook time: 30 minutes, Serves 12

Ingredients:
- 2 ½ cups almond flour
- ¼ cup coconut flour
- ¼ cup vanilla protein powder
- ½ tsp salt
- 1 Tbsp baking powder
- 2/3 cup granulated erythritol
- ½ cup butter
- ¾ cup whole milk
- 1 tsp vanilla
- 4 whole eggs
- 1 cup fresh raspberries

Instructions
1. Preheat your air fryer to 325 degrees F and grease and 8" cake pan.
2. Place the butter in a mixing bowl along with the erythritol and beat until fluffy.
3. In a separate bowl, mix the eggs, milk and vanilla together.
4. In a third bowl, combine the remaining dry ingredients.
5. Add half of the wet mixture to the bowl with the fluffy butter and beat together slowly.
6. Add half of the dry mix to the bowl and beat again until smooth.
7. Add the remaining wet ingredients, mix and add the remaining dry ingredients and blend until a smooth batter forms. Gently stir in the raspberries.
8. Pour the cake batter into the prepared pan and place in the air fryer to cook for 30 minutes. The cake will be golden brown and a toothpick will come out cleanly when inserted into the center of the cake.
9. Remove from the air fryer and cool in the pan for 20 minutes. Flip the cake out of the pan, slice and enjoy! You can also frost the cake however you'd like with a tasty keto frosting.

Nutrition Facts Per Serving
Calories 368, Total Fat 32g, Saturated Fat 12g, Total Carbs 14g, Net Carbs 10g, Protein 10g, Sugar 7g, Fiber 4g, Sodium 312mg, Potassium 192g

Blueberry Cake

Prep time: 30 minutes, Cook time: 30 minutes, Serves 12

Ingredients:
- 2 ½ cups almond flour
- ¼ cup coconut flour
- ¼ cup vanilla protein powder
- ½ tsp salt
- 1 Tbsp baking powder
- 2/3 cup granulated erythritol
- ½ cup butter
- ¾ cup whole milk
- 1 tsp vanilla
- 4 whole eggs
- 1 cup fresh blueberries

Instructions
1. Preheat your air fryer to 325 degrees F and grease and 8" cake pan.
2. Place the butter in a mixing bowl along with the erythritol and beat until fluffy.
3. In a separate bowl, mix the eggs, milk and vanilla together.
4. In a third bowl, combine the remaining dry ingredients.
5. Add half of the wet mixture to the bowl with the fluffy butter and beat together slowly.
6. Add half of the dry mix to the bowl and beat again until smooth.
7. Add the remaining wet ingredients, mix and add the remaining dry ingredients and blend until a smooth batter forms. Fold in the blueberries gently.
8. Pour the cake batter into the prepared pan and place in the air fryer to cook for 30 minutes. The cake will be golden brown and a toothpick will come out cleanly when inserted into the center of the cake.
9. Remove from the air fryer and cool in the pan for 20 minutes. Flip the cake out of the pan, slice and enjoy! You can also frost the cake however you'd like with a tasty keto frosting.

Nutrition Facts Per Serving
Calories 379, Total Fat 32g, Saturated Fat 12g, Total Carbs 13g, Net Carbs 9g, Protein 10g, Sugar 6g, Fiber 4g, Sodium 312mg, Potassium 202g

Cinnamon Cake

Prep time: 30 minutes, Cook time: 30 minutes, Serves 12

Ingredients:
- 2 ½ cups almond flour
- ¼ cup coconut flour
- ¼ cup vanilla protein powder
- ½ tsp salt
- 1 Tbsp baking powder
- 1 tsp ground cinnamon
- 2/3 cup granulated erythritol
- ½ cup butter
- ¾ cup whole milk
- 1 tsp vanilla
- 4 whole eggs

Instructions
1. Preheat your air fryer to 325 degrees F and grease and 8" cake pan.
2. Place the butter in a mixing bowl along with the erythritol and beat until fluffy.
3. In a separate bowl, mix the eggs, milk and vanilla together.
4. In a third bowl, combine the remaining dry ingredients.
5. Add half of the wet mixture to the bowl with the fluffy butter and beat together slowly.
6. Add half of the dry mix to the bowl and beat again until smooth.
7. Add the remaining wet ingredients, mix and add the remaining dry ingredients and blend until a smooth batter forms.
8. Pour the cake batter into the prepared pan and place in the air fryer to cook for 30 minutes. The cake will be golden brown and a toothpick will come out cleanly when inserted into the center of the cake.
9. Remove from the air fryer and cool in the pan for 20 minutes. Flip the cake out of the pan, slice and enjoy! You can also frost the cake however you'd like with a tasty keto frosting.

Nutrition Facts Per Serving
Calories 308, Total Fat 32g, Saturated Fat 12g, Total Carbs 8g, Net Carbs 4g, Protein 10g, Sugar 4g, Fiber 4g, Sodium 312mg, Potassium 45g

Spice Cake

Prep time: 30 minutes, Cook time: 30 minutes, Serves 12

Ingredients:
- 2 ¾ cups almond flour
- 1 tsp cinnamon
- ¼ tsp ground nutmeg
- ¼ tsp ground ginger
- ¼ cup vanilla protein powder
- ½ tsp salt
- 1 Tbsp baking powder
- 2/3 cup granulated erythritol
- ½ cup butter
- ¾ cup whole milk
- 1 tsp vanilla
- 4 whole eggs

Instructions
1. Preheat your air fryer to 325 degrees F and grease and 8" cake pan.
2. Place the butter in a mixing bowl along with the erythritol and beat until fluffy.
3. In a separate bowl, mix the eggs, milk and vanilla together.
4. In a third bowl, combine the remaining dry ingredients.
5. Add half of the wet mixture to the bowl with the fluffy butter and beat together slowly.
6. Add half of the dry mix to the bowl and beat again until smooth. Alternate wets and dries until everything is mixed together.
7. Pour the cake batter into the prepared pan and place in the air fryer to cook for 30 minutes. The cake will be golden brown and a toothpick will come out cleanly when inserted into the center of the cake.
8. Remove from the air fryer and cool in the pan for 20 minutes. Flip the cake out of the pan, slice and enjoy!

Nutrition Facts Per Serving
Calories 308, Total Fat 32g, Saturated Fat 12g, Total Carbs 8g, Net Carbs 4g, Protein 10g, Sugar 4g, Fiber 4g, Sodium 312mg, Potassium 45g

Caramel Cake

Prep time: 30 minutes, Cook time: 30 minutes, Serves 12

Ingredients:
- 2 ½ cups almond flour
- ¼ cup coconut flour
- ¼ cup vanilla protein powder
- ½ tsp salt
- 1 Tbsp baking powder
- 2/3 cup granulated erythritol
- ½ cup butter
- ¾ cup whole milk
- 1 tsp vanilla
- 4 whole eggs
- 1 cup keto caramel sauce

Instructions
1. Preheat your air fryer to 325 degrees F and grease and 8" cake pan.
2. Place the butter in a mixing bowl along with the erythritol and beat until fluffy.
3. In a separate bowl, mix the eggs, milk and vanilla together.
4. In a third bowl, combine the remaining dry ingredients.
5. Add half of the wet mixture to the bowl with the fluffy butter and beat together slowly.
6. Add half of the dry mix to the bowl and beat again until smooth.
7. Add the remaining wet ingredients, mix and add the remaining dry ingredients and blend until a smooth batter forms.
8. Pour the cake batter into the prepared pan and place in the air fryer to cook for 30 minutes. The cake will be golden brown and a toothpick will come out cleanly when inserted into the center of the cake.
9. Remove from the air fryer and cool in the pan for 20 minutes. Flip the cake out of the pan, and onto a tray. Pour the keto caramel sauce over the cake hen slice and serve!

Nutrition Facts Per Serving
Calories 388, Total Fat 35g, Saturated Fat 12g, Total Carbs 10g, Net Carbs 6g, Protein 10g, Sugar 6g, Fiber 4g, Sodium 312mg, Potassium 45g

Chocolate Chip Cake

Prep time: 30 minutes , Cook time: 30 minutes, Serves 12

Ingredients:
2 ½ cups almond flour
¼ cup coconut flour
¼ cup vanilla protein powder
½ tsp salt
1 Tbsp baking powder
2/3 cup granulated erythritol
½ cup butter
¾ cup whole milk
1 tsp vanilla
4 whole eggs
1 cup dark, unsweetened chocolate chips

Instructions
1. Preheat your air fryer to 325 degrees F and grease and 8" cake pan.
2. Place the butter in a mixing bowl along with the erythritol and beat until fluffy.
3. In a separate bowl, mix the eggs, milk and vanilla together.
4. In a third bowl, combine the remaining dry ingredients.
5. Add half of the wet mixture to the bowl with the fluffy butter and beat together slowly.
6. Add half of the dry mix to the bowl and beat again until smooth.
7. Add the remaining wet ingredients, mix and add the remaining dry ingredients and blend until a smooth batter forms. Fold in the chocolate chips.
8. Pour the cake batter into the prepared pan and place in the air fryer to cook for 30 minutes. The cake will be golden brown and a toothpick will come out cleanly when inserted into the center of the cake.
9. Remove from the air fryer and cool in the pan for 20 minutes. Flip the cake out of the pan, slice and enjoy! You can also frost the cake however you'd like with a tasty keto frosting.

Nutrition Facts Per Serving
Calories 397, Total Fat 38g, Saturated Fat 18g, Total Carbs 12g, Net Carbs 8g, Protein 10g, Sugar 7g, Fiber 4g, Sodium 312mg, Potassium 45g

Strawberry Vanilla Cake

Prep time: 30 minutes , Cook time: 30 minutes, Serves 12

Ingredients:
2 ½ cups almond flour
¼ cup coconut flour
¼ cup vanilla protein powder
½ tsp salt
1 Tbsp baking powder
2/3 cup granulated erythritol
½ cup butter
¾ cup whole milk
1 tsp vanilla
4 whole eggs
1 cup chopped strawberries

Instructions
1. Preheat your air fryer to 325 degrees F and grease and 8" cake pan.
2. Place the butter in a mixing bowl along with the erythritol and beat until fluffy.
3. In a separate bowl, mix the eggs, milk and vanilla together.
4. In a third bowl, combine the remaining dry ingredients.
5. Add half of the wet mixture to the bowl with the fluffy butter and beat together slowly.
6. Add half of the dry mix to the bowl and beat again until smooth.
7. Add the remaining wet ingredients, mix and add the remaining dry ingredients and blend until a smooth batter forms. Fold the strawberries into the cake batter.
8. Pour the cake batter into the prepared pan and place in the air fryer to cook for 30 minutes. The cake will be golden brown and a toothpick will come out cleanly when inserted into the center of the cake.
9. Remove from the air fryer and cool in the pan for 20 minutes. Flip the cake out of the pan, slice and enjoy! You can also frost the cake however you'd like with a tasty keto frosting.

Nutrition Facts Per Serving
Calories 353, Total Fat 32g, Saturated Fat 12g, Total Carbs 14g, Net Carbs 9g, Protein 10g, Sugar 8g, Fiber 5g, Sodium 312mg, Potassium 76g

Espresso Cake

Prep time: 30 minutes, Cook time: 30 minutes, Serves 12

Ingredients:
- 2 ½ cups almond flour
- ¼ cup coconut flour
- ¼ cup vanilla protein powder
- ½ tsp salt
- 1 Tbsp baking powder
- 2/3 cup granulated erythritol
- ½ cup butter
- ½ cup whole milk
- ¼ cup brewed espresso
- 1 tsp vanilla
- 4 whole eggs

Instructions
1. Preheat your air fryer to 325 degrees F and grease and 8" cake pan.
2. Place the butter in a mixing bowl along with the erythritol and beat until fluffy.
3. In a separate bowl, mix the eggs, brewed espresso, milk and vanilla together.
4. In a third bowl, combine the remaining dry ingredients.
5. Add half of the wet mixture to the bowl with the fluffy butter and beat together slowly.
6. Add half of the dry mix to the bowl and beat again until smooth.
7. Add the remaining wet ingredients, mix and add the remaining dry ingredients and blend until a smooth batter forms.
8. Pour the cake batter into the prepared pan and place in the air fryer to cook for 30 minutes. The cake will be golden brown and a toothpick will come out cleanly when inserted into the center of the cake.
9. Remove from the air fryer and cool in the pan for 20 minutes. Flip the cake out of the pan, slice and enjoy! You can also frost the cake however you'd like with a tasty keto frosting.

Nutrition Facts Per Serving
Calories 343, Total Fat 32g, Saturated Fat 12g, Total Carbs 8g, Net Carbs 4g, Protein 10g, Sugar 4g, Fiber 4g, Sodium 319mg, Potassium 45g

Almond Cake

Prep time: 30 minutes, Cook time: 30 minutes, Serves 12

Ingredients:
- 2 ¾ cups almond flour
- ¼ cup vanilla protein powder
- ½ tsp salt
- 1 Tbsp baking powder
- 2/3 cup granulated erythritol
- ½ cup butter
- ¾ cup whole milk
- 1 tsp almond extract
- 4 whole eggs

Instructions
1. Preheat your air fryer to 325 degrees F and grease and 8" cake pan.
2. Place the butter in a mixing bowl along with the erythritol and beat until fluffy.
3. In a separate bowl, mix the eggs, milk and almond extract together.
4. In a third bowl, combine the remaining dry ingredients.
5. Add half of the wet mixture to the bowl with the fluffy butter and beat together slowly.
6. Add half of the dry mix to the bowl and beat again until smooth.
7. Add the remaining wet ingredients, mix and add the remaining dry ingredients and blend until a smooth batter forms.
8. Pour the cake batter into the prepared pan and place in the air fryer to cook for 30 minutes. The cake will be golden brown and a toothpick will come out cleanly when inserted into the center of the cake.
9. Remove from the air fryer and cool in the pan for 20 minutes. Flip the cake out of the pan, slice and enjoy! You can also frost the cake however you'd like with a tasty keto frosting.

Nutrition Facts Per Serving
Calories 316, Total Fat 30g, Saturated Fat 11g, Total Carbs 8g, Net Carbs 4g, Protein 10g, Sugar 4g, Fiber 4g, Sodium 312mg, Potassium 45g

Chocolate Cake

Prep time: 30 minutes, Cook time: 30 minutes, Serves 12

Ingredients:
- 2 ½ cups almond flour
- ¼ cup coconut flour
- ¼ cup chocolate protein powder
- ½ tsp salt
- ¼ cup unsweetened cocoa powder
- 1 Tbsp baking powder
- 2/3 cup granulated erythritol
- ½ cup butter
- ¾ cup whole milk
- 1 tsp vanilla
- 4 whole eggs

Instructions
1. Preheat your air fryer to 325 degrees F and grease and 8" cake pan.
2. Place the butter in a mixing bowl along with the erythritol and beat until fluffy.
3. In a separate bowl, mix the eggs, milk and vanilla together.
4. In a third bowl, combine the remaining dry ingredients.
5. Add half of the wet mixture to the bowl with the fluffy butter and beat together slowly.
6. Add half of the dry mix to the bowl and beat again until smooth.
7. Add the remaining wet ingredients, mix and add the remaining dry ingredients and blend until a smooth batter forms.
8. Pour the cake batter into the prepared pan and place in the air fryer to cook for 30 minutes. The cake will be golden brown and a toothpick will come out cleanly when inserted into the center of the cake.
9. Remove from the air fryer and cool in the pan for 20 minutes. Flip the cake out of the pan, slice and enjoy! You can also frost the cake however you'd like with a tasty keto frosting.

Nutrition Facts Per Serving
Calories 348, Total Fat 36g, Saturated Fat 16g, Total Carbs 9g, Net Carbs 4g, Protein 11g, Sugar 4g, Fiber 5g, Sodium 321mg, Potassium 63g

Peanut Butter Cake

Prep time: 30 minutes, Cook time: 30 minutes, Serves 12

Ingredients:
- 2 ½ cups almond flour
- ¼ cup coconut flour
- ¼ cup vanilla protein powder
- ½ tsp salt
- 1 Tbsp baking powder
- 2/3 cup granulated erythritol
- ¼ cup butter
- ¼ cup peanut butter
- ¾ cup whole milk
- 1 tsp vanilla
- 4 whole eggs

Instructions
1. Preheat your air fryer to 325 degrees F and grease and 8" cake pan.
2. Place the butter and peanut butter in a mixing bowl along with the erythritol and beat until fluffy.
3. In a separate bowl, mix the eggs, milk and vanilla together.
4. In a third bowl, combine the remaining dry ingredients.
5. Add half of the wet mixture to the bowl with the fluffy butter and beat together slowly.
6. Add half of the dry mix to the bowl and beat again until smooth.
7. Add the remaining wet ingredients, mix and add the remaining dry ingredients and blend until a smooth batter forms.
8. Pour the cake batter into the prepared pan and place in the air fryer to cook for 30 minutes. The cake will be golden brown and a toothpick will come out cleanly when inserted into the center of the cake.
9. Remove from the air fryer and cool in the pan for 20 minutes. Flip the cake out of the pan, slice and enjoy!

Nutrition Facts Per Serving
Calories 351, Total Fat 36g, Saturated Fat 19g, Total Carbs 10g, Net Carbs 6g, Protein 10g, Sugar 5g, Fiber 4g, Sodium 483mg, Potassium 89g

Hazelnut Cake

Prep time: 30 minutes, Cook time: 30 minutes, Serves 12

Ingredients:
- 2 cups almond flour
- ¾ cup hazelnut flour
- ¼ cup vanilla protein powder
- ½ tsp salt
- 1 Tbsp baking powder
- 2/3 cup granulated erythritol
- ¼ cup butter
- ¼ cup hazelnut butter
- ¾ cup whole milk
- 1 tsp vanilla
- 4 whole eggs

Instructions
1. Preheat your air fryer to 325 degrees F and grease and 8" cake pan.
2. Place the butter and hazelnut butter in a mixing bowl along with the erythritol and beat until fluffy.
3. In a separate bowl, mix the eggs, milk and vanilla together.
4. In a third bowl, combine the remaining dry ingredients.
5. Add half of the wet mixture to the bowl with the fluffy butter and beat together slowly.
6. Add half of the dry mix to the bowl and beat again until smooth.
7. Add the remaining wet ingredients, mix and add the remaining dry ingredients and blend until a smooth batter forms.
8. Pour the cake batter into the prepared pan and place in the air fryer to cook for 30 minutes. The cake will be golden brown and a toothpick will come out cleanly when inserted into the center of the cake.
9. Remove from the air fryer and cool in the pan for 20 minutes. Flip the cake out of the pan, slice and enjoy!

Nutrition Facts Per Serving
Calories 429, Total Fat 43g, Saturated Fat 24g, Total Carbs 14g, Net Carbs 9g, Protein 10g, Sugar 5g, Fiber 5g, Sodium 477mg, Potassium 97g

Walnut Cake

Prep time: 30 minutes, Cook time: 30 minutes, Serves 12

Ingredients:
- 2 cups almond flour
- ¾ cup walnut flour
- ¼ cup vanilla protein powder
- ½ tsp salt
- 1 Tbsp baking powder
- 2/3 cup granulated erythritol
- ½ cup butter
- ¾ cup whole milk
- 1 tsp vanilla
- 4 whole eggs

Instructions
1. Preheat your air fryer to 325 degrees F and grease and 8" cake pan.
2. Place the butter and in a mixing bowl along with the erythritol and beat until fluffy.
3. In a separate bowl, mix the eggs, milk and vanilla together.
4. In a third bowl, combine the remaining dry ingredients.
5. Add half of the wet mixture to the bowl with the fluffy butter and beat together slowly.
6. Add half of the dry mix to the bowl and beat again until smooth.
7. Add the remaining wet ingredients, mix and add the remaining dry ingredients and blend until a smooth batter forms.
8. Pour the cake batter into the prepared pan and place in the air fryer to cook for 30 minutes. The cake will be golden brown and a toothpick will come out cleanly when inserted into the center of the cake.
9. Remove from the air fryer and cool in the pan for 20 minutes. Flip the cake out of the pan, slice and enjoy!

Nutrition Facts Per Serving
Calories 357, Total Fat 38g, Saturated Fat 21g, Total Carbs 11g, Net Carbs 6g, Protein 11g, Sugar 5g, Fiber 5g, Sodium 483mg, Potassium 102g

NY Keto Cheesecake

Prep time: 15 minutes, Cook time: 1 hour 15 minutes, Serves 12

Ingredients:
- 1 ½ pounds cream cheese
- 5 Tbsp butter
- 1 cup powdered erythritol
- 3 eggs
- 1 ½ tsp vanilla extract
- ¾ cup sour cream

Instructions
1. Preheat your air fryer to 275 degrees F and grease an 8" spring form cake pan. Place a piece of parchment in the bottom of the pan as well.
2. Place the cream cheese and butter in a large bowl and beat until combined.
3. Add the powdered erythritol and beat again until smooth.
4. Add the eggs, one at a time, allowing them to fully mix in after each addition.
5. Add the sour cream and vanilla extract and stir one last time, making sure the batter is smooth and all the ingredients are well blended.
6. Pour the batter into the prepared cake pan and then place the pan on a larger tray with high sides that will fit in the air fryer. Fill the pan with water, creating a water bath for the cheese cake.
7. Place in the pre heated air fryer and bake for an hour and 15 minutes. The cheesecake will be mostly set but may have a very slight jiggle in the center.
8. Allow the cheesecake to cool for 3 hours in the fridge before removing from the pan and serving.

Nutrition Facts Per Serving
Calories 287, Total Fat 26g, Saturated Fat 14g, Total Carbs 3g, Net Carbs 1g, Protein 5g, Sugar 1g, Fiber 2g, Sodium 192mg, Potassium 80g

Strawberry Cheesecake

Prep time: 15 minutes, Cook time: 1 hour 15 minutes, Serves 12

Ingredients:
- 1 ½ pounds cream cheese
- 5 Tbsp butter
- 1 cup powdered erythritol
- 3 eggs
- 1 ½ tsp vanilla extract
- ¾ cup sour cream
- ¾ cup chopped, fresh strawberries

Instructions
1. Preheat your air fryer to 275 degrees F and grease an 8" spring form cake pan. Place a piece of parchment in the bottom of the pan as well.
2. Place the cream cheese and butter in a large bowl and beat until combined.
3. Add the powdered erythritol and beat again until smooth.
4. Add the eggs, one at a time, allowing them to fully mix in after each addition.
5. Add the sour cream and vanilla extract and stir one last time, making sure the batter is smooth and all the ingredients are well blended.
6. Fold in the chopped strawberries
7. Pour the batter into the prepared cake pan and then place the pan on a larger tray with high sides that will fit in the air fryer. Fill the pan with water, creating a water bath for the cheese cake.
8. Place in the pre heated air fryer and bake for an hour and 15 minutes. The cheesecake will be mostly set but may have a very slight jiggle in the center.
9. Allow the cheesecake to cool for 3 hours in the fridge before removing from the pan and serving.

Nutrition Facts Per Serving
Calories 315, Total Fat 26g, Saturated Fat 14g, Total Carbs 8g, Net Carbs 6g, Protein 5g, Sugar 5g, Fiber 2g, Sodium 192mg, Potassium 110g

Blueberry Cheesecake

Prep time: 15 minutes , Cook time: 1 hour 15 minutes, Serves 12

Ingredients:

1 ½ pounds cream cheese
5 Tbsp butter
1 cup powdered erythritol
3 eggs
1 ½ tsp vanilla extract
¾ cup sour cream
1 cup fresh blueberries

Instructions

1. Preheat your air fryer to 275 degrees F and grease an 8" spring form cake pan. Place a piece of parchment in the bottom of the pan as well.
2. Place the cream cheese and butter in a large bowl and beat until combined.
3. Add the powdered erythritol and beat again until smooth.
4. Add the eggs, one at a time, allowing them to fully mix in after each addition.
5. Add the sour cream and vanilla extract and stir one last time, making sure the batter is smooth and all the ingredients are well blended.
6. Fold in the blueberries gently.
7. Pour the batter into the prepared cake pan and then place the pan on a larger tray with high sides that will fit in the air fryer. Fill the pan with water, creating a water bath for the cheese cake.
8. Place in the pre heated air fryer and bake for an hour and 15 minutes. The cheesecake will be mostly set but may have a very slight jiggle in the center.
9. Allow the cheesecake to cool for 3 hours in the fridge before removing from the pan and serving.

Nutrition Facts Per Serving

Calories 322, Total Fat 26g, Saturated Fat 14g, Total Carbs 9g, Net Carbs 7g, Protein 5g, Sugar 6g, Fiber 2g, Sodium 192mg, Potassium 125g

Raspberry Cheesecake

Prep time: 15 minutes , Cook time: 1 hour 15 minutes, Serves 12

Ingredients:

1 ½ pounds cream cheese
5 Tbsp butter
1 cup powdered erythritol
3 eggs
1 ½ tsp vanilla extract
¾ cup sour cream
1 cup fresh raspberries

Instructions

1. Preheat your air fryer to 275 degrees F and grease an 8" spring form cake pan. Place a piece of parchment in the bottom of the pan as well.
2. Place the cream cheese and butter in a large bowl and beat until combined.
3. Add the powdered erythritol and beat again until smooth.
4. Add the eggs, one at a time, allowing them to fully mix in after each addition.
5. Add the sour cream and vanilla extract and stir one last time, making sure the batter is smooth and all the ingredients are well blended.
6. Fold in the raspberries gently.
7. Pour the batter into the prepared cake pan and then place the pan on a larger tray with high sides that will fit in the air fryer. Fill the pan with water, creating a water bath for the cheese cake.
8. Place in the pre heated air fryer and bake for an hour and 15 minutes. The cheesecake will be mostly set but may have a very slight jiggle in the center.
9. Allow the cheesecake to cool for 3 hours in the fridge before removing from the pan and serving.

Nutrition Facts Per Serving

Calories 319, Total Fat 26g, Saturated Fat 14g, Total Carbs 9g, Net Carbs 7g, Protein 5g, Sugar 6g, Fiber 2g, Sodium 192mg, Potassium 121g

Cinnamon Cheesecake

Prep time: 15 minutes, Cook time: 1 hour 15 minutes, Serves 12

Ingredients:
1 ½ pounds cream cheese
5 Tbsp butter
1 cup powdered erythritol
1 tsp ground cinnamon
3 eggs
1 ½ tsp vanilla extract
¾ cup sour cream

Instructions
1. Preheat your air fryer to 275 degrees F and grease an 8" spring form cake pan. Place a piece of parchment in the bottom of the pan as well.
2. Place the cream cheese and butter in a large bowl and beat until combined.
3. Add the powdered erythritol, cinnamon and beat again until smooth.
4. Add the eggs, one at a time, allowing them to fully mix in after each addition.
5. Add the sour cream and vanilla extract and stir one last time, making sure the batter is smooth and all the ingredients are well blended.
6. Pour the batter into the prepared cake pan and then place the pan on a larger tray with high sides that will fit in the air fryer. Fill the pan with water, creating a water bath for the cheese cake.
7. Place in the pre heated air fryer and bake for an hour and 15 minutes. The cheesecake will be mostly set but may have a very slight jiggle in the center.
8. Allow the cheesecake to cool for 3 hours in the fridge before removing from the pan and serving.

Nutrition Facts Per Serving
Calories 292, Total Fat 26g, Saturated Fat 14g, Total Carbs 3g, Net Carbs 1g, Protein 5g, Sugar 1g, Fiber 2g, Sodium 192mg, Potassium 80g

Chocolate Keto Cheesecake

Prep time: 15 minutes, Cook time: 1 hour 15 minutes, Serves 12

Ingredients:
1 ½ pounds cream cheese
5 Tbsp butter
1 cup powdered erythritol
¼ cup unsweetened cocoa powder
3 eggs
1 ½ tsp vanilla extract
¾ cup sour cream

Instructions
1. Preheat your air fryer to 275 degrees F and grease an 8" spring form cake pan. Place a piece of parchment in the bottom of the pan as well.
2. Place the cream cheese and butter in a large bowl and beat until combined.
3. Add the powdered erythritol, cocoa powder and beat again until smooth.
4. Add the eggs, one at a time, allowing them to fully mix in after each addition.
5. Add the sour cream and vanilla extract and stir one last time, making sure the batter is smooth and all the ingredients are well blended.
6. Pour the batter into the prepared cake pan and then place the pan on a larger tray with high sides that will fit in the air fryer. Fill the pan with water, creating a water bath for the cheese cake.
7. Place in the pre heated air fryer and bake for an hour and 15 minutes. The cheesecake will be mostly set but may have a very slight jiggle in the center.
8. Allow the cheesecake to cool for 3 hours in the fridge before removing from the pan and serving.

Nutrition Facts Per Serving
Calories 302, Total Fat 34g, Saturated Fat 18g, Total Carbs 4g, Net Carbs 2g, Protein 5g, Sugar 2g, Fiber 2g, Sodium 192mg, Potassium 80g

Chocolate Chip Cheesecake

Prep time: 15 minutes , Cook time: 1 hour 15 minutes, Serves 12

Ingredients:
1 ½ pounds cream cheese
5 Tbsp butter
1 cup powdered erythritol
3 eggs
1 ½ tsp vanilla extract
¾ cup sour cream
1 cup dark chocolate chips

Instructions
1. Preheat your air fryer to 275 degrees F and grease an 8" spring form cake pan. Place a piece of parchment in the bottom of the pan as well.
2. Place the cream cheese and butter in a large bowl and beat until combined.
3. Add the powdered erythritol and beat again until smooth.
4. Add the eggs, one at a time, allowing them to fully mix in after each addition.
5. Add the sour cream and vanilla extract and stir one last time, making sure the batter is smooth and all the ingredients are well blended.
6. Fold in the dark chocolate chips.
7. Pour the batter into the prepared cake pan and then place the pan on a larger tray with high sides that will fit in the air fryer. Fill the pan with water, creating a water bath for the cheesecake.
8. Place in the pre heated air fryer and bake for an hour and 15 minutes. The cheesecake will be mostly set but may have a very slight jiggle in the center.
9. Allow the cheesecake to cool for 3 hours in the fridge before removing from the pan and serving.

Nutrition Facts Per Serving
Calories 364, Total Fat 36g, Saturated Fat 20g, Total Carbs 8g, Net Carbs 6g, Protein 5g, Sugar 3g, Fiber 2g, Sodium 190mg, Potassium 102g

Pumpkin Spice Cheesecake

Prep time: 15 minutes , Cook time: 1 hour 15 minutes, Serves 12

Ingredients:
1 ½ pounds cream cheese
5 Tbsp butter
1 cup powdered erythritol
2 tsp pumpkin spice
3 eggs
1 ½ tsp vanilla extract
¾ cup sour cream

Instructions
1. Preheat your air fryer to 275 degrees F and grease an 8" spring form cake pan. Place a piece of parchment in the bottom of the pan as well.
2. Place the cream cheese and butter in a large bowl and beat until combined.
3. Add the powdered erythritol and pumpkin spice and beat again until smooth.
4. Add the eggs, one at a time, allowing them to fully mix in after each addition.
5. Add the sour cream and vanilla extract and stir one last time, making sure the batter is smooth and all the ingredients are well blended.
6. Pour the batter into the prepared cake pan and then place the pan on a larger tray with high sides that will fit in the air fryer. Fill the pan with water, creating a water bath for the cheese cake.
7. Place in the pre heated air fryer and bake for an hour and 15 minutes. The cheesecake will be mostly set but may have a very slight jiggle in the center.
8. Allow the cheesecake to cool for 3 hours in the fridge before removing from the pan and serving.

Nutrition Facts Per Serving
Calories 293, Total Fat 26g, Saturated Fat 14g, Total Carbs 3g, Net Carbs 1g, Protein 5g, Sugar 1g, Fiber 2g, Sodium 195mg, Potassium 83g

Lemon Cheesecake

Prep time: 15 minutes, Cook time: 1 hour 15 minutes, Serves 12

Ingredients:

1 ½ pounds cream cheese
5 Tbsp butter
1 cup powdered erythritol
3 eggs
1 ½ tsp vanilla extract
¾ cup sour cream
1 tsp lemon zest

Instructions

1. Preheat your air fryer to 275 degrees F and grease an 8" spring form cake pan. Place a piece of parchment in the bottom of the pan as well.
2. Place the cream cheese and butter in a large bowl and beat until combined.
3. Add the powdered erythritol and beat again until smooth.
4. Add the eggs, one at a time, allowing them to fully mix in after each addition.
5. Add the sour cream, lemon zest and vanilla extract and stir one last time, making sure the batter is smooth and all the ingredients are well blended.
6. Pour the batter into the prepared cake pan and then place the pan on a larger tray with high sides that will fit in the air fryer. Fill the pan with water, creating a water bath for the cheese cake.
7. Place in the pre heated air fryer and bake for an hour and 15 minutes. The cheesecake will be mostly set but may have a very slight jiggle in the center.
8. Allow the cheesecake to cool for 3 hours in the fridge before removing from the pan and serving.

Nutrition Facts Per Serving
Calories 294, Total Fat 27g, Saturated Fat 14g, Total Carbs 5g, Net Carbs 1g, Protein 5g, Sugar 3g, Fiber 2g, Sodium 198mg, Potassium 87g

Gingerbread Cheesecake

Prep time: 15 minutes, Cook time: 1 hour 15 minutes, Serves 12

Ingredients:

1 ½ pounds cream cheese
5 Tbsp butter
1 cup powdered erythritol
½ tsp ground ginger
¼ tsp ground cinnamon
3 eggs
1 ½ tsp vanilla extract
¾ cup sour cream

Instructions

1. Preheat your air fryer to 275 degrees F and grease an 8" spring form cake pan. Place a piece of parchment in the bottom of the pan as well.
2. Place the cream cheese and butter in a large bowl and beat until combined.
3. Add the powdered erythritol, cinnamon, ginger and beat again until smooth.
4. Add the eggs, one at a time, allowing them to fully mix in after each addition.
5. Add the sour cream and vanilla extract and stir one last time, making sure the batter is smooth and all the ingredients are well blended.
6. Pour the batter into the prepared cake pan and then place the pan on a larger tray with high sides that will fit in the air fryer. Fill the pan with water, creating a water bath for the cheesecake.
7. Place in the pre heated air fryer and bake for an hour and 15 minutes. The cheesecake will be mostly set but may have a very slight jiggle in the center.
8. Allow the cheesecake to cool for 3 hours in the fridge before removing from the pan and serving.

Nutrition Facts Per Serving
Calories 293, Total Fat 26g, Saturated Fat 14g, Total Carbs 3g, Net Carbs 1g, Protein 5g, Sugar 1g, Fiber 2g, Sodium 195mg, Potassium 82g

Mascarpone Cheesecake

Prep time: 15 minutes , Cook time: 1 hour 15 minutes, Serves 12

Ingredients:
- 1 pound cream cheese
- ½ pound mascarpone cheese
- 5 Tbsp butter
- 1 cup powdered erythritol
- 3 eggs
- 1 ½ tsp vanilla extract
- ¾ cup sour cream

Instructions
1. Preheat your air fryer to 275 degrees F and grease an 8" spring form cake pan. Place a piece of parchment in the bottom of the pan as well.
2. Place the cream cheese, mascarpone and butter in a large bowl and beat until combined.
3. Add the powdered erythritol and beat again until smooth.
4. Add the eggs, one at a time, allowing them to fully mix in after each addition.
5. Add the sour cream and vanilla extract and stir one last time, making sure the batter is smooth and all the ingredients are well blended.
6. Pour the batter into the prepared cake pan and then place the pan on a larger tray with high sides that will fit in the air fryer. Fill the pan with water, creating a water bath for the cheese cake.
7. Place in the pre heated air fryer and bake for an hour and 15 minutes. The cheesecake will be mostly set but may have a very slight jiggle in the center.
8. Allow the cheesecake to cool for 3 hours in the fridge before removing from the pan and serving.

Nutrition Facts Per Serving
Calories 295, Total Fat 31g, Saturated Fat 19g, Total Carbs 4g, Net Carbs 2g, Protein 5g, Sugar 2g, Fiber 2g, Sodium 198mg, Potassium 86g

Coconut Cheesecake

Prep time: 15 minutes , Cook time: 1 hour 15 minutes, Serves 12

Ingredients:
- 1 ½ pounds cream cheese
- 5 Tbsp butter
- 1 cup powdered erythritol
- 3 eggs
- 1 ½ tsp coconut extract
- ¾ cup sour cream
- ½ cup unsweetened coconut flakes

Instructions
1. Preheat your air fryer to 275 degrees F and grease an 8" spring form cake pan. Place a piece of parchment in the bottom of the pan as well.
2. Place the cream cheese and butter in a large bowl and beat until combined.
3. Add the powdered erythritol and beat again until smooth.
4. Add the eggs, one at a time, allowing them to fully mix in after each addition.
5. Add the sour cream and coconut extract and stir one last time, making sure the batter is smooth and all the ingredients are well blended.
6. Fold in the unsweetened coconut flakes
7. Pour the batter into the prepared cake pan and then place the pan on a larger tray with high sides that will fit in the air fryer. Fill the pan with water, creating a water bath for the cheese cake.
8. Place in the pre heated air fryer and bake for an hour and 15 minutes. The cheesecake will be mostly set but may have a very slight jiggle in the center.
9. Allow the cheesecake to cool for 3 hours in the fridge before removing from the pan and serving.

Nutrition Facts Per Serving
Calories 311, Total Fat 29g, Saturated Fat 17g, Total Carbs 6g, Net Carbs 4g, Protein 5g, Sugar 3g, Fiber 2g, Sodium 192mg, Potassium 80g

Fudge Brownies

Prep time: 15 minutes, Cook time: 20 minutes, Serves 16

Ingredients:
- ½ cup melted butter
- 2/3 cup swerve
- ½ tsp vanilla extract
- 3 room temperature eggs
- ½ cup almond flour
- 1/3 cup unsweetened cocoa powder
- 1 Tbsp plain, unsweetened gelatin
- ½ tsp salt
- ½ tsp baking powder
- ¼ cup water

Instructions
1. Preheat your air fryer to 325 degrees F and grease an 8x8 inch square baking pan.
2. Combine the eggs, vanilla extract, swerve, and melted butter in a bowl and whisk together well.
3. Add the cocoa powder, almond flour, baking powder, gelatin, and salt and whisk again until smooth.
4. Add the water and stir again.
5. Pour the batter into the greased baking pan and place in the preheated air fryer. Bake for 15 minutes. The center will seem a little wet while the edges will be more firm- this is perfect.
6. Let the brownies cool in the pan before slicing and serving.

Nutrition Facts Per Serving
Calories 110, Total Fat 10g, Saturated Fat 4g, Total Carbs 4g, Net Carbs 1g, Protein 3g, Sugar 1g, Fiber 3g, Sodium 283mg, Potassium 316g

Double Chocolate Brownies

Prep time: 15 minutes, Cook time: 20 minutes, Serves 16

Ingredients:
- ½ cup melted butter
- 2/3 cup swerve
- ½ tsp vanilla extract
- 3 room temperature eggs
- ½ cup almond flour
- 1/3 cup unsweetened cocoa powder
- 1 Tbsp plain, unsweetened gelatin
- ½ tsp salt
- ½ tsp baking powder
- ¼ cup water
- ½ cup dark chocolate chips, unsweetened

Instructions
1. Preheat your air fryer to 325 degrees F and grease an 8x8 inch square baking pan.
2. Combine the eggs, vanilla extract, swerve, and melted butter in a bowl and whisk together well.
3. Add the cocoa powder, almond flour, baking powder, gelatin, and salt and whisk again until smooth.
4. Add the water and stir again.
5. Fold in the chocolate chips.
6. Pour the batter into the greased baking pan and place in the preheated air fryer. Bake for 15 minutes. The center will seem a little wet while the edges will be more firm- this is perfect.
7. Let the brownies cool in the pan before slicing and serving.

Nutrition Facts Per Serving
Calories 193, Total Fat 10g, Saturated Fat 4g, Total Carbs 6g, Net Carbs 3g, Protein 3g, Sugar 3g, Fiber 3g, Sodium 299mg, Potassium 322g

Chocolate Walnuts Brownies

Prep time: 15 minutes, Cook time: 20 minutes, Serves 16

Ingredients:
- ½ cup melted butter
- 2/3 cup swerve
- ½ tsp vanilla extract
- 3 room temperature eggs
- ½ cup almond flour
- 1/3 cup unsweetened cocoa powder
- 1 Tbsp plain, unsweetened gelatin
- ½ tsp salt
- ½ tsp baking powder
- ¼ cup water
- ½ cup chopped walnuts

Instructions
1. Preheat your air fryer to 325 degrees F and grease an 8x8 inch square baking pan.
2. Combine the eggs, vanilla extract, swerve, and melted butter in a bowl and whisk together well.
3. Add the cocoa powder, almond flour, baking powder, gelatin, and salt and whisk again until smooth.
4. Add the water and stir again.
5. Fold in walnuts.
6. Pour the batter into the greased baking pan and place in the preheated air fryer. Bake for 15 minutes. The center will seem a little wet while the edges will be more firm- this is perfect.
7. Let the brownies cool in the pan before slicing and serving.

Nutrition Facts Per Serving
Calories 178, Total Fat 19g, Saturated Fat 5g, Total Carbs 8g, Net Carbs 4g, Protein 3g, Sugar 2g, Fiber 4g, Sodium 283mg, Potassium 322g

Peanut Butter Brownies

Prep time: 15 minutes, Cook time: 20 minutes, Serves 16

Ingredients:
- ½ cup peanut butter
- 2/3 cup swerve
- ½ tsp vanilla extract
- 3 room temperature eggs
- ½ cup almond flour
- 1/3 cup unsweetened cocoa powder
- 1 Tbsp plain, unsweetened gelatin
- ½ tsp salt
- ½ tsp baking powder
- ¼ cup water

Instructions
1. Preheat your air fryer to 325 degrees F and grease an 8x8 inch square baking pan.
2. Combine the peanut butter, vanilla extract, swerve, and eggs in a bowl and whisk together well.
3. Add the cocoa powder, almond flour, baking powder, gelatin, and salt and whisk again until smooth.
4. Add the water and stir again.
5. Pour the batter into the greased baking pan and place in the preheated air fryer. Bake for 15 minutes. The center will seem a little wet while the edges will be more firm- this is perfect.
6. Let the brownies cool in the pan before slicing and serving.

Nutrition Facts Per Serving
Calories 131, Total Fat 11g, Saturated Fat 5g, Total Carbs 6g, Net Carbs 3g, Protein 6g, Sugar 4g, Fiber 3g, Sodium 283mg, Potassium 324g

Almond Brownies

Prep time: 15 minutes, Cook time: 20 minutes, Serves 16

Ingredients:
- ½ cup melted butter
- 2/3 cup swerve
- ½ tsp almond extract
- 3 room temperature eggs
- ½ cup almond flour
- 1/3 cup unsweetened cocoa powder
- 1 Tbsp plain, unsweetened gelatin
- ½ tsp salt
- ½ tsp baking powder
- ¼ cup water

Instructions
1. Preheat your air fryer to 325 degrees F and grease an 8x8 inch square baking pan.

2. Combine the eggs, almond extract, swerve, and melted butter in a bowl and whisk together well.
3. Add the cocoa powder, almond flour, baking powder, gelatin, and salt and whisk again until smooth.
4. Add the water and stir again.
5. Pour the batter into the greased baking pan and place in the preheated air fryer. Bake for 15 minutes. The center will seem a little wet while the edges will be more firm- this is perfect.
6. Let the brownies cool in the pan before slicing and serving.

Nutrition Facts Per Serving
Calories 110, Total Fat 10g, Saturated Fat 4g, Total Carbs 4g, Net Carbs 1g, Protein 3g, Sugar 1g, Fiber 3g, Sodium 283mg, Potassium 316g

Chocolate Coconut Brownies

Prep time: 15 minutes , Cook time: 20 minutes, Serves 16

Ingredients:
½ cup melted butter
2/3 cup swerve
½ tsp vanilla extract
3 room temperature eggs
½ cup almond flour
1/3 cup unsweetened cocoa powder
1 Tbsp plain, unsweetened gelatin
½ tsp salt
½ tsp baking powder
¼ cup water
½ cup unsweetened shredded coconut

Instructions
1. Preheat your air fryer to 325 degrees F and grease an 8x8 inch square baking pan.
2. Combine the eggs, vanilla extract, swerve, and melted butter in a bowl and whisk together well.
3. Add the cocoa powder, almond flour, baking powder, gelatin, and salt and whisk again until smooth.
4. Add the water and stir again.
5. Fold in the shredded coconut.
6. Pour the batter into the greased baking pan and place in the preheated air fryer. Bake for 15 minutes. The center will seem a little wet while the edges will be more firm- this is perfect.
7. Let the brownies cool in the pan before slicing and serving.

Nutrition Facts Per Serving
Calories 218, Total Fat 22g, Saturated Fat 8g, Total Carbs 9g, Net Carbs 5g, Protein 3g, Sugar 3g, Fiber 4g, Sodium 283mg, Potassium 389g

Chocolate Mint Brownies

Prep time: 15 minutes , Cook time: 20 minutes, Serves 16

Ingredients:
½ cup melted butter
2/3 cup swerve
½ tsp peppermint extract
3 room temperature eggs
½ cup almond flour
1/3 cup unsweetened cocoa powder
1 Tbsp plain, unsweetened gelatin
½ tsp salt
½ tsp baking powder
¼ cup water

Instructions
1. Preheat your air fryer to 325 degrees F and grease an 8x8 inch square baking pan.
2. Combine the eggs, peppermint extract, swerve, and melted butter in a bowl and whisk together well.
3. Add the cocoa powder, almond flour, baking powder, gelatin, and salt and whisk again until smooth.
4. Add the water and stir again.
5. Pour the batter into the greased baking pan and place in the preheated air fryer. Bake for 15 minutes. The center will seem a little wet while the edges will be more firm- this is perfect.
6. Let the brownies cool in the pan before slicing and serving.

Nutrition Facts Per Serving
Calories 110, Total Fat 10g, Saturated Fat 4g, Total Carbs 4g, Net Carbs 1g, Protein 3g, Sugar 1g, Fiber 3g, Sodium 283mg, Potassium 316g

Hazelnut Brownies

Prep time: 15 minutes, Cook time: 20 minutes, Serves 16

Ingredients:
- ½ cup melted butter
- 2/3 cup swerve
- ½ tsp vanilla extract
- 3 room temperature eggs
- ½ cup almond flour
- 1/3 cup unsweetened cocoa powder
- 1 Tbsp plain, unsweetened gelatin
- ½ tsp salt
- ½ tsp baking powder
- ¼ cup water
- ½ cup chopped hazelnuts

Instructions
1. Preheat your air fryer to 325 degrees F and grease an 8x8 inch square baking pan.
2. Combine the eggs, vanilla extract, swerve, and melted butter in a bowl and whisk together well.
3. Add the cocoa powder, almond flour, baking powder, gelatin, and salt and whisk again until smooth.
4. Add the water and stir again.
5. Pour the batter into the greased baking pan, sprinkle with the chopped hazelnuts and place in the preheated air fryer. Bake for 15 minutes. The center will seem a little wet while the edges will be more firm- this is perfect.
6. Let the brownies cool in the pan before slicing and serving.

Nutrition Facts Per Serving
Calories 152, Total Fat 23g, Saturated Fat 6g, Total Carbs 8g, Net Carbs 2g, Protein 3g, Sugar 1g, Fiber 6g, Sodium 292mg, Potassium 489g

Espresso Brownies

Prep time: 15 minutes, Cook time: 20 minutes, Serves 16

Ingredients:
- ½ cup melted butter
- 2/3 cup swerve
- ½ tsp vanilla extract
- 3 room temperature eggs
- ½ cup almond flour
- 1/3 cup unsweetened cocoa powder
- 1 Tbsp plain, unsweetened gelatin
- ½ tsp salt
- ½ tsp baking powder
- ¼ cup brewed espresso

Instructions
1. Preheat your air fryer to 325 degrees F and grease an 8x8 inch square baking pan.
2. Combine the eggs, vanilla extract, swerve, and melted butter in a bowl and whisk together well.
3. Add the cocoa powder, almond flour, baking powder, gelatin, and salt and whisk again until smooth.
4. Add the brewed espresso and stir again.
5. Pour the batter into the greased baking pan and place in the preheated air fryer. Bake for 15 minutes. The center will seem a little wet while the edges will be more firm- this is perfect.
6. Let the brownies cool in the pan before slicing and serving.

Nutrition Facts Per Serving
Calories 116, Total Fat 10g, Saturated Fat 4g, Total Carbs 4g, Net Carbs 1g, Protein 3g, Sugar 1g, Fiber 3g, Sodium 283mg, Potassium 316g

Caramel Fudge Brownies

Prep time: 15 minutes, Cook time: 20 minutes, Serves 16

Ingredients:
- ½ cup melted butter
- 2/3 cup swerve
- ½ tsp vanilla extract
- 3 room temperature eggs
- ½ cup almond flour
- 1/3 cup unsweetened cocoa powder
- 1 Tbsp plain, unsweetened gelatin
- ½ tsp salt
- ½ tsp baking powder
- ¼ cup water
- ½ cup keto caramel sauce

Instructions
1. Preheat your air fryer to 325 degrees F and grease an 8x8 inch square baking pan.

2. Combine the eggs, vanilla extract, swerve, and melted butter in a bowl and whisk together well.
3. Add the cocoa powder, almond flour, baking powder, gelatin, and salt and whisk again until smooth.
4. Add the water and stir again.
5. Pour the batter into the greased baking pan and swirl in the caramel sauce.
6. Place the pan in the preheated air fryer. Bake for 15 minutes. The center will seem a little wet while the edges will be more firm- this is perfect.
7. Let the brownies cool in the pan before slicing and serving.

Nutrition Facts Per Serving Calories 208, Total Fat 11g, Saturated Fat 4g, Total Carbs 10g, Net Carbs 7g, Protein 3g, Sugar 5g, Fiber 3g, Sodium 383mg, Potassium 316g

Raspberry Brownies

Prep time: 15 minutes , Cook time: 20 minutes, Serves 16

Ingredients:
½ cup melted butter
2/3 cup swerve
½ tsp vanilla extract
3 room temperature eggs
½ cup almond flour
1/3 cup unsweetened cocoa powder
1 Tbsp plain, unsweetened gelatin
½ tsp salt
½ tsp baking powder
¼ cup water
½ cup fresh raspberries, cut in half

Instructions
1. Preheat your air fryer to 325 degrees F and grease an 8x8 inch square baking pan.
2. Combine the eggs, vanilla extract, swerve, and melted butter in a bowl and whisk together well.
3. Add the cocoa powder, almond flour, baking powder, gelatin, and salt and whisk again until smooth.
4. Add the water and stir again.
5. Fold in the fresh raspberries.
6. Pour the batter into the greased baking pan and place in the preheated air fryer. Bake for 15 minutes. The center will seem a little wet while the edges will be more firm- this is perfect.
7. Let the brownies cool in the pan before slicing and serving.

Nutrition Facts Per Serving
Calories 170, Total Fat 10g, Saturated Fat 4g, Total Carbs 9g, Net Carbs 3g, Protein 3g, Sugar 3g, Fiber 6g, Sodium 283mg, Potassium 368g

Strawberry Fudge Brownies

Prep time: 15 minutes , Cook time: 20 minutes, Serves 16

Ingredients:
½ cup melted butter
2/3 cup swerve
½ tsp vanilla extract
3 room temperature eggs
½ cup almond flour
1/3 cup unsweetened cocoa powder
1 Tbsp plain, unsweetened gelatin
½ tsp salt
½ tsp baking powder
¼ cup water
½ cup fresh chopped strawberries

Instructions
1. Preheat your air fryer to 325 degrees F and grease an 8x8 inch square baking pan.
2. Combine the melted butter, vanilla extract, swerve, and melted butter in a bowl and whisk together well.
3. Add the cocoa powder, almond flour, baking powder, gelatin, and salt and whisk again until smooth.
4. Add the water and stir again.
5. Fold in the strawberries
6. Pour the batter into the greased baking pan and place in the preheated air fryer. Bake for 15 minutes. The center will seem a little wet while the edges will be more firm- this is perfect.
7. Let the brownies cool in the pan before slicing and serving.

Nutrition Facts Per Serving
Calories 193, Total Fat 10g, Saturated Fat 4g, Total Carbs 11g, Net Carbs 6g, Protein 3g, Sugar 5g, Fiber 5g, Sodium 283mg, Potassium 412g

Cheesecake Fudge Brownies

Prep time: 15 minutes, Cook time: 20 minutes, Serves 16

Ingredients:
- ½ cup cream cheese, softened
- 3 Tbsp erythritol sweetener
- ½ cup melted butter
- 2/3 cup swerve
- ½ tsp vanilla extract
- 3 room temperature eggs
- ½ cup almond flour
- 1/3 cup unsweetened cocoa powder
- 1 Tbsp plain, unsweetened gelatin
- ½ tsp salt
- ½ tsp baking powder
- ¼ cup water

Instructions
1. Preheat your air fryer to 325 degrees F and grease an 8x8 inch square baking pan.
2. In a small bowl, mic the cream cheese and erythritol sweetener together. Set aside.
3. Combine the melted butter, vanilla extract, swerve, and melted butter in a bowl and whisk together well.
4. Add the cocoa powder, almond flour, baking powder, gelatin, and salt and whisk again until smooth.
5. Add the water and stir again.
6. Pour the batter into the greased baking pan and swirl in the cream cheese mix.
7. Place the pan in the preheated air fryer. Bake for 15 minutes. The center will seem a little wet while the edges will be more firm- this is perfect.
8. Let the brownies cool in the pan before slicing and serving.

Nutrition Facts Per Serving
Calories 215, Total Fat 18g, Saturated Fat 5g, Total Carbs 6g, Net Carbs 3g, Protein 3g, Sugar 2g, Fiber 3g, Sodium 283mg, Potassium 316g

Chocolate Chip Cookies

Prep time: 10 minutes, Cook time: 9 minutes, Serves 12

Ingredients:
- ½ cup butter, melted
- ¾ cup erythritol
- 1 tsp vanilla extract
- 1 egg
- 1 ½ cups almond flour
- ½ tsp salt
- ½ tsp baking powder
- ¾ cup sugar free chocolate chips

Instructions
1. Preheat your air fryer to 330 degrees F and prepare your air fryer tray with a piece of parchment.
2. Beat the melted butter and erythritol together in a large bowl.
3. Add the eggs and vanilla and mix until the batter comes together.
4. Add the salt, baking powder and almond flour and mix until a nice, smooth batter forms.
5. Fold in the chocolate chips then scoop the cookie dough onto the prepared sheet tray. You will want to leave about 2 inches between the cookie dough scoops as the dough will spread slightly. If needed, you can bake the cookies in batches.
6. Bake the cookies in the air fryer for 8-9 minutes or until golden brown on the edges.
7. Let cool on the sheet tray for 5 minutes before removing and enjoying!

Nutrition Facts Per Serving
Calories 168, Total Fat 18g, Saturated Fat 6g, Total Carbs 2g, Net Carbs 1g, Protein 4g, Sugar 1g, Fiber 1g, Sodium 342mg, Potassium 110g

Butter Cookies

Prep time: 10 minutes , Cook time: 9 minutes, Serves 12

Ingredients:
- ½ cup butter, melted
- ¾ cup erythritol
- 1 tsp vanilla extract
- 1 egg
- 1 ½ cups almond flour
- ¼ tsp xanthan gum
- ½ tsp salt
- ½ tsp baking powder

Instructions
1. Preheat your air fryer to 330 degrees F and prepare your air fryer tray with a piece of parchment.
2. Beat the melted butter and erythritol together in a large bowl.
3. Add the eggs and vanilla and mix until the batter comes together.
4. Add the salt, baking powder, xanthan gum and almond flour and mix until a nice, smooth batter forms.
5. Scoop the cookie dough onto the prepared sheet tray. You will want to leave about 2 inches between the cookie dough scoops as the dough will spread slightly. If needed, you can bake the cookies in batches.
6. Bake the cookies in the air fryer for 8-9 minutes or until golden brown on the edges.
7. Let cool on the sheet tray for 5 minutes before removing and enjoying!

Nutrition Facts Per Serving
Calories 110, Total Fat 12g, Saturated Fat 3g, Total Carbs 1g, Net Carbs 0g, Protein 3g, Sugar 0g, Fiber 1g, Sodium 342mg, Potassium 46mg

Walnut Cookies

Prep time: 10 minutes , Cook time: 9 minutes, Serves 12

Ingredients:
- ½ cup butter, melted
- ¾ cup erythritol
- 1 tsp vanilla extract
- 1 egg
- 1 ½ cups almond flour
- ½ tsp salt
- ½ tsp baking powder
- ¾ cup chopped walnuts

Instructions
1. Preheat your air fryer to 330 degrees F and prepare your air fryer tray with a piece of parchment.
2. Beat the melted butter and erythritol together in a large bowl.
3. Add the eggs and vanilla and mix until the batter comes together.
4. Add the salt, baking powder and almond flour and mix until a nice, smooth batter forms.
5. Fold in the walnuts then scoop the cookie dough onto the prepared sheet tray. You will want to leave about 2 inches between the cookie dough scoops as the dough will spread slightly. If needed, you can bake the cookies in batches.
6. Bake the cookies in the air fryer for 8-9 minutes or until golden brown on the edges.
7. Let cool on the sheet tray for 5 minutes before removing and enjoying!

Nutrition Facts Per Serving
Calories 174, Total Fat 18g, Saturated Fat 6g, Total Carbs 2g, Net Carbs 1g, Protein 7g, Sugar 1g, Fiber 1g, Sodium 342mg, Potassium 178g

Coconut Cookies

Prep time: 10 minutes , Cook time: 9 minutes, Serves 12

Ingredients:
- ½ cup butter, melted
- ¾ cup erythritol
- 1 tsp vanilla extract
- 1 egg
- 1 cup almond flour
- ½ cup coconut flour
- ½ tsp salt
- ½ tsp baking powder
- ½ cup unsweetened coconut flakes

Instructions

1. Preheat your air fryer to 330 degrees F and prepare your air fryer tray with a piece of parchment.
2. Beat the melted butter and erythritol together in a large bowl.
3. Add the eggs and vanilla and mix until the batter comes together.
4. Add the salt, baking powder coconut flour and almond flour and mix until a nice, smooth batter forms.
5. Fold in the coconut flakes then scoop the cookie dough onto the prepared sheet tray. You will want to leave about 2 inches between the cookie dough scoops as the dough will spread slightly. If needed, you can bake the cookies in batches.
6. Bake the cookies in the air fryer for 8-9 minutes or until golden brown on the edges.
7. Let cool on the sheet tray for 5 minutes before removing and enjoying!

Nutrition Facts Per Serving
Calories 178, Total Fat 16g, Saturated Fat 7g, Total Carbs 7g, Net Carbs 4g, Protein 5g, Sugar 3g, Fiber 3g, Sodium 342mg, Potassium 278g

Almond Cookies

Prep time: 10 minutes , Cook time: 9 minutes, Serves 12

Ingredients:
½ cup butter, melted
¾ cup erythritol
1 tsp almond extract
1 egg
1 ½ cups almond flour
½ tsp salt
½ tsp baking powder
¾ cup chopped almonds

Instructions
1. Preheat your air fryer to 330 degrees F and prepare your air fryer tray with a piece of parchment.
2. Beat the melted butter and erythritol together in a large bowl.
3. Add the eggs and almond extract and mix until the batter comes together.
4. Add the salt, baking powder and almond flour and mix until a nice, smooth batter forms.
5. Fold in the chopped almonds then scoop the cookie dough onto the prepared sheet tray. You will want to leave about 2 inches between the cookie dough scoops as the dough will spread slightly. If needed, you can bake the cookies in batches.
6. Bake the cookies in the air fryer for 8-9 minutes or until golden brown on the edges.
7. Let cool on the sheet tray for 5 minutes before removing and enjoying!

Nutrition Facts Per Serving
Calories 176, Total Fat 24g, Saturated Fat 6g, Total Carbs 4g, Net Carbs 1g, Protein 6g, Sugar 1g, Fiber 3g, Sodium 348mg, Potassium 311g

Chocolate Chip Almond Cookies

Prep time: 10 minutes , Cook time: 9 minutes, Serves 12

Ingredients:
½ cup butter, melted
¾ cup erythritol
1 tsp almond extract
1 egg
1 ½ cups almond flour
½ tsp salt
½ tsp baking powder
½ cup sugar free chocolate chips
¼ cup sliced almonds

Instructions
1. Preheat your air fryer to 330 degrees F and prepare your air fryer tray with a piece of parchment.
2. Beat the melted butter and erythritol together in a large bowl.
3. Add the eggs and almond extract and mix until the batter comes together.
4. Add the salt, baking powder and almond flour and mix until a nice, smooth batter forms.
5. Fold in the sliced almonds then scoop the cookie dough onto the prepared sheet tray. You will want to leave about 2 inches between the cookie dough scoops as the dough will spread slightly. If needed, you can bake the cookies in batches.

6. Bake the cookies in the air fryer for 8-9 minutes or until golden brown on the edges.
7. Let cool on the sheet tray for 5 minutes before removing and enjoying!

Nutrition Facts Per Serving
Calories 174, Total Fat 19g, Saturated Fat 7g, Total Carbs 3g, Net Carbs 1g, Protein 5g, Sugar 1g, Fiber 2g, Sodium 342mg, Potassium 281g

Peanut Butter Cookies

Prep time: 10 minutes , Cook time: 9 minutes, Serves 12

Ingredients:
¼ cup butter, melted
½ cup peanut butter
¾ cup erythritol
1 tsp vanilla extract
1 egg
1 ½ cups almond flour
½ tsp salt
½ tsp baking powder

Instructions
1. Preheat your air fryer to 330 degrees F and prepare your air fryer tray with a piece of parchment.
2. Beat the melted butter, peanut butter and erythritol together in a large bowl.
3. Add the eggs and vanilla and mix until the batter comes together.
4. Add the salt, baking powder and almond flour and mix until a nice, smooth batter forms.
5. Scoop the cookie dough onto the prepared sheet tray. You will want to leave about 2 inches between the cookie dough scoops as the dough will spread slightly. If needed, you can bake the cookies in batches.
6. Bake the cookies in the air fryer for 8-9 minutes or until golden brown on the edges.
7. Let cool on the sheet tray for 5 minutes before removing and enjoying!

Nutrition Facts Per Serving
Calories 189, Total Fat 24g, Saturated Fat 8g, Total Carbs 4g, Net Carbs 2g, Protein 6g, Sugar 2g, Fiber 2g, Sodium 354mg, Potassium 199g

Peanut Butter Chocolate Chip Cookies

Prep time: 10 minutes , Cook time: 9 minutes, Serves 12

Ingredients:
¼ cup butter, melted
½ cup peanut butter
¾ cup erythritol
1 tsp vanilla extract
1 egg
1 ½ cups almond flour
½ tsp salt
½ tsp baking powder
¾ cup sugar free chocolate chips

Instructions
1. Preheat your air fryer to 330 degrees F and prepare your air fryer tray with a piece of parchment.
2. Beat the melted butter, peanut butter and erythritol together in a large bowl.
3. Add the eggs and vanilla and mix until the batter comes together.
4. Add the salt, baking powder and almond flour and mix until a nice, smooth batter forms.
5. Fold in the chocolate chips then scoop the cookie dough onto the prepared sheet tray. You will want to leave about 2 inches between the cookie dough scoops as the dough will spread slightly. If needed, you can bake the cookies in batches.
6. Bake the cookies in the air fryer for 8-9 minutes or until golden brown on the edges.
7. Let cool on the sheet tray for 5 minutes before removing and enjoying!

Nutrition Facts Per Serving
Calories 219, Total Fat 26g, Saturated Fat 9g, Total Carbs 5g, Net Carbs 2g, Protein 6g, Sugar 1g, Fiber 3g, Sodium 354mg, Potassium 199g

Hazelnut Cookies

Prep time: 10 minutes , Cook time: 9 minutes, Serves 12

Ingredients:
- ½ cup butter, melted
- ¾ cup erythritol
- 1 tsp vanilla extract
- 1 egg
- 1 ½ cups hazelnut flour
- ½ tsp salt
- ½ tsp baking powder

Instructions
1. Preheat your air fryer to 330 degrees F and prepare your air fryer tray with a piece of parchment.
2. Beat the melted butter and erythritol together in a large bowl.
3. Add the eggs and vanilla and mix until the batter comes together.
4. Add the salt, baking powder and hazelnut flour and mix until a nice, smooth batter forms.
5. Scoop the cookie dough onto the prepared sheet tray. You will want to leave about 2 inches between the cookie dough scoops as the dough will spread slightly. If needed, you can bake the cookies in batches.
6. Bake the cookies in the air fryer for 8-9 minutes or until golden brown on the edges.
7. Let cool on the sheet tray for 5 minutes before removing and enjoying!

Nutrition Facts Per Serving
Calories 134, Total Fat 11g, Saturated Fat 4g, Total Carbs 1g, Net Carbs 0g, Protein 4g, Sugar 0g, Fiber 1g, Sodium 342mg, Potassium 110g

Hazelnut Chocolate Chip Cookies

Prep time: 10 minutes , Cook time: 9 minutes, Serves 12

Ingredients:
- ½ cup butter, melted
- ¾ cup erythritol
- 1 tsp vanilla extract
- 1 egg
- 1 ½ cups hazelnut flour
- ½ tsp salt
- ½ tsp baking powder
- ¾ cup sugar free chocolate chips

Instructions
1. Preheat your air fryer to 330 degrees F and prepare your air fryer tray with a piece of parchment.
2. Beat the melted butter and erythritol together in a large bowl.
3. Add the eggs and vanilla and mix until the batter comes together.
4. Add the salt, baking powder and hazelnut flour and mix until a nice, smooth batter forms.
5. Fold in the chocolate chips then scoop the cookie dough onto the prepared sheet tray. You will want to leave about 2 inches between the cookie dough scoops as the dough will spread slightly. If needed, you can bake the cookies in batches.
6. Bake the cookies in the air fryer for 8-9 minutes or until golden brown on the edges.
7. Let cool on the sheet tray for 5 minutes before removing and enjoying!

Nutrition Facts Per Serving
Calories 173, Total Fat 18g, Saturated Fat 6g, Total Carbs 2g, Net Carbs 1g, Protein 5g, Sugar 1g, Fiber 3g, Sodium 342mg, Potassium 110g

Seedy Cookies

Prep time: 10 minutes , Cook time: 9 minutes, Serves 12

Ingredients:
- ½ cup butter, melted
- ¾ cup erythritol
- 1 tsp vanilla extract
- 1 egg
- 1 ½ cups almond flour
- ½ tsp salt
- ½ tsp baking powder
- ¼ cup chia seeds
- ¼ cup hemp seeds
- ¼ cup sesame seeds

Instructions
1. Preheat your air fryer to 330 degrees F and prepare your air fryer tray with a piece of parchment.
2. Beat the melted butter and erythritol together in a large bowl.
3. Add the eggs and vanilla and mix until the batter comes together.
4. Add the salt, baking powder and almond flour and mix until a nice, smooth batter forms.
5. Fold in all the seeds then scoop the cookie dough onto the prepared sheet tray. You will want to leave about 2 inches between the cookie dough scoops as the dough will spread slightly. If needed, you can bake the cookies in batches.
6. Bake the cookies in the air fryer for 8-9 minutes or until golden brown on the edges.
7. Let cool on the sheet tray for 5 minutes before removing and enjoying!

Nutrition Facts Per Serving
Calories 197, Total Fat 21g, Saturated Fat 5g, Total Carbs 7g, Net Carbs 4g, Protein 9g, Sugar 1g, Fiber 3g, Sodium 342mg, Potassium 188g

Raspberry Cookies

Prep time: 10 minutes , Cook time: 9 minutes, Serves 12

Ingredients:
½ cup butter, melted
¾ cup erythritol
1 tsp vanilla extract
1 egg
1 ½ cups almond flour
½ tsp salt
½ tsp baking powder
½ cup fresh raspberries

Instructions
1. Preheat your air fryer to 330 degrees F and prepare your air fryer tray with a piece of parchment.
2. Beat the melted butter and erythritol together in a large bowl.
3. Add the eggs and vanilla and mix until the batter comes together.
4. Add the salt, baking powder and almond flour and mix until a nice, smooth batter forms.
5. Fold in the raspberries, smashing them slightly into the dough, then scoop the cookie dough onto the prepared sheet tray. You will want to leave about 2 inches between the cookie dough scoops as the dough will spread slightly. If needed, you can bake the cookies in batches.
6. Bake the cookies in the air fryer for 8-9 minutes or until golden brown on the edges.
7. Let cool on the sheet tray for 5 minutes before removing and enjoying!

Nutrition Facts Per Serving
Calories 152, Total Fat 16g, Saturated Fat 4g, Total Carbs 7g, Net Carbs 4g, Protein 4g, Sugar 3g, Fiber 3g, Sodium 288mg, Potassium 67g

Cocoa Cookies

Prep time: 10 minutes , Cook time: 9 minutes, Serves 12

Ingredients:
½ cup butter, melted
¾ cup erythritol
1 tsp vanilla extract
1 egg
1 ¼ cups almond flour
¼ cup cocoa powder
½ tsp salt
½ tsp baking powder

Instructions
1. Preheat your air fryer to 330 degrees F and prepare your air fryer tray with a piece of parchment.
2. Beat the melted butter and erythritol together in a large bowl.
3. Add the eggs and vanilla and mix until the batter comes together.
4. Add the salt, baking powder, cocoa powder and almond flour and mix until a nice, smooth batter forms.

5. Scoop the cookie dough onto the prepared sheet tray. You will want to leave about 2 inches between the cookie dough scoops as the dough will spread slightly. If needed, you can bake the cookies in batches.
6. Bake the cookies in the air fryer for 8-9 minutes or until golden brown on the edges.
7. Let cool on the sheet tray for 5 minutes before removing and enjoying!

Nutrition Facts Per Serving
Calories 156, Total Fat 19g, Saturated Fat 7g, Total Carbs 2g, Net Carbs 1g, Protein 4g, Sugar 1g, Fiber 3g, Sodium 310mg, Potassium 101g

Double Chocolate Cookies

Prep time: 10 minutes , Cook time: 9 minutes, Serves 12

Ingredients:
½ cup butter, melted
¾ cup erythritol
1 tsp vanilla extract
1 egg
1 ¼ cups almond flour
¼ cup cocoa powder
½ tsp salt
½ tsp baking powder
¾ cup unsweetened chocolate chips

Instructions
1. Preheat your air fryer to 330 degrees F and prepare your air fryer tray with a piece of parchment.
2. Beat the melted butter and erythritol together in a large bowl.
3. Add the eggs and vanilla and mix until the batter comes together.
4. Add the salt, baking powder, cocoa powder and almond flour and mix until a nice, smooth batter forms.
5. Fold in the chocolate chips then scoop the cookie dough onto the prepared sheet tray. You will want to leave about 2 inches between the cookie dough scoops as the dough will spread slightly. If needed, you can bake the cookies in batches.
6. Bake the cookies in the air fryer for 8-9 minutes or until golden brown on the edges.
7. Let cool on the sheet tray for 5 minutes before removing and enjoying!

Nutrition Facts Per Serving
Calories 188, Total Fat 21g, Saturated Fat 7g, Total Carbs 2g, Net Carbs 1g, Protein 5g, Sugar 1g, Fiber 3g, Sodium 311mg, Potassium 132g

Peanut Butter Chocolate Cookies

Prep time: 10 minutes , Cook time: 9 minutes, Serves 12

Ingredients:
¼ cup butter, melted
¼ cup peanut butter
¾ cup erythritol
1 tsp vanilla extract
1 egg
1 ¼ cups almond flour
¼ cup cocoa powder
½ tsp salt
½ tsp baking powder

Instructions
1. Preheat your air fryer to 330 degrees F and prepare your air fryer tray with a piece of parchment.
2. Beat the melted butter, peanut butter and erythritol together in a large bowl.
3. Add the eggs and vanilla and mix until the batter comes together.
4. Add the salt, baking powder, cocoa powder and almond flour and mix until a nice, smooth batter forms.
5. Scoop the cookie dough onto the prepared sheet tray. You will want to leave about 2 inches between the cookie dough scoops as the dough will spread slightly. If needed, you can bake the cookies in batches.
6. Bake the cookies in the air fryer for 8-9 minutes or until golden brown on the edges.
7. Let cool on the sheet tray for 5 minutes before removing and enjoying!

Nutrition Facts Per Serving
Calories 172, Total Fat 22g, Saturated Fat 9g, Total Carbs 5g, Net Carbs 3g, Protein 6g, Sugar 1g, Fiber 2g, Sodium 310mg, Potassium 101g

Cinnamon Chocolate Chip Cookies

Prep time: 10 minutes, Cook time: 9 minutes, Serves 12

Ingredients:
½ cup butter, melted
¾ cup erythritol
1 tsp vanilla extract
1 egg
1 ½ cups almond flour
1 tsp ground cinnamon
½ tsp salt
½ tsp baking powder
¾ cup sugar free chocolate chips

Instructions
1. Preheat your air fryer to 330 degrees F and prepare your air fryer tray with a piece of parchment.
2. Beat the melted butter and erythritol together in a large bowl.
3. Add the eggs and vanilla and mix until the batter comes together.
4. Add the salt, baking powder, cinnamon and almond flour and mix until a nice, smooth batter forms.
5. Fold in the chocolate chips then scoop the cookie dough onto the prepared sheet tray. You will want to leave about 2 inches between the cookie dough scoops as the dough will spread slightly. If needed, you can bake the cookies in batches.
6. Bake the cookies in the air fryer for 8-9 minutes or until golden brown on the edges.
7. Let cool on the sheet tray for 5 minutes before removing and enjoying!

Nutrition Facts Per Serving
Calories 169, Total Fat 19g, Saturated Fat 7g, Total Carbs 2g, Net Carbs 1g, Protein 4g, Sugar 1g, Fiber 1g, Sodium 342mg, Potassium 110g

Pumpkin Spice Cookies

Prep time: 10 minutes, Cook time: 9 minutes, Serves 12

Ingredients:
¼ cup butter, melted
¼ cup pumpkin puree
¾ cup erythritol
1 tsp vanilla extract
1 egg
1 ½ cups almond flour
½ tsp salt
1 tsp pumpkin spice seasoning
½ tsp baking powder

Instructions
1. Preheat your air fryer to 330 degrees F and prepare your air fryer tray with a piece of parchment.
2. Beat the melted butter, pumpkin puree and erythritol together in a large bowl.
3. Add the eggs and vanilla and mix until the batter comes together.
4. Add the salt, baking powder, pumpkin spice seasoning and almond flour and mix until a nice, smooth batter forms.
5. Scoop the cookie dough onto the prepared sheet tray. You will want to leave about 2 inches between the cookie dough scoops as the dough will spread slightly. If needed, you can bake the cookies in batches.
6. Bake the cookies in the air fryer for 8-9 minutes or until golden brown on the edges.
7. Let cool on the sheet tray for 5 minutes before removing and enjoying!

Nutrition Facts Per Serving
Calories 188, Total Fat 16g, Saturated Fat 5g, Total Carbs 7g, Net Carbs 3g, Protein 4g, Sugar 2g, Fiber 4g, Sodium 482mg, Potassium 346g

Pumpkin Chocolate Chip Cookies

Prep time: 10 minutes, Cook time: 9 minutes, Serves 12

Ingredients:
¼ cup butter, melted
¼ cup pumpkin puree
¾ cup erythritol
1 tsp vanilla extract
1 egg
1 ½ cups almond flour
½ tsp salt
1 tsp pumpkin spice seasoning
½ tsp baking powder
¾ cup sugar free chocolate chips

Instructions

1. Preheat your air fryer to 330 degrees F and prepare your air fryer tray with a piece of parchment.
2. Beat the melted butter, pumpkin puree and erythritol together in a large bowl.
3. Add the eggs and vanilla and mix until the batter comes together.
4. Add the salt, baking powder, pumpkin spice seasoning and almond flour and mix until a nice, smooth batter forms.
5. Fold in the chocolate chips then scoop the cookie dough onto the prepared sheet tray. You will want to leave about 2 inches between the cookie dough scoops as the dough will spread slightly. If needed, you can bake the cookies in batches.
6. Bake the cookies in the air fryer for 8-9 minutes or until golden brown on the edges.
7. Let cool on the sheet tray for 5 minutes before removing and enjoying!

Nutrition Facts Per Serving
Calories 218, Total Fat 27g, Saturated Fat 8g, Total Carbs 7g, Net Carbs 3g, Protein 4g, Sugar 2g, Fiber 4g, Sodium 482mg, Potassium 346g

Cream Cheese Cookies

Prep time: 10 minutes , Cook time: 9 minutes, Serves 12

Ingredients:
½ cup cream cheese, softened
¾ cup erythritol
1 tsp vanilla extract
1 egg
1 ½ cups almond flour
½ tsp salt
½ tsp baking powder

Instructions
1. Preheat your air fryer to 330 degrees F and prepare your air fryer tray with a piece of parchment.
2. Beat the cream cheese and erythritol together in a large bowl.
3. Add the eggs and vanilla and mix until the batter comes together.
4. Add the salt, baking powder, pumpkin spice seasoning and almond flour and mix until a nice, smooth batter forms.
5. Scoop the cookie dough onto the prepared sheet tray. You will want to leave about 2 inches between the cookie dough scoops as the dough will spread slightly. If needed, you can bake the cookies in batches.
6. Bake the cookies in the air fryer for 8-9 minutes or until golden brown on the edges.
7. Let cool on the sheet tray for 5 minutes before removing and enjoying!

Nutrition Facts Per Serving
Calories 189, Total Fat 11g, Saturated Fat 6g, Total Carbs 2g, Net Carbs 1g, Protein 4g, Sugar 1g, Fiber 1g, Sodium 211 mg, Potassium 101g

Keto Shortbread

Prep time: 15 minutes , Cook time: 15 minutes, Serves 8

Ingredients:
½ cup butter
½ cup swerve sweetener
1 tsp vanilla extract
1 cup almond flour
1 tsp salt

Instructions
1. Preheat your air fryer to 300 degrees F and grease a 6 inch baking pan or tray.
2. Place the butter and swerve sweetener in a mixing bowl and beat until soft and fluffy.
3. Add the vanilla extract and beat again to incorporate fully.
4. Add the almond flour slowly, mixing it in a little at a time, until a smooth dough has formed.
5. Spread the shortbread batter in the prepared baking pan or tray and then place in the preheated air fryer.
6. Bake for 15 minutes or until the edges of the shortbread are golden brown.
7. Let cool for 10 minutes then flip the shortbread out of the pan, slice and enjoy while warm.

Nutrition Facts Per Serving
Calories 182, Total Fat 18g, Saturated Fat 7g, Total Carbs 3g, Net Carbs 2g, Protein 3g, Sugar 1g, Fiber 1g, Sodium 364mg, Potassium 78g

Lemon Shortbread

Prep time: 15 minutes, Cook time: 15 minutes, Serves 8

Ingredients:
- ½ cup butter
- ½ cup swerve sweetener
- 1 tsp vanilla extract
- 1 cup almond flour
- 1 tsp salt
- 1 tsp lemon zest

Instructions
1. Preheat your air fryer to 300 degrees F and grease a 6 inch baking pan or tray.
2. Place the butter and swerve sweetener in a mixing bowl and beat until soft and fluffy.
3. Add the vanilla extract and lemon zest and beat again to incorporate fully.
4. Add the almond flour slowly, mixing it in a little at a time, until a smooth dough has formed.
5. Spread the shortbread batter in the prepared baking pan or tray and then place in the preheated air fryer.
6. Bake for 15 minutes or until the edges of the shortbread are golden brown.
7. Let cool for 10 minutes then flip the shortbread out of the pan, slice and enjoy while warm.

Nutrition Facts Per Serving
Calories 189, Total Fat 19g, Saturated Fat 7g, Total Carbs 3g, Net Carbs 2g, Protein 3g, Sugar 1g, Fiber 1g, Sodium 364mg, Potassium 78g

Almond Shortbread

Prep time: 15 minutes, Cook time: 15 minutes, Serves 8

Ingredients:
- ½ cup butter
- ½ cup swerve sweetener
- 1 tsp almond extract
- 1 cup almond flour
- 1 tsp salt
- ½ cup sliced almonds

Instructions
1. Preheat your air fryer to 300 degrees F and grease a 6 inch baking pan or tray.
2. Place the butter and swerve sweetener in a mixing bowl and beat until soft and fluffy.
3. Add the almond extract and beat again to incorporate fully.
4. Add the almond flour slowly, mixing it in a little at a time, until a smooth dough has formed.
5. Spread the shortbread batter in the prepared baking pan or tray and then sprinkle the sliced almonds over the top of the shortbread.
6. Place in the preheated air fryer and bake for 15 minutes or until the edges of the shortbread are golden brown.
7. Let cool for 10 minutes then flip the shortbread out of the pan, slice and enjoy while warm.

Nutrition Facts Per Serving
Calories 216, Total Fat 24g, Saturated Fat 9g, Total Carbs 3g, Net Carbs 2g, Protein 3g, Sugar 1g, Fiber 1g, Sodium 364mg, Potassium 78g

Lime Shortbread

Prep time: 15 minutes, Cook time: 15 minutes, Serves 8

Ingredients:
- ½ cup butter
- ½ cup swerve sweetener
- 1 tsp vanilla extract
- 1 cup almond flour
- 1 tsp salt
- 1 tsp lime zest

Instructions
1. Preheat your air fryer to 300 degrees F and grease a 6 inch baking pan or tray.
2. Place the butter and swerve sweetener in a mixing bowl and beat until soft and fluffy.
3. Add the vanilla extract and lime zest and beat again to incorporate fully.

4. Add the almond flour slowly, mixing it in a little at a time, until a smooth dough has formed.
5. Spread the shortbread batter in the prepared baking pan or tray and then place in the preheated air fryer.
6. Bake for 15 minutes or until the edges of the shortbread are golden brown.
7. Let cool for 10 minutes then flip the shortbread out of the pan, slice and enjoy while warm.

Nutrition Facts Per Serving
Calories 184, Total Fat 18g, Saturated Fat 7g, Total Carbs 3g, Net Carbs 2g, Protein 3g, Sugar 1g, Fiber 1g, Sodium 364mg, Potassium 78g

Chocolate Shortbread

Prep time: 15 minutes , Cook time: 15 minutes, Serves 8

Ingredients:
½ cup butter
½ cup swerve sweetener
1 tsp vanilla extract
¾ cup almond flour
¼ cup cocoa powder
1 tsp salt

Instructions
1. Preheat your air fryer to 300 degrees F and grease a 6 inch baking pan or tray.
2. Place the butter and swerve sweetener in a mixing bowl and beat until soft and fluffy.
3. Add the vanilla extract and beat again to incorporate fully.
4. Add the almond flour and cocoa powder slowly, mixing them in a little at a time, until a smooth dough has formed.
5. Spread the shortbread batter in the prepared baking pan or tray and then place in the preheated air fryer.
6. Bake for 15 minutes or until the edges of the shortbread are golden brown.
7. Let cool for 10 minutes then flip the shortbread out of the pan, slice and enjoy while warm.

Nutrition Facts Per Serving
Calories 204, Total Fat 20g, Saturated Fat 7g, Total Carbs 3g, Net Carbs 2g, Protein 4g, Sugar 1g, Fiber 1g, Sodium 364mg, Potassium 89g

Chocolate Chip Shortbread

Prep time: 15 minutes , Cook time: 15 minutes, Serves 8

Ingredients:
½ cup butter
½ cup swerve sweetener
1 tsp vanilla extract
1 cup almond flour
1 tsp salt
½ cup dark chocolate chips, unsweetened

Instructions
1. Preheat your air fryer to 300 degrees F and grease a 6 inch baking pan or tray.
2. Place the butter and swerve sweetener in a mixing bowl and beat until soft and fluffy.
3. Add the vanilla extract and beat again to incorporate fully.
4. Add the almond flour slowly, mixing it in a little at a time, until a smooth dough has formed.
5. Fold in the chocolate chips gently.
6. Spread the shortbread batter in the prepared baking pan or tray and then place in the preheated air fryer.
7. Bake for 15 minutes or until the edges of the shortbread are golden brown.
8. Let cool for 10 minutes then flip the shortbread out of the pan, slice and enjoy while warm.

Nutrition Facts Per Serving
Calories 230, Total Fat 23g, Saturated Fat 9g, Total Carbs 4g, Net Carbs 2g, Protein 6g, Sugar 1g, Fiber 2g, Sodium 364mg, Potassium 78g

Peanut Butter Shortbread

Prep time: 15 minutes , Cook time: 15 minutes, Serves 8

Ingredients:
½ cup peanut butter
½ cup swerve sweetener
1 tsp vanilla extract
1 cup almond flour
1 tsp salt

Instructions
1. Preheat your air fryer to 300 degrees F and grease a 6 inch baking pan or tray.
2. Place the peanut butter and swerve sweetener in a mixing bowl and beat until soft and fluffy.
3. Add the vanilla extract and beat again to incorporate fully.
4. Add the almond flour slowly, mixing it in a little at a time, until a smooth dough has formed.
5. Spread the shortbread batter in the prepared baking pan or tray and then place in the preheated air fryer.
6. Bake for 15 minutes or until the edges of the shortbread are golden brown.
7. Let cool for 10 minutes then flip the shortbread out of the pan, slice and enjoy while warm.

Nutrition Facts Per Serving
Calories 189, Total Fat 19g, Saturated Fat 7g, Total Carbs 5g, Net Carbs 4g, Protein 3g, Sugar 2g, Fiber 1g, Sodium 364mg, Potassium 78g

Walnut Shortbread

Prep time: 15 minutes , Cook time: 15 minutes, Serves 8

Ingredients:
½ cup butter
½ cup swerve sweetener
1 tsp vanilla extract
1 cup walnut flour
1 tsp salt

Instructions
1. Preheat your air fryer to 300 degrees F and grease a 6 inch baking pan or tray.
2. Place the butter and swerve sweetener in a mixing bowl and beat until soft and fluffy.
3. Add the vanilla extract and beat again to incorporate fully.
4. Add the walnut flour slowly, mixing it in a little at a time, until a smooth dough has formed.
5. Spread the shortbread batter in the prepared baking pan or tray and then place in the preheated air fryer.
6. Bake for 15 minutes or until the edges of the shortbread are golden brown.
7. Let cool for 10 minutes then flip the shortbread out of the pan, slice and enjoy while warm.

Nutrition Facts Per Serving
Calories 188, Total Fat 18g, Saturated Fat 7g, Total Carbs 3g, Net Carbs 2g, Protein 3g, Sugar 1g, Fiber 1g, Sodium 358mg, Potassium 76g

Coconut Shortbread

Prep time: 15 minutes , Cook time: 15 minutes, Serves 8

Ingredients:
½ cup butter
½ cup swerve sweetener
1 tsp coconut extract
½ cup almond flour
½ cup coconut flour
1 tsp salt

Instructions
1. Preheat your air fryer to 300 degrees F and grease a 6 inch baking pan or tray.
2. Place the butter and swerve sweetener in a mixing bowl and beat until soft and fluffy.
3. Add the coconut extract and beat again to incorporate fully.
4. Add the almond flour and coconut flour slowly, mixing them in a little at a time, until a smooth dough has formed.
5. Spread the shortbread batter in the prepared baking pan or tray and then place in the preheated air fryer.
6. Bake for 15 minutes or until the edges of the shortbread are golden brown.
7. Let cool for 10 minutes then flip the shortbread out of the pan, slice and enjoy while warm.

Nutrition Facts Per Serving
Calories 196, Total Fat 20g, Saturated Fat 8g, Total Carbs 5g, Net Carbs 4g, Protein 3g, Sugar 3g, Fiber 1g, Sodium 364mg, Potassium 101g

Fish and Seafood

Crispy Salmon

Prep time: 10 minutes , Cook time: 10 minutes , Serves 4

Ingredients:
- 1 pound salmon filets
- ½ cup pork rinds, crushed
- ½ cup fresh grated parmesan
- 2 Tbsp dill, chopped
- ¼ tsp black pepper
- ½ tsp salt
- ¼ tsp garlic powder
- 2 Tbsp melted butter

Instructions
1. Preheat your air fryer to 450 degrees F and line your air fryer tray with foil.
2. Place the salmon filets on the foil lined tray.
3. In a small bowl or food processor, combine the remaining ingredients and mix well.
4. Press the pork rind mix onto the salmon filets, coating the whole top evenly and packing the crust into the fish filets.
5. Bake the filets in the preheated oven for 10 minutes. The top crust should be nicely browned.
6. Serve while hot.

Nutrition Facts Per Serving
Calories 346, Total Fat 21g, Saturated Fat 10g, Total Carbs 2g, Net Carbs 1g, Protein 40g, Sugar 0g, Fiber 1g, Sodium 332mg, Potassium 189g

Spicy Crunchy Salmon

Prep time: 10 minutes , Cook time: 10 minutes , Serves 4

Ingredients:
- 1 pound salmon filets
- ½ cup pork rinds, crushed
- ½ cup fresh grated parmesan
- 2 Tbsp dill, chopped
- ¼ tsp black pepper
- ½ tsp cayenne pepper
- ½ tsp salt
- ¼ tsp garlic powder
- 2 Tbsp melted butter

Instructions
1. Preheat your air fryer to 450 degrees F and line your air fryer tray with foil.
2. Place the salmon filets on the foil lined tray.
3. In a small bowl or food processor, combine the remaining ingredients and mix well.
4. Press the pork rind mix onto the salmon filets, coating the whole top evenly and packing the crust into the fish filets.
5. Bake the filets in the preheated oven for 10 minutes. The top crust should be nicely browned.
6. Serve while hot.

Nutrition Facts Per Serving
Calories 346, Total Fat 21g, Saturated Fat 10g, Total Carbs 2g, Net Carbs 1g, Protein 40g, Sugar 0g, Fiber 1g, Sodium 342mg, Potassium 192g

Crunchy Garlic Salmon

Prep time: 10 minutes , Cook time: 10 minutes , Serves 4

Ingredients:
- 1 pound salmon filets
- ½ cup pork rinds, crushed
- ½ cup fresh grated parmesan
- 2 Tbsp dill, chopped
- ¼ tsp black pepper
- ½ tsp salt
- ¼ tsp garlic powder
- 2 tsp fresh minced garlic
- 2 Tbsp melted butter

Instructions
1. Preheat your air fryer to 450 degrees F and line your air fryer tray with foil.
2. Place the salmon filets on the foil lined tray.
3. In a small bowl or food processor, combine the remaining ingredients and mix well.

4. Press the pork rind mix onto the salmon filets, coating the whole top evenly and packing the crust into the fish filets.
5. Bake the filets in the preheated oven for 10 minutes. The top crust should be nicely browned.
6. Serve while hot.

Nutrition Facts Per Serving
Calories 352, Total Fat 21g, Saturated Fat 10g, Total Carbs 2g, Net Carbs 1g, Protein 40g, Sugar 0g, Fiber 1g, Sodium 332mg, Potassium 189g

Cajun Salmon

Prep time: 10 minutes , Cook time: 10 minutes , Serves 4

Ingredients:
1 pound salmon filets
½ cup pork rinds, crushed
1 Tbsp Cajun seasoning
2 tsp fresh minced garlic
2 Tbsp melted butter

Instructions
1. Preheat your air fryer to 450 degrees F and line your air fryer tray with foil.
2. Place the salmon filets on the foil lined tray.
3. In a small bowl or food processor, combine the remaining ingredients and mix well.
4. Press the pork rind mix onto the salmon filets, coating the whole top evenly and packing the crust into the fish filets.
5. Bake the filets in the preheated oven for 10 minutes. The top crust should be nicely browned.
6. Serve while hot.

Nutrition Facts Per Serving
Calories 301, Total Fat 21g, Saturated Fat 10g, Total Carbs 2g, Net Carbs 1g, Protein 40g, Sugar 0g, Fiber 1g, Sodium 320mg, Potassium 189g

Black Pepper Parmesan Salmon

Prep time: 10 minutes , Cook time: 10 minutes , Serves 4

Ingredients:
1 pound salmon filets
½ cup pork rinds, crushed
½ cup fresh grated parmesan
1 tsp black pepper
½ tsp salt
¼ tsp garlic powder

Instructions
1. Preheat your air fryer to 450 degrees F and line your air fryer tray with foil.
2. Place the salmon filets on the foil lined tray.
3. In a small bowl or food processor, combine the remaining ingredients and mix well.
4. Press the pork rind mix onto the salmon filets, coating the whole top evenly and packing the crust into the fish filets.
5. Bake the filets in the preheated oven for 10 minutes. The top crust should be nicely browned.
6. Serve while hot.

Nutrition Facts Per Serving
Calories 354, Total Fat 21g, Saturated Fat 10g, Total Carbs 2g, Net Carbs 1g, Protein 40g, Sugar 0g, Fiber 1g, Sodium 330mg, Potassium 189g

Spicy Crunchy Garlic Salmon

Prep time: 10 minutes , Cook time: 10 minutes , Serves 4

Ingredients:
1 pound salmon filets
½ cup pork rinds, crushed
½ cup fresh grated parmesan
¼ tsp black pepper
½ tsp salt
½ tsp cayenne pepper
1 tsp erythritol sweetener
2 Tbsp melted butter

Instructions
1. Preheat your air fryer to 450 degrees F and line your air fryer tray with foil.
2. Place the salmon filets on the foil lined tray.
3. In a small bowl or food processor, combine the remaining ingredients and mix well.

4. Press the pork rind mix onto the salmon filets, coating the whole top evenly and packing the crust into the fish filets.
5. Bake the filets in the preheated oven for 10 minutes. The top crust should be nicely browned.
6. Serve while hot.

Nutrition Facts Per Serving
Calories 312, Total Fat 21g, Saturated Fat 10g, Total Carbs 2g, Net Carbs 1g, Protein 40g, Sugar 0g, Fiber 1g, Sodium 309mg, Potassium 177g

Asian Style Crunchy Salmon

Prep time: 10 minutes , Cook time: 10 minutes , Serves 4

Ingredients:
- 1 pound salmon filets
- ½ cup pork rinds, crushed
- ¼ tsp black pepper
- ½ tsp salt
- ¼ tsp garlic powder
- 2 tsp fresh minced garlic
- 1 Tbsp melted butter
- 1 Tbsp coconut aminos

Instructions
1. Preheat your air fryer to 450 degrees F and line your air fryer tray with foil.
2. Place the salmon filets on the foil lined tray.
3. In a small bowl or food processor, combine the remaining ingredients and mix well.
4. Press the pork rind mix onto the salmon filets, coating the whole top evenly and packing the crust into the fish filets.
5. Bake the filets in the preheated oven for 10 minutes. The top crust should be nicely browned.
6. Serve while hot.

Nutrition Facts Per Serving
Calories 323, Total Fat 21g, Saturated Fat 10g, Total Carbs 2g, Net Carbs 1g, Protein 40g, Sugar 0g, Fiber 1g, Sodium 482mg, Potassium 199g

Tuna Stuffed Mushrooms

Prep time: 20 minutes , Cook time: 50 minutes , Serves 5

Ingredients:
- 1 pound cremini mushrooms, stems and gills removed
- ¾ pound canned tuna in water
- ¾ cup cream cheese, softened
- 1/3 cup grated cheddar cheese
- ¼ cup sour cream
- 1 Tbsp minced garlic
- 1 Tbsp mustard
- ½ tsp salt
- ¼ tsp ground black pepper
- ½ cup grated parmesan

Instructions
1. Preheat your air fryer to 375 degrees F and line your air fryer tray with foil or parchment.
2. Place the mushroom caps on the tray and bake for 10 minutes in the air fryer. Remove from the air fryer and drain any excess water from the tray.
3. In a large mixing bowl, combine all the remaining ingredients except the parmesan cheese. Stir well to fully blend everything.
4. Stuff the mushroom caps with the crab mix and then sprinkle the parmesan over the top of the mushrooms.
5. Return the tray to the air fryer and bake for another 10 minutes or until the tops of the mushrooms are golden brown.
6. Remove from the air fryer and enjoy while hot.

Nutrition Facts Per Serving
Calories 320, Total Fat 13g, Saturated Fat 4g, Total Carbs 8g, Net Carbs 5g, Protein 24g, Sugar 1g, Fiber 3g, Sodium 494mg, Potassium 208g

Crispy Flounder

Prep time: 10 minutes, Cook time: 8 minutes, Serves 4

Ingredients:
1 pound salmon filets
½ cup pork rinds, crushed
½ cup fresh grated parmesan
2 Tbsp dill, chopped
¼ tsp black pepper
½ tsp salt
¼ tsp garlic powder
2 Tbsp melted butter

Instructions
1. Preheat your air fryer to 450 degrees F and line your air fryer tray with foil.
2. Place the flounder filets on the foil lined tray.
3. In a small bowl or food processor, combine the remaining ingredients and mix well.
4. Press the pork rind mix onto the flounder filets, coating the whole top evenly and packing the crust into the fish filets.
5. Bake the filets in the preheated oven for 10 minutes. The top crust should be nicely browned.
6. Serve while hot.

Nutrition Facts Per Serving
Calories 227, Total Fat 15g, Saturated Fat 9g, Total Carbs 2g, Net Carbs 1g, Protein 32g, Sugar 0g, Fiber 1g, Sodium 332mg, Potassium 189g

Tuna Cakes

Prep time: 30 minutes, Cook time: 60 minutes, Serves 8

Ingredients:
10 oz canned, drained tuna
4 oz pork rinds, crushed
1 cup mozzarella cheese, grated
1 Tbsp keto mayonnaise
2 eggs
½ tsp smoked paprika
3 Tbsp water
2 Tbsp olive oil

Instructions
1. Preheat your air fryer to 375 degrees F and line your air fryer tray with foil or parchment.
2. Place all the ingredients except for the olive oil, in a large bowl and blend together well using your hands.
3. Cover the bowl and refrigerate for an hour to let the flavors soak together.
4. Remove the bowl from the fridge and use your hands to form the tuna cakes, making each patty about one inch thick.
5. Place the cakes on the prepared sheet tray and drizzle with the olive oil.
6. Cook the cakes in the air fryer for about 7 minutes or until golden browned.
7. Remove from the air fryer and serve while hot.

Nutrition Facts Per Serving
Calories 313, Total Fat 25g, Saturated Fat 8g, Total Carbs 1g, Net Carbs 1g, Protein 23g, Sugar 1g, Fiber 0g, Sodium 348mg, Potassium 197g

Salmon Cakes

Prep time: 30 minutes, Cook time: 60 minutes, Serves 8

Ingredients:
10 oz canned, drained salmon
4 oz pork rinds, crushed
1 cup mozzarella cheese, grated
1 Tbsp keto mayonnaise
2 eggs
½ tsp smoked paprika
3 Tbsp water
2 Tbsp olive oil

Instructions
1. Preheat your air fryer to 375 degrees F and line your air fryer tray with foil or parchment.
2. Place all the ingredients except for the olive oil, in a large bowl and blend together well using your hands.
3. Cover the bowl and refrigerate for an hour to let the flavors soak together.
4. Remove the bowl from the fridge and use your hands to form the tuna cakes, making each patty about one inch thick.
5. Place the cakes on the prepared sheet tray and drizzle with the olive oil.

6. Cook the cakes in the air fryer for about 7 minutes or until golden browned.
7. Remove from the air fryer and serve while hot.

Nutrition Facts Per Serving
Calories 348, Total Fat 32g, Saturated Fat 8g, Total Carbs 1g, Net Carbs 1g, Protein 27g, Sugar 1g, Fiber 0g, Sodium 348mg, Potassium 197g

Red Hot Tuna Cakes

Prep time: 30 minutes , Cook time: 60 minutes , Serves 8

Ingredients:
10 oz canned, drained tuna
4 oz pork rinds, crushed
1 cup mozzarella cheese, grated
1 Tbsp keto mayonnaise
2 eggs
½ tsp smoked paprika
1 tsp red pepper flakes
3 Tbsp water
2 Tbsp olive oil

Instructions
1. Preheat your air fryer to 375 degrees F and line your air fryer tray with foil or parchment.
2. Place all the ingredients except for the olive oil, in a large bowl and blend together well using your hands.
3. Cover the bowl and refrigerate for an hour to let the flavors soak together.
4. Remove the bowl from the fridge and use your hands to form the tuna cakes, making each patty about one inch thick.
5. Place the cakes on the prepared sheet tray and drizzle with the olive oil.
6. Cook the cakes in the air fryer for about 7 minutes or until golden browned.
7. Remove from the air fryer and serve while hot.

Nutrition Facts Per Serving
Calories 318, Total Fat 25g, Saturated Fat 8g, Total Carbs 1g, Net Carbs 1g, Protein 23g, Sugar 1g, Fiber 0g, Sodium 348mg, Potassium 197g

Cajun Tuna Cakes

Prep time: 30 minutes , Cook time: 60 minutes , Serves 8

Ingredients:
10 oz canned, drained tuna
4 oz pork rinds, crushed
1 cup mozzarella cheese, grated
1 Tbsp keto mayonnaise
2 eggs
1 ½ tsp Cajun seasoning
3 Tbsp water
2 Tbsp olive oil

Instructions
1. Preheat your air fryer to 375 degrees F and line your air fryer tray with foil or parchment.
2. Place all the ingredients except for the olive oil, in a large bowl and blend together well using your hands.
3. Cover the bowl and refrigerate for an hour to let the flavors soak together.
4. Remove the bowl from the fridge and use your hands to form the tuna cakes, making each patty about one inch thick.
5. Place the cakes on the prepared sheet tray and drizzle with the olive oil.
6. Cook the cakes in the air fryer for about 7 minutes or until golden browned.
7. Remove from the air fryer and serve while hot.

Nutrition Facts Per Serving
Calories 318, Total Fat 25g, Saturated Fat 8g, Total Carbs 1g, Net Carbs 1g, Protein 23g, Sugar 1g, Fiber 0g, Sodium 376mg, Potassium 197g

Lemon Tuna Cakes

Prep time: 30 minutes, Cook time: 60 minutes, Serves 8

Ingredients:
- 10 oz canned, drained tuna
- 4 oz pork rinds, crushed
- 1 cup mozzarella cheese, grated
- 1 Tbsp keto mayonnaise
- 2 eggs
- 1 tsp lemon zest
- ½ tsp smoked paprika
- 3 Tbsp water
- 2 Tbsp olive oil

Instructions
1. Preheat your air fryer to 375 degrees F and line your air fryer tray with foil or parchment.
2. Place all the ingredients except for the olive oil, in a large bowl and blend together well using your hands.
3. Cover the bowl and refrigerate for an hour to let the flavors soak together.
4. Remove the bowl from the fridge and use your hands to form the tuna cakes, making each patty about one inch thick.
5. Place the cakes on the prepared sheet tray and drizzle with the olive oil.
6. Cook the cakes in the air fryer for about 7 minutes or until golden browned.
7. Remove from the air fryer and serve while hot.

Nutrition Facts Per Serving
Calories 318, Total Fat 25g, Saturated Fat 8g, Total Carbs 1g, Net Carbs 1g, Protein 23g, Sugar 1g, Fiber 0g, Sodium 348mg, Potassium 197g

Cod Fish Sticks

Prep time: 10 minutes, Cook time: 10 minutes, Serves 4

Ingredients:
- 1 pound cod
- ¼ cup mayonnaise
- 2 Tbsp mustard
- ½ tsp salt
- ½ tsp ground black pepper
- 1 ½ cups ground pork rinds
- 2 Tbsp whole milk

Instructions
1. Preheat your air fryer to 400 degrees F and line your air fryer tray with foil and spray with cooking grease.
2. Dry the cod filets by patting with a paper towel. Cut the fish into strips about 1 inch wide and two inches long.
3. In a small bowl, combine the mustard, mayo and milk and stir together well.
4. In a separate bowl, combine the ground pork rinds, salt and pepper.
5. Dip the fish strips into the mayonnaise mix and then into the pork rind mix, coating the fish completely. Place it on the prepared tray when done and repeat with the remaining fish sticks.
6. Place the tray in the air fryer and bake the fish for 5 minutes, flip and bake for another 5 minutes. Serve while hot!

Nutrition Facts Per Serving
Calories 263, Total Fat 16g, Saturated Fat 5g, Total Carbs 1g, Net Carbs 0g, Protein 26g, Sugar 0g, Fiber 1g, Sodium 679mg, Potassium 68g

Tuna Sticks

Prep time: 10 minutes, Cook time: 10 minutes, Serves 4

Ingredients:
- 1 pound tuna
- ¼ cup mayonnaise
- 2 Tbsp mustard
- ½ tsp salt
- ½ tsp ground black pepper
- 1 ½ cups ground pork rinds
- 2 Tbsp whole milk

Instructions
1. Preheat your air fryer to 400 degrees F and line your air fryer tray with foil and spray with cooking grease.
2. Dry the tuna filets by patting with a paper towel. Cut the fish into strips about 1 inch wide and two inches long.

3. In a small bowl, combine the mustard, mayo and milk and stir together well.
4. In a separate bowl, combine the ground pork rinds, salt and pepper.
5. Dip the fish strips into the mayonnaise mix and then into the pork rind mix, coating the fish completely. Place it on the prepared tray when done and repeat with the remaining fish sticks.
6. Place the tray in the air fryer and bake the fish for 5 minutes, flip and bake for another 5 minutes. Serve while hot!

Nutrition Facts Per Serving
Calories 274, Total Fat 18g, Saturated Fat 5g, Total Carbs 1g, Net Carbs 0g, Protein 27g, Sugar 0g, Fiber 1g, Sodium 679mg, Potassium 68g

Maple Walnut Salmon

Prep time: 10 minutes , Cook time: 15 minutes , Serves 4

Ingredients:
½ cup chopped walnuts
1 tsp smoked paprika
½ tsp onion powder
½ tsp garlic powder
3 Tbsp keto maple syrup
1 Tbsp apple cider vinegar
1 tsp coconut aminos
2 Tbsp butter
24 oz salmon filets

Instructions
1. Preheat your air fryer to 400 degrees F and line the air fryer tray with foil.
2. In a large bowl, combine the walnuts, paprika, onion powder, garlic powder, keto syrup, vinegar and coconut aminos.
3. Place the salmon on the prepared tray and spoon the walnut mix over the top of the fish.
4. Place the tray in the fridge and let cool for 2 hours.
5. Remove the tray from the fridge and dot the butter throughout the tray, dispersing it around the fish.
6. Place in the air fryer and bake for 15 minutes. Serve hot!

Nutrition Facts Per Serving
Calories 449, Total Fat 28g, Saturated Fat 7g, Total Carbs 13g, Net Carbs 1g, Protein 36g, Sugar 9g, Fiber 2g, Sodium 111mg, Potassium 943g

Almond Crusted Salmon

Prep time: 10 minutes , Cook time: 15 minutes , Serves 4

Ingredients:
½ cup sliced walnuts
1 tsp smoked paprika
½ tsp onion powder
½ tsp garlic powder
1 Tbsp apple cider vinegar
1 tsp coconut aminos
2 Tbsp butter
24 oz salmon filets

Instructions
1. Preheat your air fryer to 400 degrees F and line the air fryer tray with foil.
2. In a large bowl, combine the almonds, paprika, onion powder, garlic powder, vinegar and coconut aminos.
3. Place the salmon on the prepared tray and spoon the walnut mix over the top of the fish.
4. Place the tray in the fridge and let cool for 2 hours.
5. Remove the tray from the fridge and dot the butter throughout the tray, dispersing it around the fish.
6. Place in the air fryer and bake for 15 minutes. Serve hot!

Nutrition Facts Per Serving
Calories 402, Total Fat 28g, Saturated Fat 7g, Total Carbs 8g, Net Carbs 6g, Protein 36g, Sugar 7g, Fiber 2g, Sodium 111mg, Potassium 943g

Maple Walnut Flounder

Prep time: 10 minutes , Cook time: 15 minutes , Serves 4

Ingredients:
½ cup chopped walnuts
1 tsp smoked paprika
½ tsp onion powder
½ tsp garlic powder
3 Tbsp keto maple syrup
1 Tbsp apple cider vinegar
1 tsp coconut aminos
2 Tbsp butter
24 oz flounder filets

Instructions
1. Preheat your air fryer to 400 degrees F and line the air fryer tray with foil.
2. In a large bowl, combine the walnuts, paprika, onion powder, garlic powder, keto syrup, vinegar and coconut aminos.
3. Place the flounder on the prepared tray and spoon the walnut mix over the top of the fish.
4. Place the tray in the fridge and let cool for 2 hours.
5. Remove the tray from the fridge and dot the butter throughout the tray, dispersing it around the fish.
6. Place in the air fryer and bake for 15 minutes. Serve hot!

Nutrition Facts Per Serving
Calories 432, Total Fat 25g, Saturated Fat 6g, Total Carbs 13g, Net Carbs 1g, Protein 34g, Sugar 9g, Fiber 2g, Sodium 111mg, Potassium 943g

Sesame Walnut Tuna

Prep time: 10 minutes , Cook time: 20 minutes , Serves 4

Ingredients:
½ cup chopped walnuts
1 tsp smoked paprika
½ tsp onion powder
½ tsp garlic powder
1 Tbsp sesame seeds
1 Tbsp apple cider vinegar
2 tsp coconut aminos
2 Tbsp butter
24 oz Tuna Steaks

Instructions
1. Preheat your air fryer to 400 degrees F and line the air fryer tray with foil.
2. In a large bowl, combine the walnuts, paprika, onion powder, garlic powder, sesame seeds, vinegar and coconut aminos.
3. Place the tuna on the prepared tray and spoon the walnut mix over the top of the fish.
4. Place the tray in the fridge and let cool for 2 hours.
5. Remove the tray from the fridge and dot the butter throughout the tray, dispersing it around the fish.
6. Place in the air fryer and bake for 15 minutes. Serve hot!

Nutrition Facts Per Serving
Calories 451, Total Fat 30g, Saturated Fat 7g, Total Carbs 9g, Net Carbs 1g, Protein 34g, Sugar 6g, Fiber 2g, Sodium 111mg, Potassium 872g

Spicy Cod Fish Sticks

Prep time: 10 minutes , Cook time: 10 minutes , Serves 4

Ingredients:
1 pound cod
¼ cup mayonnaise
2 Tbsp mustard
½ tsp salt
½ tsp ground cayenne pepper
1 ½ cups ground pork rinds
2 Tbsp whole milk

Instructions
1. Preheat your air fryer to 400 degrees F and line your air fryer tray with foil and spray with cooking grease.
2. Dry the cod filets by patting with a paper towel. Cut the fish into strips about 1 inch wide and two inches long.
3. In a small bowl, combine the mustard, mayo and milk and stir together well.

4. In a separate bowl, combine the ground pork rinds, salt and cayenne pepper.
5. Dip the fish strips into the mayonnaise mix and then into the pork rind mix, coating the fish completely. Place it on the prepared tray when done and repeat with the remaining fish sticks.
6. Place the tray in the air fryer and bake the fish for 5 minutes, flip and bake for another 5 minutes. Serve while hot!

Nutrition Facts Per Serving
Calories 264, Total Fat 16g, Saturated Fat 5g, Total Carbs 1g, Net Carbs 0g, Protein 26g, Sugar 0g, Fiber 1g, Sodium 679mg, Potassium 68g

Italian Fish Sticks

Prep time: 10 minutes , Cook time: 10 minutes , Serves 4

Ingredients:
1 pound cod
¼ cup mayonnaise
2 Tbsp mustard
½ tsp salt
1 tsp Italian seasoning
½ tsp ground black pepper
1 ½ cups ground pork rinds
2 Tbsp whole milk

Instructions
1. Preheat your air fryer to 400 degrees F and line your air fryer tray with foil and spray with cooking grease.
2. Dry the cod filets by patting with a paper towel. Cut the fish into strips about 1 inch wide and two inches long.
3. In a small bowl, combine the mustard, mayo and milk and stir together well.
4. In a separate bowl, combine the ground pork rinds, salt, Italian seasoning and pepper.
5. Dip the fish strips into the mayonnaise mix and then into the pork rind mix, coating the fish completely. Place it on the prepared tray when done and repeat with the remaining fish sticks.
6. Place the tray in the air fryer and bake the fish for 5 minutes, flip and bake for another 5 minutes. Serve while hot!

Nutrition Facts Per Serving
Calories 283, Total Fat 16g, Saturated Fat 5g, Total Carbs 1g, Net Carbs 0g, Protein 26g, Sugar 0g, Fiber 1g, Sodium 683mg, Potassium 68g

Lemon Pepper Fish Sticks

Prep time: 10 minutes , Cook time: 10 minutes , Serves 4

Ingredients:
1 pound cod
¼ cup mayonnaise
2 Tbsp mustard
½ tsp salt
1 tsp lemon pepper seasoning
1 ½ cups ground pork rinds
2 Tbsp whole milk

Instructions
1. Preheat your air fryer to 400 degrees F and line your air fryer tray with foil and spray with cooking grease.
2. Dry the cod filets by patting with a paper towel. Cut the fish into strips about 1 inch wide and two inches long.
3. In a small bowl, combine the mustard, mayo and milk and stir together well.
4. In a separate bowl, combine the ground pork rinds, lemon pepper and salt.
5. Dip the fish strips into the mayonnaise mix and then into the pork rind mix, coating the fish completely. Place it on the prepared tray when done and repeat with the remaining fish sticks.
6. Place the tray in the air fryer and bake the fish for 5 minutes, flip and bake for another 5 minutes. Serve while hot!

Nutrition Facts Per Serving
Calories 265, Total Fat 16g, Saturated Fat 5g, Total Carbs 1g, Net Carbs 0g, Protein 26g, Sugar 0g, Fiber 1g, Sodium 682mg, Potassium 69g

Salmon Fish Sticks

Prep time: 10 minutes , Cook time: 10 minutes , Serves 4

Ingredients:
1 pound salmon filets
¼ cup mayonnaise
2 Tbsp mustard
½ tsp salt
½ tsp ground black pepper
1 ½ cups ground pork rinds
2 Tbsp whole milk

Instructions
1. Preheat your air fryer to 400 degrees F and line your air fryer tray with foil and spray with cooking grease.
2. Dry the salmon filets by patting with a paper towel. Cut the fish into strips about 1 inch wide and two inches long.
3. In a small bowl, combine the mustard, mayo and milk and stir together well.
4. In a separate bowl, combine the ground pork rinds, salt and pepper.
5. Dip the fish strips into the mayonnaise mix and then into the pork rind mix, coating the fish completely. Place it on the prepared tray when done and repeat with the remaining fish sticks.
6. Place the tray in the air fryer and bake the fish for 5 minutes, flip and bake for another 5 minutes. Serve while hot!

Nutrition Facts Per Serving
Calories 282, Total Fat 18g, Saturated Fat 5g, Total Carbs 1g, Net Carbs 0g, Protein 27g, Sugar 0g, Fiber 1g, Sodium 664mg, Potassium 68g

Cajun Salmon Fish Sticks

Prep time: 10 minutes , Cook time: 10 minutes , Serves 4

Ingredients:
1 pound salmon
¼ cup mayonnaise
2 Tbsp mustard
½ tsp salt
1 tsp Cajun seasoning
1 ½ cups ground pork rinds
2 Tbsp whole milk

Instructions
1. Preheat your air fryer to 400 degrees F and line your air fryer tray with foil and spray with cooking grease.
2. Dry the salmon filets by patting with a paper towel. Cut the fish into strips about 1 inch wide and two inches long.
3. In a small bowl, combine the mustard, mayo and milk and stir together well.
4. In a separate bowl, combine the ground pork rinds, Cajun seasoning, and salt.
5. Dip the fish strips into the mayonnaise mix and then into the pork rind mix, coating the fish completely. Place it on the prepared tray when done and repeat with the remaining fish sticks.
6. Place the tray in the air fryer and bake the fish for 5 minutes, flip and bake for another 5 minutes. Serve while hot!

Nutrition Facts Per Serving
Calories 288, Total Fat 18g, Saturated Fat 5g, Total Carbs 1g, Net Carbs 0g, Protein 27g, Sugar 0g, Fiber 1g, Sodium 676mg, Potassium 68g

Bacon Wrapped Fish Sticks

Prep time: 10 minutes , Cook time: 18 minutes , Serves 4

Ingredients:
1 pound cod
¼ cup mayonnaise
2 Tbsp mustard
½ tsp salt
½ tsp ground black pepper
1 ½ cups ground pork rinds
2 Tbsp whole milk
½ pound bacon, uncooked, strips

Instructions
1. Preheat your air fryer to 400 degrees F and line your air fryer tray with foil and spray with cooking grease.

2. Dry the cod filets by patting with a paper towel. Cut the fish into strips about 1 inch wide and two inches long.
3. In a small bowl, combine the mustard, mayo and milk and stir together well.
4. In a separate bowl, combine the ground pork rinds, salt and pepper.
5. Dip the fish strips into the mayonnaise mix and then into the pork rind mix, coating the fish completely. Place it on the prepared tray when done and repeat with the remaining fish sticks.
6. Wrap each fish stick in the bacon and place back onto the tray.
7. Place the tray in the air fryer and bake the fish for 10 minutes, flip and bake for another 8 minutes or until the bacon is brown and crispy. Serve while hot!

Nutrition Facts Per Serving
Calories 310, Total Fat 24g, Saturated Fat 5g, Total Carbs 1g, Net Carbs 0g, Protein 34g, Sugar 0g, Fiber 1g, Sodium 899mg, Potassium 112g

Keto Tuna Melt Cups

Prep time: 10 minutes , Cook time: 20 minutes , Serves 7

Ingredients:
5 oz canned tuna, drained
2 eggs
¼ cup sour cream
¼ cup mayonnaise
¾ cup shredded cheddar cheese
¾ cup pepper jack cheese
¼ tsp salt
¼ tsp ground black pepper
1 Tbsp parsley, chopped

Instructions
1. Preheat your air fryer to 325 degrees F and grease a muffin tin or individual muffin cups- whichever option fits in your air fryer better.
2. In a large bowl, combine the tuna, mayonnaise, sour cream, both kinds of grated cheese, parsley, salt and pepper.
3. Scoop the mix into the prepared muffin tin, filling each cup to the top.
4. Bake in the air fryer for 20 minutes or until the tops are golden brown.
5. Place on a slice of keto bread, serve with keto crackers or enjoy plain with a spoon!

Nutrition Facts Per Serving
Calories 160, Total Fat 13g, Saturated Fat 3, Total Carbs 1g, Net Carbs 1g, Protein 9g, Sugar 1g, Fiber 0g, Sodium 321mg, Potassium 197g

Garlic Shrimp Bacon Bake

Prep time: 10 minutes , Cook time: 8 minutes , Serves 4

Ingredients:
¼ cup butter
2 Tbsp minced garlic
1 pound shrimp, peeled and cleaned
¼ tsp ground black pepper
½ cup cooked, chopped bacon
1/3 cup heavy cream
¼ cup parmesan cheese

Instructions
1. Preheat your air fryer to 400 degrees F and grease an 8x8 inch baking pan.
2. Add the butter and shrimp to the pan and place in the air fryer for 3 minutes. Remove the pan from the air fryer.
3. Add the remaining ingredients to the pan and return to the air fryer to cook for another 5 minutes. The mix should be bubbling and the shrimp should be pink.
4. Serve with zucchini noodles or enjoy plain.

Nutrition Facts Per Serving
Calories 350, Total Fat 27g, Saturated Fat 15g, Total Carbs 3g, Net Carbs 3g, Protein 36g, Sugar 0g, Fiber 0g, Sodium 924mg, Potassium 16g

Gruyere Shrimp Bacon Bake

Prep time: 10 minutes , Cook time: 10 minutes , Serves 4

Ingredients:
- ¼ cup butter
- 2 Tbsp minced garlic
- 1 pound shrimp, peeled and cleaned
- ¼ tsp ground black pepper
- ½ cup cooked, chopped bacon
- 1/3 cup heavy cream
- ¼ cup parmesan cheese
- ½ cup gruyere cheese, grated

Instructions
1. Preheat your air fryer to 400 degrees F and grease an 8x8 inch baking pan.
2. Add the butter and shrimp to the pan and place in the air fryer for 3 minutes. Remove the pan from the air fryer.
3. Add the remaining ingredients to the pan and return to the air fryer to cook for another 5 minutes. The mix should be bubbling and the shrimp should be pink.
4. Sprinkle the gruyere over the shrimp and return to the air fryer for another 2 minutes to brown the top of the cheese.
5. Serve with zucchini noodles or enjoy plain.

Nutrition Facts Per Serving
Calories 410, Total Fat 32g, Saturated Fat 18g, Total Carbs 4g, Net Carbs 3g, Protein 38g, Sugar 0g, Fiber 0g, Sodium 988mg, Potassium 24g

Cajun Shrimp Bacon Bake

Prep time: 10 minutes , Cook time: 10 minutes , Serves 4

Ingredients:
- ¼ cup butter
- 2 Tbsp minced garlic
- 1 pound shrimp, peeled and cleaned
- ½ tsp Cajun seasoning
- ½ cup cooked, chopped bacon
- 1/3 cup heavy cream
- ¼ cup parmesan cheese

Instructions
1. Preheat your air fryer to 400 degrees F and grease an 8x8 inch baking pan.
2. Add the butter and shrimp to the pan and place in the air fryer for 3 minutes. Remove the pan from the air fryer.
3. Add the remaining ingredients to the pan and return to the air fryer to cook for another 5 minutes. The mix should be bubbling and the shrimp should be pink.
4. Serve with zucchini noodles or enjoy plain.

Nutrition Facts Per Serving
Calories 352, Total Fat 27g, Saturated Fat 15g, Total Carbs 3g, Net Carbs 3g, Protein 36g, Sugar 0g, Fiber 0g, Sodium 930mg, Potassium 18g

Garlic Shrimp Prosciutto Bake

Prep time: 10 minutes , Cook time: 10 minutes , Serves 4

Ingredients:
- ¼ cup butter
- 2 Tbsp minced garlic
- 1 pound shrimp, peeled and cleaned
- ¼ tsp ground black pepper
- 2 oz thinly sliced, shredded prosciutto
- 1/3 cup heavy cream
- ¼ cup parmesan cheese

Instructions
1. Preheat your air fryer to 400 degrees F and grease an 8x8 inch baking pan.
2. Add the butter and shrimp to the pan and place in the air fryer for 3 minutes. Remove the pan from the air fryer.
3. Add the remaining ingredients to the pan and return to the air fryer to cook for another 5 minutes. The mix should be bubbling and the shrimp should be pink.
4. Serve with zucchini noodles or enjoy plain.

Nutrition Facts Per Serving
Calories 358, Total Fat 27g, Saturated Fat 15g, Total Carbs 3g, Net Carbs 3g, Protein 36g, Sugar 0g, Fiber 0g, Sodium 1026mg, Potassium 16g

Garlic Shrimp Tuna Bake

Prep time: 10 minutes , Cook time: 10 minutes , Serves 4

Ingredients:
- ¼ cup butter
- 2 Tbsp minced garlic
- 1 pound shrimp, peeled and cleaned
- ¼ tsp ground black pepper
- 1 tin canned tuna, drained well
- 1/3 cup heavy cream
- ¼ cup parmesan cheese

Instructions
1. Preheat your air fryer to 400 degrees F and grease an 8x8 inch baking pan.
2. Add the butter and shrimp to the pan and place in the air fryer for 3 minutes. Remove the pan from the air fryer.
3. Add the remaining ingredients to the pan and return to the air fryer to cook for another 5 minutes. The mix should be bubbling and the shrimp should be pink.
4. Serve with zucchini noodles or enjoy plain.

Nutrition Facts Per Serving
Calories 376, Total Fat 30g, Saturated Fat 15g, Total Carbs 3g, Net Carbs 3g, Protein 43g, Sugar 0g, Fiber 0g, Sodium 924mg, Potassium 16g

Jalapeno Tuna Melt Cups

Prep time: 10 minutes , Cook time: 20 minutes , Serves 7

Ingredients:
- 5 oz canned tuna, drained
- 2 eggs
- ¼ cup sour cream
- ¼ cup mayonnaise
- ¾ cup shredded cheddar cheese
- ¾ cup pepper jack cheese
- ¼ tsp salt
- ¼ tsp ground black pepper
- 1 Tbsp parsley, chopped
- ½ cup jalapeno slices

Instructions
1. Preheat your air fryer to 325 degrees F and grease a muffin tin or individual muffin cups- whichever option fits in your air fryer better.
2. In a large bowl, combine the tuna, mayonnaise, sour cream, both kinds of grated cheese, parsley, jalapeno slices, salt, and pepper.
3. Scoop the mix into the prepared muffin tin, filling each cup to the top.
4. Bake in the air fryer for 20 minutes or until the tops are golden brown.
5. Place on a slice of keto bread, serve with keto crackers or enjoy plain with a spoon!

Nutrition Facts Per Serving
Calories 167, Total Fat 13g, Saturated Fat 3, Total Carbs 2g, Net Carbs 1g, Protein 9g, Sugar 2g, Fiber 0g, Sodium 321mg, Potassium 197g

Herbed Tuna Melt Cups

Prep time: 10 minutes , Cook time: 20 minutes , Serves 7

Ingredients:
- 5 oz canned tuna, drained
- 2 eggs
- ¼ cup sour cream
- ¼ cup mayonnaise
- ¾ cup shredded cheddar cheese
- ¾ cup pepper jack cheese
- ¼ tsp salt
- ¼ tsp ground black pepper
- 1 Tbsp parsley, chopped
- 1 tsp fresh chopped rosemary
- 1 tsp fresh chopped basil

Instructions
1. Preheat your air fryer to 325 degrees F and grease a muffin tin or individual muffin cups- whichever option fits in your air fryer better.
2. In a large bowl, combine the tuna, mayonnaise, sour cream, both kinds of grated cheese, parsley, rosemary, basil, salt, and pepper.
3. Scoop the mix into the prepared muffin tin, filling each cup to the top.

4. Bake in the air fryer for 20 minutes or until the tops are golden brown.
5. Place on a slice of keto bread, serve with keto crackers or enjoy plain with a spoon!

Nutrition Facts Per Serving
Calories 163, Total Fat 13g, Saturated Fat 3, Total Carbs 1g, Net Carbs 1g, Protein 9g, Sugar 1g, Fiber 0g, Sodium 325mg, Potassium 197g

Cajun Tuna Melt Cups

Prep time: 10 minutes , Cook time: 20 minutes , Serves 7

Ingredients:
5 oz canned tuna, drained
2 eggs
¼ cup sour cream
¼ cup mayonnaise
¾ cup shredded cheddar cheese
¾ cup pepper jack cheese
¼ tsp salt
½ tsp Cajun seasoning
1 Tbsp parsley, chopped

Instructions
1. Preheat your air fryer to 325 degrees F and grease a muffin tin or individual muffin cups- whichever option fits in your air fryer better.
2. In a large bowl, combine the tuna, mayonnaise, sour cream, both kinds of grated cheese, parsley, Cajun seasoning, salt, and pepper.
3. Scoop the mix into the prepared muffin tin, filling each cup to the top.
4. Bake in the air fryer for 20 minutes or until the tops are golden brown.
5. Place on a slice of keto bread, serve with keto crackers or enjoy plain with a spoon!

Nutrition Facts Per Serving
Calories 161, Total Fat 13g, Saturated Fat 3, Total Carbs 1g, Net Carbs 1g, Protein 9g, Sugar 1g, Fiber 0g, Sodium 321mg, Potassium 197g

Cheddar Tuna Melt Cups

Prep time: 10 minutes , Cook time: 20 minutes , Serves 7

Ingredients:
5 oz canned tuna, drained
2 eggs
¼ cup sour cream
¼ cup mayonnaise
1 ½ cups shredded cheddar cheese
¼ tsp salt
¼ tsp ground black pepper
1 Tbsp parsley, chopped

Instructions
1. Preheat your air fryer to 325 degrees F and grease a muffin tin or individual muffin cups- whichever option fits in your air fryer better.
2. In a large bowl, combine the tuna, mayonnaise, sour cream, cheese, parsley, salt and pepper.
3. Scoop the mix into the prepared muffin tin, filling each cup to the top.
4. Bake in the air fryer for 20 minutes or until the tops are golden brown.
5. Place on a slice of keto bread, serve with keto crackers or enjoy plain with a spoon!

Nutrition Facts Per Serving
Calories 160, Total Fat 13g, Saturated Fat 3, Total Carbs 1g, Net Carbs 1g, Protein 9g, Sugar 1g, Fiber 0g, Sodium 321mg, Potassium 197g

Sesame Tuna Melt Cups

Prep time: 10 minutes , Cook time: 20 minutes , Serves 7

Ingredients:
5 oz canned tuna, drained
2 eggs
¼ cup sour cream
¼ cup mayonnaise
1 Tbsp sesame seeds
1 Tbsp coconut aminos
¾ cup shredded cheddar cheese
¾ cup pepper jack cheese
¼ tsp salt
¼ tsp ground black pepper
1 Tbsp parsley, chopped

Instructions

1. Preheat your air fryer to 325 degrees F and grease a muffin tin or individual muffin cups- whichever option fits in your air fryer better.
2. In a large bowl, combine the tuna, mayonnaise, sour cream, sesame seeds, coconut aminos, both kinds of grated cheese, parsley, salt and pepper.
3. Scoop the mix into the prepared muffin tin, filling each cup to the top.
4. Bake in the air fryer for 20 minutes or until the tops are golden brown.
5. Place on a slice of keto bread, serve with keto crackers or enjoy plain with a spoon!

Nutrition Facts Per Serving
Calories 172, Total Fat 16g, Saturated Fat 3, Total Carbs 4g, Net Carbs 2g, Protein 9g, Sugar 1g, Fiber 2g, Sodium 327mg, Potassium 202g

Asian Style Crunchy Flounder

Prep time: 10 minutes , Cook time: 10 minutes , Serves 4

Ingredients:
1 pound flounder filets
½ cup pork rinds, crushed
¼ tsp black pepper
½ tsp salt
¼ tsp garlic powder
2 tsp fresh minced garlic
1 Tbsp melted butter
1 Tbsp coconut aminos

Instructions
1. Preheat your air fryer to 450 degrees F and line your air fryer tray with foil.
2. Place the flounder filets on the foil lined tray.
3. In a small bowl or food processor, combine the remaining ingredients and mix well.
4. Press the pork rind mix onto the salmon filets, coating the whole top evenly and packing the crust into the fish filets.
5. Bake the filets in the preheated oven for 10 minutes. The top crust should be nicely browned.
6. Serve while hot.

Nutrition Facts Per Serving
Calories 323, Total Fat 21g, Saturated Fat 10g, Total Carbs 2g, Net Carbs 1g, Protein 40g, Sugar 0g, Fiber 1g, Sodium 482mg, Potassium 199g

Prosciutto Wrapped Cod

Prep time: 5 minutes , Cook time: 15 minutes , Serves 2

Ingredients:
1 pound cod fillets
¼ tsp salt
¼ tsp ground black pepper
2 oz prosciutto de parma, very thinly sliced
2 Tbsp olive oil
1 tsp minced garlic
4 cups baby spinach
2 tsp lemon juice

Instructions
1. Preheat your air fryer to 325 degrees F and line your air fryer tray with foil.
2. Dry the cod fillets by patting with a paper towel the sprinkle with salt and pepper.
3. Wrap the filets in the prosciutto, enclosing them as fully as possible.
4. Place the wrapped filets on the prepared tray.
5. Toss the spinach with the olive oil, garlic and lemon juice and place on the tray as well, around the wrapped cod.
6. Place in the air fryer and bake for 12 minutes. The spinach should be nicely wilted and the fish 145 degrees F internally.
7. Serve hot!

Nutrition Facts Per Serving
Calories 416, Total Fat 19g, Saturated Fat 3g, Total Carbs 11g, Net Carbs 9g, Protein 49g, Sugar 3g, Fiber 2g, Sodium 482mg, Potassium 582g

Prosciutto Wrapped Salmon

Prep time: 5 minutes , Cook time: 16 minutes , Serves 2

Ingredients:
- 1 pound salmon fillets
- ¼ tsp salt
- ¼ tsp ground black pepper
- 2 oz prosciutto de parma, very thinly sliced
- 2 Tbsp olive oil
- 1 tsp minced garlic
- 4 cups baby spinach
- 2 tsp lemon juice

Instructions
1. Preheat your air fryer to 325 degrees F and line your air fryer tray with foil.
2. Dry the salmon fillets by patting with a paper towel the sprinkle with salt and pepper.
3. Wrap the filets in the prosciutto, enclosing them as fully as possible.
4. Place the wrapped filets on the prepared tray.
5. Toss the spinach with the olive oil, garlic and lemon juice and place on the tray as well, around the wrapped salmon.
6. Place in the air fryer and bake for 12 minutes. The spinach should be nicely wilted and the fish 145 degrees F internally.
7. Serve hot!

Nutrition Facts Per Serving
Calories 464, Total Fat 22g, Saturated Fat 5g, Total Carbs 11g, Net Carbs 9g, Protein 49g, Sugar 3g, Fiber 2g, Sodium 482mg, Potassium 582g

Fast Seared Scallops

Prep time: 5 minutes , Cook time: 5 minutes , Serves 4

Ingredients:
- 1 pound jumbo scallops
- 2 Tbsp butter
- ¼ tsp salt
- ¼ tsp ground black pepper

Instructions
1. Preheat your air fryer to 400 degrees F and line your air fryer tray with foil.
2. Place the butter on the air fryer tray and place inside the air fryer for one minute to melt.
3. Remove the tray and add the scallops and seasonings, toss together and return to the air fryer for 5 minutes. The bottom of the scallops should be golden brown.
4. Serve hot.

Nutrition Facts Per Serving
Calories 160, Total Fat 9g, Saturated Fat 4g, Total Carbs 3g, Net Carbs 2g, Protein 13g, Sugar 0g, Fiber 1g, Sodium 640mg, Potassium 232g

Lemon Scallops

Prep time: 5 minutes , Cook time: 5 minutes , Serves 4

Ingredients:
- 1 pound jumbo scallops
- 2 Tbsp butter
- 1 tsp lemon zest
- ¼ tsp salt
- ¼ tsp ground black pepper

Instructions
1. Preheat your air fryer to 400 degrees F and line your air fryer tray with foil.
2. Place the butter on the air fryer tray and place inside the air fryer for one minute to melt.
3. Remove the tray and add the scallops and seasonings, toss together and return to the air fryer for 5 minutes. The bottom of the scallops should be golden brown.
4. Serve hot.

Nutrition Facts Per Serving
Calories 163, Total Fat 9g, Saturated Fat 4g, Total Carbs 3g, Net Carbs 2g, Protein 13g, Sugar 0g, Fiber 1g, Sodium 640mg, Potassium 232g

Dijon Baked Salmon

Prep time: 5 minutes , Cook time: 18 minutes , Serves 5

Ingredients:
1 ½ pounds salmon
¼ cup parsley, freshly chopped
¼ cup Dijon mustard
1 Tbsp olive oil
1 Tbsp fresh squeezed lemon juice
1 Tbsp minced garlic
¼ tsp salt
¼ tsp ground black pepper

Instructions
1. Preheat your air fryer to 375 degrees F line your air fryer tray with a piece of parchment paper.
2. Place the salmon on the parchment lined tray.
3. In a small bowl, mix together the remaining ingredients and then spread over the top of the salmon.
4. Place the salmon in the air fryer and bake for 18 minutes. Slice and serve hot!

Nutrition Facts Per Serving
Calories 250, Total Fat 13g, Saturated Fat 2g, Total Carbs 2g, Net Carbs 1g, Protein 31g, Sugar 0g, Fiber 1g, Sodium 371mg, Potassium 42g

Garlic Dijon Baked Salmon

Prep time: 5 minutes , Cook time: 18 minutes , Serves 5

Ingredients:
1 ½ pounds salmon
¼ cup parsley, freshly chopped
¼ cup Dijon mustard
1 Tbsp olive oil
1 Tbsp fresh squeezed lemon juice
3 Tbsp minced garlic
¼ tsp salt
¼ tsp ground black pepper

Instructions
1. Preheat your air fryer to 375 degrees F line your air fryer tray with a piece of parchment paper.
2. Place the salmon on the parchment lined tray.
3. In a small bowl, mix together the remaining ingredients and then spread over the top of the salmon.
4. Place the salmon in the air fryer and bake for 18 minutes. Slice and serve hot!

Nutrition Facts Per Serving
Calories 272, Total Fat 13g, Saturated Fat 2g, Total Carbs 3g, Net Carbs 1g, Protein 31g, Sugar 1g, Fiber 1g, Sodium 371mg, Potassium 42g

Maple Dijon Baked Salmon

Prep time: 5 minutes , Cook time: 18 minutes , Serves 5

Ingredients:
1 ½ pounds salmon
¼ cup parsley, freshly chopped
¼ cup Dijon mustard
1 Tbsp olive oil
1 tsp maple extract
1 Tbsp fresh squeezed lemon juice
1 Tbsp minced garlic
¼ tsp salt
¼ tsp ground black pepper

Instructions
1. Preheat your air fryer to 375 degrees F line your air fryer tray with a piece of parchment paper.
2. Place the salmon on the parchment lined tray.
3. In a small bowl, mix together the remaining ingredients and then spread over the top of the salmon.
4. Place the salmon in the air fryer and bake for 18 minutes. Slice and serve hot!

Nutrition Facts Per Serving
Calories 254, Total Fat 13g, Saturated Fat 2g, Total Carbs 2g, Net Carbs 1g, Protein 31g, Sugar 0g, Fiber 1g, Sodium 373mg, Potassium 42g

Creamy Baked Scallops

Prep time: 5 minutes , Cook time: 5 minutes , Serves 4

Ingredients:
- 1 pound jumbo scallops
- 1 Tbsp butter
- 1 Tbsp heavy cream
- ¼ tsp salt
- ¼ tsp ground black pepper

Instructions
1. Preheat your air fryer to 400 degrees F and line your air fryer tray with foil.
2. Place the butter on the air fryer tray and place inside the air fryer for one minute to melt.
3. Remove the tray and add the scallops, heavy cream, and seasonings, toss together and return to the air fryer for 5 minutes. The bottom of the scallops should be golden brown.
4. Serve hot.

Nutrition Facts Per Serving
Calories 174, Total Fat 10g, Saturated Fat 45g, Total Carbs 3g, Net Carbs 2g, Protein 13g, Sugar 0g, Fiber 1g, Sodium 644mg, Potassium 232g

Cajun Seared Scallops

Prep time: 5 minutes , Cook time: 5 minutes , Serves 4

Ingredients:
- 1 pound jumbo scallops
- 2 Tbsp butter
- ½ tsp Cajun seasoning

Instructions
1. Preheat your air fryer to 400 degrees F and line your air fryer tray with foil.
2. Place the butter on the air fryer tray and place inside the air fryer for one minute to melt.
3. Remove the tray and add the scallops and seasonings, toss together and return to the air fryer for 5 minutes. The bottom of the scallops should be golden brown.
4. Serve hot.

Nutrition Facts Per Serving
Calories 161, Total Fat 9g, Saturated Fat 4g, Total Carbs 3g, Net Carbs 2g, Protein 13g, Sugar 0g, Fiber 1g, Sodium 627mg, Potassium 230g

Crispy Scallops

Prep time: 5 minutes , Cook time: 5 minutes , Serves 4

Ingredients:
- 1 pound jumbo scallops
- 2 Tbsp butter
- ¼ tsp salt
- ¼ tsp ground black pepper
- ¼ cup ground pork rinds

Instructions
1. Preheat your air fryer to 400 degrees F and line your air fryer tray with foil.
2. Place the butter on the air fryer tray and place inside the air fryer for one minute to melt.
3. Remove the tray and add the scallops, pork rinds, and seasonings, toss together and return to the air fryer for 5 minutes. The bottom of the scallops should be golden brown.
4. Serve hot.

Nutrition Facts Per Serving
Calories 182, Total Fat 11g, Saturated Fat 6g, Total Carbs 3g, Net Carbs 2g, Protein 13g, Sugar 0g, Fiber 1g, Sodium 647mg, Potassium 241g

Bacon Scallops

Prep time: 5 minutes , Cook time: 5 minutes , Serves 4

Ingredients:
- 1 pound jumbo scallops
- 1 Tbsp butter
- ¼ cup cooked, crumbled bacon
- ¼ tsp salt
- ¼ tsp ground black pepper

Instructions
1. Preheat your air fryer to 400 degrees F and line your air fryer tray with foil.
2. Place the butter on the air fryer tray and place inside the air fryer for one minute to melt.

3. Remove the tray and add the scallops, bacon and seasonings, toss together and return to the air fryer for 5 minutes. The bottom of the scallops should be golden brown.
4. Serve hot.

Nutrition Facts Per Serving
Calories 189, Total Fat 12g, Saturated Fat 6g, Total Carbs 3g, Net Carbs 2g, Protein 13g, Sugar 0g, Fiber 1g, Sodium 640mg, Potassium 232g

Scallops and Spinach

Prep time: 5 minutes , Cook time: 5 minutes , Serves 4

Ingredients:
1 pound jumbo scallops
3 cups baby spinach
2 Tbsp butter
¼ tsp salt
¼ tsp ground black pepper

Instructions
1. Preheat your air fryer to 400 degrees F and line your air fryer tray with foil.
2. Place the butter on the air fryer tray and place inside the air fryer for one minute to melt.
3. Remove the tray and add the scallops, spinach and seasonings, toss together and return to the air fryer for 5 minutes. The bottom of the scallops should be golden brown.
4. Serve hot.

Nutrition Facts Per Serving
Calories 174, Total Fat 9g, Saturated Fat 4g, Total Carbs 5g, Net Carbs 2g, Protein 13g, Sugar 0g, Fiber 3g, Sodium 640mg, Potassium 267g

Salmon and Asparagus

Prep time: 20 minutes , Cook time: 20 minutes , Serves 5

Ingredients:
1 ¾ pound salmon fillets
¼ tsp salt
¼ tsp ground black pepper
3 Tbsp olive oil
1 pound asparagus spears
1 Tbsp lemon juice
1 Tbsp fresh chopped parsley

Instructions
1. Preheat your air fryer to 400 degrees F and line your air fryer tray with a long piece of parchment paper.
2. Place the salmon filets on the parchment and sprinkle with the salt and pepper and rub the spices into the fish.
3. Top the fish with the remaining ingredients and then wrap the parchment paper up around the fish filets, enclosing them completely.
4. Place the tray in the air fryer and bake for 20 minutes.
5. Remove from the air fryer, unwrap the parchment and serve while hot!

Nutrition Facts Per Serving
Calories 257, Total Fat 10g, Saturated Fat 4g, Total Carbs 10g, Net Carbs 6g, Protein 33g, Sugar 3g, Fiber 4g, Sodium 492mg, Potassium 325g

Cod and Asparagus

Prep time: 20 minutes , Cook time: 20 minutes , Serves 5

Ingredients:
1 ¾ pound cod fillets
¼ tsp salt
¼ tsp ground black pepper
3 Tbsp olive oil
1 pound asparagus spears
1 Tbsp lemon juice
1 Tbsp fresh chopped parsley

Instructions
1. Preheat your air fryer to 400 degrees F and line your air fryer tray with a long piece of parchment paper.
2. Place the cod filets on the parchment and sprinkle with the salt and pepper and rub the spices into the fish.

3. Top the fish with the remaining ingredients and then wrap the parchment paper up around the fish filets, enclosing them completely.
4. Place the tray in the air fryer and bake for 20 minutes.
5. Remove from the air fryer, unwrap the parchment and serve while hot!

Nutrition Facts Per Serving
Calories 235, Total Fat 8g, Saturated Fat 4g, Total Carbs 10g, Net Carbs 6g, Protein 33g, Sugar 3g, Fiber 4g, Sodium 492mg, Potassium 325g

Parmesan Salmon and Asparagus

Prep time: 20 minutes , Cook time: 20 minutes , Serves 5

Ingredients:
1 ¾ pound salmon fillets
¼ tsp salt
¼ tsp ground black pepper
3 Tbsp olive oil
1 pound asparagus spears
½ cup grated parmesan cheese
1 Tbsp lemon juice
1 Tbsp fresh chopped parsley

Instructions
1. Preheat your air fryer to 400 degrees F and line your air fryer tray with a long piece of parchment paper.
2. Place the salmon filets on the parchment and sprinkle with the salt and pepper and rub the spices into the fish.
3. Top the fish with the olive oil, asparagus, and lemon juice Sprinkle the parmesan on top along with the parsley.
4. Place the tray in the air fryer and bake for 20 minutes.
5. Remove from the air fryer and serve while hot!

Nutrition Facts Per Serving
Calories 282, Total Fat 14g, Saturated Fat 5g, Total Carbs 11g, Net Carbs 6g, Protein 34g, Sugar 4g, Fiber 4g, Sodium 496mg, Potassium 325g

Parmesan Flounder and Asparagus

Prep time: 20 minutes , Cook time: 15 minutes , Serves 5

Ingredients:
1 ¾ pound flounder fillets
¼ tsp salt
¼ tsp ground black pepper
3 Tbsp olive oil
1 pound asparagus spears
½ cup grated parmesan cheese
1 Tbsp lemon juice
1 Tbsp fresh chopped parsley

Instructions
1. Preheat your air fryer to 400 degrees F and line your air fryer tray with a long piece of parchment paper.
2. Place the flounder filets on the parchment and sprinkle with the salt and pepper and rub the spices into the fish.
3. Top the fish with the olive oil, asparagus, and lemon juice Sprinkle the parmesan on top along with the parsley.
4. Place the tray in the air fryer and bake for 15 minutes.
5. Remove from the air fryer and serve while hot!

Nutrition Facts Per Serving
Calories 269, Total Fat 13g, Saturated Fat 5g, Total Carbs 11g, Net Carbs 6g, Protein 32g, Sugar 4g, Fiber 4g, Sodium 496mg, Potassium 325g

Crispy Shrimp

Prep time: 2 minutes , Cook time: 12 minutes , Serves 4

Ingredients:
1 pound shrimp, fully cleaned and peeled
½ cup pork rinds, crushed
½ cup fresh grated parmesan
2 Tbsp dill, chopped
¼ tsp black pepper
½ tsp salt
¼ tsp garlic powder
2 Tbsp melted butter

Instructions
1. Preheat your air fryer to 350 degrees F and line the air fryer tray or baking pan with foil.
2. Place the pork rinds, parmesan, dill, pepper, salt, garlic powder and melted butter in a bowl and mix well.
3. Add the shrimp to the bowl and toss to coat completely.
4. Bake for 12 minutes, stirring occasionally to flip the shrimp.
5. Divide on to plates and enjoy hot!

Nutrition Facts Per Serving
Calories 389, Total Fat 27g, Saturated Fat 18g, Total Carbs 5g, Net Carbs 4g, Protein 27g, Sugar 1g, Fiber 1g, Sodium 1537mg, Potassium 329g

Parmesan Salmon and Brussel Sprouts

Prep time: 20 minutes , Cook time: 20 minutes , Serves 5

Ingredients:
1 ¾ pound salmon fillets
¼ tsp salt
¼ tsp ground black pepper
3 Tbsp olive oil
1 pound sliced Brussel sprouts
½ cup grated parmesan cheese
1 Tbsp lemon juice
1 Tbsp fresh chopped parsley

Instructions
1. Preheat your air fryer to 400 degrees F and line your air fryer tray with a long piece of parchment paper.
2. Place the salmon filets on the parchment and sprinkle with the salt and pepper and rub the spices into the fish.
3. Top the fish with the olive oil, Brussels sprouts, and lemon juice Sprinkle the parmesan on top along with the parsley.
4. Place the tray in the air fryer and bake for 20 minutes.
5. Remove from the air fryer and serve while hot!

Nutrition Facts Per Serving
Calories 274, Total Fat 13g, Saturated Fat 5g, Total Carbs 11g, Net Carbs 6g, Protein 34g, Sugar 4g, Fiber 4g, Sodium 496mg, Potassium 325g

Parmesan Tuna and Brussel Sprouts

Prep time: 20 minutes , Cook time: 20 minutes , Serves 5

Ingredients:
1 ¾ pound tuna fillets
¼ tsp salt
¼ tsp ground black pepper
3 Tbsp olive oil
1 pound sliced Brussel sprouts
½ cup grated parmesan cheese
1 Tbsp lemon juice
1 Tbsp fresh chopped parsley

Instructions
1. Preheat your air fryer to 400 degrees F and line your air fryer tray with a long piece of parchment paper.
2. Place the tuna filets on the parchment and sprinkle with the salt and pepper and rub the spices into the fish.
3. Top the fish with the olive oil, Brussels sprouts, and lemon juice Sprinkle the parmesan on top along with the parsley.
4. Place the tray in the air fryer and bake for 20 minutes.
5. Remove from the air fryer and serve while hot!

Nutrition Facts Per Serving
Calories 285, Total Fat 13g, Saturated Fat 5g, Total Carbs 11g, Net Carbs 6g, Protein 34g, Sugar 4g, Fiber 4g, Sodium 496mg, Potassium 325g

Lemon Dill Wrapped Cod

Prep time: 5 minutes , Cook time: 15 minutes , Serves 2

Ingredients:
1 pound cod fillets
¼ tsp salt
¼ tsp ground black pepper
1 tsp lemon zest
1 Tbsp chopped fresh dill
2 oz prosciutto de parma, very thinly sliced

2 Tbsp olive oil
1 tsp minced garlic
4 cups baby spinach
2 tsp lemon juice

Instructions
1. Preheat your air fryer to 325 degrees F and line your air fryer tray with foil.
2. Dry the cod fillets by patting with a paper towel the sprinkle with salt and pepper.
3. Sprinkle the lemon zest and dill on the filets as well.
4. Wrap the filets in the prosciutto, enclosing them as fully as possible.
5. Place the wrapped filets on the prepared tray.
6. Toss the spinach with the olive oil, garlic and lemon juice and place on the tray as well, around the wrapped cod.
7. Place in the air fryer and bake for 12 minutes. The spinach should be nicely wilted and the fish 145 degrees F internally.
8. Serve hot!

Nutrition Facts Per Serving
Calories 430, Total Fat 20g, Saturated Fat 3g, Total Carbs 11g, Net Carbs 9g, Protein 49g, Sugar 3g, Fiber 2g, Sodium 482mg, Potassium 582g

Mediterranean Salmon

Prep time: 20 minutes , Cook time: 20 minutes , Serves 5

Ingredients:
1 ¾ pound salmon fillets
¼ tsp salt
1 tsp smoked paprika
1 tsp ground dried ginger
¼ cup pitted olives
¼ cup sundried tomatoes
¼ cup capers
1 Tbsp fresh chopped dill
1/3 cup keto pesto sauce

Instructions
1. Preheat your air fryer to 400 degrees F and line your air fryer tray with a long piece of parchment paper.
2. Place the salmon filets on the parchment and sprinkle with the salt, paprika, and ginger and rub the spices into the fish.
3. Top the fish with the remaining ingredients and then wrap the parchment paper up around the fish filets, enclosing them completely.
4. Place the tray in the air fryer and bake for 20 minutes.
5. Remove from the air fryer, unwrap the parchment and serve while hot!

Nutrition Facts Per Serving
Calories 243, Total Fat 10g, Saturated Fat 4g, Total Carbs 7g, Net Carbs 3g, Protein 33g, Sugar 1g, Fiber 4g, Sodium 489mg, Potassium 321g

Lemon Dill Parchment Salmon

Prep time: 20 minutes , Cook time: 20 minutes , Serves 5

Ingredients:
1 ¾ pound salmon fillets
¼ tsp salt
1 TBSP fresh chopped dill
1 tsp lemon zest
¼ cup pitted olives
¼ cup sundried tomatoes
¼ cup capers
2 Tbsp olive oil

Instructions
1. Preheat your air fryer to 400 degrees F and line your air fryer tray with a long piece of parchment paper.
2. Place the salmon filets on the parchment and sprinkle with the salt, lemon zest, and dill and rub the spices into the fish.
3. Top the fish with the remaining ingredients and then wrap the parchment paper up around the fish filets, enclosing them completely.
4. Place the tray in the air fryer and bake for 20 minutes.
5. Remove from the air fryer, unwrap the parchment and serve while hot!

Nutrition Facts Per Serving
Calories 214, Total Fat 10g, Saturated Fat 4g, Total Carbs 5g, Net Carbs 1g, Protein 33g, Sugar 1g, Fiber 4g, Sodium 489mg, Potassium 321g

Mediterranean Flounder

Prep time: 20 minutes, Cook time: 12 minutes, Serves 5

Ingredients:
1 ¾ pound salmon fillets
¼ tsp salt
1 tsp smoked paprika
1 tsp ground dried ginger
¼ cup pitted olives
¼ cup sundried tomatoes
¼ cup capers
1 Tbsp fresh chopped dill
1/3 cup keto pesto sauce

Instructions
1. Preheat your air fryer to 400 degrees F and line your air fryer tray with a long piece of parchment paper.
2. Place the flounder filets on the parchment and sprinkle with the salt, paprika, and ginger and rub the spices into the fish.
3. Top the fish with the remaining ingredients and then wrap the parchment paper up around the fish filets, enclosing them completely.
4. Place the tray in the air fryer and bake for 12 minutes.
5. Remove from the air fryer, unwrap the parchment and serve while hot!

Nutrition Facts Per Serving
Calories 211, Total Fat 8g, Saturated Fat 3g, Total Carbs 6g, Net Carbs 3g, Protein 33g, Sugar 1g, Fiber 3g, Sodium 489mg, Potassium 321g

Tomato Parchment Cod

Prep time: 20 minutes, Cook time: 15 minutes, Serves 5

Ingredients:
1 ¾ pound cod fillets
¼ tsp salt
1 tsp smoked paprika
1 tsp ground dried ginger
¼ cup pitted olives
¼ cup sundried tomatoes
¼ cup capers
1 Tbsp fresh chopped dill
1/3 cup keto marinara

Instructions
1. Preheat your air fryer to 400 degrees F and line your air fryer tray with a long piece of parchment paper.
2. Place the cod filets on the parchment and sprinkle with the salt, paprika, and ginger and rub the spices into the fish.
3. Top the fish with the remaining ingredients and then wrap the parchment paper up around the fish filets, enclosing them completely.
4. Place the tray in the air fryer and bake for 15 minutes.
5. Remove from the air fryer, unwrap the parchment and serve while hot!

Nutrition Facts Per Serving
Calories 373, Total Fat 7g, Saturated Fat 3g, Total Carbs 5g, Net Carbs 3g, Protein 33g, Sugar 1g, Fiber 2g, Sodium 489mg, Potassium 321g

Italian Style Flounder

Prep time: 20 minutes, Cook time: 15 minutes, Serves 5

Ingredients:
1 ¾ pound salmon fillets
¼ tsp salt
2 tsp Italian seasoning
1 cup baby spinach
¼ cup sundried tomatoes
1 Tbsp fresh chopped dill
1/3 cup keto pesto sauce

Instructions
1. Preheat your air fryer to 400 degrees F and line your air fryer tray with a long piece of parchment paper.
2. Place the flounder filets on the parchment and sprinkle with the salt and Italian seasoning and rub the spices into the fish.
3. Top the fish with the remaining ingredients and then wrap the parchment paper up around the fish filets, enclosing them completely.
4. Place the tray in the air fryer and bake for 20 minutes.
5. Remove from the air fryer, unwrap the parchment and serve while hot!

Nutrition Facts Per Serving
Calories 226, Total Fat 8g, Saturated Fat 3g, Total Carbs 7g, Net Carbs 3g, Protein 30g, Sugar 2g, Fiber 4g, Sodium 487mg, Potassium 321g

Lemon Parchment Salmon

Prep time: 20 minutes , Cook time: 20 minutes , Serves 5

Ingredients:
1 ¾ pound salmon fillets
¼ tsp salt
½ tsp ground black pepper
2 cups baby spinach
1 lemon, sliced thinly

Instructions
1. Preheat your air fryer to 400 degrees F and line your air fryer tray with a long piece of parchment paper.
2. Place the salmon filets on the parchment and sprinkle with the salt and pepper and rub the spices into the fish.
3. Top the fish with the remaining ingredients and then wrap the parchment paper up around the fish filets, enclosing them completely.
4. Place the tray in the air fryer and bake for 20 minutes.
5. Remove from the air fryer, unwrap the parchment and serve while hot!

Nutrition Facts Per Serving
Calories 264, Total Fat 9g, Saturated Fat 4g, Total Carbs 8g, Net Carbs 3g, Protein 33g, Sugar 1g, Fiber 5g, Sodium 492mg, Potassium 324g

Prosciutto Wrapped Ahi Ahi

Prep time: 5 minutes , Cook time: 20 minutes , Serves 2

Ingredients:
1 pound cod Ahi Ahi
¼ tsp salt
¼ tsp ground black pepper
2 oz prosciutto de parma, very thinly sliced
2 Tbsp olive oil
1 tsp minced garlic
4 cups baby spinach
2 tsp lemon juice

Instructions
1. Preheat your air fryer to 325 degrees F and line your air fryer tray with foil.
2. Dry the cod fillets by patting with a paper towel the sprinkle with salt and pepper.
3. Wrap the filets in the prosciutto, enclosing them as fully as possible.
4. Place the wrapped filets on the prepared tray.
5. Place the tray in the air fryer and bake for 10 minutes.
6. Toss the spinach with the olive oil, garlic and lemon juice and remove the tray from the air fryer and place the spinach mix on the tray as well, around the wrapped cod.
7. Place in the air fryer and bake for another 10 minutes. The spinach should be nicely wilted and the fish 145 degrees F internally.
8. Serve hot!

Nutrition Facts Per Serving
Calories 420, Total Fat 20g, Saturated Fat 4g, Total Carbs 11g, Net Carbs 9g, Protein 49g, Sugar 3g, Fiber 2g, Sodium 480mg, Potassium 579g

Prosciutto Wrapped Tuna Bites

Prep time: 5 minutes , Cook time: 10 minutes , Serves 2

Ingredients:
1 pound tuna cut into 1" pieces
¼ tsp salt
¼ tsp ground black pepper
2 oz prosciutto de parma, very thinly sliced
2 Tbsp olive oil
1 tsp minced garlic
4 cups baby spinach
2 tsp lemon juice

Instructions
1. Preheat your air fryer to 325 degrees F and line your air fryer tray with foil.
2. Dry the tuna bites by patting with a paper towel the sprinkle with salt and pepper.
3. Wrap the bites in the prosciutto, enclosing them as fully as possible.
4. Place the wrapped bites on the prepared tray.
5. Toss the spinach with the olive oil, garlic and lemon juice and place on the tray as well, around the wrapped tuna.
6. Place in the air fryer and bake for 12 minutes. The spinach should be nicely wilted and the fish 145 degrees F internally.
7. Serve hot!

Nutrition Facts Per Serving
Calories 430, Total Fat 20g, Saturated Fat 3g, Total Carbs 11g, Net Carbs 9g, Protein 49g, Sugar 3g, Fiber 2g, Sodium 480mg, Potassium 580g

Crab Stuffed Mushrooms

Prep time: 20 minutes , Cook time: 50 minutes , Serves 5

Ingredients:
- 1 pound cremini mushrooms, stems and gills removed
- ¾ pound fresh crab meat
- ¾ cup cream cheese, softened
- 1/3 cup grated cheddar cheese
- ¼ cup sour cream
- 1 Tbsp minced garlic
- 1 Tbsp mustard
- ½ tsp salt
- ¼ tsp ground black pepper
- ½ cup grated parmesan

Instructions
1. Preheat your air fryer to 375 degrees F and line your air fryer tray with foil or parchment.
2. Place the mushroom caps on the tray and bake for 10 minutes in the air fryer. Remove from the air fryer and drain any excess water from the tray.
3. In a large mixing bowl, combine all the remaining ingredients except the parmesan cheese. Stir well to fully blend everything.
4. Stuff the mushroom caps with the crab mix and then sprinkle the parmesan over the top of the mushrooms.
5. Return the tray to the air fryer and bake for another 10 minutes or until the tops of the mushrooms are golden brown.
6. Remove from the air fryer and enjoy while hot.

Nutrition Facts Per Serving
Calories 334, Total Fat 18g, Saturated Fat 6g, Total Carbs 10g, Net Carbs 6g, Protein 24g, Sugar 1g, Fiber 4g, Sodium 487mg, Potassium 211g

Bacon and Crab Stuffed Mushrooms

Prep time: 20 minutes , Cook time: 50 minutes , Serves 5

Ingredients:
- 1 pound cremini mushrooms, stems and gills removed
- ¾ pound fresh crab meat
- ½ cup cooked, crumbled bacon
- ¾ cup cream cheese, softened
- 1/3 cup grated cheddar cheese
- ¼ cup sour cream
- 1 Tbsp minced garlic
- 1 Tbsp mustard
- ½ tsp salt
- ¼ tsp ground black pepper
- ½ cup grated parmesan

Instructions
1. Preheat your air fryer to 375 degrees F and line your air fryer tray with foil or parchment.
2. Place the mushroom caps on the tray and bake for 10 minutes in the air fryer. Remove from the air fryer and drain any excess water from the tray.
3. In a large mixing bowl, combine all the remaining ingredients except the parmesan cheese. Stir well to fully blend everything.
4. Stuff the mushroom caps with the crab mix and then sprinkle the parmesan over the top of the mushrooms.
5. Return the tray to the air fryer and bake for another 10 minutes or until the tops of the mushrooms are golden brown.
6. Remove from the air fryer and enjoy while hot.

Nutrition Facts Per Serving
Calories 399, Total Fat 25g, Saturated Fat 10g, Total Carbs 10g, Net Carbs 6g, Protein 24g, Sugar 1g, Fiber 4g, Sodium 487mg, Potassium 211g

Crab and Spinach Mushrooms

Prep time: 20 minutes , Cook time: 50 minutes , Serves 5

Ingredients:
- 1 pound cremini mushrooms, stems and gills removed
- ¾ pound fresh crab meat
- 3 cups baby spinach, wilted
- ¾ cup cream cheese, softened
- 1/3 cup grated cheddar cheese
- ¼ cup sour cream
- 1 Tbsp minced garlic
- 1 Tbsp mustard
- ½ tsp salt

¼ tsp ground black pepper
½ cup grated parmesan

Instructions
1. Preheat your air fryer to 375 degrees F and line your air fryer tray with foil or parchment.
2. Place the mushroom caps on the tray and bake for 10 minutes in the air fryer. Remove from the air fryer and drain any excess water from the tray.
3. In a large mixing bowl, combine all the remaining ingredients except the parmesan cheese. Stir well to fully blend everything.
4. Stuff the mushroom caps with the crab mix and then sprinkle the parmesan over the top of the mushrooms.
5. Return the tray to the air fryer and bake for another 10 minutes or until the tops of the mushrooms are golden brown.
6. Remove from the air fryer and enjoy while hot.

Nutrition Facts Per Serving
Calories 348, Total Fat 20g, Saturated Fat 6g, Total Carbs 14g, Net Carbs 6g, Protein 24g, Sugar 2g, Fiber 7g, Sodium 501mg, Potassium 468g

Garlicy and Crab Stuffed Mushrooms

Prep time: 20 minutes , Cook time: 50 minutes , Serves 5

Ingredients:
1 pound cremini mushrooms, stems and gills removed
¾ pound fresh crab meat
¾ cup cream cheese, softened
1/3 cup grated cheddar cheese
¼ cup sour cream
2 Tbsp minced garlic
1 Tbsp mustard
½ tsp salt
¼ tsp ground black pepper
½ cup grated parmesan

Instructions
1. Preheat your air fryer to 375 degrees F and line your air fryer tray with foil or parchment.
2. Place the mushroom caps on the tray and bake for 10 minutes in the air fryer. Remove from the air fryer and drain any excess water from the tray.
3. In a large mixing bowl, combine all the remaining ingredients except the parmesan cheese. Stir well to fully blend everything.
4. Stuff the mushroom caps with the crab mix and then sprinkle the parmesan over the top of the mushrooms.
5. Return the tray to the air fryer and bake for another 10 minutes or until the tops of the mushrooms are golden brown.
6. Remove from the air fryer and enjoy while hot.

Nutrition Facts Per Serving
Calories 346, Total Fat 18g, Saturated Fat 6g, Total Carbs 10g, Net Carbs 6g, Protein 24g, Sugar 1g, Fiber 4g, Sodium 487mg, Potassium 211g

Black Pepper Flounder

Prep time: 5 minutes , Cook time: 8 minutes , Serves 4

Ingredients:
1 pound flounder filets
¾ tsp black pepper
½ tsp salt
¼ tsp garlic powder
2 Tbsp softened butter

Instructions
1. Preheat your air fryer to 450 degrees F and line your air fryer tray with foil.
2. Place the flounder filets on the foil lined tray.
3. In a small bowl combine the remaining ingredients and mix well to make a cohesive butter.
4. Spread the seasoned butter over the fish filets.
5. Bake the filets in the preheated oven for 8 minutes until nicely browned.
6. Serve while hot.

Nutrition Facts Per Serving
Calories 209, Total Fat 12g, Saturated Fat 7g, Total Carbs 2g, Net Carbs 1g, Protein 32g, Sugar 0g, Fiber 1g, Sodium 108mg, Potassium 63g

Parmesan Butter Flounder

Prep time: 5 minutes , Cook time: 8 minutes , Serves 4

Ingredients:
1 pound salmon filets
½ cup fresh grated parmesan
¼ tsp black pepper
½ tsp salt
¼ tsp garlic powder
2 Tbsp softened butter

Instructions
1. Preheat your air fryer to 450 degrees F and line your air fryer tray with foil.
2. Place the flounder filets on the foil lined tray.
3. In a small bowl combine the remaining ingredients and mix well to make a cohesive butter.
4. Spread the seasoned butter over the fish filets.
5. Bake the filets in the preheated oven for 8 minutes until nicely browned.
6. Serve while hot.

Nutrition Facts Per Serving
Calories 287, Total Fat 16g, Saturated Fat 9g, Total Carbs 2g, Net Carbs 1g, Protein 40g, Sugar 0g, Fiber 1g, Sodium 108mg, Potassium 63g

Herbed Butter Flounder

Prep time: 5 minutes , Cook time: 8 minutes , Serves 4

Ingredients:
1 pound flounder filets
½ cup fresh grated parmesan
¼ tsp black pepper
½ tsp salt
¼ tsp garlic powder
½ tsp dried basil
½ tsp dried thyme
2 Tbsp softened butter

Instructions
1. Preheat your air fryer to 450 degrees F and line your air fryer tray with foil.
2. Place the flounder filets on the foil lined tray.
3. In a small bowl combine the remaining ingredients and mix well to make a cohesive butter.
4. Spread the seasoned butter over the fish filets.
5. Bake the filets in the preheated oven for 8 minutes until nicely browned.
6. Serve while hot.

Nutrition Facts Per Serving
Calories 209, Total Fat 12g, Saturated Fat 7g, Total Carbs 2g, Net Carbs 1g, Protein 32g, Sugar 0g, Fiber 1g, Sodium 108mg, Potassium 63g

Garlic Butter Shrimp

Prep time: 2 minutes , Cook time: 12 minutes , Serves 4

Ingredients:
1 pound shrimp, cleaned completely
5 Tbsp butter, melted
½ tsp ground black pepper
½ tsp salt
½ cup vegetable stock
2 Tbsp lemon juice
¼ cup minced garlic
2 Tbsp parsley

Instructions
1. Preheat your air fryer to 350 degrees F and line the air fryer tray or baking pan with foil.
2. Place the shrimp, butter, pepper, salt, vegetable stock, and garlic in a large bowl and toss together well. Pour the mix onto the prepared tray or pan.
3. Bake for 12 minutes, stirring occasionally to flip the shrimp.
4. Divide on to plates and garnish with the lemon juice and garlic. Enjoy hot!

Nutrition Facts Per Serving
Calories 307, Total Fat 20g, Saturated Fat 12g, Total Carbs 3g, Net Carbs 3g, Protein 27g, Sugar 1g, Fiber 0g, Sodium 1522mg, Potassium 229g

Cajun Butter Shrimp

Prep time: 2 minutes , Cook time: 12 minutes , Serves 4

Ingredients:
1 pound shrimp, cleaned completely
5 Tbsp butter, melted
½ tsp ground black pepper
½ tsp salt
1 tsp Cajun seasoning
½ cup vegetable stock
2 Tbsp lemon juice
2 Tbsp parsley

Instructions
1. Preheat your air fryer to 350 degrees F and line the air fryer tray or baking pan with foil.
2. Place the shrimp, butter, pepper, salt, Cajun seasoning and vegetable stock in a large bowl and toss together well. Pour the mix onto the prepared tray or pan.
3. Bake for 12 minutes, stirring occasionally to flip the shrimp.
4. Divide on to plates and garnish with the lemon juice and garlic. Enjoy hot!

Nutrition Facts Per Serving
Calories 287, Total Fat 20g, Saturated Fat 12g, Total Carbs 3g, Net Carbs 3g, Protein 27g, Sugar 0g, Fiber 0g, Sodium 1501mg, Potassium 201g

Parmesan Shrimp

Prep time: 2 minutes , Cook time: 12 minutes , Serves 4

Ingredients:
1 pound shrimp, cleaned completely
5 Tbsp butter, melted
½ tsp ground black pepper
½ tsp salt
½ cup vegetable stock
2 Tbsp lemon juice
¼ cup minced garlic
½ cup parmesan cheese
2 Tbsp parsley

Instructions
1. Preheat your air fryer to 350 degrees F and line the air fryer tray or baking pan with foil.
2. Place the shrimp, butter, pepper, salt, vegetable stock, and garlic in a large bowl and toss together well. Pour the mix onto the prepared tray or pan.
3. Sprinkle the parmesan cheese over the top of the shrimp and place in the air fryer.
4. Bake for 12 minutes.
5. Divide on to plates and garnish with the lemon juice and garlic. Enjoy hot!

Nutrition Facts Per Serving
Calories 352, Total Fat 32g, Saturated Fat 22g, Total Carbs 7g, Net Carbs 6g, Protein 32g, Sugar 1g, Fiber 1g, Sodium 1672mg, Potassium 301g

Salmon Egg Salad

Prep time: 5 minutes , Cook time: 16 minutes , Serves 6

Ingredients:
6 Tbsp Mayonnaise
8 Large Eggs
2 Tbsp apple cider vinegar
1 tsp ground black pepper
1 tsp salt
1 cup smoked salmon, shredded

Instructions
1. Preheat your air fryer to 250 degrees F.
2. Place a wire rack in the air fryer and place the eggs on top of the rack.
3. Cook for 16 minutes then remove the eggs and place them directly into an ice water bath to cool and stop the cooking process.
4. Peel the eggs and place in a large bowl.
5. Mash the eggs with a fork.
6. Add in the mayonnaise, cider vinegar, pepper and salt.
7. Gently fold in the smoked salmon and serve chilled.

Nutrition Facts Per Serving
Calories 278, Total Fat 34g, Saturated Fat 10g, Total Carbs 9g, Net Carbs 6g, Protein 12g, Sugar 2g, Fiber 3g, Sodium 876mg, Potassium 348g

Poultry

Keto Fried Chicken

Prep time: 10 minutes , Cook time: 15 minutes , Serves 4

Ingredients:
- 1 pound chicken tenders
- ½ cup whole milk
- ¼ cup whey protein powder
- ½ cup grated parmesan
- ¼ tsp salt
- ¼ tsp ground black pepper
- ½ tsp paprika
- 2 eggs
- 2 Tbsp olive oil

Instructions
1. Preheat your air fryer to 450 degrees F and line the air fryer tray or baking pan with foil.
2. Place the chicken tenders and whole milk in a large bowl. Cover and marinate in the fridge overnight.
3. On a shallow bowl, toss the protein powder, parmesan, salt, pepper and paprika together.
4. Whisk the egg in a separate bowl.
5. Dip the chicken into the egg and then into the protein powder mix. Place the chicken tenders on the prepared sheet tray and, once they are all dipped, drizzle with the olive oil.
6. Bake in the air fryer for 15 minutes or until the tenders are golden brown. Enjoy hot!

Nutrition Facts Per Serving
Calories 342, Total Fat 15g, Saturated Fat 7g, Total Carbs 3g, Net Carbs 1g, Protein 48g, Sugar 1g, Fiber 2g, Sodium 321mg, Potassium 578g

Buffalo Chicken Pizza

Prep time: 20 minutes , Cook time: 20 minutes , Serves 3

Ingredients:
- 1 cup almond flour
- 1 egg
- 3 Tbsp water
- 4 Tbsp fresh grated parmesan
- 1 Tbsp fresh chopped basil
- ½ cup fresh diced mozzarella
- 1 cup shredded cooked chicken
- 1/3 cup keto buffalo sauce

Instructions
1. Preheat your air fryer to 375 degrees F and line the air fryer tray or baking pan with foil.
2. In a medium sized bowl, mix together the almond flour and water.
3. Add the egg and parmesan to the bowl and knead into a soft dough.
4. Place the dough on the prepared tray and press into a flat circle, about ¼ inch thick. Wet your hands if needed in order to make it easier to push the dough down.
5. In a separate bowl, toss the shredded chicken with the buffalo sauce.
6. Spread the chicken mix over the dough and then top with the fresh basil and mozzarella.
7. Place in the preheated air fryer and bake for 18 minutes or until the cheese is melted and bubbling.
8. Slice and serve

Nutrition Facts Per Serving
Calories 389, Total Fat 26g, Saturated Fat 13g, Total Carbs 14g, Net Carbs 10g, Protein 25g, Sugar 9g, Fiber 4g, Sodium 418mg, Potassium 219g

Spicy Fried Chicken

Prep time: 10 minutes, Cook time: 15 minutes, Serves 4

Ingredients:
- 1 pound chicken tenders
- ½ cup whole milk
- ¼ cup whey protein powder
- ½ cup grated parmesan
- ¼ tsp salt
- ½ tsp paprika
- 1 tsp ground cayenne pepper
- 2 eggs
- 2 Tbsp olive oil

Instructions
1. Preheat your air fryer to 450 degrees F and line the air fryer tray or baking pan with foil.
2. Place the chicken tenders and whole milk in a large bowl. Cover and marinate in the fridge overnight.
3. On a shallow bowl, toss the protein powder, parmesan, salt, cayenne pepper and paprika together.
4. Whisk the egg in a separate bowl.
5. Dip the chicken into the egg and then into the protein powder mix. Place the chicken tenders on the prepared sheet tray and, once they are all dipped, drizzle with the olive oil.
6. Bake in the air fryer for 15 minutes or until the tenders are golden brown. Enjoy hot!

Nutrition Facts Per Serving
Calories 342, Total Fat 15g, Saturated Fat 7g, Total Carbs 3g, Net Carbs 1g, Protein 48g, Sugar 1g, Fiber 2g, Sodium 321mg, Potassium 578g

Dijon Baked Chicken Breast

Prep time: 5 minutes, Cook time: 24 minutes, Serves 5

Ingredients:
- 1 ½ pounds Chicken Breast, thinly sliced
- ¼ cup parsley, freshly chopped
- ¼ cup Dijon mustard
- 1 Tbsp olive oil
- 1 Tbsp fresh squeezed lemon juice
- 1 Tbsp minced garlic
- ¼ tsp salt
- ¼ tsp ground black pepper

Instructions
1. Preheat your air fryer to 375 degrees F line your air fryer tray with a piece of parchment paper.
2. Place the chicken breast on the parchment lined tray.
3. In a small bowl, mix together the remaining ingredients and then spread over the top of the chicken breast.
4. Place the chicken breast in the air fryer and bake for 18 minutes. Slice and serve hot!

Nutrition Facts Per Serving
Calories 279, Total Fat 11g, Saturated Fat 2g, Total Carbs 2g, Net Carbs 1g, Protein 35g, Sugar 0g, Fiber 1g, Sodium 389mg, Potassium 47g

Maple Dijon Baked Chicken Breast

Prep time: 5 minutes, Cook time: 24 minutes, Serves 5

Ingredients:
- 1 ½ pounds Chicken Breast, thinly sliced
- ¼ cup parsley, freshly chopped
- ¼ cup Dijon mustard
- 1 Tbsp olive oil
- 1 tsp maple extract
- 1 Tbsp fresh squeezed lemon juice
- 1 Tbsp minced garlic
- ¼ tsp salt
- ¼ tsp ground black pepper

Instructions
1. Preheat your air fryer to 375 degrees F line your air fryer tray with a piece of parchment paper.
2. Place the chicken breast on the parchment lined tray.
3. In a small bowl, mix together the remaining ingredients and then spread over the top of the chicken breast.
4. Place the chicken breast in the air fryer and bake for 18 minutes. Slice and serve hot!

Nutrition Facts Per Serving
Calories 281, Total Fat 11g, Saturated Fat 2g, Total Carbs 2g, Net Carbs 1g, Protein 35g, Sugar 0g, Fiber 1g, Sodium 389mg, Potassium 47g

Sweet and Spicy Dijon Baked Chicken Breast

Prep time: 5 minutes , Cook time: 24 minutes , Serves 5

Ingredients:
1 ½ pounds Chicken Breast, thinly sliced
¼ cup parsley, freshly chopped
¼ cup Dijon mustard
1 Tbsp olive oil
1 Tbsp fresh squeezed lemon juice
1 tsp maple extract
½ tsp cayenne pepper
1 Tbsp minced garlic
¼ tsp salt
¼ tsp ground black pepper

Instructions
1. Preheat your air fryer to 375 degrees F line your air fryer tray with a piece of parchment paper.
2. Place the chicken breast on the parchment lined tray.
3. In a small bowl, mix together the remaining ingredients and then spread over the top of the chicken breast.
4. Place the chicken breast in the air fryer and bake for 18 minutes. Slice and serve hot!

Nutrition Facts Per Serving
Calories 284, Total Fat 11g, Saturated Fat 2g, Total Carbs 2g, Net Carbs 1g, Protein 35g, Sugar 0g, Fiber 1g, Sodium 392mg, Potassium 51g

Herbed Fried Chicken

Prep time: 10 minutes , Cook time: 15 minutes , Serves 4

Ingredients:
1 pound chicken tenders
½ cup whole milk
1 bay leaf
¼ cup whey protein powder
½ cup grated parmesan
¼ tsp salt
¼ tsp ground black pepper
½ tsp dried basil
½ tsp dried parsley
2 eggs
2 Tbsp olive oil

Instructions
1. Preheat your air fryer to 450 degrees F and line the air fryer tray or baking pan with foil.
2. Place the chicken tenders, bay leaf and whole milk in a large bowl. Cover and marinate in the fridge overnight.
3. On a shallow bowl, toss the protein powder, parmesan, salt, pepper and paprika together.
4. Whisk the egg in a separate bowl.
5. Remove the chicken from the milk and dip the chicken into the egg and then into the protein powder mix. Place the chicken tenders on the prepared sheet tray and, once they are all dipped, drizzle with the olive oil.
6. Bake in the air fryer for 15 minutes or until the tenders are golden brown. Enjoy hot!

Nutrition Facts Per Serving
Calories 344, Total Fat 15g, Saturated Fat 7g, Total Carbs 3g, Net Carbs 1g, Protein 48g, Sugar 1g, Fiber 2g, Sodium 321mg, Potassium 578g

BBQ Fried Chicken

Prep time: 10 minutes , Cook time: 15 minutes , Serves 4

Ingredients:
1 pound chicken tenders
½ cup whole milk
¼ cup whey protein powder
½ cup grated parmesan
¼ tsp salt
¼ tsp ground black pepper
½ tsp paprika
2 eggs
2 Tbsp olive oil
½ cup keto BBQ sauce

Instructions
1. Preheat your air fryer to 450 degrees F and line the air fryer tray or baking pan with foil.
2. Place the chicken tenders and whole milk in a large bowl. Cover and marinate in the fridge overnight.

3. On a shallow bowl, toss the protein powder, parmesan, salt, pepper and paprika together.
4. Whisk the egg in a separate bowl.
5. Dip the chicken into the egg and then into the protein powder mix. Place the chicken tenders on the prepared sheet tray and, once they are all dipped, drizzle with the olive oil.
6. Bake in the air fryer for 15 minutes or until the tenders are golden brown.
7. Serve with the BBQ sauce on the side for dipping and enjoy hot!

Nutrition Facts Per Serving
Calories 412, Total Fat 19g, Saturated Fat 10g, Total Carbs 4g, Net Carbs 2g, Protein 48g, Sugar 1g, Fiber 2g, Sodium 451mg, Potassium 540g

Chicken Nuggets

Prep time: 10 minutes , Cook time: 15 minutes , Serves 4

Ingredients:
1 pound chicken breast
¼ cup mayonnaise
2 Tbsp mustard
½ tsp salt
½ tsp ground black pepper
1 ½ cups ground pork rinds
2 Tbsp whole milk

Instructions
1. Preheat your air fryer to 400 degrees F and line your air fryer tray with foil and spray with cooking grease.
2. Dry the chicken breast by patting with a paper towel. Cut the chicken into strips about 1 ½ inches wide and two inches long. You can, however cut it into any shape you'd like- larger pieces will have a longer cooking time.
3. In a small bowl, combine the mustard, mayo and milk and stir together well.
4. In a separate bowl, combine the ground pork rinds, salt and pepper.
5. Dip the chicken nuggets into the mayonnaise mix and then into the pork rind mix, coating the chicken completely. Place it on the prepared tray when done and repeat with the remaining chicken pieces.
6. Place the tray in the air fryer and bake the chicken for 8 minutes, flip and bake for another 7 minutes. Serve while hot!

Nutrition Facts Per Serving
Calories 278, Total Fat 18g, Saturated Fat 5g, Total Carbs 1g, Net Carbs 0g, Protein 24g, Sugar 0g, Fiber 1g, Sodium 654mg, Potassium 71g

Greek Garlic Chicken

Prep time: 20 minutes , Cook time: 30 minutes , Serves 4

Ingredients:
3 Tbsp olive oil
3 Tbsp lemon juice
3 Tbsp minced garlic
1 tsp oregano, dried
1 pound chicken thighs
½ tsp sea salt
¼ tsp ground black pepper
½ pound asparagus
1 zucchini, sliced thinly
1 lemon, sliced thinly

Instructions
1. Preheat your air fryer to 400 degrees F and prepare your air fryer tray with a piece of foil.
2. In a large bowl, whisk together 2 Tbsp of the olive oil, lemon juice, dried oregano and garlic.
3. Add the chicken to the bowl and toss to coat. Cover the bowl and place in the fridge for two hours.
4. Add the remaining tablespoon of olive oil to a sauté pan and heat over high. Sear the marinated chicken on each side for 3 minutes, just to brown.
5. Move the browned chicken to the prepared, foil lined tray and pour the remaining marinade from the bowl over the chicken.
6. Add the asparagus, zucchini and lemon slices, layering them over and around the chicken.
7. Place the tray in the preheated air fryer for 20 minutes. Serve hot.

Nutrition Facts Per Serving
Calories 244, Total Fat 15g, Saturated Fat 2g, Total Carbs 6g, Net Carbs 4g, Protein 24g, Sugar 3g, Fiber 2g, Sodium 398mg, Potassium 263g

Creamy Garlic Chicken Thighs

Prep time: 20 minutes , Cook time: 30 minutes , Serves 4

Ingredients:
- 3 Tbsp olive oil
- 3 Tbsp lemon juice
- 3 Tbsp minced garlic
- 1 tsp oregano, dried
- 1 pound chicken thighs
- ½ tsp sea salt
- ¼ tsp ground black pepper
- ½ pound asparagus
- 1 zucchini, sliced thinly
- 1 lemon, sliced thinly
- ¼ cup heavy cream

Instructions
1. Preheat your air fryer to 400 degrees F and prepare your air fryer tray with a piece of foil.
2. In a large bowl, whisk together 2 Tbsp of the olive oil, lemon juice, dried oregano and garlic.
3. Add the chicken to the bowl and toss to coat. Cover the bowl and place in the fridge for two hours.
4. Add the remaining tablespoon of olive oil to a sauté pan and heat over high. Sear the marinated chicken on each side for 3 minutes, just to brown.
5. Move the browned chicken to the prepared, foil lined tray and pour the remaining marinade from the bowl over the chicken.
6. Add the asparagus, zucchini and lemon slices, layering them over and around the chicken.
7. Place the tray in the preheated air fryer for 20 minutes. Add the cream to the pan and cook for another 5 minutes. Serve hot

Nutrition Facts Per Serving
Calories 264, Total Fat 18g, Saturated Fat 6g, Total Carbs 10g, Net Carbs 8g, Protein 24g, Sugar 4g, Fiber 2g, Sodium 398mg, Potassium 263g

Lemon Garlic Chicken Thighs

Prep time: 20 minutes , Cook time: 30 minutes , Serves 4

Ingredients:
- 3 Tbsp olive oil
- 3 Tbsp lemon juice
- 3 Tbsp minced garlic
- 1 pound chicken thighs
- ½ tsp sea salt
- ¼ tsp ground black pepper
- 1 lemon, sliced thinly

Instructions
1. Preheat your air fryer to 400 degrees F and prepare your air fryer tray with a piece of foil.
2. In a large bowl, whisk together 2 Tbsp of the olive oil, lemon juice, and garlic.
3. Add the chicken to the bowl and toss to coat. Cover the bowl and place in the fridge for two hours.
4. Add the remaining tablespoon of olive oil to a sauté pan and heat over high. Sear the marinated chicken on each side for 3 minutes, just to brown.
5. Move the browned chicken to the prepared, foil lined tray and pour the remaining marinade from the bowl over the chicken.
6. Add the lemon slices, layering them over and around the chicken.
7. Place the tray in the preheated air fryer for 20 minutes. Serve hot.

Nutrition Facts Per Serving
Calories 201, Total Fat 14g, Saturated Fat 2g, Total Carbs 2g, Net Carbs 1g, Protein 24g, Sugar 0g, Fiber 1g, Sodium 304mg, Potassium 263g

Brussels and Garlic Chicken

Prep time: 20 minutes , Cook time: 30 minutes , Serves 4

Ingredients:
- 3 Tbsp olive oil
- 3 Tbsp lemon juice
- 3 Tbsp minced garlic
- 1 tsp oregano, dried
- 1 pound chicken thighs
- ½ tsp sea salt
- ¼ tsp ground black pepper
- 1 pound Brussel sprouts, cut in half

1 lemon, sliced thinly

Instructions
1. Preheat your air fryer to 400 degrees F and prepare your air fryer tray with a piece of foil.
2. In a large bowl, whisk together 2 Tbsp of the olive oil, lemon juice, dried oregano and garlic.
3. Add the chicken to the bowl and toss to coat. Cover the bowl and place in the fridge for two hours.
4. Add the remaining tablespoon of olive oil to a sauté pan and heat over high. Sear the marinated chicken on each side for 3 minutes, just to brown.
5. Move the browned chicken to the prepared, foil lined tray and pour the remaining marinade from the bowl over the chicken.
6. Add the Brussels and lemon slices, layering them over and around the chicken.
7. Place the tray in the preheated air fryer for 20 minutes. Serve hot

Nutrition Facts Per Serving
Calories 228, Total Fat 13g, Saturated Fat 2g, Total Carbs 4g, Net Carbs 2g, Protein 24g, Sugar 1g, Fiber 2g, Sodium 398mg, Potassium 201g

Creamy Brussels and Garlic Chicken

Prep time: 20 minutes , Cook time: 30 minutes , Serves 4

Ingredients:
3 Tbsp olive oil
3 Tbsp lemon juice
3 Tbsp minced garlic
1 tsp oregano, dried
1 pound chicken thighs
½ tsp sea salt
¼ tsp ground black pepper
1 pound Brussels Sprouts, sliced in half
½ cup heavy cream

Instructions
1. Preheat your air fryer to 400 degrees F and prepare your air fryer tray with a piece of foil.
2. In a large bowl, whisk together 2 Tbsp of the olive oil, lemon juice, dried oregano and garlic.
3. Add the chicken to the bowl and toss to coat. Cover the bowl and place in the fridge for two hours.
4. Add the remaining tablespoon of olive oil to a sauté pan and heat over high. Sear the marinated chicken on each side for 3 minutes, just to brown.
5. Move the browned chicken to the prepared, foil lined tray and pour the remaining marinade from the bowl and the heavy cream over the chicken.
6. Add the Brussels, layering them over and around the chicken.
7. Place the tray in the preheated air fryer for 20 minutes. Serve hot.

Nutrition Facts Per Serving
Calories 265, Total Fat 15g, Saturated Fat 2g, Total Carbs 5g, Net Carbs 3g, Protein 24g, Sugar 2g, Fiber 2g, Sodium 367mg, Potassium 222g

Bacon Chicken Thighs

Prep time: 20 minutes , Cook time: 30 minutes , Serves 4

Ingredients:
3 Tbsp olive oil
3 Tbsp lemon juice
3 Tbsp minced garlic
1 tsp oregano, dried
1 pound chicken thighs
½ tsp sea salt
¼ tsp ground black pepper
1 cup cooked, chopped bacon

Instructions
1. Preheat your air fryer to 400 degrees F and prepare your air fryer tray with a piece of foil.
2. In a large bowl, whisk together 2 Tbsp of the olive oil, lemon juice, dried oregano and garlic.
3. Add the chicken to the bowl and toss to coat. Cover the bowl and place in the fridge for two hours.
4. Add the remaining tablespoon of olive oil to a sauté pan and heat over high. Sear the marinated chicken on each side for 3 minutes, just to brown.

5. Move the browned chicken to the prepared, foil lined tray and pour the remaining marinade from the bowl over the chicken.
6. Add the bacon, placing it over and around the chicken.
7. Place the tray in the preheated air fryer for 20 minutes. Serve hot.

Nutrition Facts Per Serving
Calories 278, Total Fat 25g, Saturated Fat 2g, Total Carbs 6g, Net Carbs 4g, Protein 29g, Sugar 3g, Fiber 2g, Sodium 865mg, Potassium 245g

Maple Chicken Thighs with Brussels

Prep time: 20 minutes , Cook time: 30 minutes , Serves 4

Ingredients:
- 3 Tbsp olive oil
- 3 Tbsp lemon juice
- 3 Tbsp minced garlic
- 1 tsp oregano, dried
- 1 pound chicken thighs
- ½ tsp sea salt
- ¼ tsp ground black pepper
- 1 pound Brussels Sprouts, sliced in half
- 1 tsp maple extract

Instructions
1. Preheat your air fryer to 400 degrees F and prepare your air fryer tray with a piece of foil.
2. In a large bowl, whisk together 2 Tbsp of the olive oil, lemon juice, maple extract, dried oregano and garlic.
3. Add the chicken to the bowl and toss to coat. Cover the bowl and place in the fridge for two hours.
4. Add the remaining tablespoon of olive oil to a sauté pan and heat over high. Sear the marinated chicken on each side for 3 minutes, just to brown.
5. Move the browned chicken to the prepared, foil lined tray and pour the remaining marinade from the bowl over the chicken.
6. Add the Brussels, layering them over and around the chicken.
7. Place the tray in the preheated air fryer for 20 minutes. Serve hot

Nutrition Facts Per Serving
Calories 250, Total Fat 15g, Saturated Fat 2g, Total Carbs 8g, Net Carbs 4g, Protein 24g, Sugar 3g, Fiber 4g, Sodium 405mg, Potassium 263g

Maple Bacon Chicken Thighs

Prep time: 20 minutes , Cook time: 30 minutes , Serves 4

Ingredients:
- 3 Tbsp olive oil
- 3 Tbsp lemon juice
- 3 Tbsp minced garlic
- 1 tsp oregano, dried
- 1 pound chicken thighs
- ½ tsp sea salt
- ¼ tsp ground black pepper
- 1 tsp maple extract
- ½ cup cooked, chopped bacon

Instructions
1. Preheat your air fryer to 400 degrees F and prepare your air fryer tray with a piece of foil.
2. In a large bowl, whisk together 2 Tbsp of the olive oil, lemon juice, dried oregano and garlic.
3. Add the chicken to the bowl and toss to coat. Cover the bowl and place in the fridge for two hours.
4. Add the remaining tablespoon of olive oil to a sauté pan and heat over high. Sear the marinated chicken on each side for 3 minutes, just to brown.
5. Move the browned chicken to the prepared, foil lined tray and pour the remaining marinade from the bowl over the chicken.
6. Add the asparagus, zucchini and lemon slices, layering them over and around the chicken.
7. Place the tray in the preheated air fryer for 20 minutes.

Nutrition Facts Per Serving
Calories 280, Total Fat 25g, Saturated Fat 2g, Total Carbs 6g, Net Carbs 4g, Protein 29g, Sugar 3g, Fiber 2g, Sodium 865mg, Potassium 245g

Lemon Feta Garlic Chicken

Prep time: 20 minutes , Cook time: 30 minutes , Serves 4

Ingredients:
3 Tbsp olive oil
3 Tbsp lemon juice
3 Tbsp minced garlic
1 tsp oregano, dried
1 pound chicken thighs
½ tsp sea salt
¼ tsp ground black pepper
1 cup feta cheese
1 lemon, sliced thinly

Instructions
1. Preheat your air fryer to 400 degrees F and prepare your air fryer tray with a piece of foil.
2. In a large bowl, whisk together 2 Tbsp of the olive oil, lemon juice, dried oregano and garlic.
3. Add the chicken to the bowl and toss to coat. Cover the bowl and place in the fridge for two hours.
4. Add the remaining tablespoon of olive oil to a sauté pan and heat over high. Sear the marinated chicken on each side for 3 minutes, just to brown.
5. Move the browned chicken to the prepared, foil lined tray and pour the remaining marinade from the bowl over the chicken.
6. Add the lemon slices, layering them over and around the chicken.
7. Place the tray in the preheated air fryer for 20 minutes. Add the feta cheese to the pan and stir. Cook for another 5 minutes to melt the feta then serve hot.

Nutrition Facts Per Serving
Calories 268, Total Fat 18g, Saturated Fat 4g, Total Carbs 6g, Net Carbs 4g, Protein 25g, Sugar 3g, Fiber 2g, Sodium 398mg, Potassium 263g

Garlic Parmesan Chicken Thighs

Prep time: 20 minutes , Cook time: 30 minutes , Serves 4

Ingredients:
3 Tbsp olive oil
3 Tbsp lemon juice
3 Tbsp minced garlic
1 tsp oregano, dried
1 pound chicken thighs
½ tsp sea salt
¼ tsp ground black pepper
½ cup grated parmesan cheese

Instructions
1. Preheat your air fryer to 400 degrees F and prepare your air fryer tray with a piece of foil.
2. In a large bowl, whisk together 2 Tbsp of the olive oil, lemon juice, dried oregano and garlic.
3. Add the chicken to the bowl and toss to coat. Cover the bowl and place in the fridge for two hours.
4. Add the remaining tablespoon of olive oil to a sauté pan and heat over high. Sear the marinated chicken on each side for 3 minutes, just to brown.
5. Move the browned chicken to the prepared, foil lined tray and pour the remaining marinade from the bowl over the chicken.
6. Place the tray in the preheated air fryer for 20 minutes.
7. Remove the pan and sprinkle the parmesan over the chicken. Return to the oven and bake for another 5 minutes. Serve hot.

Nutrition Facts Per Serving
Calories 289, Total Fat 17g, Saturated Fat 3g, Total Carbs 6g, Net Carbs 4g, Protein 26g, Sugar 3g, Fiber 2g, Sodium 478mg, Potassium 263g

Black Pepper Chicken Thighs

Prep time: 20 minutes , Cook time: 30 minutes , Serves 4

Ingredients:
3 Tbsp olive oil
3 Tbsp minced garlic
1 pound chicken thighs
½ tsp sea salt
1 tsp ground black pepper

Instructions
1. Preheat your air fryer to 400 degrees F and prepare your air fryer tray with a piece of foil.

2. In a large bowl, whisk together 2 Tbsp of the olive oil, salt, pepper, and garlic.
3. Add the chicken to the bowl and toss to coat. Cover the bowl and place in the fridge for two hours.
4. Add the remaining tablespoon of olive oil to a sauté pan and heat over high. Sear the marinated chicken on each side for 3 minutes, just to brown.
5. Move the browned chicken to the prepared, foil lined tray and pour the remaining marinade from the bowl over the chicken.
6. Place the tray in the preheated air fryer for 20 minutes. Serve hot.

Nutrition Facts Per Serving
Calories 206, Total Fat 15g, Saturated Fat 2g, Total Carbs 1g, Net Carbs 0g, Protein 24g, Sugar 0g, Fiber 1g, Sodium 341mg, Potassium 201g

Garlic Chicken and Spinach

Prep time: 20 minutes , Cook time: 30 minutes , Serves 4

Ingredients:
3 Tbsp olive oil
3 Tbsp lemon juice
3 Tbsp minced garlic
1 tsp oregano, dried
1 pound chicken thighs
½ tsp sea salt
¼ tsp ground black pepper
1 lemon, sliced thinly
4 cups baby spinach

Instructions
1. Preheat your air fryer to 400 degrees F and prepare your air fryer tray with a piece of foil.
2. In a large bowl, whisk together 2 Tbsp of the olive oil, lemon juice, dried oregano and garlic.
3. Add the chicken to the bowl and toss to coat. Cover the bowl and place in the fridge for two hours.
4. Add the remaining tablespoon of olive oil to a sauté pan and heat over high. Sear the marinated chicken on each side for 3 minutes, just to brown.
5. Move the browned chicken to the prepared, foil lined tray and pour the remaining marinade from the bowl over the chicken.
6. Add the lemon slices, layering them over and around the chicken.
7. Place the tray in the preheated air fryer for 20 minutes.
8. Remove the tray from the fryer and add the spinach around the chicken. Return to the air fryer for another 5 minutes to wilt the spinach then serve hot.

Nutrition Facts Per Serving
Calories 209, Total Fat 15g, Saturated Fat 2g, Total Carbs 8g, Net Carbs 3g, Protein 24g, Sugar 1g, Fiber 5g, Sodium 388mg, Potassium 261g

Rotisserie Style Chicken Thighs

Prep time: 20 minutes , Cook time: 30 minutes , Serves 4

Ingredients:
3 Tbsp olive oil
1 pound chicken thighs
½ tsp sea salt
¼ tsp ground black pepper

Instructions
1. Preheat your air fryer to 400 degrees F and prepare your air fryer tray with a piece of foil.
2. In a large bowl, whisk together 2 Tbsp of the olive oil, salt and pepper.
3. Add the chicken to the bowl and toss to coat. Cover the bowl and place in the fridge for two hours.
4. Add the remaining tablespoon of olive oil to a sauté pan and heat over high. Sear the marinated chicken on each side for 3 minutes, just to brown.
5. Move the browned chicken to the prepared, foil lined tray and pour the remaining marinade from the bowl over the chicken.
6. Place the tray in the preheated air fryer for 20 minutes until the skin is crispy. Serve hot.

Nutrition Facts Per Serving
Calories 199, Total Fat 13g, Saturated Fat 2g, Total Carbs 1g, Net Carbs 0g, Protein 24g, Sugar 0g, Fiber 1g, Sodium 233mg, Potassium 0g

Spicy Chicken Nuggets

Prep time: 10 minutes , Cook time: 15 minutes , Serves 4

Ingredients:
1 pound chicken breast
¼ cup mayonnaise
2 Tbsp mustard
½ tsp salt
½ tsp ground cayenne pepper
1 ½ cups ground pork rinds
2 Tbsp whole milk

Instructions
1. Preheat your air fryer to 400 degrees F and line your air fryer tray with foil and spray with cooking grease.
2. Dry the chicken breast by patting with a paper towel. Cut the chicken into strips about 1 ½ inches wide and two inches long. You can, however cut it into any shape you'd like- larger pieces will have a longer cooking time.
3. In a small bowl, combine the mustard, mayo and milk and stir together well.
4. In a separate bowl, combine the ground pork rinds, salt and cayenne pepper.
5. Dip the chicken nuggets into the mayonnaise mix and then into the pork rind mix, coating the chicken completely. Place it on the prepared tray when done and repeat with the remaining chicken pieces.
6. Place the tray in the air fryer and bake the chicken for 8 minutes, flip and bake for another 7 minutes. Serve while hot!

Nutrition Facts Per Serving
Calories 278, Total Fat 18g, Saturated Fat 5g, Total Carbs 1g, Net Carbs 0g, Protein 24g, Sugar 0g, Fiber 1g, Sodium 656mg, Potassium 71g

Italian Seasoned Chicken Nuggets

Prep time: 10 minutes , Cook time: 15 minutes , Serves 4

Ingredients:
1 pound chicken breast
¼ cup mayonnaise
2 Tbsp mustard
½ tsp salt
1 tsp Italian Seasoning
½ tsp ground black pepper
1 ½ cups ground pork rinds
2 Tbsp whole milk

Instructions
1. Preheat your air fryer to 400 degrees F and line your air fryer tray with foil and spray with cooking grease.
2. Dry the chicken breast by patting with a paper towel. Cut the chicken into strips about 1 ½ inches wide and two inches long. You can, however cut it into any shape you'd like- larger pieces will have a longer cooking time.
3. In a small bowl, combine the mustard, mayo and milk and stir together well.
4. In a separate bowl, combine the ground pork rinds, salt, Italian seasoning and pepper.
5. Dip the chicken nuggets into the mayonnaise mix and then into the pork rind mix, coating the chicken completely. Place it on the prepared tray when done and repeat with the remaining chicken pieces.
6. Place the tray in the air fryer and bake the chicken for 8 minutes, flip and bake for another 7 minutes. Serve while hot!

Nutrition Facts Per Serving
Calories 280, Total Fat 18g, Saturated Fat 5g, Total Carbs 1g, Net Carbs 0g, Protein 24g, Sugar 0g, Fiber 1g, Sodium 662mg, Potassium 74g

Sweet and Spicy Chicken Nuggets

Prep time: 10 minutes , Cook time: 15 minutes , Serves 4

Ingredients:
1 pound chicken breast
¼ cup mayonnaise
2 Tbsp mustard
½ tsp salt
½ tsp ground cayenne pepper
1 tsp powdered erythritol
1 ½ cups ground pork rinds
2 Tbsp whole milk

Instructions
1. Preheat your air fryer to 400 degrees F and line your air fryer tray with foil and spray with cooking grease.

2. Dry the chicken breast by patting with a paper towel. Cut the chicken into strips about 1 ½ inches wide and two inches long. You can, however cut it into any shape you'd like- larger pieces will have a longer cooking time.
3. In a small bowl, combine the mustard, mayo and milk and stir together well.
4. In a separate bowl, combine the ground pork rinds, salt, erythritol and cayenne pepper.
5. Dip the chicken nuggets into the mayonnaise mix and then into the pork rind mix, coating the chicken completely. Place it on the prepared tray when done and repeat with the remaining chicken pieces.
6. Place the tray in the air fryer and bake the chicken for 8 minutes, flip and bake for another 7 minutes. Serve while hot!

Nutrition Facts Per Serving
Calories 278, Total Fat 18g, Saturated Fat 5g, Total Carbs 2g, Net Carbs 0g, Protein 24g, Sugar 0g, Fiber 2g, Sodium 654mg, Potassium 71g

Creamy Tuscan Chicken

Prep time: 10 minutes , Cook time: 15 minutes , Serves 6

Ingredients:
1 ½ pounds chicken breast, thinly sliced
2 Tbsp olive oil
1 cup heavy cream
½ cup chicken broth
1 tsp garlic powder
½ cup grated parmesan cheese
½ cup chopped sundried tomatoes
2 cups baby spinach
1 tsp Italian seasoning

Instructions
1. Preheat your air fryer to 375 degrees F and prepare a baking tray that will fit inside your air fryer.
2. Place the chicken and olive oil in your baking tray and then into your air fryer for 4 minutes.
3. Remove the pan, flip the chicken and return to the air fryer for another 4 minutes.
4. Whisk the remaining ingredients in a small bowl.
5. Remove the tray again and add all the remaining ingredients to the pan, stirring briefly.
6. Return the pan to the air fryer and cook for 10 minutes. The sauce should be bubbling and the spinach wilted.
7. Serve while hot!

Nutrition Facts Per Serving
Calories 371, Total Fat 23g, Saturated Fat 12g, Total Carbs 9g, Net Carbs 8g, Protein 28g, Sugar 3g, Fiber 1g, Sodium 456mg, Potassium 100g

Creamy Tomato Chicken

Prep time: 10 minutes , Cook time: 15 minutes , Serves 6

Ingredients:
1 ½ pounds chicken breast, thinly sliced
2 Tbsp olive oil
1 cup heavy cream
1 Tbsp tomato paste
½ cup chicken broth
1 tsp garlic powder
½ cup grated parmesan cheese
½ cup chopped sundried tomatoes
2 cups baby spinach
1 tsp Italian seasoning

Instructions
1. Preheat your air fryer to 375 degrees F and prepare a baking tray that will fit inside your air fryer.
2. Place the chicken and olive oil in your baking tray and then into your air fryer for 4 minutes.
3. Remove the pan, flip the chicken and return to the air fryer for another 4 minutes.
4. Whisk the remaining ingredients in a small bowl.
5. Remove the tray again and add all the remaining ingredients to the pan, stirring briefly.
6. Return the pan to the air fryer and cook for 10 minutes. The sauce should be bubbling and the spinach wilted.
7. Serve while hot!

Nutrition Facts Per Serving
Calories 392, Total Fat 23g, Saturated Fat 12g, Total Carbs 10g, Net Carbs 9g, Protein 28g, Sugar 3g, Fiber 1g, Sodium 456mg, Potassium 104g

Marinara Chicken

Prep time: 10 minutes , Cook time: 15 minutes , Serves 6

Ingredients:
- 1 ½ pounds chicken breast, thinly sliced
- 2 Tbsp olive oil
- 1 cup keto marinara
- 1 Tbsp tomato paste
- ½ cup chicken broth
- 1 tsp garlic powder
- ½ cup grated parmesan cheese
- ½ cup chopped sundried tomatoes
- 2 cups baby spinach
- 1 tsp Italian seasoning

Instructions
1. Preheat your air fryer to 375 degrees F and prepare a baking tray that will fit inside your air fryer.
2. Place the chicken and olive oil in your baking tray and then into your air fryer for 4 minutes.
3. Remove the pan, flip the chicken and return to the air fryer for another 4 minutes.
4. Whisk the remaining ingredients in a small bowl.
5. Remove the tray again and add all the remaining ingredients to the pan, stirring briefly.
6. Return the pan to the air fryer and cook for 10 minutes. The sauce should be bubbling and the spinach wilted.
7. Serve while hot!

Nutrition Facts Per Serving
Calories 415, Total Fat 23g, Saturated Fat 12g, Total Carbs 13g, Net Carbs 9g, Protein 28g, Sugar 3g, Fiber 4g, Sodium 456mg, Potassium 104g

Creamy Tomato Turkey

Prep time: 10 minutes , Cook time: 15 minutes , Serves 6

Ingredients:
- 1 ½ pounds turkey breast, thinly sliced
- 2 Tbsp olive oil
- 1 cup heavy cream
- 1 Tbsp tomato paste
- ½ cup chicken broth
- 1 tsp garlic powder
- ½ cup grated parmesan cheese
- ½ cup chopped sundried tomatoes
- 2 cups baby spinach
- 1 tsp Italian seasoning

Instructions
1. Preheat your air fryer to 375 degrees F and prepare a baking tray that will fit inside your air fryer.
2. Place the turkey and olive oil in your baking tray and then into your air fryer for 4 minutes.
3. Remove the pan, flip the turkey and return to the air fryer for another 4 minutes.
4. Whisk the remaining ingredients in a small bowl.
5. Remove the tray again and add all the remaining ingredients to the pan, stirring briefly.
6. Return the pan to the air fryer and cook for 10 minutes. The sauce should be bubbling and the spinach wilted.
7. Serve while hot!

Nutrition Facts Per Serving
Calories 392, Total Fat 23g, Saturated Fat 12g, Total Carbs 10g, Net Carbs 9g, Protein 28g, Sugar 3g, Fiber 1g, Sodium 456mg, Potassium 104g

Creamy Tomato Chicken

Prep time: 10 minutes , Cook time: 15 minutes , Serves 6

Ingredients:
- 1 ½ pounds chicken breast, thinly sliced
- 2 Tbsp olive oil
- 1 cup heavy cream
- 1 Tbsp tomato paste
- ½ cup chicken broth
- 1 tsp garlic powder
- ½ cup grated parmesan cheese
- ½ cup chopped sundried tomatoes
- 2 cups baby spinach
- 1 tsp Italian seasoning

Instructions

1. Preheat your air fryer to 375 degrees F and prepare a baking tray that will fit inside your air fryer.
2. Place the chicken and olive oil in your baking tray and then into your air fryer for 4 minutes.
3. Remove the pan, flip the chicken and return to the air fryer for another 4 minutes.
4. Whisk the remaining ingredients in a small bowl.
5. Remove the tray again and add all the remaining ingredients to the pan, stirring briefly.
6. Return the pan to the air fryer and cook for 10 minutes. The sauce should be bubbling and the spinach wilted.
7. Serve while hot!

Nutrition Facts Per Serving
Calories 392, Total Fat 23g, Saturated Fat 12g, Total Carbs 10g, Net Carbs 9g, Protein 28g, Sugar 3g, Fiber 1g, Sodium 456mg, Potassium 104g

Creamy Garlic Ground Chicken

Prep time: 10 minutes , Cook time: 15 minutes , Serves 6

Ingredients:
1 ½ pounds ground chicken
2 Tbsp olive oil
1 cup heavy cream
½ cup chicken broth
1 Tbsp garlic powder
½ cup grated parmesan cheese
½ cup chopped sundried tomatoes
2 cups baby spinach
1 tsp Italian seasoning

Instructions
1. Preheat your air fryer to 375 degrees F and prepare a baking tray that will fit inside your air fryer.
2. Place the ground chicken and olive oil in the pan and use a spatula to break up the chicken as much as possible. Place the pan in your air fryer for 4 minutes.
3. Remove the pan, break up the chicken more and return to the air fryer for another 4 minutes.
4. Whisk the remaining ingredients in a small bowl.
5. Remove the tray again, break up the chicken, and add all the remaining ingredients to the pan, stirring briefly.
6. Return the pan to the air fryer and cook for 10 minutes. The sauce should be bubbling and the spinach wilted.
7. Serve while hot!

Nutrition Facts Per Serving
Calories 378, Total Fat 21g, Saturated Fat 12g, Total Carbs 9g, Net Carbs 8g, Protein 28g, Sugar 3g, Fiber 1g, Sodium 456mg, Potassium 100g

Creamy Garlic Ground Turkey

Prep time: 10 minutes , Cook time: 15 minutes , Serves 6

Ingredients:
1 ½ pounds ground turkey
2 Tbsp olive oil
1 cup heavy cream
½ cup chicken broth
1 Tbsp garlic powder
½ cup grated parmesan cheese
½ cup chopped sundried tomatoes
2 cups baby spinach
1 tsp Italian seasoning

Instructions
1. Preheat your air fryer to 375 degrees F and prepare a baking tray that will fit inside your air fryer.
2. Place the ground turkey and olive oil in the pan and use a spatula to break up the chicken as much as possible. Place the pan in your air fryer for 4 minutes.
3. Remove the pan, break up the turkey more and return to the air fryer for another 4 minutes.
4. Whisk the remaining ingredients in a small bowl.
5. Remove the tray again, break up the turkey, and add all the remaining ingredients to the pan, stirring briefly.

6. Return the pan to the air fryer and cook for 10 minutes. The sauce should be bubbling and the spinach wilted.
7. Serve while hot!

Nutrition Facts Per Serving
Calories 378, Total Fat 21g, Saturated Fat 12g, Total Carbs 9g, Net Carbs 8g, Protein 28g, Sugar 3g, Fiber 1g, Sodium 456mg, Potassium 100g

Creamy Olive Chicken

Prep time: 10 minutes , Cook time: 15 minutes , Serves 6

Ingredients:
1 ½ pounds chicken breast, thinly sliced
2 Tbsp olive oil
1 cup heavy cream
½ cup chicken broth
1 tsp garlic powder
½ cup grated parmesan cheese
½ cup chopped olives
2 cups baby spinach
1 tsp Italian seasoning

Instructions
1. Preheat your air fryer to 375 degrees F and prepare a baking tray that will fit inside your air fryer.
2. Place the chicken and olive oil in your baking tray and then into your air fryer for 4 minutes.
3. Remove the pan, flip the chicken and return to the air fryer for another 4 minutes.
4. Stir the remaining ingredients in a small bowl.
5. Remove the tray again and add all the remaining ingredients to the pan, stirring briefly.
6. Return the pan to the air fryer and cook for 10 minutes. The sauce should be bubbling and the spinach wilted.
7. Serve while hot!

Nutrition Facts Per Serving
Calories 393, Total Fat 26g, Saturated Fat 12g, Total Carbs 11g, Net Carbs 8g, Protein 28g, Sugar 3g, Fiber 1g, Sodium 456mg, Potassium 100g

Cream Cheese and Spinach Stuffed Chicken

Prep time: 15 minutes , Cook time: 20 minutes , Serves 4

Ingredients:
1 pound chicken breast
1 tsp chili powder
1 tsp Italian seasoning
½ tsp ground black pepper
½ tsp salt
3 cups baby spinach
¼ cup cream cheese
½ cup grated parmesan cheese
1 Tbsp minced garlic
¼ tsp ground black pepper

Instructions
1. Preheat your air fryer to 375 degrees F and prepare your air fryer tray with a piece of foil.
2. In a small bowl, mix together the cream cheese, parmesan, garlic and ¼ tsp black pepper.
3. Slice each chicken breast in half, cutting it almost all the through.
4. Divide the cream cheese mix between the chicken breast, spreading it in the center of each chicken breast.
5. Stuff the baby spinach in the middle of the chicken with the cream cheese and close the chicken again, so it is stuffed with the cream cheese and spinach.
6. Place the stuffed chicken breast on the sheet tray and sprinkle with the chili powder, Italian seasoning, ground black pepper and salt.
7. Place in the air fryer and cook for 20 minutes. The chicken should be golden brown and crisp and have no pink in the center.
8. Serve while hot.

Nutrition Facts Per Serving
Calories 281, Total Fat 16g, Saturated Fat 8g, Total Carbs 3g, Net Carbs 0g, Protein 30g, Sugar 1g, Fiber 0g, Sodium 677mg, Potassium 552g

Cream Cheese and Kale Stuffed Chicken

Prep time: 15 minutes , Cook time: 20 minutes , Serves 4

Ingredients:
1 pound chicken breast
1 tsp chili powder
1 tsp Italian seasoning
½ tsp ground black pepper
½ tsp salt
3 cups chopped kale
¼ cup cream cheese
½ cup grated parmesan cheese
1 Tbsp minced garlic
¼ tsp ground black pepper

Instructions
1. Preheat your air fryer to 375 degrees F and prepare your air fryer tray with a piece of foil.
2. In a small bowl, mix together the cream cheese, parmesan, garlic and ¼ tsp black pepper.
3. Slice each chicken breast in half, cutting it almost all the through.
4. Divide the cream cheese mix between the chicken breast, spreading it in the center of each chicken breast.
5. Stuff the kale in the middle of the chicken with the cream cheese and close the chicken again, so it is stuffed with the cream cheese and kale.
6. Place the stuffed chicken breast on the sheet tray and sprinkle with the chili powder, Italian seasoning, ground black pepper and salt.
7. Place in the air fryer and cook for 20 minutes. The chicken should be golden brown and crisp and have no pink in the center.
8. Serve while hot.

Nutrition Facts Per Serving
Calories 267, Total Fat 16g, Saturated Fat 8g, Total Carbs 4g, Net Carbs 3g, Protein 30g, Sugar 1g, Fiber 1g, Sodium 677mg, Potassium 552g

Cream Cheese and Asparagus Stuffed Chicken

Prep time: 15 minutes , Cook time: 20 minutes , Serves 4

Ingredients:
1 pound chicken breast
1 tsp chili powder
1 tsp Italian seasoning
½ tsp ground black pepper
½ tsp salt
2 cups chopped asparagus
¼ cup cream cheese
½ cup grated parmesan cheese
1 Tbsp minced garlic
¼ tsp ground black pepper

Instructions
1. Preheat your air fryer to 375 degrees F and prepare your air fryer tray with a piece of foil.
2. In a small bowl, mix together the cream cheese, parmesan, garlic and ¼ tsp black pepper.
3. Slice each chicken breast in half, cutting it almost all the through.
4. Divide the cream cheese mix between the chicken breast, spreading it in the center of each chicken breast.
5. Stuff the asparagus in the middle of the chicken with the cream cheese and close the chicken again, so it is stuffed with the cream cheese and spinach.
6. Place the stuffed chicken breast on the sheet tray and sprinkle with the chili powder, Italian seasoning, ground black pepper and salt.
7. Place in the air fryer and cook for 20 minutes. The chicken should be golden brown and crisp and have no pink in the center.
8. Serve while hot.

Nutrition Facts Per Serving
Calories 287, Total Fat 16g, Saturated Fat 8g, Total Carbs 3g, Net Carbs 0g, Protein 30g, Sugar 1g, Fiber 0g, Sodium 679mg, Potassium 550g

Buffalo Fried Chicken

Prep time: 10 minutes , Cook time: 15 minutes , Serves 4

Ingredients:
1 pound chicken tenders
½ cup whole milk
¼ cup whey protein powder
½ cup grated parmesan
¼ tsp salt
¼ tsp ground black pepper
½ tsp paprika
2 eggs
2 Tbsp olive oil
½ cup keto buffalo sauce

Instructions
1. Preheat your air fryer to 450 degrees F and line the air fryer tray or baking pan with foil.
2. Place the chicken tenders and whole milk in a large bowl. Cover and marinate in the fridge overnight.
3. On a shallow bowl, toss the protein powder, parmesan, salt, pepper and paprika together.
4. Whisk the egg in a separate bowl.
5. Dip the chicken into the egg and then into the protein powder mix. Place the chicken tenders on the prepared sheet tray and, once they are all dipped, drizzle with the olive oil.
6. Bake in the air fryer for 15 minutes or until the tenders are golden brown.
7. Serve with the buffalo sauce on the side as a dip and enjoy hot!

Nutrition Facts Per Serving
Calories 399, Total Fat 19g, Saturated Fat 10g, Total Carbs 4g, Net Carbs 2g, Protein 48g, Sugar 1g, Fiber 2g, Sodium 321mg, Potassium 578g

Chicken Melt Cups

Prep time: 10 minutes , Cook time: 20 minutes , Serves 7

Ingredients:
1 ¼ cup shredded cooked chicken (rotisserie chicken works well
2 eggs
¼ cup sour cream
¼ cup mayonnaise
¾ cup shredded cheddar cheese
¾ cup pepper jack cheese
¼ tsp salt
¼ tsp ground black pepper
1 Tbsp parsley, chopped

Instructions
1. Preheat your air fryer to 325 degrees F and grease a muffin tin or individual muffin cups- whichever option fits in your air fryer better.
2. In a large bowl, combine the chicken, mayonnaise, sour cream, both kinds of grated cheese, parsley, salt and pepper.
3. Scoop the mix into the prepared muffin tin, filling each cup to the top.
4. Bake in the air fryer for 20 minutes or until the tops are golden brown.
5. Place on a slice of keto bread, serve with keto crackers or enjoy plain with a spoon!

Nutrition Facts Per Serving
Calories 199, Total Fat 13g, Saturated Fat 3, Total Carbs 3g, Net Carbs 1g, Protein 12g, Sugar 1g, Fiber 2g, Sodium 336mg, Potassium 202g

Spicy Chicken Melt Cups

Prep time: 10 minutes , Cook time: 20 minutes , Serves 7

Ingredients:
1 ¼ cup shredded cooked chicken (rotisserie chicken works well
2 eggs
¼ cup sour cream
¼ cup mayonnaise
1 tsp cayenne pepper
¾ cup shredded cheddar cheese
¾ cup pepper jack cheese
¼ tsp salt
¼ tsp ground black pepper
1 Tbsp parsley, chopped

Instructions
1. Preheat your air fryer to 325 degrees F and grease a muffin tin or individual muffin cups- whichever option fits in your air fryer better.

2. In a large bowl, combine the chicken, mayonnaise, cayenne pepper, sour cream, both kinds of grated cheese, parsley, salt and pepper.
3. Scoop the mix into the prepared muffin tin, filling each cup to the top.
4. Bake in the air fryer for 20 minutes or until the tops are golden brown.
5. Place on a slice of keto bread, serve with keto crackers or enjoy plain with a spoon!

Nutrition Facts Per Serving
Calories 201, Total Fat 13g, Saturated Fat 3, Total Carbs 3g, Net Carbs 1g, Protein 12g, Sugar 1g, Fiber 2g, Sodium 339mg, Potassium 202g

Jalapeno Chicken Melt Cups

Prep time: 10 minutes , Cook time: 20 minutes , Serves 7

Ingredients:
1 ¼ cup shredded cooked chicken (rotisserie chicken works well
2 eggs
¼ cup sour cream
¼ cup mayonnaise
¾ cup shredded cheddar cheese
¾ cup pepper jack cheese
¼ tsp salt
¼ tsp ground black pepper
1 Tbsp parsley, chopped
½ cup jalapeno slices

Instructions
1. Preheat your air fryer to 325 degrees F and grease a muffin tin or individual muffin cups- whichever option fits in your air fryer better.
2. In a large bowl, combine the chicken, mayonnaise, sour cream, both kinds of grated cheese, parsley, jalapenos, salt and pepper.
3. Scoop the mix into the prepared muffin tin, filling each cup to the top.
4. Bake in the air fryer for 20 minutes or until the tops are golden brown.
5. Place on a slice of keto bread, serve with keto crackers or enjoy plain with a spoon!

Nutrition Facts Per Serving
Calories 212, Total Fat 13g, Saturated Fat 3, Total Carbs 6g, Net Carbs 4g, Protein 12g, Sugar 3g, Fiber 2g, Sodium 343mg, Potassium 207g

Cheddar Chicken Melt Cups

Prep time: 10 minutes , Cook time: 20 minutes , Serves 7

Ingredients:
1 ¼ cup shredded cooked chicken (rotisserie chicken works well
2 eggs
¼ cup sour cream
¼ cup mayonnaise
1 ½ cup shredded cheddar cheese
¼ tsp salt
¼ tsp ground black pepper
1 Tbsp parsley, chopped

Instructions
1. Preheat your air fryer to 325 degrees F and grease a muffin tin or individual muffin cups- whichever option fits in your air fryer better.
2. In a large bowl, combine the chicken, mayonnaise, sour cream, grated cheese, parsley, salt and pepper.
3. Scoop the mix into the prepared muffin tin, filling each cup to the top.
4. Bake in the air fryer for 20 minutes or until the tops are golden brown.
5. Place on a slice of keto bread, serve with keto crackers or enjoy plain with a spoon!

Nutrition Facts Per Serving
Calories 199, Total Fat 13g, Saturated Fat 3, Total Carbs 3g, Net Carbs 1g, Protein 12g, Sugar 1g, Fiber 2g, Sodium 336mg, Potassium 202g

BBQ Chicken Melt Cups

Prep time: 10 minutes , Cook time: 20 minutes , Serves 7

Ingredients:
- 1 ¼ cup shredded cooked chicken (rotisserie chicken works well
- 2 eggs
- ¼ cup sour cream
- ¼ cup mayonnaise
- 2 Tbsp Keto BBQ sauce
- ¾ cup shredded cheddar cheese
- ¾ cup pepper jack cheese
- ¼ tsp salt
- ¼ tsp ground black pepper
- 1 Tbsp parsley, chopped

Instructions
1. Preheat your air fryer to 325 degrees F and grease a muffin tin or individual muffin cups- whichever option fits in your air fryer better.
2. In a large bowl, combine the chicken, mayonnaise, sour cream, keto BBQ sauce, both kinds of grated cheese, parsley, salt and pepper.
3. Scoop the mix into the prepared muffin tin, filling each cup to the top.
4. Bake in the air fryer for 20 minutes or until the tops are golden brown.
5. Place on a slice of keto bread, serve with keto crackers or enjoy plain with a spoon!

Nutrition Facts Per Serving
Calories 219, Total Fat 14g, Saturated Fat 3, Total Carbs 5g, Net Carbs 3g, Protein 12g, Sugar 3g, Fiber 2g, Sodium 336mg, Potassium 202g

Teriyaki Chicken Melt Cups

Prep time: 10 minutes , Cook time: 20 minutes , Serves 7

Ingredients:
- 1 ¼ cup shredded cooked chicken (rotisserie chicken works well
- 2 eggs
- ¼ cup sour cream
- ¼ cup mayonnaise
- 2 Tbsp keto teriyaki sauce
- ¾ cup shredded cheddar cheese
- ¾ cup pepper jack cheese
- ¼ tsp salt
- ¼ tsp ground black pepper
- 1 Tbsp parsley, chopped

Instructions
1. Preheat your air fryer to 325 degrees F and grease a muffin tin or individual muffin cups- whichever option fits in your air fryer better.
2. In a large bowl, combine the chicken, mayonnaise, sour cream, both kinds of grated cheese, parsley, teriyaki sauce, salt and pepper.
3. Scoop the mix into the prepared muffin tin, filling each cup to the top.
4. Bake in the air fryer for 20 minutes or until the tops are golden brown.
5. Place on a slice of keto bread, serve with keto crackers or enjoy plain with a spoon!

Nutrition Facts Per Serving
Calories 216, Total Fat 14g, Saturated Fat 3, Total Carbs 6g, Net Carbs 4g, Protein 12g, Sugar 2g, Fiber 2g, Sodium 349mg, Potassium 211g

Buffalo Chicken Melt Cups

Prep time: 10 minutes , Cook time: 20 minutes , Serves 7

Ingredients:
- 1 ¼ cup shredded cooked chicken (rotisserie chicken works well
- 2 eggs
- ¼ cup sour cream
- ¼ cup mayonnaise
- 2 Tbsp Keto buffalo sauce
- ¾ cup shredded cheddar cheese
- ¾ cup pepper jack cheese
- ¼ tsp salt
- ¼ tsp ground black pepper
- 1 Tbsp parsley, chopped

Instructions
1. Preheat your air fryer to 325 degrees F and grease a muffin tin or individual muffin cups- whichever option fits in your air fryer better.

2. In a large bowl, combine the chicken, mayonnaise, sour cream, both kinds of grated cheese, parsley, buffalo sauce, salt, and pepper.
3. Scoop the mix into the prepared muffin tin, filling each cup to the top.
4. Bake in the air fryer for 20 minutes or until the tops are golden brown.
5. Place on a slice of keto bread, serve with keto crackers or enjoy plain with a spoon!

Nutrition Facts Per Serving
Calories 219, Total Fat 14g, Saturated Fat 3, Total Carbs 7g, Net Carbs 5g, Protein 12g, Sugar 3g, Fiber 2g, Sodium 347mg, Potassium 202g

Chicken Patties

Prep time: 30 minutes , Cook time: 60 minutes , Serves 8

Ingredients:
10 shredded, cooked chicken
4 oz pork rinds, crushed
1 cup mozzarella cheese, grated
1 Tbsp keto mayonnaise
2 eggs
½ tsp smoked paprika
3 Tbsp water
2 Tbsp olive oil

Instructions
1. Preheat your air fryer to 375 degrees F and line your air fryer tray with foil or parchment.
2. Place all the ingredients except for the olive oil, in a large bowl and blend together well using your hands.
3. Cover the bowl and refrigerate for an hour to let the flavors soak together.
4. Remove the bowl from the fridge and use your hands to form the tuna cakes, making each patty about one inch thick.
5. Place the cakes on the prepared sheet tray and drizzle with the olive oil.
6. Cook the cakes in the air fryer for about 7 minutes or until golden browned.
7. Remove from the air fryer and serve while hot.

Nutrition Facts Per Serving
Calories 343, Total Fat 27g, Saturated Fat 8g, Total Carbs 1g, Net Carbs 1g, Protein 30g, Sugar 1g, Fiber 0g, Sodium 301mg, Potassium 194g

BBQ Chicken Patties

Prep time: 30 minutes , Cook time: 60 minutes , Serves 8

Ingredients:
10 oz shredded rotisserie chicken
4 oz pork rinds, crushed
½ cup mozzarella cheese, grated
½ cup keto BBQ sauce
2 eggs
½ tsp smoked paprika
3 Tbsp water
2 Tbsp olive oil

Instructions
1. Preheat your air fryer to 375 degrees F and line your air fryer tray with foil or parchment.
2. Place all the ingredients except for the olive oil, in a large bowl and blend together well using your hands.
3. Cover the bowl and refrigerate for an hour to let the flavors soak together.
4. Remove the bowl from the fridge and use your hands to form the tuna cakes, making each patty about one inch thick.
5. Place the cakes on the prepared sheet tray and drizzle with the olive oil.
6. Cook the cakes in the air fryer for about 7 minutes or until golden browned.
7. Remove from the air fryer and serve while hot.

Nutrition Facts Per Serving
Calories 367, Total Fat 30g, Saturated Fat 8g, Total Carbs 6g, Net Carbs 4g, Protein 30g, Sugar 2g, Fiber 2g, Sodium 378mg, Potassium 213g

Lemon Pepper Chicken Patties

Prep time: 30 minutes , Cook time: 60 minutes , Serves 8

Ingredients:
- 10 shredded, cooked chicken
- 4 oz pork rinds, crushed
- 1 cup mozzarella cheese, grated
- 1 Tbsp keto mayonnaise
- 2 eggs
- ½ tsp ground black pepper
- 1 Tbsp lemon zest
- 3 Tbsp water
- 2 Tbsp olive oil

Instructions
1. Preheat your air fryer to 375 degrees F and line your air fryer tray with foil or parchment.
2. Place all the ingredients except for the olive oil, in a large bowl and blend together well using your hands.
3. Cover the bowl and refrigerate for an hour to let the flavors soak together.
4. Remove the bowl from the fridge and use your hands to form the tuna cakes, making each patty about one inch thick.
5. Place the cakes on the prepared sheet tray and drizzle with the olive oil.
6. Cook the cakes in the air fryer for about 7 minutes or until golden browned.
7. Remove from the air fryer and serve while hot.

Nutrition Facts Per Serving
Calories 341, Total Fat 29g, Saturated Fat 9g, Total Carbs 1g, Net Carbs 1g, Protein 30g, Sugar 1g, Fiber 0g, Sodium 301mg, Potassium 194g

Garlic Chicken Patties

Prep time: 30 minutes , Cook time: 60 minutes , Serves 8

Ingredients:
- 10 shredded, cooked chicken
- 4 oz pork rinds, crushed
- 1 cup mozzarella cheese, grated
- 1 Tbsp keto mayonnaise
- 2 eggs
- 1 tsp garlic powder
- 1 Tbsp minced garlic
- 3 Tbsp water
- 2 Tbsp olive oil

Instructions
1. Preheat your air fryer to 375 degrees F and line your air fryer tray with foil or parchment.
2. Place all the ingredients except for the olive oil, in a large bowl and blend together well using your hands.
3. Cover the bowl and refrigerate for an hour to let the flavors soak together.
4. Remove the bowl from the fridge and use your hands to form the tuna cakes, making each patty about one inch thick.
5. Place the cakes on the prepared sheet tray and drizzle with the olive oil.
6. Cook the cakes in the air fryer for about 7 minutes or until golden browned.
7. Remove from the air fryer and serve while hot.

Nutrition Facts Per Serving
Calories 352, Total Fat 28g, Saturated Fat 8g, Total Carbs 2g, Net Carbs 2g, Protein 30g, Sugar 2g, Fiber 0g, Sodium 316mg, Potassium 202g

Prosciutto Wrapped Chicken

Prep time: 5 minutes , Cook time: 15 minutes , Serves 2

Ingredients:
- 1 pound chicken breast
- ¼ tsp salt
- ¼ tsp ground black pepper
- 2 oz prosciutto de parma, very thinly sliced
- 2 Tbsp olive oil
- 1 tsp minced garlic
- 4 cups baby spinach
- 2 tsp lemon juice

Instructions
1. Preheat your air fryer to 325 degrees F and line your air fryer tray with foil.
2. Dry the chicken by patting with a paper towel then cut into strips and sprinkle with salt and pepper.
3. Wrap the chicken breast in the prosciutto, enclosing them as fully as possible.

4. Place the wrapped chicken breast on the prepared tray.
5. Toss the spinach with the olive oil, garlic and lemon juice and place on the tray as well, around the wrapped chicken.
6. Place in the air fryer and bake for 12 minutes. The spinach should be nicely wilted and the chicken 145 degrees F internally.
7. Serve hot!

Nutrition Facts Per Serving
Calories 437, Total Fat 17g, Saturated Fat 3g, Total Carbs 11g, Net Carbs 9g, Protein 41g, Sugar 3g, Fiber 2g, Sodium 482mg, Potassium 582g

Pepper and Prosciutto Chicken

Prep time: 5 minutes , Cook time: 15 minutes , Serves 2

Ingredients:
1 pound chicken breast
¼ tsp salt
½ tsp ground black pepper
2 oz prosciutto de parma, very thinly sliced
2 Tbsp olive oil
1 tsp minced garlic
4 cups baby spinach
2 tsp lemon juice

Instructions
1. Preheat your air fryer to 325 degrees F and line your air fryer tray with foil.
2. Dry the chicken by patting with a paper towel then cut into strips and sprinkle with salt and pepper.
3. Wrap the chicken breast in the prosciutto, enclosing them as fully as possible.
4. Place the wrapped chicken breast on the prepared tray.
5. Toss the spinach with the olive oil, garlic and lemon juice and place on the tray as well, around the wrapped chicken.
6. Place in the air fryer and bake for 12 minutes. The spinach should be nicely wilted and the fish 145 degrees F internally.
7. Serve hot!

Nutrition Facts Per Serving
Calories 437, Total Fat 17g, Saturated Fat 3g, Total Carbs 11g, Net Carbs 9g, Protein 41g, Sugar 3g, Fiber 2g, Sodium 482mg, Potassium 582g

Roasted Chicken Thighs

Prep time: 20 minutes , Cook time: 30 minutes , Serves 6

Ingredients:
2 pounds chicken thighs, bone in, skin on
½ tsp salt
½ tsp ground black pepper
3 carrots, chopped
2 celery stalks, chopped
1 Tbsp minced garlic
3 Tbsp butter, melted
½ cup white onion, chopped
1 tsp dried thyme
½ tsp dried rosemary

Instructions
1. Preheat your air fryer to 425 degrees F and prepare your air fryer tray with a piece of foil.
2. Rub the chicken thighs with the salt and pepper, wrap and let sit overnight to season.
3. Place the onion, carrot, celery and garlic on the prepared foil lined tray.
4. Place the chicken thighs on top of the veggies.
5. Brush the chicken with the melted butter and sprinkle with the thyme and rosemary.
6. Bake in the air fryer for 20 minutes or until the chicken thighs are browned and the veggies are beginning to brown as well.
7. Serve hot.

Nutrition Facts Per Serving
Calories 243, Total Fat 12g, Saturated Fat 5g, Total Carbs 4g, Net Carbs 3g, Protein 30g, Sugar 2g, Fiber 1g, Sodium 350mg, Potassium 104g

Dijon Roasted Chicken Thighs

Prep time: 20 minutes , Cook time: 30 minutes , Serves 6

Ingredients:
- 2 pounds chicken thighs, bone in, skin on
- ½ tsp salt
- ½ tsp ground black pepper
- ¼ cup Dijon mustard
- 3 carrots, chopped
- 2 celery stalks, chopped
- 1 Tbsp minced garlic
- 3 Tbsp butter, melted
- ½ cup white onion, chopped
- 1 tsp dried thyme
- ½ tsp dried rosemary

Instructions
1. Preheat your air fryer to 425 degrees F and prepare your air fryer tray with a piece of foil.
2. Rub the chicken thighs with the salt, pepper and Dijon mustard, wrap and let sit overnight to season.
3. Place the onion, carrot, celery and garlic on the prepared foil lined tray.
4. Place the chicken thighs on top of the veggies.
5. Brush the chicken with the melted butter and sprinkle with the thyme and rosemary.
6. Bake in the air fryer for 20 minutes or until the chicken thighs are browned and the veggies are beginning to brown as well.
7. Serve hot.

Nutrition Facts Per Serving
Calories 256, Total Fat 13g, Saturated Fat 5g, Total Carbs 5g, Net Carbs 4g, Protein 30g, Sugar 3g, Fiber 1g, Sodium 350mg, Potassium 104g

Cajun Roasted Chicken Thighs

Prep time: 20 minutes , Cook time: 30 minutes , Serves 6

Ingredients:
- 2 pounds chicken thighs, bone in, skin on
- ½ tsp salt
- 1 tsp Cajun seasoning
- 3 carrots, chopped
- 2 celery stalks, chopped
- 1 Tbsp minced garlic
- 3 Tbsp butter, melted
- ½ cup white onion, chopped
- 1 tsp dried thyme
- ½ tsp dried rosemary

Instructions
1. Preheat your air fryer to 425 degrees F and prepare your air fryer tray with a piece of foil.
2. Rub the chicken thighs with the salt and Cajun seasoning, wrap and let sit overnight to season.
3. Place the onion, carrot, celery and garlic on the prepared foil lined tray.
4. Place the chicken thighs on top of the veggies.
5. Brush the chicken with the melted butter and sprinkle with the thyme and rosemary.
6. Bake in the air fryer for 20 minutes or until the chicken thighs are browned and the veggies are beginning to brown as well.
7. Serve hot.

Nutrition Facts Per Serving
Calories 245, Total Fat 12g, Saturated Fat 5g, Total Carbs 4g, Net Carbs 3g, Protein 30g, Sugar 2g, Fiber 1g, Sodium 353mg, Potassium 104g

Lemon Roasted Chicken Thighs

Prep time: 20 minutes , Cook time: 30 minutes , Serves 6

Ingredients:
- 2 pounds chicken thighs, bone in, skin on
- ½ tsp salt
- ½ tsp ground black pepper
- 3 carrots, chopped
- 2 celery stalks, chopped
- 1 Tbsp minced garlic
- 3 Tbsp butter, melted
- ½ cup white onion, chopped
- 1 tsp dried thyme
- ½ tsp dried rosemary
- 1 lemon, sliced thinly

Instructions

1. Preheat your air fryer to 425 degrees F and prepare your air fryer tray with a piece of foil.
2. Rub the chicken thighs with the salt and pepper, wrap and let sit overnight to season.
3. Place the onion, carrot, celery, lemon slices and garlic on the prepared foil lined tray.
4. Place the chicken thighs on top of the veggies.
5. Brush the chicken with the melted butter and sprinkle with the thyme and rosemary.
6. Bake in the air fryer for 20 minutes or until the chicken thighs are browned and the veggies are beginning to brown as well.
7. Serve hot.

Nutrition Facts Per Serving
Calories 252, Total Fat 12g, Saturated Fat 5g, Total Carbs 6g, Net Carbs 4g, Protein 30g, Sugar 2g, Fiber 2g, Sodium 350mg, Potassium 119g

Roasted Chicken Thighs and Brussels

Prep time: 20 minutes , Cook time: 30 minutes , Serves 6

Ingredients:
2 pounds chicken thighs, bone in, skin on
½ tsp salt
½ tsp ground black pepper
3 carrots, chopped
2 celery stalks, chopped
4 cups sliced Brussels sprouts
1 Tbsp minced garlic
3 Tbsp butter, melted
½ cup white onion, chopped
1 tsp dried thyme
½ tsp dried rosemary

Instructions
1. Preheat your air fryer to 425 degrees F and prepare your air fryer tray with a piece of foil.
2. Rub the chicken thighs with the salt and pepper, wrap and let sit overnight to season.
3. Place the onion, carrot, celery, Brussels sprouts and garlic on the prepared foil lined tray.
4. Place the chicken thighs on top of the veggies.
5. Brush the chicken with the melted butter and sprinkle with the thyme and rosemary.
6. Bake in the air fryer for 20 minutes or until the chicken thighs are browned and the veggies are beginning to brown as well.
7. Serve hot.

Nutrition Facts Per Serving
Calories 277, Total Fat 12g, Saturated Fat 5g, Total Carbs 10g, Net Carbs 4g, Protein 30g, Sugar 3g, Fiber 6g, Sodium 386mg, Potassium 104g

Maple Roasted Chicken Thighs

Prep time: 20 minutes , Cook time: 30 minutes , Serves 6

Ingredients:
2 pounds chicken thighs, bone in, skin on
½ tsp salt
½ tsp ground black pepper
1 tsp maple extract
3 carrots, chopped
2 celery stalks, chopped
1 Tbsp minced garlic
3 Tbsp butter, melted
½ cup white onion, chopped
1 tsp dried thyme
½ tsp dried rosemary

Instructions
1. Preheat your air fryer to 425 degrees F and prepare your air fryer tray with a piece of foil.
2. Rub the chicken thighs with the salt, pepper, and maple extract, wrap and let sit overnight to season.
3. Place the onion, carrot, celery and garlic on the prepared foil lined tray.
4. Place the chicken thighs on top of the veggies.
5. Brush the chicken with the melted butter and sprinkle with the thyme and rosemary.
6. Bake in the air fryer for 20 minutes or until the chicken thighs are browned and the veggies are beginning to brown as well.
7. Serve hot.

Nutrition Facts Per Serving
Calories 243, Total Fat 12g, Saturated Fat 5g, Total Carbs 4g, Net Carbs 3g, Protein 30g, Sugar 2g, Fiber 1g, Sodium 350mg, Potassium 104g

Prosciutto and Lemon Chicken

Prep time: 5 minutes , Cook time: 15 minutes , Serves 2

Ingredients:
1 pound chicken breast
¼ tsp salt
¼ tsp ground black pepper
2 oz prosciutto de parma, very thinly sliced
½ lemon sliced thinly
2 Tbsp olive oil
1 tsp minced garlic
4 cups baby spinach
2 tsp lemon juice

Instructions
1. Preheat your air fryer to 325 degrees F and line your air fryer tray with foil.
2. Dry the chicken by patting with a paper towel then cut into strips and sprinkle with salt and pepper.
3. Wrap the chicken breast in the prosciutto, enclosing them as fully as possible.
4. Place the wrapped chicken breast on the prepared tray and place the lemon slices on top of each wrap.
5. Toss the spinach with the olive oil, garlic and lemon juice and place on the tray as well, around the wrapped chicken.
6. Place in the air fryer and bake for 12 minutes. The spinach should be nicely wilted and the fish 145 degrees F internally.
7. Serve hot!

Nutrition Facts Per Serving
Calories 449, Total Fat 17g, Saturated Fat 3g, Total Carbs 14g, Net Carbs 12g, Protein 41g, Sugar 4g, Fiber 2g, Sodium 482mg, Potassium 582g

Blackened Chicken Patties

Prep time: 30 minutes , Cook time: 60 minutes , Serves 8

Ingredients:
10 shredded, cooked chicken
4 oz pork rinds, crushed
1 cup mozzarella cheese, grated
1 Tbsp keto mayonnaise
2 eggs
½ tsp smoked paprika
1 Tbsp activated charcoal
3 Tbsp water
2 Tbsp olive oil

Instructions
1. Preheat your air fryer to 375 degrees F and line your air fryer tray with foil or parchment.
2. Place all the ingredients except for the olive oil, in a large bowl and blend together well using your hands.
3. Cover the bowl and refrigerate for an hour to let the flavors soak together.
4. Remove the bowl from the fridge and use your hands to form the tuna cakes, making each patty about one inch thick.
5. Place the cakes on the prepared sheet tray and drizzle with the olive oil.
6. Cook the cakes in the air fryer for about 7 minutes or until golden browned.
7. Remove from the air fryer and serve while hot.

Nutrition Facts Per Serving
Calories 345, Total Fat 28g, Saturated Fat 8g, Total Carbs 1g, Net Carbs 1g, Protein 30g, Sugar 1g, Fiber 0g, Sodium 301mg, Potassium 194g

Garlic Chicken Bacon Bake

Prep time: 10 minutes , Cook time: 10 minutes , Serves 4

Ingredients:
¼ cup butter
2 Tbsp minced garlic
1 pound cooked, shredded chicken
¼ tsp ground black pepper
½ cup cooked, chopped bacon
1/3 cup heavy cream
¼ cup parmesan cheese

Instructions
1. Preheat your air fryer to 400 degrees F and grease an 8x8 inch baking pan.

2. Add the butter and chicken to the pan and place in the air fryer for 3 minutes. Remove the pan from the air fryer.
3. Add the remaining ingredients to the pan and return to the air fryer to cook for another 5 minutes. The mix should be bubbling.
4. Serve with zucchini noodles or enjoy plain.

Nutrition Facts Per Serving
Calories 302, Total Fat 21g, Saturated Fat 13g, Total Carbs 3g, Net Carbs 3g, Protein 31g, Sugar 0g, Fiber 0g, Sodium 924mg, Potassium 24g

Garlic Chicken Bake

Prep time: 10 minutes , Cook time: 10 minutes , Serves 4

Ingredients:
¼ cup butter
2 Tbsp minced garlic
1 pound cooked, shredded chicken
¼ tsp ground black pepper
1/3 cup heavy cream
¼ cup parmesan cheese

Instructions
1. Preheat your air fryer to 400 degrees F and grease an 8x8 inch baking pan.
2. Add the butter and chicken to the pan and place in the air fryer for 3 minutes. Remove the pan from the air fryer.
3. Add the remaining ingredients to the pan and return to the air fryer to cook for another 5 minutes. The mix should be bubbling.
4. Serve with zucchini noodles or enjoy plain.

Nutrition Facts Per Serving
Calories 273, Total Fat 16g, Saturated Fat 9g, Total Carbs 3g, Net Carbs 3g, Protein 25g, Sugar 0g, Fiber 0g, Sodium 432mg, Potassium 24g

Spicy Chicken Bacon Bake

Prep time: 10 minutes , Cook time: 10 minutes , Serves 4

Ingredients:
¼ cup butter
2 Tbsp minced garlic
1 pound cooked, shredded chicken
1 tsp cayenne seasoning
½ cup cooked, chopped bacon
1/3 cup heavy cream
¼ cup parmesan cheese

Instructions
1. Preheat your air fryer to 400 degrees F and grease an 8x8 inch baking pan.
2. Add the butter and chicken to the pan and place in the air fryer for 3 minutes. Remove the pan from the air fryer.
3. Add the remaining ingredients to the pan and return to the air fryer to cook for another 5 minutes. The mix should be bubbling.
4. Serve with zucchini noodles or enjoy plain.

Nutrition Facts Per Serving
Calories 301, Total Fat 21g, Saturated Fat 13g, Total Carbs 3g, Net Carbs 3g, Protein 31g, Sugar 0g, Fiber 0g, Sodium 929mg, Potassium 24g

Chicken Zucchini Boats

Prep time: 20 minutes , Cook time: 20 minutes , Serves 6

Ingredients:
3 zucchini, sliced in half, seeds scooped out
1 tsp salt
½ tsp ground black pepper
1 tsp olive oil
2 tsp smoked paprika
1 cup chopped mushrooms
1 cup cooked, shredded chicken (rotisserie chicken works well!)
1 cup shredded cheddar cheese
3 Tbsp sour cream
2 Tbsp chopped chives

Instructions
1. Preheat your air fryer to 375 degrees F and line the air fryer tray or baking pan with foil.
2. Place the zucchini skins on the prepared tray and sprinkle with the salt. Let sit for 30 minutes then pat the skins dry to remove the water which the salt has extracted.

3. Spread the mushrooms inside the zucchini boats, dividing the filling evenly.
4. Sprinkle the zucchini with the black pepper, paprika and olive oil.
5. Bake for 10 minutes to soften.
6. Remove from the air fryer and top with the shredded chicken and cheese. Return to the air fryer for another 10 minutes or until the cheese is bubbly.
7. Remove from the air fryer and top with the sour cream and chives. Serve hot

Nutrition Facts Per Serving
Calories 187, Total Fat 18g, Saturated Fat 9g, Total Carbs 7g, Net Carbs 3g, Protein 12g, Sugar 3g, Fiber 4g, Sodium 515mg, Potassium 219g

Chicken Stuffed Mushrooms

Prep time: 20 minutes , Cook time: 50 minutes , Serves 5

Ingredients:
1 pound cremini mushrooms, stems and gills removed
¾ pound cooked, shredded chicken
¾ cup cream cheese, softened
1/3 cup grated cheddar cheese
¼ cup sour cream
1 Tbsp minced garlic
1 Tbsp mustard
½ tsp salt
¼ tsp ground black pepper
½ cup grated parmesan

Instructions
1. Preheat your air fryer to 375 degrees F and line your air fryer tray with foil or parchment.
2. Place the mushroom caps on the tray and bake for 10 minutes in the air fryer. Remove from the air fryer and drain any excess water from the tray.
3. In a large mixing bowl, combine all the remaining ingredients except the parmesan cheese. Stir well to fully blend everything.
4. Stuff the mushroom caps with the crab mix and then sprinkle the parmesan over the top of the mushrooms.
5. Return the tray to the air fryer and bake for another 10 minutes or until the tops of the mushrooms are golden brown.
6. Remove from the air fryer and enjoy while hot.

Nutrition Facts Per Serving
Calories 320, Total Fat 18g, Saturated Fat 6g, Total Carbs 8g, Net Carbs 6g, Protein 24g, Sugar 1g, Fiber 2g, Sodium 487mg, Potassium 211g

Bacon Chicken Stuffed Mushrooms

Prep time: 20 minutes , Cook time: 50 minutes , Serves 5

Ingredients:
1 pound cremini mushrooms, stems and gills removed
¾ pound cooked, shredded chicken
½ cup cooked, crumbled bacon
¾ cup cream cheese, softened
1/3 cup grated cheddar cheese
¼ cup sour cream
1 Tbsp minced garlic
1 Tbsp mustard
½ tsp salt
¼ tsp ground black pepper
½ cup grated parmesan

Instructions
1. Preheat your air fryer to 375 degrees F and line your air fryer tray with foil or parchment.
2. Place the mushroom caps on the tray and bake for 10 minutes in the air fryer. Remove from the air fryer and drain any excess water from the tray.
3. In a large mixing bowl, combine all the remaining ingredients except the parmesan cheese. Stir well to fully blend everything.
4. Stuff the mushroom caps with the crab mix and then sprinkle the parmesan over the top of the mushrooms.
5. Return the tray to the air fryer and bake for another 10 minutes or until the tops of the mushrooms are golden brown.
6. Remove from the air fryer and enjoy while hot.

Nutrition Facts Per Serving
Calories 411, Total Fat 32g, Saturated Fat 16g, Total Carbs 10g, Net Carbs 6g, Protein 32g, Sugar 1g, Fiber 4g, Sodium 863mg, Potassium 254g

Turkey Stuffed Mushrooms

Prep time: 20 minutes , Cook time: 50 minutes , Serves 5

Ingredients:
1 pound cremini mushrooms, stems and gills removed
¾ pound cooked ground turkey
¾ cup cream cheese, softened
1/3 cup grated cheddar cheese
¼ cup sour cream
1 Tbsp minced garlic
1 Tbsp mustard
½ tsp salt
¼ tsp ground black pepper
½ cup grated parmesan

Instructions
1. Preheat your air fryer to 375 degrees F and line your air fryer tray with foil or parchment.
2. Place the mushroom caps on the tray and bake for 10 minutes in the air fryer. Remove from the air fryer and drain any excess water from the tray.
3. In a large mixing bowl, combine all the remaining ingredients except the parmesan cheese. Stir well to fully blend everything.
4. Stuff the mushroom caps with the crab mix and then sprinkle the parmesan over the top of the mushrooms.
5. Return the tray to the air fryer and bake for another 10 minutes or until the tops of the mushrooms are golden brown.
6. Remove from the air fryer and enjoy while hot.

Nutrition Facts Per Serving
Calories 324, Total Fat 15g, Saturated Fat 3g, Total Carbs 8g, Net Carbs 4g, Protein 20g, Sugar 1g, Fiber 4g, Sodium 487mg, Potassium 211g

Turkey Garlic Mushrooms

Prep time: 20 minutes , Cook time: 50 minutes , Serves 5

Ingredients:
1 pound cremini mushrooms, stems and gills removed
¾ pound cooked, crumbled turkey
¾ cup cream cheese, softened
1/3 cup grated cheddar cheese
¼ cup sour cream
2 Tbsp minced garlic
1 Tbsp mustard
½ tsp salt
¼ tsp ground black pepper
½ cup grated parmesan

Instructions
1. Preheat your air fryer to 375 degrees F and line your air fryer tray with foil or parchment.
2. Place the mushroom caps on the tray and bake for 10 minutes in the air fryer. Remove from the air fryer and drain any excess water from the tray.
3. In a large mixing bowl, combine all the remaining ingredients except the parmesan cheese. Stir well to fully blend everything.
4. Stuff the mushroom caps with the crab mix and then sprinkle the parmesan over the top of the mushrooms.
5. Return the tray to the air fryer and bake for another 10 minutes or until the tops of the mushrooms are golden brown.
6. Remove from the air fryer and enjoy while hot.

Nutrition Facts Per Serving
Calories 326, Total Fat 15g, Saturated Fat 3g, Total Carbs 8g, Net Carbs 4g, Protein 20g, Sugar 1g, Fiber 4g, Sodium 487mg, Potassium 211g

Mediterranean Chicken

Prep time: 20 minutes , Cook time: 30 minutes , Serves 5

Ingredients:
1 ¾ pound chicken breast, cut thinly
¼ tsp salt
1 tsp smoked paprika
1 tsp ground dried ginger
¼ cup pitted olives
¼ cup sundried tomatoes
¼ cup capers
1 Tbsp fresh chopped dill

1/3 cup keto pesto sauce

Instructions
1. Preheat your air fryer to 400 degrees F and line your air fryer tray with a long piece of parchment paper.
2. Place the chicken breast on the parchment and sprinkle with the salt, paprika, and ginger and rub the spices into the chicken.
3. Top the chicken with the remaining ingredients and then wrap the parchment paper up around the chicken breast, enclosing them completely.
4. Place the tray in the air fryer and bake for 30 minutes.
5. Remove from the air fryer, unwrap the parchment and serve while hot!

Nutrition Facts Per Serving
Calories 267, Total Fat 11g, Saturated Fat 5g, Total Carbs 8g, Net Carbs 3g, Protein 37g, Sugar 2g, Fiber 5g, Sodium 453mg, Potassium 311g

Lemon Parchment Chicken

Prep time: 20 minutes , Cook time: 30 minutes , Serves 5

Ingredients:
1 ¾ pound chicken breast, cut thinly
¼ tsp salt
1 tsp ground black pepper
2 cups baby spinach
1/3 cup keto pesto sauce

Instructions
1. Preheat your air fryer to 400 degrees F and line your air fryer tray with a long piece of parchment paper.
2. Place the chicken breast on the parchment and sprinkle with the salt and pepper and rub the spices into the chicken.
3. Top the chicken with the remaining ingredients and then wrap the parchment paper up around the chicken breast, enclosing them completely.
4. Place the tray in the air fryer and bake for 30 minutes.
5. Remove from the air fryer, unwrap the parchment and serve while hot!

Nutrition Facts Per Serving
Calories 267, Total Fat 11g, Saturated Fat 5g, Total Carbs 8g, Net Carbs 3g, Protein 37g, Sugar 2g, Fiber 5g, Sodium 453mg, Potassium 311g

Maple Walnut Chicken Breast

Prep time: 10 minutes , Cook time: 15 minutes , Serves 4

Ingredients:
½ cup chopped walnuts
1 tsp smoked paprika
½ tsp onion powder
½ tsp garlic powder
3 Tbsp keto maple syrup
1 Tbsp apple cider vinegar
1 tsp coconut aminos
2 Tbsp butter
24 oz chicken breast, sliced thinly

Instructions
1. Preheat your air fryer to 400 degrees F and line the air fryer tray with foil.
2. In a large bowl, combine the walnuts, paprika, onion powder, garlic powder, keto syrup, vinegar and coconut aminos.
3. Place the chicken breast on the prepared tray and spoon the walnut mix over the top of the fish.
4. Place the tray in the fridge and let cool for 2 hours.
5. Remove the tray from the fridge and dot the butter throughout the tray, dispersing it around the salmon.
6. Place in the air fryer and bake for 15 minutes. Serve hot!

Nutrition Facts Per Serving
Calories 408, Total Fat 26g, Saturated Fat 7g, Total Carbs 11g, Net Carbs 9g, Protein 42g, Sugar 8g, Fiber 2g, Sodium 111mg, Potassium 943g

Maple Sesame Chicken Breast

Prep time: 10 minutes , Cook time: 20 minutes , Serves 4

Ingredients:
- 2 Tbsp sesame seeds
- 1 tsp smoked paprika
- ½ tsp onion powder
- ½ tsp garlic powder
- 3 Tbsp keto maple syrup
- 1 Tbsp apple cider vinegar
- 1 tsp coconut aminos
- 2 Tbsp butter
- 24 oz chicken breast, sliced thinly

Instructions
1. Preheat your air fryer to 400 degrees F and line the air fryer tray with foil.
2. In a large bowl, combine the sesame seeds, paprika, onion powder, garlic powder, keto syrup, vinegar and coconut aminos.
3. Place the chicken breast on the prepared tray and spoon the walnut mix over the top of the fish.
4. Place the tray in the fridge and let cool for 2 hours.
5. Remove the tray from the fridge and dot the butter throughout the tray, dispersing it around the salmon.
6. Place in the air fryer and bake for 15 minutes. Serve hot!

Nutrition Facts Per Serving
Calories 454, Total Fat 26g, Saturated Fat 11g, Total Carbs 11g, Net Carbs 9g, Protein 43g, Sugar 8g, Fiber 2g, Sodium 111mg, Potassium 945g

Maple Walnut Chicken Breast with Spinach

Prep time: 10 minutes , Cook time: 15 minutes , Serves 4

Ingredients:
- ½ cup chopped walnuts
- 1 tsp smoked paprika
- ½ tsp onion powder
- ½ tsp garlic powder
- 3 Tbsp keto maple syrup
- 1 Tbsp apple cider vinegar
- 1 tsp coconut aminos
- 2 Tbsp butter
- 24 oz chicken breast, sliced thinly
- 4 cups baby spinach

Instructions
1. Preheat your air fryer to 400 degrees F and line the air fryer tray with foil.
2. In a large bowl, combine the walnuts, paprika, onion powder, garlic powder, keto syrup, vinegar and coconut aminos.
3. Place the chicken breast on the prepared tray and spoon the walnut mix over the top of the fish.
4. Place the tray in the fridge and let cool for 2 hours.
5. Remove the tray from the fridge and dot the butter throughout the tray, dispersing it around the salmon.
6. Arrange the spinach around the salmon as well.
7. Place in the air fryer and bake for 15 minutes. Serve hot!

Nutrition Facts Per Serving
Calories 445, Total Fat 26g, Saturated Fat 7g, Total Carbs 14g, Net Carbs 9g, Protein 42g, Sugar 8g, Fiber 5g, Sodium 121mg, Potassium 932g

Tomato Parchment Chicken

Prep time: 20 minutes , Cook time: 30 minutes , Serves 5

Ingredients:
- 1 ¾ pound chicken breast, cut thinly
- ¼ tsp salt
- ½ tsp ground black pepper
- 1 tsp smoked paprika
- ½ cup fresh chopped tomatoes
- ¼ cup sundried tomatoes
- 1/3 cup keto marinara sauce

Instructions
1. Preheat your air fryer to 400 degrees F and line your air fryer tray with a long piece of parchment paper.
2. Place the chicken breast on the parchment and sprinkle with the salt, paprika, and pepper and rub the spices into the chicken.

3. Top the chicken with the remaining ingredients and then wrap the parchment paper up around the chicken breast, enclosing them completely.
4. Place the tray in the air fryer and bake for 20 minutes.
5. Remove from the air fryer, unwrap the parchment and serve while hot!

Nutrition Facts Per Serving
Calories 327, Total Fat 11g, Saturated Fat 5g, Total Carbs 10g, Net Carbs 4g, Protein 37g, Sugar 4g, Fiber 6g, Sodium 453mg, Potassium 311g

Fajita Chicken

Prep time: 20 minutes , Cook time: 20 minutes , Serves 5

Ingredients:
1 ¾ pound chicken breast, cut thinly into strips
2 tsp fajita seasoning
½ cup sliced green bell peppers
4 Tbsp olive oil

Instructions
1. Preheat your air fryer to 400 degrees F and line your air fryer tray with a long piece of parchment paper.
2. Place the chicken breast on the parchment and sprinkle with the fajita seasoning and rub the spices into the chicken.
3. Add the remaining ingredients and then wrap the parchment paper up around the chicken breast, enclosing them completely.
4. Place the tray in the air fryer and bake for 20 minutes.
5. Remove from the air fryer, unwrap the parchment and serve while hot!

Nutrition Facts Per Serving
Calories 272, Total Fat 11g, Saturated Fat 5g, Total Carbs 8g, Net Carbs 3g, Protein 37g, Sugar 2g, Fiber 5g, Sodium 453mg, Potassium 311g

Sweet and Salty Chicken

Prep time: 10 minutes , Cook time: 15 minutes , Serves 4

Ingredients:
1 pound chicken tenders
½ cup whole milk
¼ cup whey protein powder
½ cup grated parmesan
1 tsp erythritol
¼ tsp salt
¼ tsp ground black pepper
½ tsp paprika
2 eggs
2 Tbsp olive oil

Instructions
1. Preheat your air fryer to 450 degrees F and line the air fryer tray or baking pan with foil.
2. Place the chicken tenders and whole milk in a large bowl. Cover and marinate in the fridge overnight.
3. On a shallow bowl, toss the protein powder, parmesan, salt, erythritol, pepper and paprika together.
4. Whisk the egg in a separate bowl.
5. Dip the chicken into the egg and then into the protein powder mix. Place the chicken tenders on the prepared sheet tray and, once they are all dipped, drizzle with the olive oil.
6. Bake in the air fryer for 15 minutes or until the tenders are golden brown. Enjoy hot!

Nutrition Facts Per Serving
Calories 342, Total Fat 15g, Saturated Fat 7g, Total Carbs 3g, Net Carbs 1g, Protein 48g, Sugar 1g, Fiber 2g, Sodium 321mg, Potassium 578g

Chicken and Egg Salad

Prep time: 5 minutes, Cook time: 16 minutes, Serves 6

Ingredients:
- 6 Tbsp Mayonnaise
- 8 Large Eggs
- 2 Tbsp apple cider vinegar
- 1 tsp ground black pepper
- 1 tsp salt
- 1 cup cooked shredded chicken (rotisserie chicken works great!)

Instructions
1. Preheat your air fryer to 250 degrees F.
2. Place a wire rack in the air fryer and place the eggs on top of the rack.
3. Cook for 16 minutes then remove the eggs and place them directly into an ice water bath to cool and stop the cooking process.
4. Peel the eggs and place in a large bowl.
5. Mash the eggs with a fork.
6. Add in the mayonnaise, cider vinegar, pepper and salt.
7. Stir in the chicken and serve chilled.

Nutrition Facts Per Serving
Calories 245, Total Fat 12g, Saturated Fat 6g, Total Carbs 2g, Net Carbs 1g, Protein 22g, Sugar 0g, Fiber 1g, Sodium 454mg, Potassium 289g

Pesto Fried Chicken

Prep time: 10 minutes, Cook time: 15 minutes, Serves 4

Ingredients:
- 1 pound chicken tenders
- ½ cup whole milk
- ¼ cup whey protein powder
- ½ cup grated parmesan
- 1 tsp garlic powder
- 2 tsp dried basil
- ¼ tsp salt
- ¼ tsp ground black pepper
- ½ tsp paprika
- 2 eggs
- 2 Tbsp olive oil

Instructions
1. Preheat your air fryer to 450 degrees F and line the air fryer tray or baking pan with foil.
2. Place the chicken tenders and whole milk in a large bowl. Cover and marinate in the fridge overnight.
3. On a shallow bowl, toss the protein powder, basil, garlic powder, parmesan, salt, pepper and paprika together.
4. Whisk the egg in a separate bowl.
5. Dip the chicken into the egg and then into the protein powder mix. Place the chicken tenders on the prepared sheet tray and, once they are all dipped, drizzle with the olive oil.
6. Bake in the air fryer for 15 minutes or until the tenders are golden brown. Enjoy hot!

Nutrition Facts Per Serving
Calories 342, Total Fat 15g, Saturated Fat 7g, Total Carbs 3g, Net Carbs 1g, Protein 48g, Sugar 1g, Fiber 2g, Sodium 321mg, Potassium 578g

Vegan and Vegetarian

Egg Salad

Prep time: 5 minutes, Cook time: 16 minutes, Serves 6

Ingredients:
- 6 Tbsp Mayonnaise
- 8 Large Eggs
- 2 Tbsp apple cider vinegar
- 1 tsp ground black pepper
- 1 tsp salt

Instructions
1. Preheat your air fryer to 250 degrees F.
2. Place a wire rack in the air fryer and place the eggs on top of the rack.
3. Cook for 16 minutes then remove the eggs and place them directly into an ice water bath to cool and stop the cooking process.
4. Peel the eggs and place in a large bowl.
5. Mash the eggs with a fork.
6. Add in the mayonnaise, cider vinegar, pepper and salt

Nutrition Facts Per Serving
Calories 189, Total Fat 12g, Saturated Fat 6g, Total Carbs 2g, Net Carbs 1g, Protein 12g, Sugar 0g, Fiber 1g, Sodium 454mg, Potassium 289g

Cream of Asparagus Soup

Prep time: 15 minutes, Cook time: 20 minutes, Serves 4

Ingredients:
- 1 pound chopped asparagus
- 3 Tbsp olive oil
- 1 tsp sea salt
- ¼ tsp ground black pepper
- 2 cups chopped cauliflower
- ½ cup diced onion
- 1 Tbsp dried chopped thyme
- 1 qt chicken broth
- 1 cup heavy cream

Instructions
1. Preheat your air fryer to 400 degrees F and line the air fryer tray or baking pan with foil.
2. Place the asparagus, cauliflower, and onion on the prepared sheet tray.
3. Sprinkle the veggies with the salt, black pepper, thyme and olive oil.
4. Roast in the air fryer for 20 minutes or until the squash is tender.
5. Add the roasted veggies to a blender or food processor and add the chicken broth and heavy cream.
6. Puree until smooth. Serve hot.

Nutrition Facts Per Serving
Calories 152, Total Fat 16g, Saturated Fat 8g, Total Carbs 14g, Net Carbs 9g, Protein 4g, Sugar 3g, Fiber 5g, Sodium 328mg, Potassium 154g

Roasted Mushrooms and Grits

Prep time: 20 minutes, Cook time: 23 minutes, Serves 4

Ingredients:
- ½ pound sliced mushrooms
- 1 Tbsp minced garlic
- 1 Tbsp fresh chopped rosemary
- ½ cup chopped walnuts
- 2 Tbsp olive oil
- 2 cups chopped cauliflower florets
- 1 cup heavy cream
- ½ cup water
- 1 cup shredded cheddar cheese
- 2 Tbsp butter
- 1 tsp salt
- ¼ tsp ground black pepper

Instructions
1. Preheat your air fryer to 400 degrees F and line the air fryer tray or baking pan with foil.
2. Place the mushrooms, garlic, rosemary, olive oil and walnuts on the tray and toss to coat everything in the oil.

3. Place the tray in the air fryer and cook for 15 minutes.
4. While the mushrooms are cooking, place the cauliflower in a blender or food processor and pulse until the cauliflower is like rice.
5. Place the cauliflower in a pot along with the water and cook over medium heat for 5 minutes.
6. Add the heavy cream and cook for another 3 minutes.
7. Stir in the cheese, butter, salt and pepper and mix to melt the cheese.
8. Divide between bowls and top with the roasted mushrooms. Enjoy hot!

Nutrition Facts Per Serving
Calories 455, Total Fat 36g, Saturated Fat 8g, Total Carbs 17g, Net Carbs 11g, Protein 16g, Sugar 4g, Fiber 6g, Sodium 463mg, Potassium 163g

Roasted Pepper Grits

Prep time: 20 minutes , Cook time: 23 minutes , Serves 4

Ingredients:
2 cups green bell pepper slices
1 Tbsp minced garlic
1 Tbsp fresh chopped rosemary
½ cup chopped walnuts
2 Tbsp olive oil
2 cups chopped cauliflower florets
1 cup heavy cream
½ cup water
1 cup shredded cheddar cheese
2 Tbsp butter
1 tsp salt
¼ tsp ground black pepper

Instructions
1. Preheat your air fryer to 400 degrees F and line the air fryer tray or baking pan with foil.
2. Place the green bell pepper, garlic, rosemary, olive oil and walnuts on the tray and toss to coat everything in the oil.
3. Place the tray in the air fryer and cook for 15 minutes.
4. While the peppers are cooking, place the cauliflower in a blender or food processor and pulse until the cauliflower is like rice.
5. Place the cauliflower in a pot along with the water and cook over medium heat for 5 minutes.
6. Add the heavy cream and cook for another 3 minutes.
7. Stir in the cheese, butter, salt and pepper and mix to melt the cheese.
8. Divide between bowls and top with the roasted mushrooms. Enjoy hot!

Nutrition Facts Per Serving
Calories 423, Total Fat 31g, Saturated Fat 7g, Total Carbs 14g, Net Carbs 10g, Protein 13g, Sugar 3g, Fiber 4g, Sodium 463mg, Potassium 163g

Loaded Baked Zucchini

Prep time: 20 minutes , Cook time: 20 minutes , Serves 6

Ingredients:
3 zucchini, sliced in half, seeds scooped out
1 tsp salt
½ tsp ground black pepper
1 tsp olive oil
2 tsp smoked paprika
1 cup shredded cheddar cheese
3 Tbsp sour cream
2 Tbsp chopped chives

Instructions
1. Preheat your air fryer to 375 degrees F and line the air fryer tray or baking pan with foil.
2. Place the zucchini skins on the prepared tray and sprinkle with the salt. Let sit for 30 minutes then pat the skins dry to remove the water which the salt has extracted.
3. Sprinkle the zucchini with the black pepper, paprika and olive oil.
4. Bake for 10 minutes to soften.
5. Remove from the air fryer and top with the cheese. Return to the air fryer for another 10 minutes or until the cheese is bubbly.
6. Remove from the air fryer and top with the sour cream and chives. Serve hot

Nutrition Facts Per Serving
Calories 108, Total Fat 8g, Saturated Fat 4g, Total Carbs 4g, Net Carbs 3g, Protein 6g, Sugar 1g, Fiber 1g, Sodium 485mg, Potassium 189g

Butternut Squash Soup

Prep time: 15 minutes , Cook time: 20 minutes , Serves 4

Ingredients:
4 cups chopped butternut squash
3 Tbsp olive oil
1 tsp sea salt
¼ tsp ground black pepper
2 cups chopped carrots
½ cup diced onion
1 Tbsp dried chopped thyme
1 qt chicken broth
1 cup heavy cream

Instructions
1. Preheat your air fryer to 400 degrees F and line the air fryer tray or baking pan with foil.
2. Place the squash, carrots, and onion on the prepared sheet tray.
3. Sprinkle the veggies with the salt, black pepper, thyme and olive oil.
4. Roast in the air fryer for 20 minutes or until the squash is tender.
5. Add the roasted veggies to a blender or food processor and add the chicken broth and heavy cream.
6. Puree until smooth. Serve hot.

Nutrition Facts Per Serving
Calories 193, Total Fat 22g, Saturated Fat 10g, Total Carbs 12g, Net Carbs 8g, Protein 6g, Sugar 2g, Fiber 2g, Sodium 328mg, Potassium 154g

Spinach and Artichoke Casserole

Prep time: 10 minutes , Cook time: 30 minutes , Serves 12

Ingredients:
16 eggs
¼ cup whole milk
1 can (14 oz) artichokes, drained
10 oz frozen, chopped spinach, thawed, drained
1 cup cheddar cheese, grated
½ cup grated parmesan cheese
½ cup whole milk ricotta
¼ cup chopped white onion
1 tsp minced garlic
1 tsp sea salt
½ tsp dried thyme
½ tsp ground black pepper

Instructions
1. Preheat your air fryer to 350 degrees F and prepare a large baking dish with baking grease (make sure the pan will fit in your air fryer.
2. Whisk the eggs and milk in a large bowl.
3. Add the artichokes and spinach to the egg mix.
4. Add all the remaining ingredients, except the ricotta, and stir well.
5. Pour the egg and veggie mix into the prepared tray.
6. Dollop the ricotta around the pan, dispersing it evenly.
7. Bake in the air fryer for 30 minutes or until the eggs are completely set.

Nutrition Facts Per Serving
Calories 230, Total Fat 16g, Saturated Fat 6g, Total Carbs 4g, Net Carbs 3g, Protein 16g, Sugar 13g, Fiber 1g, Sodium 578mg, Potassium 222g

Spinach Parmesan Egg Casserole

Prep time: 10 minutes , Cook time: 30 minutes , Serves 12

Ingredients:
16 eggs
¼ cup whole milk
20 oz frozen, chopped spinach, thawed, drained
½ cup cheddar cheese, grated
1 cup grated parmesan cheese
½ cup whole milk ricotta
¼ cup chopped white onion
1 tsp minced garlic
1 tsp sea salt
½ tsp dried thyme
½ tsp ground black pepper

Instructions
1. Preheat your air fryer to 350 degrees F and prepare a large baking dish with baking grease (make sure the pan will fit in your air fryer.
2. Whisk the eggs and milk in a large bowl.

3. Add the spinach to the egg mix.
4. Add all the remaining ingredients, except the ricotta, and stir well.
5. Pour the egg and veggie mix into the prepared tray.
6. Dollop the ricotta around the pan, dispersing it evenly.
7. Bake in the air fryer for 30 minutes or until the eggs are completely set.

Nutrition Facts Per Serving
Calories 236, Total Fat 16g, Saturated Fat 6g, Total Carbs 4g, Net Carbs 3g, Protein 16g, Sugar 1g, Fiber 1g, Sodium 578mg, Potassium 222g

Garlic, Spinach and Artichoke Casserole

Prep time: 10 minutes , Cook time: 30 minutes , Serves 12

Ingredients:
16 eggs
¼ cup whole milk
1 can (14 oz) artichokes, drained
10 oz frozen, chopped spinach, thawed, drained
1 cup cheddar cheese, grated
½ cup grated parmesan cheese
½ cup whole milk ricotta
¼ cup chopped white onion
1 Tbsp minced garlic
1 tsp garlic powder
1 tsp sea salt
½ tsp dried thyme
½ tsp ground black pepper

Instructions
1. Preheat your air fryer to 350 degrees F and prepare a large baking dish with baking grease (make sure the pan will fit in your air fryer.
2. Whisk the eggs and milk in a large bowl.
3. Add the artichokes and spinach to the egg mix.
4. Add all the remaining ingredients, except the ricotta, and stir well.
5. Pour the egg and veggie mix into the prepared tray.
6. Dollop the ricotta around the pan, dispersing it evenly.
7. Bake in the air fryer for 30 minutes or until the eggs are completely set.

Nutrition Facts Per Serving
Calories 244, Total Fat 16g, Saturated Fat 6g, Total Carbs 5g, Net Carbs 3g, Protein 16g, Sugar 1g, Fiber 1g, Sodium 578mg, Potassium 222g

Spinach and Sundried Tomato Casserole

Prep time: 10 minutes , Cook time: 30 minutes , Serves 12

Ingredients:
16 eggs
¼ cup whole milk
½ cup chopped sundried tomatoes
10 oz frozen, chopped spinach, thawed, drained
1 cup cheddar cheese, grated
½ cup grated parmesan cheese
½ cup whole milk ricotta
¼ cup chopped white onion
1 tsp minced garlic
1 tsp sea salt
½ tsp dried thyme
½ tsp ground black pepper

Instructions
1. Preheat your air fryer to 350 degrees F and prepare a large baking dish with baking grease (make sure the pan will fit in your air fryer.
2. Whisk the eggs and milk in a large bowl.
3. Add the sundried tomatoes and spinach to the egg mix.
4. Add all the remaining ingredients, except the ricotta, and stir well.
5. Pour the egg and veggie mix into the prepared tray.
6. Dollop the ricotta around the pan, dispersing it evenly.
7. Bake in the air fryer for 30 minutes or until the eggs are completely set.

Nutrition Facts Per Serving
Calories 247, Total Fat 16g, Saturated Fat 6g, Total Carbs 8g, Net Carbs 7 g, Protein 16g, Sugar 1g, Fiber 1g, Sodium 578mg, Potassium 297g

Brussels Sprout Casserole

Prep time: 10 minutes, Cook time: 30 minutes, Serves 12

Ingredients:
- 16 eggs
- ¼ cup whole milk
- 1 pound sliced Brussels Sprouts
- 1 cup cheddar cheese, grated
- ½ cup grated parmesan cheese
- ½ cup whole milk ricotta
- ¼ cup chopped white onion
- 1 tsp minced garlic
- 1 tsp sea salt
- ½ tsp dried thyme
- ½ tsp ground black pepper

Instructions
1. Preheat your air fryer to 350 degrees F and prepare a large baking dish with baking grease (make sure the pan will fit in your air fryer.
2. Whisk the eggs and milk in a large bowl.
3. Add the Brussels to the egg mix.
4. Add all the remaining ingredients, except the ricotta, and stir well.
5. Pour the egg and veggie mix into the prepared tray.
6. Dollop the ricotta around the pan, dispersing it evenly.
7. Bake in the air fryer for 30 minutes or until the eggs are completely set.

Nutrition Facts Per Serving
Calories 246, Total Fat 16g, Saturated Fat 6g, Total Carbs 8g, Net Carbs 3g, Protein 16g, Sugar 3g, Fiber 5g, Sodium 578mg, Potassium 222g

Asparagus and Tomato Casserole

Prep time: 10 minutes, Cook time: 30 minutes, Serves 12

Ingredients:
- 16 eggs
- ¼ cup whole milk
- 1 pound chopped asparagus
- ½ cup sundried tomatoes, chopped
- ½ cup cheddar cheese, grated
- 1 cup grated parmesan cheese
- ½ cup whole milk ricotta
- ¼ cup chopped white onion
- 1 tsp minced garlic
- 1 tsp sea salt
- ½ tsp dried thyme
- ½ tsp ground black pepper

Instructions
1. Preheat your air fryer to 350 degrees F and prepare a large baking dish with baking grease (make sure the pan will fit in your air fryer.
2. Whisk the eggs and milk in a large bowl.
3. Add the asparagus and sundried tomatoes to the egg mix.
4. Add all the remaining ingredients, except the ricotta, and stir well.
5. Pour the egg and veggie mix into the prepared tray.
6. Dollop the ricotta around the pan, dispersing it evenly.
7. Bake in the air fryer for 30 minutes or until the eggs are completely set.

Nutrition Facts Per Serving
Calories 277, Total Fat 16g, Saturated Fat 6g, Total Carbs 9g, Net Carbs 6g, Protein 16g, Sugar 3g, Fiber 3g, Sodium 582mg, Potassium 222g

Asparagus Egg White Casserole

Prep time: 10 minutes, Cook time: 30 minutes, Serves 12

Ingredients:
- 20 egg whites
- ¼ cup whole milk
- 1 pound chopped asparagus
- 1 cup cheddar cheese, grated
- ½ cup grated parmesan cheese
- ½ cup whole milk ricotta
- ¼ cup chopped white onion
- 1 tsp minced garlic
- 1 tsp sea salt
- ½ tsp dried thyme
- ½ tsp ground black pepper

Instructions

1. Preheat your air fryer to 350 degrees F and prepare a large baking dish with baking grease (make sure the pan will fit in your air fryer.
2. Whisk the egg whites and milk in a large bowl.
3. Add the asparagus to the egg mix.
4. Add all the remaining ingredients, except the ricotta, and stir well.
5. Pour the egg and veggie mix into the prepared tray.
6. Dollop the ricotta around the pan, dispersing it evenly.
7. Bake in the air fryer for 30 minutes or until the eggs are completely set.

Nutrition Facts Per Serving
Calories 154, Total Fat 6g, Saturated Fat 1g, Total Carbs 6g, Net Carbs 3g, Protein 16g, Sugar 1g, Fiber 3g, Sodium 458mg, Potassium 124g

Cheesy Egg Casserole

Prep time: 10 minutes , Cook time: 30 minutes , Serves 12

Ingredients:
16 eggs
¼ cup whole milk
1 cup cheddar cheese, grated
½ cup grated parmesan cheese
½ cup whole milk ricotta
¼ cup chopped white onion
1 tsp minced garlic
1 tsp sea salt
½ tsp dried thyme
½ tsp ground black pepper

Instructions
1. Preheat your air fryer to 350 degrees F and prepare a large baking dish with baking grease (make sure the pan will fit in your air fryer.
2. Whisk the eggs and milk in a large bowl.
3. Add all the remaining ingredients, except the ricotta, and stir well.
4. Pour the egg and veggie mix into the prepared tray.
5. Dollop the ricotta around the pan, dispersing it evenly.
6. Bake in the air fryer for 30 minutes or until the eggs are completely set.

Nutrition Facts Per Serving
Calories 187, Total Fat 16g, Saturated Fat 6g, Total Carbs 2g, Net Carbs 1g, Protein 16g, Sugar 0g, Fiber 1g, Sodium 533mg, Potassium 78g

Broccoli Cheese Soup

Prep time: 15 minutes , Cook time: 20 minutes , Serves 4

Ingredients:
6 cups chopped broccoli
3 Tbsp olive oil
1 tsp sea salt
¼ tsp ground black pepper
½ cup diced onion
2 Tbsp minced garlic
1 Tbsp dried chopped thyme
1 qt chicken broth
½ cup heavy cream
1 cup grated cheddar cheese

Instructions
1. Preheat your air fryer to 400 degrees F and line the air fryer tray or baking pan with foil.
2. Place the broccoli, garlic, and onion on the prepared sheet tray.
3. Sprinkle the veggies with the salt, black pepper, thyme and olive oil.
4. Roast in the air fryer for 20 minutes or until the broccoli is tender.
5. Add the roasted veggies to a blender or food processor and add the chicken broth, cheese and heavy cream.
6. Puree until smooth. Serve hot.

Nutrition Facts Per Serving
Calories 346, Total Fat 16g, Saturated Fat 7g, Total Carbs 9g, Net Carbs 3g, Protein 4g, Sugar 2g, Fiber 6g, Sodium 345mg, Potassium 178g

Pepper Stuffed Mushrooms

Prep time: 20 minutes , Cook time: 50 minutes , Serves 5

Ingredients:
1 pound cremini mushrooms, stems and gills removed
1 cup minced bell pepper
¾ cup cream cheese, softened
1/3 cup grated cheddar cheese
¼ cup sour cream
2 Tbsp minced garlic
1 Tbsp mustard
½ tsp salt
¼ tsp ground black pepper
½ cup grated parmesan

Instructions
1. Preheat your air fryer to 375 degrees F and line your air fryer tray with foil or parchment.
2. Place the mushroom caps on the tray and bake for 10 minutes in the air fryer. Remove from the air fryer and drain any excess water from the tray.
3. In a large mixing bowl, combine all the remaining ingredients except the parmesan cheese. Stir well to fully blend everything.
4. Stuff the mushroom caps with the crab mix and then sprinkle the parmesan over the top of the mushrooms.
5. Return the tray to the air fryer and bake for another 10 minutes or until the tops of the mushrooms are golden brown.
6. Remove from the air fryer and enjoy while hot.

Nutrition Facts Per Serving
Calories 276, Total Fat 10g, Saturated Fat 1g, Total Carbs 8g, Net Carbs 4g, Protein 11g, Sugar 1g, Fiber 4g, Sodium 487mg, Potassium 211g

Spinach Stuffed Mushrooms

Prep time: 20 minutes , Cook time: 50 minutes , Serves 5

Ingredients:
1 pound cremini mushrooms, stems and gills removed
3 cups baby spinach, wilted
¾ cup cream cheese, softened
1/3 cup grated cheddar cheese
¼ cup sour cream
2 Tbsp minced garlic
1 Tbsp mustard
½ tsp salt
¼ tsp ground black pepper
½ cup grated parmesan

Instructions
1. Preheat your air fryer to 375 degrees F and line your air fryer tray with foil or parchment.
2. Place the mushroom caps on the tray and bake for 10 minutes in the air fryer. Remove from the air fryer and drain any excess water from the tray.
3. In a large mixing bowl, combine all the remaining ingredients except the parmesan cheese. Stir well to fully blend everything.
4. Stuff the mushroom caps with the crab mix and then sprinkle the parmesan over the top of the mushrooms.
5. Return the tray to the air fryer and bake for another 10 minutes or until the tops of the mushrooms are golden brown.
6. Remove from the air fryer and enjoy while hot.

Nutrition Facts Per Serving
Calories 289, Total Fat 10g, Saturated Fat 2g, Total Carbs 6g, Net Carbs 3g, Protein 11g, Sugar 1g, Fiber 3g, Sodium 487mg, Potassium 211g

Cauliflower Soup

Prep time: 15 minutes , Cook time: 20 minutes , Serves 4

Ingredients:
6 cups chopped cauliflower
3 Tbsp olive oil
1 tsp sea salt
¼ tsp ground black pepper
2 Tbsp minced garlic
½ cup diced onion
1 Tbsp dried chopped thyme
1 qt vegetable broth

1 cup heavy cream

Instructions
1. Preheat your air fryer to 400 degrees F and line the air fryer tray or baking pan with foil.
2. Place the cauliflower, garlic and onion on the prepared sheet tray.
3. Sprinkle the veggies with the salt, black pepper, thyme and olive oil.
4. Roast in the air fryer for 20 minutes or until the cauliflower is tender.
5. Add the roasted veggies to a blender or food processor and add the veggie broth and heavy cream.
6. Puree until smooth. Serve hot.

Nutrition Facts Per Serving
Calories 211, Total Fat 15g, Saturated Fat 10g, Total Carbs 10g, Net Carbs 4g, Protein 3g, Sugar 1g, Fiber 6g, Sodium 128mg, Potassium 432g

Roasted Veggie Soup

Prep time: 15 minutes , Cook time: 20 minutes , Serves 4

Ingredients:
2 cups chopped cauliflower
2 cups chopped broccoli
1 cup green bell pepper
1 cup chopped carrot
3 Tbsp olive oil
1 tsp sea salt
¼ tsp ground black pepper
2 Tbsp minced garlic
½ cup diced onion
1 Tbsp dried chopped thyme
1 qt vegetable broth
1 cup heavy cream

Instructions
1. Preheat your air fryer to 400 degrees F and line the air fryer tray or baking pan with foil.
2. Place the cauliflower, broccoli, bell pepper, carrots, garlic and onion on the prepared sheet tray.
3. Sprinkle the veggies with the salt, black pepper, thyme and olive oil.
4. Roast in the air fryer for 20 minutes or until the cauliflower is tender.
5. Add the roasted veggies to a blender or food processor and add the veggie broth and heavy cream.
6. Puree until smooth. Serve hot.

Nutrition Facts Per Serving
Calories 209, Total Fat 8g, Saturated Fat 4g, Total Carbs 9g, Net Carbs 2g, Protein 4g, Sugar 3g, Fiber 7g, Sodium 127mg, Potassium 272g

Loaded Veggie Pizza

Prep time: 20 minutes , Cook time: 20 minutes , Serves 3

Ingredients:
1 cup almond flour
1 egg
3 Tbsp water
4 Tbsp fresh grated parmesan
1 Tbsp fresh chopped basil
½ cup fresh diced mozzarella
¼ cup chopped tomatoes
½ cup sliced mushrooms
1 cup fresh arugula
¼ cup keto tomato sauce

Instructions
1. Preheat your air fryer to 375 degrees F and line the air fryer tray or baking pan with foil.
2. In a medium sized bowl, mix together the almond flour and water.
3. Add the egg and parmesan to the bowl and knead into a soft dough.
4. Place the dough on the prepared tray and press into a flat circle, about ¼ inch thick. Wet your hands if needed in order to make it easier to push the dough down.
5. Spread the tomato sauce over the dough and then top with the fresh basil, tomatoes, mushrooms and mozzarella.
6. Place in the preheated air fryer and bake for 18 minutes or until the cheese is melted and bubbling.
7. Top with the fresh arugula.
8. Slice and serve

Nutrition Facts Per Serving
Calories 372, Total Fat 14g, Saturated Fat 9g, Total Carbs 10g, Net Carbs 5g, Protein 13g, Sugar 3g, Fiber 5g, Sodium 220mg, Potassium 546g

Strawberry Arugula Pizza

Prep time: 20 minutes , Cook time: 20 minutes , Serves 3

Ingredients:
- 1 cup almond flour
- 1 egg
- 3 Tbsp water
- 4 Tbsp fresh grated parmesan
- ½ cup cream cheese, softened
- 1 tsp erythritol
- 1 cup sliced strawberries
- 1 cup fresh arugula

Instructions
1. Preheat your air fryer to 375 degrees F and line the air fryer tray or baking pan with foil.
2. In a medium sized bowl, mix together the almond flour and water.
3. Add the egg and parmesan to the bowl and knead into a soft dough.
4. Place the dough on the prepared tray and press into a flat circle, about ¼ inch thick. Wet your hands if needed in order to make it easier to push the dough down.
5. In a separate bowl, beat the cream cheese and erythritol until very soft.
6. Spread the cream cheese mix over the dough and then top with the strawberries
7. Place in the preheated air fryer and bake for 15 minutes.
8. Remove from the fryer and top with the arugula.
9. Slice and serve

Nutrition Facts Per Serving
Calories 279, Total Fat 16g, Saturated Fat 8g, Total Carbs 14g, Net Carbs 8g, Protein 25g, Sugar 7g, Fiber 6g, Sodium 342mg, Potassium 189g

Green Power Soup

Prep time: 15 minutes , Cook time: 20 minutes , Serves 4

Ingredients:
- 2 cups chopped broccoli
- 4 cups baby spinach
- 3 Tbsp olive oil
- 1 tsp sea salt
- ¼ tsp ground black pepper
- 2 Tbsp minced garlic
- ½ cup diced onion
- 1 Tbsp dried chopped thyme
- 1 qt vegetable broth
- 1 cup heavy cream

Instructions
1. Preheat your air fryer to 400 degrees F and line the air fryer tray or baking pan with foil.
2. Place the broccoli, garlic and onion on the prepared sheet tray.
3. Sprinkle the veggies with the salt, black pepper, thyme and olive oil.
4. Roast in the air fryer for 20 minutes or until the cauliflower is tender.
5. Add the roasted veggies to a blender or food processor and add the veggie broth, spinach and heavy cream.
6. Puree until smooth. Serve hot.

Nutrition Facts Per Serving
Calories 283, Total Fat 12g, Saturated Fat 8g, Total Carbs 8g, Net Carbs 3g, Protein 3g, Sugar 1g, Fiber 5g, Sodium 134mg, Potassium 232g

Pumpkin Soup

Prep time: 15 minutes , Cook time: 20 minutes , Serves 4

Ingredients:
- 4 cups chopped fresh pumpkin
- 3 Tbsp olive oil
- 1 tsp sea salt
- ¼ tsp ground black pepper
- 2 cups chopped carrots
- ½ cup diced onion
- 1 Tbsp dried chopped thyme
- 1 qt chicken broth
- 1 cup heavy cream

Instructions
1. Preheat your air fryer to 400 degrees F and line the air fryer tray or baking pan with foil.
2. Place the pumpkin, carrots, and onion on the prepared sheet tray.

3. Sprinkle the veggies with the salt, black pepper, thyme and olive oil.
4. Roast in the air fryer for 20 minutes or until the squash is tender.
5. Add the roasted veggies to a blender or food processor and add the chicken broth and heavy cream.
6. Puree until smooth. Serve hot.

Nutrition Facts Per Serving
Calories 215, Total Fat 22g, Saturated Fat 10g, Total Carbs 13g, Net Carbs 9g, Protein 5g, Sugar 2g, Fiber 2g, Sodium 328mg, Potassium 154g

Broccoli Cheese Fritters

Prep time: 10 minutes , Cook time: 30 minutes , Serves 4

Ingredients:
¾ cup almond flour
7 Tbsp ground flaxseeds
1 cup broccoli, fresh
4 ounces grated mozzarella cheese
2 eggs
2 tsp baking powder
1 tsp salt
¼ tsp ground black pepper
1 Tbsp olive oil

Instructions
1. Preheat your air fryer to 400 degrees F and prepare a large baking dish with foil.
2. Place the broccoli in a food processor along with the mozzarella, almond flour, 4 tablespoons of the flaxseeds and baking powder. Pulse until the mixture reaches a crumbly texture.
3. Add the eggs, salt and pepper and pulse until a dough forms.
4. Scoop the mix into bite sized balls, rolling them between your hands.
5. Roll the balls in the remaining flaxseeds and place on the prepared baking tray.
6. Drizzle with the olive oil and roll the balls around on the tray so the olive oil is coating the outside.
7. Place in the preheated air fryer and bake for 10 minutes or until nicely golden brown. Enjoy hot.

Nutrition Facts Per Serving
Calories 237, Total Fat 19g, Saturated Fat 6g, Total Carbs 7g, Net Carbs 3g, Protein 15g, Sugar 1g, Fiber 4g, Sodium 1083mg, Potassium 190g

Carrot Cheese Fritters

Prep time: 10 minutes , Cook time: 30 minutes , Serves 4

Ingredients:
¾ cup almond flour
7 Tbsp ground flaxseeds
1 ½ cups chopped carrots
4 ounces grated mozzarella cheese
2 eggs
2 tsp baking powder
1 tsp salt
¼ tsp ground black pepper
1 Tbsp olive oil

Instructions
1. Preheat your air fryer to 400 degrees F and prepare a large baking dish with foil.
2. Place the carrots in a food processor along with the mozzarella, almond flour, 4 tablespoons of the flaxseeds and baking powder. Pulse until the mixture reaches a crumbly texture.
3. Add the eggs, salt and pepper and pulse until a dough forms.
4. Scoop the mix into bite sized balls, rolling them between your hands.
5. Roll the balls in the remaining flaxseeds and place on the prepared baking tray.
6. Drizzle with the olive oil and roll the balls around on the tray so the olive oil is coating the outside.
7. Place in the preheated air fryer and bake for 10 minutes or until nicely golden brown. Enjoy hot.

Nutrition Facts Per Serving
Calories 289, Total Fat 19g, Saturated Fat 6g, Total Carbs 10g, Net Carbs 7g, Protein 15g, Sugar 3g, Fiber 4g, Sodium 1083mg, Potassium 106g

Broccoli and Mushroom Fritters

Prep time: 10 minutes , Cook time: 30 minutes , Serves 4

Ingredients:
¾ cup almond flour
7 Tbsp ground flaxseeds
½ cup broccoli, fresh
½ cup sliced mushrooms
4 ounces grated mozzarella cheese
2 eggs
2 tsp baking powder
1 tsp salt
¼ tsp ground black pepper
1 Tbsp olive oil

Instructions
1. Preheat your air fryer to 400 degrees F and prepare a large baking dish with foil.
2. Place the broccoli and mushrooms in a food processor along with the mozzarella, almond flour, 4 tablespoons of the flaxseeds and baking powder. Pulse until the mixture reaches a crumbly texture.
3. Add the eggs, salt and pepper and pulse until a dough forms.
4. Scoop the mix into bite sized balls, rolling them between your hands.
5. Roll the balls in the remaining flaxseeds and place on the prepared baking tray.
6. Drizzle with the olive oil and roll the balls around on the tray so the olive oil is coating the outside.
7. Place in the preheated air fryer and bake for 10 minutes or until nicely golden brown. Enjoy hot.

Nutrition Facts Per Serving
Calories 241, Total Fat 19g, Saturated Fat 6g, Total Carbs 7g, Net Carbs 3g, Protein 15g, Sugar 1g, Fiber 4g, Sodium 1083mg, Potassium 165g

Broccoli Parmesan Fritters

Prep time: 10 minutes , Cook time: 30 minutes , Serves 4

Ingredients:
¾ cup almond flour
7 Tbsp ground flaxseeds
1 cup broccoli, fresh
4 ounces grated parmesan cheese
2 eggs
2 tsp baking powder
1 tsp salt
¼ tsp ground black pepper
1 Tbsp olive oil

Instructions
1. Preheat your air fryer to 400 degrees F and prepare a large baking dish with foil.
2. Place the broccoli in a food processor along with the parmesan, almond flour, 4 tablespoons of the flaxseeds and baking powder. Pulse until the mixture reaches a crumbly texture.
3. Add the eggs, salt and pepper and pulse until a dough forms.
4. Scoop the mix into bite sized balls, rolling them between your hands.
5. Roll the balls in the remaining flaxseeds and place on the prepared baking tray.
6. Drizzle with the olive oil and roll the balls around on the tray so the olive oil is coating the outside.
7. Place in the preheated air fryer and bake for 10 minutes or until nicely golden brown. Enjoy hot.

Nutrition Facts Per Serving
Calories 243, Total Fat 20g, Saturated Fat 6g, Total Carbs 7g, Net Carbs 3g, Protein 15g, Sugar 1g, Fiber 4g, Sodium 1098mg, Potassium 190g

Spicy Broccoli Cheese Fritters

Prep time: 10 minutes , Cook time: 30 minutes , Serves 4

Ingredients:
¾ cup almond flour
7 Tbsp ground flaxseeds
1 cup broccoli, fresh
4 ounces grated mozzarella cheese
2 eggs
2 tsp baking powder

1 tsp salt
½ tsp red pepper flakes
1 Tbsp olive oil

Instructions
1. Preheat your air fryer to 400 degrees F and prepare a large baking dish with foil.
2. Place the broccoli in a food processor along with the mozzarella, almond flour, 4 tablespoons of the flaxseeds and baking powder. Pulse until the mixture reaches a crumbly texture.
3. Add the eggs, salt and red pepper flakes and pulse until a dough forms.
4. Scoop the mix into bite sized balls, rolling them between your hands.
5. Roll the balls in the remaining flaxseeds and place on the prepared baking tray.
6. Drizzle with the olive oil and roll the balls around on the tray so the olive oil is coating the outside.
7. Place in the preheated air fryer and bake for 10 minutes or until nicely golden brown. Enjoy hot.

Nutrition Facts Per Serving
Calories 239, Total Fat 19g, Saturated Fat 6g, Total Carbs 7g, Net Carbs 3g, Protein 15g, Sugar 1g, Fiber 4g, Sodium 1086mg, Potassium 190g

Broccoli Red Pepper Fritters

Prep time: 10 minutes , Cook time: 30 minutes , Serves 4

Ingredients:
¾ cup almond flour
7 Tbsp ground flaxseeds
1 cup broccoli, fresh
½ cup chopped red bell pepper
4 ounces grated mozzarella cheese
2 eggs
2 tsp baking powder
1 tsp salt
¼ tsp ground black pepper
1 Tbsp olive oil

Instructions
1. Preheat your air fryer to 400 degrees F and prepare a large baking dish with foil.
2. Place the broccoli in a food processor along with the mozzarella, red peppers, almond flour, 4 tablespoons of the flaxseeds and baking powder. Pulse until the mixture reaches a crumbly texture.
3. Add the eggs, salt and pepper and pulse until a dough forms.
4. Scoop the mix into bite sized balls, rolling them between your hands.
5. Roll the balls in the remaining flaxseeds and place on the prepared baking tray.
6. Drizzle with the olive oil and roll the balls around on the tray so the olive oil is coating the outside.
7. Place in the preheated air fryer and bake for 10 minutes or until nicely golden brown. Enjoy hot.

Nutrition Facts Per Serving
Calories 289, Total Fat 19g, Saturated Fat 6g, Total Carbs 10g, Net Carbs 6g, Protein 15g, Sugar 3g, Fiber 4g, Sodium 1097mg, Potassium 220g

Veggie Baked Zucchini Boats

Prep time: 20 minutes , Cook time: 20 minutes , Serves 6

Ingredients:
3 zucchini, sliced in half, seeds scooped out
1 tsp salt
½ tsp ground black pepper
1 tsp olive oil
2 tsp smoked paprika
1 cup chopped mushrooms
1 cup baby spinach
1 cup shredded cheddar cheese
3 Tbsp sour cream
2 Tbsp chopped chives

Instructions
1. Preheat your air fryer to 375 degrees F and line the air fryer tray or baking pan with foil.
2. Place the zucchini skins on the prepared tray and sprinkle with the salt. Let sit for 30 minutes then pat the skins dry to remove the water which the salt has extracted.
3. Spread the mushrooms and baby spinach inside the zucchini boats, dividing the filling evenly.

4. Sprinkle the zucchini with the black pepper, paprika and olive oil.
5. Bake for 10 minutes to soften.
6. Remove from the air fryer and top with the cheese. Return to the air fryer for another 10 minutes or until the cheese is bubbly.
7. Remove from the air fryer and top with the sour cream and chives. Serve hot

Nutrition Facts Per Serving
Calories 158, Total Fat 8g, Saturated Fat 4g, Total Carbs 6g, Net Carbs 4g, Protein 6g, Sugar 3g, Fiber 2g, Sodium 498mg, Potassium 192g

Warmed Nuts and Grits

Prep time: 20 minutes , Cook time: 13 minutes , Serves 4

Ingredients:
½ cup chopped pecans
½ cup chopped almonds
½ cup chopped walnuts
¼ tsp dried sage
2 Tbsp olive oil
2 cups chopped cauliflower florets
1 cup heavy cream
½ cup water
1 cup shredded cheddar cheese
2 Tbsp butter
1 tsp salt
¼ tsp ground black pepper

Instructions
1. Preheat your air fryer to 400 degrees F and line the air fryer tray or baking pan with foil.
2. Place the nuts, olive oil, and sage on the tray and toss to coat everything in the oil.
3. Place the tray in the air fryer and cook for 15 minutes.
4. While the nuts are cooking, place the cauliflower in a blender or food processor and pulse until the cauliflower is like rice.
5. Place the cauliflower in a pot along with the water and cook over medium heat for 5 minutes.
6. Add the heavy cream and cook for another 3 minutes.
7. Stir in the cheese, butter, salt and pepper and mix to melt the cheese.
8. Divide between bowls and top with the roasted mushrooms. Enjoy hot!

Nutrition Facts Per Serving
Calories 455, Total Fat 36g, Saturated Fat 8g, Total Carbs 17g, Net Carbs 11g, Protein 16g, Sugar 4g, Fiber 6g, Sodium 463mg, Potassium 163g

Keto Pizza

Prep time: 20 minutes , Cook time: 20 minutes , Serves 3

Ingredients:
1 cup almond flour
1 egg
3 Tbsp water
1 tsp minced garlic
1 Tbsp fresh chopped basil
4 Tbsp fresh grated parmesan
¼ cup keto tomato sauce
½ cup fresh diced mozzarella

Instructions
1. Preheat your air fryer to 375 degrees F and line the air fryer tray or baking pan with foil.
2. In a medium sized bowl, mix together the almond flour and water.
3. Add the egg and parmesan to the bowl and knead into a soft dough.
4. Place the dough on the prepared tray and press into a flat circle, about ¼ inch thick. Wet your hands if needed in order to make it easier to push the dough down.
5. Spread the tomato sauce over the dough and then top with the minced garlic, fresh basil and mozzarella.
6. Place in the preheated air fryer and bake for 18 minutes or until the cheese is melted and bubbling.
7. Slice and serve

Nutrition Facts Per Serving
Calories 323, Total Fat 24g, Saturated Fat 12g, Total Carbs 11g, Net Carbs 8g, Protein 14g, Sugar 6g, Fiber 3g, Sodium 342mg, Potassium 98g

Extra Cheese Pizza

Prep time: 20 minutes , Cook time: 20 minutes , Serves 3

Ingredients:
- 1 cup almond flour
- 1 egg
- 3 Tbsp water
- 1 tsp minced garlic
- 1 Tbsp fresh chopped basil
- 4 Tbsp fresh grated parmesan
- ¼ cup keto tomato sauce
- ½ cup fresh diced mozzarella
- ½ cup shaved parmesan
- ¼ cup shredded cheddar cheese

Instructions
1. Preheat your air fryer to 375 degrees F and line the air fryer tray or baking pan with foil.
2. In a medium sized bowl, mix together the almond flour and water.
3. Add the egg and parmesan to the bowl and knead into a soft dough.
4. Place the dough on the prepared tray and press into a flat circle, about ¼ inch thick. Wet your hands if needed in order to make it easier to push the dough down.
5. Spread the tomato sauce over the dough and then top with the minced garlic, fresh basil, shaved parmesan, cheddar, and mozzarella.
6. Place in the preheated air fryer and bake for 18 minutes or until the cheese is melted and bubbling.
7. Slice and serve

Nutrition Facts Per Serving
Calories 419, Total Fat 36g, Saturated Fat 24g, Total Carbs 13g, Net Carbs 9g, Protein 19g, Sugar 8g, Fiber 4g, Sodium 452mg, Potassium 110g

Roasted Squash Grits

Prep time: 20 minutes , Cook time: 23 minutes , Serves 4

Ingredients:
- ½ pound chopped butternut squash
- 1 Tbsp minced garlic
- 1 Tbsp fresh chopped rosemary
- ½ cup chopped walnuts
- 2 Tbsp olive oil
- 2 cups chopped cauliflower florets
- 1 cup heavy cream
- ½ cup water
- 1 cup shredded cheddar cheese
- 2 Tbsp butter
- 1 tsp salt
- ¼ tsp ground black pepper

Instructions
1. Preheat your air fryer to 400 degrees F and line the air fryer tray or baking pan with foil.
2. Place the butternut squash, garlic, rosemary, olive oil and walnuts on the tray and toss to coat everything in the olive oil.
3. Place the tray in the air fryer and cook for 15 minutes.
4. While the squash is cooking, place the cauliflower in a blender or food processor and pulse until the cauliflower is like rice.
5. Place the cauliflower in a pot along with the water and cook over medium heat for 5 minutes.
6. Add the heavy cream and cook for another 3 minutes.
7. Stir in the cheese, butter, salt and pepper and mix to melt the cheese.
8. Divide between bowls and top with the roasted mushrooms. Enjoy hot!

Nutrition Facts Per Serving
Calories 485, Total Fat 37g, Saturated Fat 8g, Total Carbs 18g, Net Carbs 12g, Protein 13g, Sugar 4g, Fiber 6g, Sodium 463mg, Potassium 163g

Broccoli and Grits

Prep time: 20 minutes , Cook time: 23 minutes , Serves 4

Ingredients:
- ½ pound chopped broccoli florets
- 1 Tbsp minced garlic
- 1 Tbsp fresh chopped rosemary
- ½ cup chopped pecans
- 2 Tbsp olive oil
- 2 cups chopped cauliflower florets

1 cup heavy cream
½ cup water
1 cup shredded cheddar cheese
2 Tbsp butter
1 tsp salt
¼ tsp ground black pepper

Instructions
1. Preheat your air fryer to 400 degrees F and line the air fryer tray or baking pan with foil.
2. Place the broccoli, garlic, rosemary, olive oil and pecans on the tray and toss to coat everything in the oil.
3. Place the tray in the air fryer and cook for 15 minutes.
4. While the broccoli is cooking, place the cauliflower in a blender or food processor and pulse until the cauliflower is like rice.
5. Place the cauliflower in a pot along with the water and cook over medium heat for 5 minutes.
6. Add the heavy cream and cook for another 3 minutes.
7. Stir in the cheese, butter, salt and pepper and mix to melt the cheese.
8. Divide between bowls and top with the roasted mushrooms. Enjoy hot!

Nutrition Facts Per Serving
Calories 455, Total Fat 36g, Saturated Fat 8g, Total Carbs 17g, Net Carbs 11g, Protein 16g, Sugar 4g, Fiber 6g, Sodium 463mg, Potassium 163g

Mug Lasagna

Prep time: 5 minutes , Cook time: 15 minutes , Serves 1

Ingredients:
½ large zucchini, sliced thinly
3 Tbsp keto marinara sauce
2 Tbsp ricotta, whole milk
¼ cup fresh chopped mozzarella

Instructions
1. Preheat your air fryer to 400 degrees F.
2. Get an oven safe large ramekin or mug.
3. Lay some of the zucchini slices in the bottom of the cup.
4. Spread about 1 tablespoon of the ricotta on top of the zucchini then top with a tablespoon of the marinara sauce.
5. Layer more zucchini on top of the marinara and repeat the layering process until you have used all the zucchini, ricotta and marinara.
6. Top with the mozzarella.
7. Place the lasagna in the oven and bake for 15 minutes or until the mozzarella is melted and bubbly. Enjoy hot

Nutrition Facts Per Serving
Calories 318, Total Fat 24g, Saturated Fat 15g, Total Carbs 7g, Net Carbs 6g, Protein 20g, Sugar 3g, Fiber 1g, Sodium 562mg, Potassium 248g

Mushroom Lunch Lasagna

Prep time: 5 minutes , Cook time: 15 minutes , Serves 1

Ingredients:
½ large zucchini, sliced thinly
½ cup thinly sliced mushrooms
3 Tbsp keto marinara sauce
2 Tbsp ricotta, whole milk
¼ cup fresh chopped mozzarella

Instructions
1. Preheat your air fryer to 400 degrees F.
2. Get an oven safe large ramekin or mug.
3. Lay some of the zucchini and mushroom slices in the bottom of the cup.
4. Spread about 1 tablespoon of the ricotta on top of the zucchini then top with a tablespoon of the marinara sauce.
5. Layer more zucchini and mushrooms on top of the marinara and repeat the layering process until you have used all the zucchini, mushrooms, ricotta and marinara.
6. Top with the mozzarella.
7. Place the lasagna in the oven and bake for 15 minutes or until the mozzarella is melted and bubbly. Enjoy hot

Nutrition Facts Per Serving
Calories 343, Total Fat 24g, Saturated Fat 15g, Total Carbs 9g, Net Carbs 6g, Protein 20g, Sugar 4g, Fiber 2g, Sodium 562mg, Potassium 248g

Eggplant Caprese Rollups

Prep time: 5 minutes, Cook time: 8 minutes, Serves 8

Ingredients:
- 1 eggplant, sliced thinly lengthwise
- 4 oz mozzarella cheese, sliced
- 1 tomato, sliced
- 2 Tbsp chopped fresh basil
- 2 Tbsp olive oil

Instructions
1. Preheat your air fryer to 400 degrees F and prepare a large baking dish with foil.
2. Lay the eggplant slices out on a clean work surface.
3. Place a piece of tomato, cheese and a little basil on each eggplant slice and then roll up to enclose the filling.
4. Secure using a toothpick and then place the eggplant rolls on the prepared foil lined baking dish.
5. Drizzle with the olive oil and place in the air fryer to cook for 8 minutes. The eggplant should be lightly brown and the cheese melted. Serve warm.

Nutrition Facts Per Serving
Calories 59, Total Fat 3g, Saturated Fat 1g, Total Carbs 4g, Net Carbs 3g, Protein 3g, Sugar 2g, Fiber 1g, Sodium 90mg, Potassium 178mg

Eggplant Parmesan Rollups

Prep time: 5 minutes, Cook time: 8 minutes, Serves 8

Ingredients:
- 1 eggplant, sliced thinly lengthwise
- 4 oz grated parmesan
- 1 tomato, sliced
- 2 Tbsp chopped fresh basil
- 2 Tbsp olive oil

Instructions
1. Preheat your air fryer to 400 degrees F and prepare a large baking dish with foil.
2. Lay the eggplant slices out on a clean work surface.
3. Place a piece of tomato, cheese and a little basil on each eggplant slice and then roll up to enclose the filling.
4. Secure using a toothpick and then place the eggplant rolls on the prepared foil lined baking dish.
5. Drizzle with the olive oil and place in the air fryer to cook for 8 minutes. The eggplant should be lightly brown and the cheese melted. Serve warm.

Nutrition Facts Per Serving
Calories 57, Total Fat 3g, Saturated Fat 1g, Total Carbs 4g, Net Carbs 3g, Protein 3g, Sugar 2g, Fiber 1g, Sodium 90mg, Potassium 178mg

Eggplant Zucchini Rollups

Prep time: 5 minutes, Cook time: 8 minutes, Serves 8

Ingredients:
- 1 eggplant, sliced thinly lengthwise
- 4 oz mozzarella cheese, sliced
- 1 zucchini, sliced lengthwise
- 2 Tbsp chopped fresh basil
- 2 Tbsp olive oil

Instructions
1. Preheat your air fryer to 400 degrees F and prepare a large baking dish with foil.
2. Lay the eggplant slices out on a clean work surface.
3. Place a piece of zucchini, cheese and a little basil on each eggplant slice and then roll up to enclose the filling.
4. Secure using a toothpick and then place the eggplant rolls on the prepared foil lined baking dish.
5. Drizzle with the olive oil and place in the air fryer to cook for 8 minutes. The eggplant should be lightly brown and the cheese melted. Serve warm.

Nutrition Facts Per Serving
Calories 68, Total Fat 3g, Saturated Fat 1g, Total Carbs 5g, Net Carbs 4g, Protein 3g, Sugar 1g, Fiber 1g, Sodium 90mg, Potassium 178mg

Zucchini Caprese Rollups

Prep time: 5 minutes , Cook time: 8 minutes , Serves 8

Ingredients:
1 Zucchini, sliced thinly lengthwise
4 oz mozzarella cheese, sliced
1 tomato, sliced
2 Tbsp chopped fresh basil
2 Tbsp olive oil

Instructions
1. Preheat your air fryer to 400 degrees F and prepare a large baking dish with foil.
2. Lay the zucchini slices out on a clean work surface.
3. Place a piece of tomato, cheese and a little basil on each zucchini slice and then roll up to enclose the filling.
4. Secure using a toothpick and then place the eggplant rolls on the prepared foil lined baking dish.
5. Drizzle with the olive oil and place in the air fryer to cook for 8 minutes. The zucchini should be lightly brown and the cheese melted. Serve warm.

Nutrition Facts Per Serving
Calories 61, Total Fat 3g, Saturated Fat 1g, Total Carbs 5g, Net Carbs 4g, Protein 3g, Sugar 3g, Fiber 1g, Sodium 90mg, Potassium 178mg

Spicy Eggplant Rollups

Prep time: 5 minutes , Cook time: 8 minutes , Serves 8

Ingredients:
1 eggplant, sliced thinly lengthwise
4 oz parmesan cheese, sliced
1 tomato, sliced
2 Tbsp chopped fresh basil
2 Tbsp olive oil
1 tsp cayenne pepper

Instructions
1. Preheat your air fryer to 400 degrees F and prepare a large baking dish with foil.
2. Lay the eggplant slices out on a clean work surface.
3. Place a piece of tomato, cheese and a little basil on each eggplant slice and then roll up to enclose the filling.
4. Secure using a toothpick and then place the eggplant rolls on the prepared foil lined baking dish.
5. Drizzle with the olive oil, sprinkle with the cayenne and place in the air fryer to cook for 8 minutes. The eggplant should be lightly brown and the cheese melted. Serve warm.

Nutrition Facts Per Serving
Calories 60, Total Fat 3g, Saturated Fat 1g, Total Carbs 4g, Net Carbs 3g, Protein 3g, Sugar 2g, Fiber 1g, Sodium 90mg, Potassium 178mg

Eggplant Tahini Rollups

Prep time: 5 minutes , Cook time: 8 minutes , Serves 8

Ingredients:
1 eggplant, sliced thinly lengthwise
4 oz mozzarella cheese, sliced
¼ cup tahini paste
2 Tbsp chopped fresh basil
2 Tbsp olive oil

Instructions
1. Preheat your air fryer to 400 degrees F and prepare a large baking dish with foil.
2. Lay the eggplant slices out on a clean work surface.
3. Spread tahini on each eggplant then top with a slice of cheese and a little basil on each eggplant slice and then roll up to enclose the filling.
4. Secure using a toothpick and then place the eggplant rolls on the prepared foil lined baking dish.
5. Drizzle with the olive oil and place in the air fryer to cook for 8 minutes. The eggplant should be lightly brown and the cheese melted. Serve warm.

Nutrition Facts Per Serving
Calories 68, Total Fat 4g, Saturated Fat 2g, Total Carbs 4g, Net Carbs 3g, Protein 4g, Sugar 2g, Fiber 1g, Sodium 105 mg, Potassium 178mg

Lemon Eggplant Rollups

Prep time: 5 minutes , Cook time: 8 minutes , Serves 8

Ingredients:
- 1 eggplant, sliced thinly lengthwise
- 4 oz mozzarella cheese, sliced
- 2 Tbsp chopped fresh basil
- 2 Tbsp olive oil
- 1 tsp lemon zest

Instructions
1. Preheat your air fryer to 400 degrees F and prepare a large baking dish with foil.
2. Lay the eggplant slices out on a clean work surface.
3. Place a piece of tomato, cheese and a little basil on each eggplant slice and then roll up to enclose the filling.
4. Secure using a toothpick and then place the eggplant rolls on the prepares foil lined baking dish.
5. Drizzle with the olive oil, sprinkle with the lemon zest and place in the air fryer to cook for 8 minutes. The eggplant should be lightly brown and the cheese melted. Serve warm.

Nutrition Facts Per Serving
Calories 60, Total Fat 3g, Saturated Fat 1g, Total Carbs 4g, Net Carbs 3g, Protein 3g, Sugar 2g, Fiber 1g, Sodium 90mg, Potassium 178mg

Tomato Lasagna

Prep time: 5 minutes , Cook time: 15 minutes , Serves 1

Ingredients:
- ½ large zucchini, sliced thinly
- ½ cup sliced cherry tomatoes
- 3 Tbsp keto marinara sauce
- 2 Tbsp ricotta, whole milk
- ¼ cup fresh chopped mozzarella

Instructions
1. Preheat your air fryer to 400 degrees F.
2. Get an oven safe large ramekin or mug.
3. Lay some of the zucchini slices in the bottom of the cup and top with a few tomato slices.
4. Spread about 1 tablespoon of the ricotta on top of the zucchini and tomatoes then top with a tablespoon of the marinara sauce.
5. Layer more zucchini and tomatoes on top of the marinara and repeat the layering process until you have used all the zucchini, tomatoes, ricotta and marinara.
6. Top with the mozzarella.
7. Place the lasagna in the oven and bake for 15 minutes or until the mozzarella is melted and bubbly. Enjoy hot

Nutrition Facts Per Serving
Calories 345, Total Fat 24g, Saturated Fat 15g, Total Carbs 10g, Net Carbs 8g, Protein 20g, Sugar 4g, Fiber 1g, Sodium 562mg, Potassium 248g

Spicy Egg Salad

Prep time: 5 minutes , Cook time: 16 minutes , Serves 6

Ingredients:
- 6 Tbsp Mayonnaise
- 8 Large Eggs
- 2 Tbsp apple cider vinegar
- 1 tsp ground black pepper
- 1 tsp salt
- ¼ tsp paprika
- 1 tsp cayenne pepper, ground

Instructions
1. Preheat your air fryer to 250 degrees F.
2. Place a wire rack in the air fryer and place the eggs on top of the rack.
3. Cook for 16 minutes then remove the eggs and place them directly into an ice water bath to cool and stop the cooking process.
4. Peel the eggs and place in a large bowl.
5. Mash the eggs with a fork.
6. Add in the mayonnaise, cider vinegar, pepper, cayenne, paprika and salt

Nutrition Facts Per Serving
Calories 189, Total Fat 12g, Saturated Fat 6g, Total Carbs 2g, Net Carbs 1g, Protein 12g, Sugar 0g, Fiber 1g, Sodium 458mg, Potassium 289g

Roasted Brussels Sprout Salad

Prep time: 7 minutes , Cook time: 15 minutes , Serves 4

Ingredients:
- 1 pound Brussel sprouts, sliced in quarters
- 1 tsp minced, fresh rosemary
- ¼ cup olive oil
- 1 Tbsp apple cider vinegar
- 2 Tbsp lemon juice
- ½ tsp Dijon mustard
- ½ tsp kosher salt

Instructions
1. Preheat your air fryer to 450 degrees F and line the air fryer tray or baking pan with foil.
2. Toss the Brussels sprouts with the rosemary and olive oil and place on the prepared tray.
3. Roast in the air fryer for 15 minutes.
4. Place the hot, roasted sprouts in a large bowl and add the remaining ingredients to make a dressing. Toss well and serve hot or cold.

Nutrition Facts Per Serving
Calories 157, Total Fat 14g, Saturated Fat 2g, Total Carbs 9g, Net Carbs 6g, Protein 3g, Sugar 2g, Fiber 3g, Sodium 27mg, Potassium 509g

Spicy Pepper Lasagna

Prep time: 5 minutes , Cook time: 15 minutes , Serves 1

Ingredients:
- ½ large zucchini, sliced thinly
- ¼ cup chopped red bell peppers
- 3 Tbsp keto marinara sauce
- 2 Tbsp ricotta, whole milk
- ¼ cup fresh chopped mozzarella

Instructions
1. Preheat your air fryer to 400 degrees F.
2. Get an oven safe large ramekin or mug.
3. Lay some of the zucchini slices and chopped bell peppers in the bottom of the cup.
4. Spread about 1 tablespoon of the ricotta on top of the zucchini then top with a tablespoon of the marinara sauce.
5. Layer more zucchini and peppers on top of the marinara and repeat the layering process until you have used all the zucchini, peppers ricotta and marinara.
6. Top with the mozzarella.
7. Place the lasagna in the oven and bake for 15 minutes or until the mozzarella is melted and bubbly. Enjoy hot

Nutrition Facts Per Serving
Calories 325, Total Fat 24g, Saturated Fat 15g, Total Carbs 9g, Net Carbs 7g, Protein 20g, Sugar 4g, Fiber 2g, Sodium 573mg, Potassium 249g

Onion Lasagna

Prep time: 5 minutes , Cook time: 15 minutes , Serves 1

Ingredients:
- ½ large zucchini, sliced thinly
- ¼ cup thinly sliced red onion
- 3 Tbsp keto marinara sauce
- 2 Tbsp ricotta, whole milk
- ¼ cup fresh chopped mozzarella

Instructions
1. Preheat your air fryer to 400 degrees F.
2. Get an oven safe large ramekin or mug.
3. Lay some of the zucchini slices and onion slices in the bottom of the cup.
4. Spread about 1 tablespoon of the ricotta on top of the zucchini then top with a tablespoon of the marinara sauce.
5. Layer more zucchini and onion on top of the marinara and repeat the layering process until you have used all the zucchini, onion ricotta and marinara.
6. Top with the mozzarella.
7. Place the lasagna in the oven and bake for 15 minutes or until the mozzarella is melted and bubbly. Enjoy hot

Nutrition Facts Per Serving
Calories 325, Total Fat 24g, Saturated Fat 15g, Total Carbs 8g, Net Carbs 7g, Protein 20g, Sugar 4g, Fiber 1g, Sodium 562mg, Potassium 248g

Cheesey Stromboli

Prep time: 5 minutes , Cook time: 15 minutes , Serves 4

Ingredients:
- 1 ¼ cups grated mozzarella cheese
- 4 Tbsp almond flour
- 3 Tbsp coconut flour
- 1 egg
- 1 tsp dried basil
- ¼ cup sliced mozzarella cheese
- ½ cup grated cheddar cheese

Instructions
1. Preheat your air fryer to 400 degrees F.
2. Melt the grated mozzarella in a large bowl using the microwave, stirring occasionally.
3. Add the flours and dried basil to the bowl with the mozzarella and mix together for one minute.
4. Add the egg and continue to mix until a nice dough forms.
5. Place the dough on a piece of parchment and then roll into a rectangle about 4 inches wide.
6. Place the sliced mozzarella and cheese slices on top of the dough, in the center.
7. Cover the sliced mozzarella and cheese with the dough, enclosing the filling in the center.
8. Place the Stromboli on a sheet tray and in the preheated air fryer and bake for 20 minutes. Slice and serve!

Nutrition Facts Per Serving
Calories 401, Total Fat 22g, Saturated Fat 15g, Total Carbs 8g, Net Carbs 5g, Protein 21g, Sugar 3g, Fiber 3g, Sodium 723mg, Potassium 321g

Maple Brussels Sprout Salad

Prep time: 7 minutes , Cook time: 15 minutes , Serves 4

Ingredients:
- 1 pound Brussel sprouts, sliced in quarters
- 1 tsp minced, fresh rosemary
- ¼ cup olive oil
- 1 Tbsp apple cider vinegar
- 1 tsp maple extract
- 2 Tbsp lemon juice
- ½ tsp Dijon mustard
- ½ tsp kosher salt

Instructions
1. Preheat your air fryer to 450 degrees F and line the air fryer tray or baking pan with foil.
2. Toss the Brussels sprouts with the rosemary and olive oil and place on the prepared tray.
3. Roast in the air fryer for 15 minutes.
4. Place the hot, roasted sprouts in a large bowl and add the remaining ingredients to make a dressing. Toss well and serve hot or cold.

Nutrition Facts Per Serving
Calories 157, Total Fat 14g, Saturated Fat 2g, Total Carbs 9g, Net Carbs 6g, Protein 3g, Sugar 2g, Fiber 3g, Sodium 27mg, Potassium 509g

Avocado Egg Salad

Prep time: 5 minutes , Cook time: 16 minutes , Serves 6

Ingredients:
- 6 Tbsp Mayonnaise
- 8 Large Eggs
- 2 Tbsp apple cider vinegar
- 1 tsp ground black pepper
- 1 tsp salt
- 1 avocado, chopped

Instructions
1. Preheat your air fryer to 250 degrees F.
2. Place a wire rack in the air fryer and place the eggs on top of the rack.
3. Cook for 16 minutes then remove the eggs and place them directly into an ice water bath to cool and stop the cooking process.
4. Peel the eggs and place in a large bowl.
5. Mash the eggs with a fork.
6. Add in the mayonnaise, cider vinegar, pepper and salt.
7. Gently stir in the avocado and then serve chilled.

Nutrition Facts Per Serving
Calories 289, Total Fat 22g, Saturated Fat 9g, Total Carbs 5g, Net Carbs 4g, Protein 12g, Sugar 0g, Fiber 1g, Sodium 488mg, Potassium 254g

Deviled Egg Salad

Prep time: 5 minutes , Cook time: 16 minutes , Serves 6

Ingredients:
6 Tbsp Mayonnaise
8 Large Eggs
2 Tbsp apple cider vinegar
1 tsp ground black pepper
1 tsp salt
1 tsp smoked paprika, ground

Instructions
1. Preheat your air fryer to 250 degrees F.
2. Place a wire rack in the air fryer and place the eggs on top of the rack.
3. Cook for 16 minutes then remove the eggs and place them directly into an ice water bath to cool and stop the cooking process.
4. Peel the eggs and place in a large bowl.
5. Mash the eggs with a fork.
6. Add in the mayonnaise, cider vinegar, pepper, smoked paprika and salt

Nutrition Facts Per Serving
Calories 189, Total Fat 12g, Saturated Fat 6g, Total Carbs 2g, Net Carbs 1g, Protein 12g, Sugar 0g, Fiber 1g, Sodium 489mg, Potassium 311g

Spicy Sriracha Egg Salad

Prep time: 5 minutes , Cook time: 16 minutes , Serves 6

Ingredients:
6 Tbsp Mayonnaise
8 Large Eggs
2 Tbsp apple cider vinegar
1 tsp ground black pepper
1 tsp salt
1 Tbsp sriracha sauce

Instructions
1. Preheat your air fryer to 250 degrees F.
2. Place a wire rack in the air fryer and place the eggs on top of the rack.
3. Cook for 16 minutes then remove the eggs and place them directly into an ice water bath to cool and stop the cooking process.
4. Peel the eggs and place in a large bowl.
5. Mash the eggs with a fork.
6. Add in the mayonnaise, cider vinegar, pepper, sriracha and salt

Nutrition Facts Per Serving
Calories 189, Total Fat 12g, Saturated Fat 6g, Total Carbs 2g, Net Carbs 1g, Protein 12g, Sugar 1g, Fiber 1g, Sodium 467mg, Potassium 289g

Cheesy Brussels Sprout Salad

Prep time: 7 minutes , Cook time: 15 minutes , Serves 4

Ingredients:
1 pound Brussel sprouts, sliced in quarters
1 tsp minced, fresh rosemary
¼ cup olive oil
1 Tbsp apple cider vinegar
2 Tbsp lemon juice
½ tsp Dijon mustard
½ tsp kosher salt
½ cup grated parmesan cheese

Instructions
1. Preheat your air fryer to 450 degrees F and line the air fryer tray or baking pan with foil.
2. Toss the Brussels sprouts with the rosemary and olive oil and place on the prepared tray.
3. Roast in the air fryer for 15 minutes.
4. Place the hot, roasted sprouts in a large bowl and add the remaining ingredients to make a dressing. Toss well and serve hot or cold.

Nutrition Facts Per Serving
Calories 209, Total Fat 23g, Saturated Fat 6g, Total Carbs 14g, Net Carbs 7g, Protein 36g, Sugar 3g, Fiber 7g, Sodium 324mg, Potassium 578g

Roasted Broccoli Salad

Prep time: 7 minutes , Cook time: 15 minutes , Serves 4

Ingredients:
- 1 pound chopped broccoli florets
- 1 tsp minced, fresh rosemary
- ¼ cup olive oil
- 2 Tbsp balsamic vinegar
- ½ tsp Dijon mustard
- ½ tsp kosher salt

Instructions
1. Preheat your air fryer to 450 degrees F and line the air fryer tray or baking pan with foil.
2. Toss the chopped broccoli with the rosemary and olive oil and place on the prepared tray.
3. Roast in the air fryer for 15 minutes.
4. Place the hot, roasted sprouts in a large bowl and add the remaining ingredients to make a dressing. Toss well and serve hot or cold.

Nutrition Facts Per Serving
Calories 197, Total Fat 22g, Saturated Fat 6g, Total Carbs 14g, Net Carbs 7g, Protein 18g, Sugar 7g, Fiber 7g, Sodium 321mg, Potassium 578g

Asian Broccoli Salad

Prep time: 7 minutes , Cook time: 15 minutes , Serves 4

Ingredients:
- 1 pound chopped broccoli florets
- ¼ cup olive oil
- 2 Tbsp rice wine vinegar
- 2 Tbsp soy sauce
- ½ tsp red chili pepper flakes
- ½ tsp kosher salt

Instructions
1. Preheat your air fryer to 450 degrees F and line the air fryer tray or baking pan with foil.
2. Toss the chopped broccoli with the olive oil and place on the prepared tray.
3. Roast in the air fryer for 15 minutes.
4. Place the hot, roasted sprouts in a large bowl and add the remaining ingredients to make a dressing. Toss well and serve hot or cold.

Nutrition Facts Per Serving
Calories 208, Total Fat 17g, Saturated Fat 8g, Total Carbs 15g, Net Carbs 7g, Protein 18g, Sugar 9g, Fiber 8g, Sodium 378mg, Potassium 578g

Fall Broccoli Salad

Prep time: 7 minutes , Cook time: 15 minutes , Serves 4

Ingredients:
- 1 pound chopped broccoli florets
- 1 tsp minced, fresh rosemary
- ¼ tsp dried sage
- ¼ cup olive oil
- 1 tsp maple extract
- ½ tsp Dijon mustard
- ½ tsp kosher salt

Instructions
1. Preheat your air fryer to 450 degrees F and line the air fryer tray or baking pan with foil.
2. Toss the chopped broccoli with the rosemary, sage and olive oil and place on the prepared tray.
3. Roast in the air fryer for 15 minutes.
4. Place the hot, roasted sprouts in a large bowl and add the remaining ingredients to make a dressing. Toss well and serve hot or cold.

Nutrition Facts Per Serving
Calories 209, Total Fat 22g, Saturated Fat 6g, Total Carbs 12g, Net Carbs 7g, Protein 18g, Sugar 7g, Fiber 5g, Sodium 321mg, Potassium 578g

Beef, Lamb and Pork

Cheesy Italian Meatloaf

Prep time: 15 minutes, Cook time: 35 minutes, Serves 4

Ingredients:
- 1 pound ground beef
- ¾ cup mozzarella cheese, shredded
- ¼ cup fresh grated parmesan
- 1 tsp Italian seasoning
- ¼ tsp ground black pepper
- ¼ tsp salt
- 1 Tbsp almond flour
- 1 Tbsp tomato paste
- 1 Tbsp monk fruit sweetener
- 1 tsp apple cider vinegar
- 1 tsp Dijon mustard

Instructions
1. Preheat your air fryer to 350 degrees F and grease a loaf pans that will fit in the air fryer basket.
2. In a large mixing bowl, combine the beef, cheeses, Italian seasoning, pepper, salt and almond flour. Blend together well and then place in a greased loaf pan.
3. Bake for 35 minutes.
4. While the meatloaf is baking, combine the tomato paste, monk fruit sweetener, vinegar and mustard. Mix well.
5. Once the meatloaf is done, spoon the sauce over the top and then slice and serve.

Nutrition Facts Per Serving
Calories 267, Total Fat 5g, Saturated Fat 3g, Total Carbs 7g, Net Carbs 5g, Protein 33g, Sugar 2g, Fiber 2g, Sodium 678mg, Potassium 279g

Pepper and Cheese Meatloaf

Prep time: 15 minutes, Cook time: 35 minutes, Serves 4

Ingredients:
- 1 pound ground beef
- ¾ cup mozzarella cheese, shredded
- ¼ cup fresh grated parmesan
- 1 tsp Italian seasoning
- ½ cup diced red bell pepper
- ¼ tsp ground black pepper
- ¼ tsp salt
- 1 Tbsp almond flour
- 1 Tbsp tomato paste
- 1 Tbsp monk fruit sweetener
- 1 tsp apple cider vinegar
- 1 tsp Dijon mustard

Instructions
1. Preheat your air fryer to 350 degrees F and grease a loaf pan that will fit in the air fryer basket.
2. In a large mixing bowl, combine the beef, cheeses, Italian seasoning, diced red pepper, ground black pepper, salt and almond flour. Blend together well and then place in a greased loaf pan.
3. Bake for 35 minutes.
4. While the meatloaf is baking, combine the tomato paste, monk fruit sweetener, vinegar and mustard. Mix well.
5. Once the meatloaf is done, spoon the sauce over the top and then slice and serve.

Nutrition Facts Per Serving
Calories 289, Total Fat 5g, Saturated Fat 3g, Total Carbs 9g, Net Carbs 7g, Protein 33g, Sugar 2g, Fiber 2g, Sodium 678mg, Potassium 279g

Garlic Meatloaf

Prep time: 15 minutes, Cook time: 35 minutes, Serves 4

Ingredients:
- 1 pound ground beef
- 1 Tbsp minced garlic
- ¼ cup fresh grated parmesan
- 1 tsp Italian seasoning
- ¼ tsp ground black pepper
- ¼ tsp salt
- 1 Tbsp almond flour
- 1 Tbsp tomato paste
- 1 Tbsp monk fruit sweetener
- 1 tsp apple cider vinegar
- 1 tsp Dijon mustard

Instructions
1. Preheat your air fryer to 350 degrees F and grease a loaf pan that will fit in the air fryer basket.
2. In a large mixing bowl, combine the beef, minced garlic, Italian seasoning, cheese, pepper, salt and almond flour. Blend together well and then place in a greased loaf pan.
3. Bake for 35 minutes.
4. While the meatloaf is baking, combine the tomato paste, monk fruit sweetener, vinegar and mustard. Mix well.
5. Once the meatloaf is done, spoon the sauce over the top and then slice and serve.

Nutrition Facts Per Serving
Calories 201, Total Fat 3g, Saturated Fat 1g, Total Carbs 6g, Net Carbs 2g, Protein 33g, Sugar 2g, Fiber 4g, Sodium 342mg, Potassium 189g

Asian Style Meatloaf

Prep time: 15 minutes, Cook time: 35 minutes, Serves 4

Ingredients:
- 1 pound ground beef
- ½ tsp ground ginger
- 1 Tbsp soy sauce
- ¼ tsp ground black pepper
- ¼ tsp salt
- 1 Tbsp almond flour
- 1 Tbsp tomato paste
- 1 Tbsp monk fruit sweetener
- 1 tsp rice wine vinegar
- 1 tsp Dijon mustard

Instructions
1. Preheat your air fryer to 350 degrees F and grease a loaf pan that will fit in the air fryer basket.
2. In a large mixing bowl, combine the beef, ginger, soy sauce, pepper, salt and almond flour. Blend together well and then place in a greased loaf pan.
3. Bake for 35 minutes.
4. While the meatloaf is baking, combine the tomato paste, monk fruit sweetener, vinegar and mustard. Mix well.
5. Once the meatloaf is done, spoon the sauce over the top and then slice and serve.

Nutrition Facts Per Serving
Calories 267, Total Fat 5g, Saturated Fat 3g, Total Carbs 7g, Net Carbs 5g, Protein 33g, Sugar 2g, Fiber 2g, Sodium 678mg, Potassium 279g

Classic Meatballs

Prep time: 10 minutes, Cook time: 25 minutes, Serves 4

Ingredients:
- 1 pound ground beef
- ¾ cup mozzarella cheese, shredded
- ¼ cup fresh grated parmesan
- 1 tsp Italian seasoning
- ¼ tsp ground black pepper
- ¼ tsp salt
- 1 Tbsp almond flour

Instructions
1. Preheat your air fryer to 350 degrees F and line the air fryer tray with a piece of foil.
2. In a large mixing bowl, combine the beef, cheeses, Italian seasoning, pepper, salt and almond flour. Blend together well.
3. Roll the meat mixture into evenly sized balls and place on the prepared tray.
4. Bake for 25 minutes.
5. Serve the meatballs while hot!

Nutrition Facts Per Serving
Calories 201, Total Fat 4g, Saturated Fat 2g, Total Carbs 6g, Net Carbs 5g, Protein 33g, Sugar 2g, Fiber 1g, Sodium 381mg, Potassium 180g

Asian Style Meatballs

Prep time: 10 minutes , Cook time: 25 minutes , Serves 4

Ingredients:
1 pound ground beef
¼ cup fresh grated parmesan
¼ tsp ground black pepper
¼ tsp salt
1 Tbsp soy Sauce
¼ tsp ground ginger
1 Tbsp coconut flour

Instructions
1. Preheat your air fryer to 350 degrees F and line the air fryer tray with a piece of foil.
2. In a large mixing bowl, combine the beef, cheese, ground ginger, soy sauce, pepper, salt and coconut flour. Blend together well.
3. Roll the meat mixture into evenly sized balls and place on the prepared tray.
4. Bake for 25 minutes.
5. Serve the meatballs while hot!

Nutrition Facts Per Serving
Calories 185, Total Fat 3g, Saturated Fat 1g, Total Carbs 6g, Net Carbs 5g, Protein 33g, Sugar 2g, Fiber 1g, Sodium 381mg, Potassium 180g

Bacon Wrapped Meatballs

Prep time: 10 minutes , Cook time: 25 minutes , Serves 4

Ingredients:
1 pound ground beef
¾ cup mozzarella cheese, shredded
¼ cup fresh grated parmesan
1 tsp Italian seasoning
¼ tsp ground black pepper
¼ tsp salt
1 Tbsp almond flour
¾ pound bacon strips

Instructions
1. Preheat your air fryer to 350 degrees F and line the air fryer tray with a piece of foil.
2. In a large mixing bowl, combine the beef, cheeses, Italian seasoning, pepper, salt and almond flour. Blend together well.
3. Roll the meat mixture into evenly sized balls and place on the prepared tray.
4. Wrap each meatball in a strip of bacon.
5. Bake for 25 minutes.
6. Serve the meatballs while hot!

Nutrition Facts Per Serving
Calories 310, Total Fat 8g, Saturated Fat 6g, Total Carbs 9g, Net Carbs 5g, Protein 45g, Sugar 3g, Fiber 4g, Sodium 877mg, Potassium 190g

Spicy Meatballs

Prep time: 10 minutes , Cook time: 25 minutes , Serves 4

Ingredients:
1 pound ground beef
¾ cup mozzarella cheese, shredded
¼ cup fresh grated parmesan
1 tsp cayenne pepper
1 tsp sriracha sauce
¼ tsp ground black pepper
¼ tsp salt
1 Tbsp almond flour

Instructions
1. Preheat your air fryer to 350 degrees F and line the air fryer tray with a piece of foil.
2. In a large mixing bowl, combine the beef, cheeses, cayenne pepper, sriracha sauce, pepper, salt and almond flour. Blend together well.
3. Roll the meat mixture into evenly sized balls and place on the prepared tray.
4. Bake for 25 minutes.
5. Serve the meatballs while hot!

Nutrition Facts Per Serving
Calories 212, Total Fat 4g, Saturated Fat 2g, Total Carbs 7g, Net Carbs 6g, Protein 33g, Sugar 2g, Fiber 1g, Sodium 397mg, Potassium 152g

Egg Cobb Salad

Prep time: 5 minutes , Cook time: 16 minutes , Serves 6

Ingredients:
- 6 Tbsp Mayonnaise
- 8 Large Eggs
- 2 Tbsp apple cider vinegar
- ½ tsp ground black pepper
- ½ tsp salt
- 1 cup cooked bacon, chopped
- 1 avocado, diced
- ½ cup blue cheese, crumbled
- ½ cup tomatoes, diced

Instructions
1. Preheat your air fryer to 250 degrees F.
2. Place a wire rack in the air fryer and place the eggs on top of the rack.
3. Cook for 16 minutes then remove the eggs and place them directly into an ice water bath to cool and stop the cooking process.
4. Peel the eggs and place in a large bowl.
5. Mash the eggs with a fork.
6. Add in the mayonnaise, cider vinegar, pepper and salt and stir well.
7. Divide between bowls and top with the avocado, blue cheese and tomatoes.

Nutrition Facts Per Serving
Calories 315, Total Fat 18g, Saturated Fat 8g, Total Carbs 7, Net Carbs 4g, Protein 8g, Sugar 0g, Fiber 3g, Sodium 454mg, Potassium 289g

Beef Stuffed Mushrooms

Prep time: 20 minutes , Cook time: 20 minutes , Serves 5

Ingredients:
- 1 pound cremini mushrooms, stems and gills removed
- ¾ pound cooked, ground beef
- ¾ cup cream cheese, softened
- 1/3 cup grated cheddar cheese
- ¼ cup sour cream
- 2 Tbsp minced garlic
- 1 Tbsp mustard
- ½ tsp salt
- ¼ tsp ground black pepper
- ½ cup grated parmesan

Instructions
1. Preheat your air fryer to 375 degrees F and line your air fryer tray with foil or parchment.
2. Place the mushroom caps on the tray and bake for 10 minutes in the air fryer. Remove from the air fryer and drain any excess water from the tray.
3. In a large mixing bowl, combine all the remaining ingredients except the parmesan cheese. Stir well to fully blend everything.
4. Stuff the mushroom caps with the crab mix and then sprinkle the parmesan over the top of the mushrooms.
5. Return the tray to the air fryer and bake for another 10 minutes or until the tops of the mushrooms are golden brown.
6. Remove from the air fryer and enjoy while hot.

Nutrition Facts Per Serving
Calories 382, Total Fat 17g, Saturated Fat 6g, Total Carbs 8g, Net Carbs 4g, Protein 24g, Sugar 1g, Fiber 4g, Sodium 487mg, Potassium 211g

Mexican Stuffed Mushrooms

Prep time: 20 minutes , Cook time: 20 minutes , Serves 5

Ingredients:
- 1 pound cremini mushrooms, stems and gills removed
- ¾ pound cooked, ground beef
- ¾ cup cream cheese, softened
- 1/3 cup grated cheddar cheese
- ¼ cup sour cream
- 2 Tbsp minced garlic
- 1 Tbsp mustard
- 1 tsp Mexican seasoning
- ½ cup grated parmesan

Instructions
1. Preheat your air fryer to 375 degrees F and line your air fryer tray with foil or parchment.
2. Place the mushroom caps on the tray and bake for 10 minutes in the air fryer. Remove from

the air fryer and drain any excess water from the tray.
3. In a large mixing bowl, combine all the remaining ingredients except the parmesan cheese. Stir well to fully blend everything.
4. Stuff the mushroom caps with the crab mix and then sprinkle the parmesan over the top of the mushrooms.
5. Return the tray to the air fryer and bake for another 10 minutes or until the tops of the mushrooms are golden brown.
6. Remove from the air fryer and enjoy while hot.

Nutrition Facts Per Serving
Calories 382, Total Fat 17g, Saturated Fat 6g, Total Carbs 8g, Net Carbs 4g, Protein 24g, Sugar 1g, Fiber 4g, Sodium 487mg, Potassium 211g

Bacon Stuffed Mushrooms

Prep time: 20 minutes , Cook time: 20 minutes , Serves 5

Ingredients:
1 pound cremini mushrooms, stems and gills removed
1 cup cooked crumbled bacon
1 cup almond flour
¾ cup cream cheese, softened
1/3 cup grated cheddar cheese
¼ cup sour cream
2 Tbsp minced garlic
1 Tbsp mustard
½ tsp salt
¼ tsp ground black pepper
½ cup grated parmesan

Instructions
1. Preheat your air fryer to 375 degrees F and line your air fryer tray with foil or parchment.
2. Place the mushroom caps on the tray and bake for 10 minutes in the air fryer. Remove from the air fryer and drain any excess water from the tray.
3. In a large mixing bowl, combine all the remaining ingredients except the parmesan cheese. Stir well to fully blend everything.
4. Stuff the mushroom caps with the crab mix and then sprinkle the parmesan over the top of the mushrooms.
5. Return the tray to the air fryer and bake for another 10 minutes or until the tops of the mushrooms are golden brown.
6. Remove from the air fryer and enjoy while hot.

Nutrition Facts Per Serving
Calories 412, Total Fat 22g, Saturated Fat 12g, Total Carbs 13g, Net Carbs 7g, Protein 24g, Sugar 3g, Fiber 6g, Sodium 854mg, Potassium 265g

Bacon and Mushroom Baked Zucchini

Prep time: 20 minutes , Cook time: 20 minutes , Serves 6

Ingredients:
3 zucchini, sliced in half, seeds scooped out
1 tsp salt
½ tsp ground black pepper
1 tsp olive oil
2 tsp smoked paprika
½ cup chopped white onion
1 ½ cups cooked sausage
1 cup shredded cheddar cheese
3 Tbsp sour cream
2 Tbsp chopped chives

Instructions
1. Preheat your air fryer to 375 degrees F and line the air fryer tray or baking pan with foil.
2. Place the zucchini skins on the prepared tray and sprinkle with the salt. Let sit for 30 minutes then pat the skins dry to remove the water which the salt has extracted.
3. Spread the onions inside the zucchini boats, dividing the filling evenly.
4. Sprinkle the zucchini with the black pepper, paprika and olive oil.
5. Bake for 10 minutes to soften.
6. Remove from the air fryer and top with the sausage and cheese. Return to the air fryer for another 10 minutes or until the cheese is bubbly.
7. Remove from the air fryer and top with the sour cream and chives. Serve hot

Nutrition Facts Per Serving
Calories 216, Total Fat 21g, Saturated Fat 10g, Total Carbs 6g, Net Carbs 4g, Protein 10g, Sugar 3g, Fiber 2g, Sodium 515mg, Potassium 219g

Bacon Pizza

Prep time: 20 minutes , Cook time: 20 minutes , Serves 3

Ingredients:
- 1 cup almond flour
- 1 egg
- 3 Tbsp water
- 1 tsp minced garlic
- 4 Tbsp fresh grated parmesan
- ¼ cup keto tomato sauce
- ½ cup fresh grated mozzarella
- 1 cup cooked, crumbled bacon

Instructions
1. Preheat your air fryer to 375 degrees F and line the air fryer tray or baking pan with foil.
2. In a medium sized bowl, mix together the almond flour and water.
3. Add the egg and parmesan to the bowl and knead into a soft dough.
4. Place the dough on the prepared tray and press into a flat circle, about ¼ inch thick. Wet your hands if needed in order to make it easier to push the dough down.
5. Spread the tomato sauce over the dough and then top with the minced garlic, bacon crumbles, and mozzarella.
6. Place in the preheated air fryer and bake for 18 minutes or until the cheese is melted and bubbling.
7. Slice and serve

Nutrition Facts Per Serving
Calories 411, Total Fat 33g, Saturated Fat 19g, Total Carbs 13g, Net Carbs 8g, Protein 22g, Sugar 8g, Fiber 5g, Sodium 892mg, Potassium 342g

Bacon and Cheese Egg Salad

Prep time: 5 minutes , Cook time: 16 minutes , Serves 6

Ingredients:
- 6 Tbsp Mayonnaise
- 8 Large Eggs
- 2 Tbsp apple cider vinegar
- 1 tsp ground black pepper
- 1 tsp salt
- 1 cup cooked, chopped bacon
- 1 cup grated cheddar cheese

Instructions
1. Preheat your air fryer to 250 degrees F.
2. Place a wire rack in the air fryer and place the eggs on top of the rack.
3. Cook for 16 minutes then remove the eggs and place them directly into an ice water bath to cool and stop the cooking process.
4. Peel the eggs and place in a large bowl.
5. Mash the eggs with a fork.
6. Add in the mayonnaise, cider vinegar, pepper and salt.
7. Fold in the bacon and cheddar cheese.

Nutrition Facts Per Serving
Calories 312, Total Fat 24g, Saturated Fat 14g, Total Carbs 6g, Net Carbs 4g, Protein 12g, Sugar 2g, Fiber 2g, Sodium 983mg, Potassium 438g

Bacon and Mushroom Baked Zucchini

Prep time: 20 minutes , Cook time: 20 minutes , Serves 6

Ingredients:
- 3 zucchini, sliced in half, seeds scooped out
- 1 tsp salt
- ½ tsp ground black pepper
- 1 tsp olive oil
- 2 tsp smoked paprika
- 1 cup chopped mushrooms
- 1 cup cooked, crumbled bacon
- 1 cup shredded cheddar cheese
- 3 Tbsp sour cream
- 2 Tbsp chopped chives

Instructions
1. Preheat your air fryer to 375 degrees F and line the air fryer tray or baking pan with foil.
2. Place the zucchini skins on the prepared tray and sprinkle with the salt. Let sit for 30 minutes then pat the skins dry to remove the water which the salt has extracted.
3. Spread the mushrooms and bacon inside the zucchini boats, dividing the filling evenly.
4. Sprinkle the zucchini with the black pepper, paprika and olive oil.
5. Bake for 10 minutes to soften.

6. Remove from the air fryer and top with the cheese. Return to the air fryer for another 10 minutes or until the cheese is bubbly.
7. Remove from the air fryer and top with the sour cream and chives. Serve hot

Nutrition Facts Per Serving
Calories 211, Total Fat 23g, Saturated Fat 12g, Total Carbs 8g, Net Carbs 5g, Protein 10g, Sugar 3g, Fiber 3g, Sodium 515mg, Potassium 219g

Prosciutto and Parmesan Pizza

Prep time: 20 minutes , Cook time: 20 minutes , Serves 3

Ingredients:
1 cup almond flour
1 egg
3 Tbsp water
4 Tbsp fresh grated parmesan
1 Tbsp minced garlic
2 ounces thinly sliced prosciutto
¾ cup shaved parmesan
2 Tbsp olive oil

Instructions
1. Preheat your air fryer to 375 degrees F and line the air fryer tray or baking pan with foil.
2. In a medium sized bowl, mix together the almond flour and water.
3. Add the egg and parmesan to the bowl and knead into a soft dough.
4. Place the dough on the prepared tray and press into a flat circle, about ¼ inch thick. Wet your hands if needed in order to make it easier to push the dough down.
5. Spread the olive oil over the dough and then top with the garlic, prosciutto and parmesan.
6. Place in the preheated air fryer and bake for 18 minutes or until the cheese is melted and bubbling.
7. Slice and serve

Nutrition Facts Per Serving
Calories 375, Total Fat 21g, Saturated Fat 10g, Total Carbs 10g, Net Carbs 6g, Protein 18g, Sugar 6g, Fiber 4g, Sodium 768mg, Potassium 319g

BBQ Pork Pizza

Prep time: 20 minutes , Cook time: 20 minutes , Serves 3

Ingredients:
1 cup almond flour
1 egg
3 Tbsp water
4 Tbsp fresh grated parmesan
½ cup fresh blue cheese crumbles
1 cup shredded cooked pork shoulder
1/3 cup keto BBQ sauce

Instructions
1. Preheat your air fryer to 375 degrees F and line the air fryer tray or baking pan with foil.
2. In a medium sized bowl, mix together the almond flour and water.
3. Add the egg and parmesan to the bowl and knead into a soft dough.
4. Place the dough on the prepared tray and press into a flat circle, about ¼ inch thick. Wet your hands if needed in order to make it easier to push the dough down.
5. In a separate bowl, toss the shredded pork shoulder with the BBQ sauce.
6. Spread the chicken mix over the dough and then top with the fresh basil and blue cheese.
7. Place in the preheated air fryer and bake for 18 minutes or until the cheese is melted and bubbling.
8. Slice and serve

Nutrition Facts Per Serving
Calories 435, Total Fat 36g, Saturated Fat 23g, Total Carbs 13g, Net Carbs 6g, Protein 34g, Sugar 9g, Fiber 7g, Sodium 522mg, Potassium 329g

Bacon Lasagna

Prep time: 5 minutes, Cook time: 15 minutes, Serves 1

Ingredients:
- ½ large zucchini, sliced thinly
- ¼ cup cooked, chopped bacon
- 3 Tbsp keto marinara sauce
- 2 Tbsp ricotta, whole milk
- ¼ cup fresh chopped mozzarella

Instructions
1. Preheat your air fryer to 400 degrees F.
2. Get an oven safe large ramekin or mug.
3. Lay some of the zucchini slices in the bottom of the cup.
4. Spread about 1 tablespoon of the ricotta on top of the zucchini then top with a tablespoon of the marinara sauce.
5. Top with some of the crumbled bacon.
6. Layer more zucchini on top of the marinara and repeat the layering process until you have used all the zucchini, ricotta, bacon crumbles and marinara.
7. Top with the mozzarella.
8. Place the lasagna in the oven and bake for 15 minutes or until the mozzarella is melted and bubbly. Enjoy hot

Nutrition Facts Per Serving
Calories 386, Total Fat 36g, Saturated Fat 25g, Total Carbs 7g, Net Carbs 6g, Protein 27g, Sugar 3g, Fiber 1g, Sodium 872mg, Potassium 563g

Italian Lunch Lasagna

Prep time: 5 minutes, Cook time: 15 minutes, Serves 1

Ingredients:
- ½ large zucchini, sliced thinly
- ¼ cup crumbled, cooked ground beef
- 3 Tbsp keto marinara sauce
- 2 Tbsp ricotta, whole milk
- 1 tsp Italian seasoning
- ¼ cup fresh chopped mozzarella

Instructions
1. Preheat your air fryer to 400 degrees F.
2. Mix the ricotta and Italian seasoning together.
3. Get an oven safe large ramekin or mug.
4. Lay some of the zucchini slices in the bottom of the cup.
5. Spread about 1 tablespoon of the ricotta on top of the zucchini then top with a tablespoon of the marinara sauce.
6. Top with the ground beef.
7. Layer more zucchini on top of the marinara and repeat the layering process until you have used all the zucchini, ricotta, ground beef and marinara.
8. Top with the mozzarella.
9. Place the lasagna in the oven and bake for 15 minutes or until the mozzarella is melted and bubbly. Enjoy hot

Nutrition Facts Per Serving
Calories 389, Total Fat 31g, Saturated Fat 18g, Total Carbs 8g, Net Carbs 6g, Protein 29g, Sugar 4g, Fiber 1g, Sodium 562mg, Potassium 248g

Bacon and Cheese Stromboli

Prep time: 5 minutes, Cook time: 15 minutes, Serves 4

Ingredients:
- 1 ¼ cups grated mozzarella cheese
- 4 Tbsp almond flour
- 3 Tbsp coconut flour
- 1 egg
- 1 tsp dried basil
- ¼ pound cooked, crumbled bacon
- ½ cup grated cheddar cheese

Instructions
1. Preheat your air fryer to 400 degrees F.
2. Melt the mozzarella in a large bowl using the microwave, stirring occasionally.
3. Add the flours and dried basil to the bowl with the mozzarella and mix together for one minute.
4. Add the egg and continue to mix until a nice dough forms.
5. Place the dough on a piece of parchment and then roll into a rectangle about 4 inches wide.

6. Place the bacon and cheese slices on top of the dough, in the center.
7. Cover the bacon and cheese with the dough, enclosing the filling in the center.
8. Place the Stromboli on a sheet tray and in the preheated air fryer and bake for 20 minutes. Slice and serve!

Nutrition Facts Per Serving
Calories 412, Total Fat 21g, Saturated Fat 16g, Total Carbs 8g, Net Carbs 5g, Protein 21g, Sugar 3g, Fiber 3g, Sodium 879mg, Potassium 327g

Pepperoni Mozzarella Stromboli

Prep time: 5 minutes , Cook time: 15 minutes , Serves 4

Ingredients:
1 ¼ cups grated mozzarella cheese
4 Tbsp almond flour
3 Tbsp coconut flour
1 egg
1 tsp dried basil
¼ pound sliced pepperoni
½ cup sliced mozzarella

Instructions
1. Preheat your air fryer to 400 degrees F.
2. Melt the grated mozzarella in a large bowl using the microwave, stirring occasionally.
3. Add the flours and dried basil to the bowl with the mozzarella and mix together for one minute.
4. Add the egg and continue to mix until a nice dough forms.
5. Place the dough on a piece of parchment and then roll into a rectangle about 4 inches wide.
6. Place the pepperoni and cheese slices on top of the dough, in the center.
7. Cover the pepperoni and cheese with the dough, enclosing the filling in the center.
8. Place the Stromboli on a sheet tray and in the preheated air fryer and bake for 20 minutes. Slice and serve!

Nutrition Facts Per Serving
Calories 399, Total Fat 20g, Saturated Fat 16g, Total Carbs 8g, Net Carbs 5g, Protein 19g, Sugar 3g, Fiber 3g, Sodium 876mg, Potassium 321g

Ham and Cheese Stromboli

Prep time: 5 minutes , Cook time: 15 minutes , Serves 4

Ingredients:
1 ¼ cups grated mozzarella cheese
4 Tbsp almond flour
3 Tbsp coconut flour
1 egg
1 tsp dried basil
¼ pound sliced ham
½ cup grated cheddar cheese

Instructions
1. Preheat your air fryer to 400 degrees F.
2. Melt the mozzarella in a large bowl using the microwave, stirring occasionally.
3. Add the flours and dried basil to the bowl with the mozzarella and mix together for one minute.
4. Add the egg and continue to mix until a nice dough forms.
5. Place the dough on a piece of parchment and then roll into a rectangle about 4 inches wide.
6. Place the ham and cheese slices on top of the dough, in the center.
7. Cover the ham and cheese with the dough, enclosing the filling in the center.
8. Place the Stromboli on a sheet tray and in the preheated air fryer and bake for 20 minutes. Slice and serve!

Nutrition Facts Per Serving
Calories 420, Total Fat 22g, Saturated Fat 15g, Total Carbs 8g, Net Carbs 5g, Protein 23g, Sugar 3g, Fiber 3g, Sodium 876mg, Potassium 321g

Dijon Baked Pork Chops

Prep time: 5 minutes , Cook time: 24 minutes , Serves 5

Ingredients:
- 1 ½ pounds Bone In Pork Chops
- ¼ cup parsley, freshly chopped
- ¼ cup Dijon mustard
- 1 Tbsp olive oil
- 1 Tbsp fresh squeezed lemon juice
- 1 Tbsp minced garlic
- ¼ tsp salt
- ¼ tsp ground black pepper

Instructions
1. Preheat your air fryer to 375 degrees F line your air fryer tray with a piece of parchment paper.
2. Place the pork chops on the parchment lined tray.
3. In a small bowl, mix together the remaining ingredients and then spread over the top of the pork chops.
4. Place the pork chops in the air fryer and bake for 18 minutes. Slice and serve hot!

Nutrition Facts Per Serving
Calories 309, Total Fat 11g, Saturated Fat 2g, Total Carbs 2g, Net Carbs 1g, Protein 33g, Sugar 0g, Fiber 1g, Sodium 652mg, Potassium 47g

Maple Dijon Baked Pork Chops

Prep time: 5 minutes , Cook time: 24 minutes , Serves 5

Ingredients:
- 1 ½ pounds Bone In Pork Chops
- ¼ cup parsley, freshly chopped
- ¼ cup Dijon mustard
- 1 Tbsp olive oil
- 1 tsp maple extract
- 1 Tbsp fresh squeezed lemon juice
- 1 Tbsp minced garlic
- ¼ tsp salt
- ¼ tsp ground black pepper

Instructions
1. Preheat your air fryer to 375 degrees F line your air fryer tray with a piece of parchment paper.
2. Place the pork chops on the parchment lined tray.
3. In a small bowl, mix together the remaining ingredients and then spread over the top of the pork chops.
4. Place the pork chops in the air fryer and bake for 18 minutes. Slice and serve hot!

Nutrition Facts Per Serving
Calories 310, Total Fat 11g, Saturated Fat 2g, Total Carbs 2g, Net Carbs 1g, Protein 33g, Sugar 0g, Fiber 1g, Sodium 657mg, Potassium 47g

Sweet and Spicy Dijon Baked Pork Chops

Prep time: 5 minutes , Cook time: 24 minutes , Serves 5

Ingredients:
- 1 ½ pounds Bone In Pork Chops
- ¼ cup parsley, freshly chopped
- ¼ cup Dijon mustard
- ½ tsp cayenne pepper
- 1 Tbsp olive oil
- 1 Tbsp fresh squeezed lemon juice
- 1 Tbsp minced garlic
- ¼ tsp salt
- ¼ tsp ground black pepper

Instructions
1. Preheat your air fryer to 375 degrees F line your air fryer tray with a piece of parchment paper.
2. Place the pork chops on the parchment lined tray.
3. In a small bowl, mix together the remaining ingredients and then spread over the top of the pork chops.
4. Place the pork chops in the air fryer and bake for 18 minutes. Slice and serve hot!

Nutrition Facts Per Serving
Calories 313, Total Fat 11g, Saturated Fat 2g, Total Carbs 2g, Net Carbs 1g, Protein 33g, Sugar 0g, Fiber 1g, Sodium 663mg, Potassium 49g

Creamy Tuscan Pork Chops

Prep time: 10 minutes , Cook time: 15 minutes , Serves 6

Ingredients:
1 ½ pounds pork chops
2 Tbsp olive oil
1 cup heavy cream
½ cup chicken broth
1 tsp garlic powder
½ cup grated parmesan cheese
½ cup chopped sundried tomatoes
2 cups baby spinach
1 tsp Italian seasoning

Instructions
1. Preheat your air fryer to 375 degrees F and prepare a baking tray that will fit inside your air fryer.
2. Place the pork chops and olive oil in your baking tray and then into your air fryer for 4 minutes.
3. Remove the pan, flip the pork chops and return to the air fryer for another 4 minutes.
4. Whisk the remaining ingredients in a small bowl.
5. Remove the tray again and add all the remaining ingredients to the pan, stirring briefly.
6. Return the pan to the air fryer and cook for 10 minutes. The sauce should be bubbling and the spinach wilted.
7. Serve while hot!

Nutrition Facts Per Serving
Calories 399, Total Fat 20g, Saturated Fat 12g, Total Carbs 9g, Net Carbs 8g, Protein 31g, Sugar 3g, Fiber 1g, Sodium 456mg, Potassium 105g

Greek Garlic Pork Chops

Prep time: 20 minutes , Cook time: 30 minutes , Serves 4

Ingredients:
3 Tbsp olive oil
3 Tbsp lemon juice
3 Tbsp minced garlic
1 tsp oregano, dried
1 pound pork chops
½ tsp sea salt
¼ tsp ground black pepper
½ pound asparagus
1 zucchini, sliced thinly
1 lemon, sliced thinly

Instructions
1. Preheat your air fryer to 400 degrees F and prepare your air fryer tray with a piece of foil.
2. In a large bowl, whisk together 2 Tbsp of the olive oil, lemon juice, dried oregano and garlic.
3. Add the pork chops to the bowl and toss to coat. Cover the bowl and place in the fridge for two hours.
4. Add the remaining tablespoon of olive oil to a saute pan and heat over high. Sear the marinated pork chops on each side for 3 minutes, just to brown.
5. Move the browned pork chops to the prepared, foil lined tray and pour the remaining marinade from the bowl over the chops.
6. Add the asparagus, zucchini and lemon slices, layering them over and around the pork chops.
7. Place the tray in the preheated air fryer for 20 minutes. Serve hot.

Nutrition Facts Per Serving
Calories 223, Total Fat 10g, Saturated Fat 2g, Total Carbs 6g, Net Carbs 4g, Protein 27g, Sugar 3g, Fiber 2g, Sodium 398mg, Potassium 263g

Lemon Garlic Pork Chops

Prep time: 20 minutes , Cook time: 30 minutes , Serves 4

Ingredients:
3 Tbsp olive oil
3 Tbsp lemon juice
3 Tbsp minced garlic
1 pound pork chops
½ tsp sea salt
¼ tsp ground black pepper
½ pound asparagus
1 zucchini, sliced thinly
1 lemon, sliced thinly

Instructions
1. Preheat your air fryer to 400 degrees F and prepare your air fryer tray with a piece of foil.
2. In a large bowl, whisk together 2 Tbsp of the olive oil, lemon juice, and garlic.
3. Add the pork chops to the bowl and toss to coat. Cover the bowl and place in the fridge for two hours.
4. Add the remaining tablespoon of olive oil to a saute pan and heat over high. Sear the marinated pork chops on each side for 3 minutes, just to brown.
5. Move the browned pork chops to the prepared, foil lined tray and pour the remaining marinade from the bowl over the chops.
6. Add the asparagus, zucchini and lemon slices, layering them over and around the pork chops.
7. Place the tray in the preheated air fryer for 20 minutes. Serve hot.

Nutrition Facts Per Serving
Calories 220, Total Fat 10g, Saturated Fat 2g, Total Carbs 6g, Net Carbs 4g, Protein 27g, Sugar 3g, Fiber 2g, Sodium 397mg, Potassium 263g

Creamy Garlic Pork Chops

Prep time: 20 minutes , Cook time: 30 minutes , Serves 4

Ingredients:
3 Tbsp olive oil
3 Tbsp lemon juice
3 Tbsp minced garlic
1 tsp oregano, dried
1 pound pork chops
½ tsp sea salt
¼ tsp ground black pepper
½ pound asparagus
1 zucchini, sliced thinly
1 lemon, sliced thinly
½ cup heavy cream

Instructions
1. Preheat your air fryer to 400 degrees F and prepare your air fryer tray with a piece of foil.
2. In a large bowl, whisk together 2 Tbsp of the olive oil, lemon juice, dried oregano and garlic.
3. Add the pork chops to the bowl and toss to coat. Cover the bowl and place in the fridge for two hours.
4. Add the remaining tablespoon of olive oil to a saute pan and heat over high. Sear the marinated pork chops on each side for 3 minutes, just to brown.
5. Move the browned pork chops to the prepared, foil lined tray and pour the remaining marinade from the bowl over the chops.
6. Add the asparagus, zucchini and lemon slices, layering them over and around the pork chops.
7. Place the tray in the preheated air fryer for 20 minutes. Remove the tray from the fryer and whisk in the heavy cream. Return to the air fryer for another 5 minutes then serve hot.

Nutrition Facts Per Serving
Calories 248, Total Fat 18g, Saturated Fat 4g, Total Carbs 6g, Net Carbs 4g, Protein 27g, Sugar 4g, Fiber 2g, Sodium 405mg, Potassium 278g

Lemon Pepper Pork Chops

Prep time: 20 minutes , Cook time: 30 minutes , Serves 4

Ingredients:

3 Tbsp olive oil
3 Tbsp lemon juice
1 pound pork chops
½ tsp sea salt
1 tsp ground black pepper
½ pound asparagus
1 zucchini, sliced thinly
1 lemon, sliced thinly

Instructions

1. Preheat your air fryer to 400 degrees F and prepare your air fryer tray with a piece of foil.
2. In a large bowl, whisk together 2 Tbsp of the olive oil, lemon juice, salt and pepper.
3. Add the pork chops to the bowl and toss to coat. Cover the bowl and place in the fridge for two hours.
4. Add the remaining tablespoon of olive oil to a saute pan and heat over high. Sear the marinated pork chops on each side for 3 minutes, just to brown.
5. Move the browned pork chops to the prepared, foil lined tray and pour the remaining marinade from the bowl over the chops.
6. Add the asparagus, zucchini and lemon slices, layering them over and around the pork chops.
7. Place the tray in the preheated air fryer for 20 minutes. Serve hot.

Nutrition Facts Per Serving

Calories 222, Total Fat 10g, Saturated Fat 2g, Total Carbs 6g, Net Carbs 4g, Protein 27g, Sugar 3g, Fiber 2g, Sodium 398mg, Potassium 263g

Brussels and Pork Chops

Prep time: 20 minutes , Cook time: 30 minutes , Serves 4

Ingredients:

3 Tbsp olive oil
3 Tbsp lemon juice
3 Tbsp minced garlic
1 tsp oregano, dried
1 pound pork chops
½ tsp sea salt
¼ tsp ground black pepper
1 pound Brussel sprouts sliced in half
1 lemon, sliced thinly

Instructions

1. Preheat your air fryer to 400 degrees F and prepare your air fryer tray with a piece of foil.
2. In a large bowl, whisk together 2 Tbsp of the olive oil, lemon juice, dried oregano and garlic.
3. Add the pork chops to the bowl and toss to coat. Cover the bowl and place in the fridge for two hours.
4. Add the remaining tablespoon of olive oil to a saute pan and heat over high. Sear the marinated pork chops on each side for 3 minutes, just to brown.
5. Move the browned pork chops to the prepared, foil lined tray and pour the remaining marinade from the bowl over the chops.
6. Add the Brussels and lemon slices, layering them over and around the pork chops.
7. Place the tray in the preheated air fryer for 20 minutes. Serve hot.

Nutrition Facts Per Serving

Calories 203, Total Fat 10g, Saturated Fat 2g, Total Carbs 7g, Net Carbs 4g, Protein 27g, Sugar 3g, Fiber 3g, Sodium 388mg, Potassium 232g

Maple Brussels and Pork Chops

Prep time: 20 minutes, Cook time: 30 minutes, Serves 4

Ingredients:
- 3 Tbsp olive oil
- 3 Tbsp lemon juice
- 3 Tbsp minced garlic
- 1 tsp maple extract
- 1 tsp oregano, dried
- 1 pound pork chops
- ½ tsp sea salt
- ¼ tsp ground black pepper
- 1 pound Brussel sprouts sliced in half
- 1 lemon, sliced thinly

Instructions
1. Preheat your air fryer to 400 degrees F and prepare your air fryer tray with a piece of foil.
2. In a large bowl, whisk together 2 Tbsp of the olive oil, lemon juice, maple extract dried oregano and garlic.
3. Add the pork chops to the bowl and toss to coat. Cover the bowl and place in the fridge for two hours.
4. Add the remaining tablespoon of olive oil to a saute pan and heat over high. Sear the marinated pork chops on each side for 3 minutes, just to brown.
5. Move the browned pork chops to the prepared, foil lined tray and pour the remaining marinade from the bowl over the chops.
6. Add the Brussels and lemon slices, layering them over and around the pork chops.
7. Place the tray in the preheated air fryer for 20 minutes. Serve hot.

Nutrition Facts Per Serving
Calories 205, Total Fat 10g, Saturated Fat 2g, Total Carbs 7g, Net Carbs 4g, Protein 27g, Sugar 3g, Fiber 3g, Sodium 388mg, Potassium 232g

Bacon Brussels and Pork Chops

Prep time: 20 minutes, Cook time: 30 minutes, Serves 4

Ingredients:
- 3 Tbsp olive oil
- 3 Tbsp lemon juice
- 3 Tbsp minced garlic
- 1 tsp oregano, dried
- 1 pound pork chops
- ½ tsp sea salt
- ¼ tsp ground black pepper
- 1 pound Brussel sprouts sliced in half
- ½ cup cooked crumbled bacon

Instructions
1. Preheat your air fryer to 400 degrees F and prepare your air fryer tray with a piece of foil.
2. In a large bowl, whisk together 2 Tbsp of the olive oil, lemon juice, dried oregano and garlic.
3. Add the pork chops to the bowl and toss to coat. Cover the bowl and place in the fridge for two hours.
4. Add the remaining tablespoon of olive oil to a saute pan and heat over high. Sear the marinated pork chops on each side for 3 minutes, just to brown.
5. Move the browned pork chops to the prepared, foil lined tray and pour the remaining marinade from the bowl over the chops.
6. Add the Brussels and bacon, layering them over and around the pork chops.
7. Place the tray in the preheated air fryer for 20 minutes. Serve hot.

Nutrition Facts Per Serving
Calories 299, Total Fat 10g, Saturated Fat 2g, Total Carbs 7g, Net Carbs 4g, Protein 34g, Sugar 3g, Fiber 3g, Sodium 776mg, Potassium 267g

Brussels, Tomatoes and Pork Chops

Prep time: 20 minutes , Cook time: 30 minutes , Serves 4

Ingredients:
- 3 Tbsp olive oil
- 3 Tbsp lemon juice
- 3 Tbsp minced garlic
- 1 tsp oregano, dried
- 1 pound pork chops
- ½ tsp sea salt
- ¼ tsp ground black pepper
- 1 pound Brussel sprouts sliced in half
- ¼ cup chopped sundried tomatoes
- 1 lemon, sliced thinly

Instructions
1. Preheat your air fryer to 400 degrees F and prepare your air fryer tray with a piece of foil.
2. In a large bowl, whisk together 2 Tbsp of the olive oil, lemon juice, dried oregano and garlic.
3. Add the pork chops to the bowl and toss to coat. Cover the bowl and place in the fridge for two hours.
4. Add the remaining tablespoon of olive oil to a saute pan and heat over high. Sear the marinated pork chops on each side for 3 minutes, just to brown.
5. Move the browned pork chops to the prepared, foil lined tray and pour the remaining marinade from the bowl over the chops.
6. Add the Brussels, sundried tomatoes and lemon slices, layering them over and around the pork chops.
7. Place the tray in the preheated air fryer for 20 minutes. Serve hot.

Nutrition Facts Per Serving
Calories 253, Total Fat 10g, Saturated Fat 2g, Total Carbs 11g, Net Carbs 6g, Protein 27g, Sugar 4g, Fiber 5g, Sodium 388mg, Potassium 232g

Veggies Roasted Pork Chops

Prep time: 20 minutes , Cook time: 30 minutes , Serves 6

Ingredients:
- 2 pounds Pork Chops, bone-in
- ½ tsp salt
- ½ tsp ground black pepper
- 3 carrots, chopped
- 2 celery stalks, chopped
- 1 Tbsp minced garlic
- 3 Tbsp butter, melted
- ½ cup white onion, chopped
- 1 tsp dried thyme
- ½ tsp dried rosemary

Instructions
1. Preheat your air fryer to 425 degrees F and prepare your air fryer tray with a piece of foil.
2. Rub the pork chops with the salt and pepper, wrap and let sit overnight to season.
3. Place the onion, carrot, celery and garlic on the prepared foil lined tray.
4. Place the pork chops on top of the veggies.
5. Brush the pork chops with the melted butter and sprinkle with the thyme and rosemary.
6. Bake in the air fryer for 30 minutes or until the chicken thighs are browned and the veggies are beginning to brown as well.
7. Serve hot.

Nutrition Facts Per Serving
Calories 243, Total Fat 12g, Saturated Fat 6g, Total Carbs 6g, Net Carbs 5g, Protein 31g, Sugar 3g, Fiber 1g, Sodium 496mg, Potassium 104g

Dijon Roasted Pork Chops

Prep time: 20 minutes , Cook time: 30 minutes , Serves 6

Ingredients:
- 2 pounds Pork Chops, bone-in
- ½ tsp salt
- ½ tsp ground black pepper
- ¼ cup Dijon mustard
- 3 carrots, chopped
- 2 celery stalks, chopped
- 1 Tbsp minced garlic
- 3 Tbsp butter, melted
- ½ cup white onion, chopped
- 1 tsp dried thyme
- ½ tsp dried rosemary

Instructions
1. Preheat your air fryer to 425 degrees F and prepare your air fryer tray with a piece of foil.
2. Rub the pork chops with the salt, pepper, and Dijon and wrap and let sit overnight to season.
3. Place the onion, carrot, celery and garlic on the prepared foil lined tray.
4. Place the pork chops on top of the veggies.
5. Brush the pork chops with the melted butter and sprinkle with the thyme and rosemary.
6. Bake in the air fryer for 30 minutes or until the chicken thighs are browned and the veggies are beginning to brown as well.
7. Serve hot.

Nutrition Facts Per Serving
Calories 254, Total Fat 13g, Saturated Fat 6g, Total Carbs 8g, Net Carbs 7g, Protein 31g, Sugar 4g, Fiber 1g, Sodium 504mg, Potassium 110g

Maple Roasted Pork Chops and Veggies

Prep time: 20 minutes , Cook time: 30 minutes , Serves 6

Ingredients:
- 2 pounds Pork Chops, bone-in
- ½ tsp salt
- ½ tsp ground black pepper
- 1 tsp maple extract
- 3 carrots, chopped
- 2 celery stalks, chopped
- 1 Tbsp minced garlic
- 3 Tbsp butter, melted
- ½ cup white onion, chopped
- 1 tsp dried thyme
- ½ tsp dried rosemary

Instructions
1. Preheat your air fryer to 425 degrees F and prepare your air fryer tray with a piece of foil.
2. Rub the pork chops with the salt, pepper, and maple extract and wrap and let sit overnight to season.
3. Place the onion, carrot, celery and garlic on the prepared foil lined tray.
4. Place the pork chops on top of the veggies.
5. Brush the pork chops with the melted butter and sprinkle with the thyme and rosemary.
6. Bake in the air fryer for 30 minutes or until the chicken thighs are browned and the veggies are beginning to brown as well.
7. Serve hot.

Nutrition Facts Per Serving
Calories 243, Total Fat 12g, Saturated Fat 6g, Total Carbs 6g, Net Carbs 5g, Protein 31g, Sugar 3g, Fiber 1g, Sodium 496mg, Potassium 104g

Brussels and Roasted Pork Chops

Prep time: 20 minutes , Cook time: 30 minutes , Serves 6

Ingredients:
- 2 pounds Pork Chops, bone-in
- ½ tsp salt
- ½ tsp ground black pepper
- 3 carrots, chopped
- 2 celery stalks, chopped
- ½ pound Brussels Sprouts, sliced in half
- 1 Tbsp minced garlic
- 3 Tbsp butter, melted
- ½ cup white onion, chopped
- 1 tsp dried thyme
- ½ tsp dried rosemary

Instructions

1. Preheat your air fryer to 425 degrees F and prepare your air fryer tray with a piece of foil.
2. Rub the pork chops with the salt and pepper, wrap and let sit overnight to season.
3. Place the onion, carrot, celery, Brussels and garlic on the prepared foil lined tray.
4. Place the pork chops on top of the veggies.
5. Brush the pork chops with the melted butter and sprinkle with the thyme and rosemary.
6. Bake in the air fryer for 30 minutes or until the chicken thighs are browned and the veggies are beginning to brown as well.
7. Serve hot.

Nutrition Facts Per Serving
Calories 289, Total Fat 12g, Saturated Fat 6g, Total Carbs 11g, Net Carbs 9g, Protein 31g, Sugar 5g, Fiber 2g, Sodium 496mg, Potassium 104g

Sweet Veggies Roasted Pork Chops

Prep time: 20 minutes , Cook time: 30 minutes , Serves 6

Ingredients:
2 pounds Pork Chops, bone-in
½ tsp salt
½ tsp ground black pepper
3 carrots, chopped
2 celery stalks, chopped
1 Tbsp minced garlic
3 Tbsp butter, melted
2 Tbsp erythritol sweetener
½ cup white onion, chopped
1 tsp dried thyme
½ tsp dried rosemary

Instructions
1. Preheat your air fryer to 425 degrees F and prepare your air fryer tray with a piece of foil.
2. Rub the pork chops with the salt and pepper, wrap and let sit overnight to season.
3. Place the onion, carrot, celery and garlic on the prepared foil lined tray. Sprinkle the erythritol over the veggies.
4. Place the pork chops on top of the veggies.
5. Brush the pork chops with the melted butter and sprinkle with the thyme and rosemary.
6. Bake in the air fryer for 30 minutes or until the chicken thighs are browned and the veggies are beginning to brown as well.
7. Serve hot.

Nutrition Facts Per Serving
Calories 243, Total Fat 12g, Saturated Fat 6g, Total Carbs 6g, Net Carbs 5g, Protein 31g, Sugar 3g, Fiber 1g, Sodium 496mg, Potassium 104g

Spinach and Bacon Casserole

Prep time: 10 minutes , Cook time: 30 minutes , Serves 12

Ingredients:
16 eggs
¼ cup whole milk
1 cup cooked, sliced bacon
10 oz frozen, chopped spinach, thawed, drained
1 cup cheddar cheese, grated
½ cup grated parmesan cheese
½ cup whole milk ricotta
¼ cup chopped white onion
1 tsp minced garlic
1 tsp sea salt
½ tsp dried thyme
½ tsp ground black pepper

Instructions
1. Preheat your air fryer to 350 degrees F and prepare a large baking dish with baking grease (make sure the pan will fit in your air fryer.
2. Whisk the eggs and milk in a large bowl.
3. Add the bacon and spinach to the egg mix.
4. Add all the remaining ingredients, except the ricotta, and stir well.
5. Pour the egg and veggie mix into the prepared tray.
6. Dollop the ricotta around the pan, dispersing it evenly.
7. Bake in the air fryer for 30 minutes or until the eggs are completely set.

Nutrition Facts Per Serving
Calories 319, Total Fat 22g, Saturated Fat 8g, Total Carbs 4g, Net Carbs 3g, Protein 20g, Sugar 3g, Fiber 1g, Sodium 689mg, Potassium 222g

Asparagus and Bacon Casserole

Prep time: 10 minutes , Cook time: 30 minutes , Serves 12

Ingredients:

16 eggs
¼ cup whole milk
1 cup cooked, sliced bacon
1 pound chopped asparagus
1 cup cheddar cheese, grated
½ cup grated parmesan cheese
½ cup whole milk ricotta
¼ cup chopped white onion
1 tsp minced garlic
1 tsp sea salt
½ tsp dried thyme
½ tsp ground black pepper

Instructions

1. Preheat your air fryer to 350 degrees F and prepare a large baking dish with baking grease (make sure the pan will fit in your air fryer.
2. Whisk the eggs and milk in a large bowl.
3. Add the bacon and asparagus to the egg mix.
4. Add all the remaining ingredients, except the ricotta, and stir well.
5. Pour the egg and veggie mix into the prepared tray.
6. Dollop the ricotta around the pan, dispersing it evenly.
7. Bake in the air fryer for 30 minutes or until the eggs are completely set.

Nutrition Facts Per Serving

Calories 322, Total Fat 22g, Saturated Fat 8g, Total Carbs 5g, Net Carbs 3g, Protein 20g, Sugar 3g, Fiber 2g, Sodium 689mg, Potassium 222g

Spinach and Maple Bacon Casserole

Prep time: 10 minutes , Cook time: 30 minutes , Serves 12

Ingredients:

16 eggs
¼ cup whole milk
1 cup cooked, sliced maple seasoned bacon
10 oz frozen, chopped spinach, thawed, drained
1 cup cheddar cheese, grated
½ cup grated parmesan cheese
½ cup whole milk ricotta
¼ cup chopped white onion
1 tsp minced garlic
1 tsp sea salt
½ tsp dried thyme
½ tsp ground black pepper

Instructions

1. Preheat your air fryer to 350 degrees F and prepare a large baking dish with baking grease (make sure the pan will fit in your air fryer.
2. Whisk the eggs and milk in a large bowl.
3. Add the bacon and spinach to the egg mix.
4. Add all the remaining ingredients, except the ricotta, and stir well.
5. Pour the egg and veggie mix into the prepared tray.
6. Dollop the ricotta around the pan, dispersing it evenly.
7. Bake in the air fryer for 30 minutes or until the eggs are completely set.

Nutrition Facts Per Serving

Calories 368, Total Fat 22g, Saturated Fat 8g, Total Carbs 9g, Net Carbs 8g, Protein 20g, Sugar 5g, Fiber 1g, Sodium 689mg, Potassium 222g

Bacon and Cheese Casserole

Prep time: 10 minutes , Cook time: 30 minutes , Serves 12

Ingredients:

16 eggs
¼ cup whole milk
1 cup cooked, sliced bacon
1 cup cheddar cheese, grated
½ cup grated parmesan cheese
½ cup whole milk ricotta
¼ cup chopped white onion
1 tsp minced garlic
1 tsp sea salt
½ tsp dried thyme
½ tsp ground black pepper

Instructions

1. Preheat your air fryer to 350 degrees F and prepare a large baking dish with baking grease (make sure the pan will fit in your air fryer.

2. Whisk the eggs and milk in a large bowl.
3. Add the bacon to the egg mix.
4. Add all the remaining ingredients, except the ricotta, and stir well.
5. Pour the egg and veggie mix into the prepared tray.
6. Dollop the ricotta around the pan, dispersing it evenly.
7. Bake in the air fryer for 30 minutes or until the eggs are completely set.

Nutrition Facts Per Serving
Calories 301, Total Fat 22g, Saturated Fat 8g, Total Carbs 4g, Net Carbs 3g, Protein 20g, Sugar 3g, Fiber 1g, Sodium 689mg, Potassium 222g

Bacon Veggie Casserole

Prep time: 10 minutes , Cook time: 30 minutes , Serves 12

Ingredients:
16 eggs
¼ cup whole milk
1 cup cooked, sliced bacon
10 oz frozen, chopped spinach, thawed, drained
2 cups chopped asparagus
½ cup sundried tomatoes, chopped
1 cup cheddar cheese, grated
½ cup grated parmesan cheese
½ cup whole milk ricotta
¼ cup chopped white onion
1 tsp minced garlic
1 tsp sea salt
½ tsp dried thyme
½ tsp ground black pepper

Instructions
1. Preheat your air fryer to 350 degrees F and prepare a large baking dish with baking grease (make sure the pan will fit in your air fryer.
2. Whisk the eggs and milk in a large bowl.
3. Add the bacon, asparagus, tomatoes and spinach to the egg mix.
4. Add all the remaining ingredients, except the ricotta, and stir well.
5. Pour the egg and veggie mix into the prepared tray.
6. Dollop the ricotta around the pan, dispersing it evenly.
7. Bake in the air fryer for 30 minutes or until the eggs are completely set.

Nutrition Facts Per Serving
Calories 349, Total Fat 22g, Saturated Fat 8g, Total Carbs 11g, Net Carbs 9g, Protein 20g, Sugar 3g, Fiber 2g, Sodium 689mg, Potassium 222g

Broccoli and Bacon Fritters

Prep time: 10 minutes , Cook time: 30 minutes , Serves 4

Ingredients:
¾ cup almond flour
7 Tbsp ground flaxseeds
1 cup broccoli, fresh
½ cup cooked, crumbled bacon
4 ounces grated mozzarella cheese
2 eggs
2 tsp baking powder
1 tsp salt
¼ tsp ground black pepper
1 Tbsp olive oil

Instructions
1. Preheat your air fryer to 400 degrees F and prepare a large baking dish with foil.
2. Place the broccoli in a food processor along with the mozzarella, bacon, almond flour, 4 tablespoons of the flaxseeds and baking powder. Pulse until the mixture reaches a crumbly texture.
3. Add the eggs, salt and pepper and pulse until a dough forms.
4. Scoop the mix into bite sized balls, rolling them between your hands.
5. Roll the balls in the remaining flaxseeds and place on the prepared baking tray.
6. Drizzle with the olive oil and roll the balls around on the tray so the olive oil is coating the outside.
7. Place in the preheated air fryer and bake for 10 minutes or until nicely golden brown. Enjoy hot.

Nutrition Facts Per Serving
Calories 278, Total Fat 26g, Saturated Fat 12g, Total Carbs 7g, Net Carbs 3g, Protein 21g, Sugar 1g, Fiber 4g, Sodium 1346mg, Potassium 190g

Cauliflower and Bacon Fritters

Prep time: 10 minutes , Cook time: 30 minutes , Serves 4

Ingredients:
- ¾ cup almond flour
- 7 Tbsp ground flaxseeds
- 1 cup cauliflower, fresh
- ½ cup cooked, crumbled bacon
- 4 ounces grated mozzarella cheese
- 2 eggs
- 2 tsp baking powder
- 1 tsp salt
- ¼ tsp ground black pepper
- 1 Tbsp olive oil

Instructions
1. Preheat your air fryer to 400 degrees F and prepare a large baking dish with foil.
2. Place the cauliflower in a food processor along with the mozzarella, bacon, almond flour, 4 tablespoons of the flaxseeds and baking powder. Pulse until the mixture reaches a crumbly texture.
3. Add the eggs, salt and pepper and pulse until a dough forms.
4. Scoop the mix into bite sized balls, rolling them between your hands.
5. Roll the balls in the remaining flaxseeds and place on the prepared baking tray.
6. Drizzle with the olive oil and roll the balls around on the tray so the olive oil is coating the outside.
7. Place in the preheated air fryer and bake for 10 minutes or until nicely golden brown. Enjoy hot.

Nutrition Facts Per Serving
Calories 270, Total Fat 26g, Saturated Fat 12g, Total Carbs 6g, Net Carbs 4g, Protein 21g, Sugar 1g, Fiber 4g, Sodium 1207mg, Potassium 167g

Mushroom and Bacon Fritters

Prep time: 10 minutes , Cook time: 30 minutes , Serves 4

Ingredients:
- ¾ cup almond flour
- 7 Tbsp ground flaxseeds
- 1 ½ cup chopped mushrooms, fresh
- ½ cup cooked, crumbled bacon
- 4 ounces grated mozzarella cheese
- 2 eggs
- 2 tsp baking powder
- 1 tsp salt
- ¼ tsp ground black pepper
- 1 Tbsp olive oil

Instructions
1. Preheat your air fryer to 400 degrees F and prepare a large baking dish with foil.
2. Place the mushrooms in a food processor along with the mozzarella, bacon, almond flour, 4 tablespoons of the flaxseeds and baking powder. Pulse until the mixture reaches a crumbly texture.
3. Add the eggs, salt and pepper and pulse until a dough forms.
4. Scoop the mix into bite sized balls, rolling them between your hands.
5. Roll the balls in the remaining flaxseeds and place on the prepared baking tray.
6. Drizzle with the olive oil and roll the balls around on the tray so the olive oil is coating the outside.
7. Place in the preheated air fryer and bake for 10 minutes or until nicely golden brown. Enjoy hot.

Nutrition Facts Per Serving
Calories 265, Total Fat 26g, Saturated Fat 12g, Total Carbs 6g, Net Carbs 2g, Protein 21g, Sugar 1g, Fiber 4g, Sodium 1300mg, Potassium 177g

Cheesy Bacon Fritters

Prep time: 10 minutes , Cook time: 30 minutes , Serves 4

Ingredients:
- ¾ cup almond flour
- 7 Tbsp ground flaxseeds
- 1 cup cooked, crumbled bacon
- 4 ounces grated mozzarella cheese
- ½ cup grated parmesan
- 2 eggs

2 tsp baking powder
1 tsp salt
¼ tsp ground black pepper
1 Tbsp olive oil

Instructions
1. Preheat your air fryer to 400 degrees F and prepare a large baking dish with foil.
2. Place the mozzarella, parmesan, bacon, almond flour, 4 tablespoons of the flaxseeds and baking powder. Pulse until the mixture reaches a crumbly texture.
3. Add the eggs, salt and pepper and pulse until a dough forms.
4. Scoop the mix into bite sized balls, rolling them between your hands.
5. Roll the balls in the remaining flaxseeds and place on the prepared baking tray.
6. Drizzle with the olive oil and roll the balls around on the tray so the olive oil is coating the outside.
7. Place in the preheated air fryer and bake for 10 minutes or until nicely golden brown. Enjoy hot.

Nutrition Facts Per Serving
Calories 288, Total Fat 29g, Saturated Fat 15g, Total Carbs 7g, Net Carbs 3g, Protein 21g, Sugar 1g, Fiber 4g, Sodium 1368mg, Potassium 190g

Eggplant Bacon Caprese Rollups

Prep time: 5 minutes , Cook time: 8 minutes , Serves 8

Ingredients:
1 eggplant, sliced thinly lengthwise
4 oz mozzarella cheese, sliced
8 strips bacon
1 tomato, sliced
2 Tbsp chopped fresh basil
2 Tbsp olive oil

Instructions
1. Preheat your air fryer to 400 degrees F and prepare a large baking dish with foil.
2. Lay the eggplant slices out on a clean work surface.
3. Place a piece of tomato, cheese and a little basil on each eggplant slice and then roll up to enclose the filling.
4. Wrap a strip of bacon around the outside of each rollup.
5. Secure using a toothpick and then place the eggplant rolls on the prepared foil lined baking dish.
6. Drizzle with the olive oil and place in the air fryer to cook for 8 minutes. The eggplant should be lightly brown and the cheese melted. Serve warm.

Nutrition Facts Per Serving
Calories 98, Total Fat 5g, Saturated Fat 3g, Total Carbs 4g, Net Carbs 3g, Protein 4g, Sugar 2g, Fiber 1g, Sodium 310mg, Potassium 178mg

Cheesy Bacon Rollups

Prep time: 5 minutes , Cook time: 8 minutes , Serves 8

Ingredients:
1 eggplant, sliced thinly lengthwise
4 oz mozzarella cheese, sliced
½ cup grated parmesan
8 strips bacon
2 Tbsp chopped fresh basil
2 Tbsp olive oil

Instructions
1. Preheat your air fryer to 400 degrees F and prepare a large baking dish with foil.
2. Lay the eggplant slices out on a clean work surface.
3. Place mozzarella, parmesan and a little basil on each eggplant slice and then roll up to enclose the filling.
4. Wrap a strip of bacon around the outside of each rollup.
5. Secure using a toothpick and then place the eggplant rolls on the prepared foil lined baking dish.
6. Drizzle with the olive oil and place in the air fryer to cook for 8 minutes. The eggplant should be lightly brown and the cheese melted. Serve warm.

Nutrition Facts Per Serving
Calories 98, Total Fat 5g, Saturated Fat 3g, Total Carbs 4g, Net Carbs 3g, Protein 4g, Sugar 2g, Fiber 1g, Sodium 310mg, Potassium 178mg

Zucchini Bacon Rollups

Prep time: 5 minutes, Cook time: 8 minutes, Serves 8

Ingredients:
1 eggplant, sliced thinly lengthwise
4 oz mozzarella cheese, sliced
8 strips bacon
2 Tbsp chopped fresh basil
2 Tbsp olive oil

Instructions
1. Preheat your air fryer to 400 degrees F and prepare a large baking dish with foil.
2. Lay the eggplant slices out on a clean work surface.
3. Place a piece of cheese and a little basil on each eggplant slice and then roll up to enclose the filling.
4. Wrap a strip of bacon around the outside of each rollup.
5. Secure using a toothpick and then place the eggplant rolls on the prepared foil lined baking dish.
6. Drizzle with the olive oil and place in the air fryer to cook for 8 minutes. The eggplant should be lightly brown and the cheese melted. Serve warm.

Nutrition Facts Per Serving
Calories 103, Total Fat 5g, Saturated Fat 3g, Total Carbs 5g, Net Carbs 3g, Protein 4g, Sugar 2g, Fiber 2g, Sodium 310mg, Potassium 178mg

Eggplant Bacon Hummus Rollups

Prep time: 5 minutes, Cook time: 8 minutes, Serves 8

Ingredients:
1 eggplant, sliced thinly lengthwise
¼ cup keto hummus
4 oz mozzarella cheese, sliced
8 strips bacon
2 Tbsp chopped fresh basil
2 Tbsp olive oil

Instructions
1. Preheat your air fryer to 400 degrees F and prepare a large baking dish with foil.
2. Lay the eggplant slices out on a clean work surface.
3. Spread hummus on each eggplant slice.
4. Place a piece of cheese and a little basil on each eggplant slice and then roll up to enclose the filling.
5. Wrap a strip of bacon around the outside of each rollup.
6. Secure using a toothpick and then place the eggplant rolls on the prepared foil lined baking dish.
7. Drizzle with the olive oil and place in the air fryer to cook for 8 minutes. The eggplant should be lightly brown and the cheese melted. Serve warm.

Nutrition Facts Per Serving
Calories 107, Total Fat 5g, Saturated Fat 3g, Total Carbs 5g, Net Carbs 3g, Protein 5g, Sugar 2g, Fiber 2g, Sodium 310mg, Potassium 178mg

Red Pepper Meatballs

Prep time: 10 minutes, Cook time: 25 minutes, Serves 4

Ingredients:
1 pound ground beef
¾ cup mozzarella cheese, shredded
½ cup diced red peppers
¼ cup fresh grated parmesan
1 tsp Italian seasoning
¼ tsp ground black pepper
¼ tsp salt
1 Tbsp almond flour

Instructions
1. Preheat your air fryer to 350 degrees F and line the air fryer tray with a piece of foil.
2. In a large mixing bowl, combine the beef, cheeses, red peppers, Italian seasoning, pepper, salt and almond flour. Blend together well.
3. Roll the meat mixture into evenly sized balls and place on the prepared tray.
4. Bake for 25 minutes.
5. Serve the meatballs while hot!

Nutrition Facts Per Serving
Calories 253, Total Fat 4g, Saturated Fat 2g, Total Carbs 8g, Net Carbs 5g, Protein 33g, Sugar 2g, Fiber 3g, Sodium 381mg, Potassium 180g

Spicy Meatballs

Prep time: 10 minutes , Cook time: 25 minutes , Serves 4

Ingredients:
1 pound ground beef
¾ cup mozzarella cheese, shredded
¼ cup fresh grated parmesan
1 tsp Italian seasoning
1 tsp cayenne pepper
¼ tsp ground black pepper
¼ tsp salt
1 Tbsp almond flour

Instructions
1. Preheat your air fryer to 350 degrees F and line the air fryer tray with a piece of foil.
2. In a large mixing bowl, combine the beef, cayenne pepper, cheeses, Italian seasoning, pepper, salt and almond flour. Blend together well.
3. Roll the meat mixture into evenly sized balls and place on the prepared tray.
4. Bake for 25 minutes.
5. Serve the meatballs while hot!

Nutrition Facts Per Serving
Calories 204, Total Fat 4g, Saturated Fat 2g, Total Carbs 6g, Net Carbs 5g, Protein 33g, Sugar 2g, Fiber 1g, Sodium 381mg, Potassium 180mg

Extra Juicy Meatballs

Prep time: 10 minutes , Cook time: 25 minutes , Serves 4

Ingredients:
1 pound ground beef
¾ cup mozzarella cheese, shredded
¼ cup mayonnaise
1 egg
¼ cup fresh grated parmesan
1 tsp Italian seasoning
¼ tsp ground black pepper
¼ tsp salt
1 Tbsp almond flour

Instructions
1. Preheat your air fryer to 350 degrees F and line the air fryer tray with a piece of foil.
2. In a large mixing bowl, combine the beef, cheeses, mayonnaise, egg, Italian seasoning, pepper, salt and almond flour. Blend together well.
3. Roll the meat mixture into evenly sized balls and place on the prepared tray.
4. Bake for 25 minutes.
5. Serve the meatballs while hot!

Nutrition Facts Per Serving
Calories 265, Total Fat 8g, Saturated Fat 4g, Total Carbs 6g, Net Carbs 5g, Protein 33g, Sugar 2g, Fiber 1g, Sodium 381mg, Potassium 180g

Lamb Meatballs

Prep time: 10 minutes , Cook time: 25 minutes , Serves 4

Ingredients:
1 pound ground lamb
¾ cup mozzarella cheese, shredded
¼ cup fresh grated parmesan
1 tsp Italian seasoning
¼ tsp ground black pepper
¼ tsp salt
1 Tbsp almond flour

Instructions
1. Preheat your air fryer to 350 degrees F and line the air fryer tray with a piece of foil.
2. In a large mixing bowl, combine the lamb, cheeses, Italian seasoning, pepper, salt and almond flour. Blend together well.
3. Roll the meat mixture into evenly sized balls and place on the prepared tray.
4. Bake for 25 minutes.
5. Serve the meatballs while hot!

Nutrition Facts Per Serving
Calories 197, Total Fat 4g, Saturated Fat 1g, Total Carbs 6g, Net Carbs 5g, Protein 33g, Sugar 2g, Fiber 1g, Sodium 381mg, Potassium 180g

Indian Style Lamb Meatballs

Prep time: 10 minutes , Cook time: 25 minutes , Serves 4

Ingredients:
1 pound ground lamb
¾ cup halloumi cheese, shredded
¼ cup fresh grated parmesan
1 tsp cumin
½ tsp turmeric
¼ tsp ground black pepper
¼ tsp salt
1 Tbsp almond flour

Instructions
1. Preheat your air fryer to 350 degrees F and line the air fryer tray with a piece of foil.
2. In a large mixing bowl, combine the lamb, cheeses, cumin, turmeric, pepper, salt and almond flour. Blend together well.
3. Roll the meat mixture into evenly sized balls and place on the prepared tray.
4. Bake for 25 minutes.
5. Serve the meatballs while hot!

Nutrition Facts Per Serving
Calories 199, Total Fat 4g, Saturated Fat 1g, Total Carbs 6g, Net Carbs 5g, Protein 33g, Sugar 2g, Fiber 1g, Sodium 381mg, Potassium 180g

Baharat Lamb Meatballs

Prep time: 10 minutes , Cook time: 25 minutes , Serves 4

Ingredients:
1 pound ground lamb
¾ cup halloumi cheese, shredded
¼ cup fresh grated parmesan
1 tsp Baharat seasoning
¼ tsp ground black pepper
¼ tsp salt
1 Tbsp coconut flour

Instructions
1. Preheat your air fryer to 350 degrees F and line the air fryer tray with a piece of foil.
2. In a large mixing bowl, combine the lamb, cheeses, Baharat seasoning, pepper, salt and coconut flour. Blend together well.
3. Roll the meat mixture into evenly sized balls and place on the prepared tray.
4. Bake for 25 minutes.
5. Serve the meatballs while hot!

Nutrition Facts Per Serving
Calories 203, Total Fat 4g, Saturated Fat 1g, Total Carbs 7g, Net Carbs 6g, Protein 33g, Sugar 4g, Fiber 1g, Sodium 381mg, Potassium 180g

Curried Lamb Meatballs

Prep time: 10 minutes , Cook time: 25 minutes , Serves 4

Ingredients:
1 pound ground lamb
¾ cup feta cheese
¼ cup fresh grated parmesan
1 tsp curry seasoning
¼ tsp ground black pepper
¼ tsp salt
1 Tbsp coconut flour

Instructions
1. Preheat your air fryer to 350 degrees F and line the air fryer tray with a piece of foil.
2. In a large mixing bowl, combine the lamb, cheeses, curry seasoning, pepper, salt and almond flour. Blend together well.
3. Roll the meat mixture into evenly sized balls and place on the prepared tray.
4. Bake for 25 minutes.
5. Serve the meatballs while hot!

Nutrition Facts Per Serving
Calories 217, Total Fat 5g, Saturated Fat 1g, Total Carbs 7g, Net Carbs 6g, Protein 33g, Sugar 3g, Fiber 1g, Sodium 381mg, Potassium 180g

Lemon Garlic Lamb Chops

Prep time: 20 minutes , Cook time: 30 minutes , Serves 4

Ingredients:
3 Tbsp olive oil
3 Tbsp lemon juice
3 Tbsp minced garlic
1 pound lamb chops
½ tsp sea salt
¼ tsp ground black pepper
½ pound asparagus
1 zucchini, sliced thinly
1 lemon, sliced thinly

Instructions

1. Preheat your air fryer to 400 degrees F and prepare your air fryer tray with a piece of foil.
2. In a large bowl, whisk together 2 Tbsp of the olive oil, lemon juice, and garlic.
3. Add the lamb chops to the bowl and toss to coat. Cover the bowl and place in the fridge for two hours.
4. Add the remaining tablespoon of olive oil to a saute pan and heat over high. Sear the marinated lamb chops on each side for 3 minutes, just to brown.
5. Move the browned pork lamb to the prepared, foil lined tray and pour the remaining marinade from the bowl over the chops.
6. Add the asparagus, zucchini and lemon slices, layering them over and around the lamb chops.
7. Place the tray in the preheated air fryer for 20 minutes. Serve hot.

Nutrition Facts Per Serving
Calories 215, Total Fat 8g, Saturated Fat 2g, Total Carbs 6g, Net Carbs 4g, Protein 25g, Sugar 3g, Fiber 2g, Sodium 397mg, Potassium 263g

Minty Lamb Chops

Prep time: 20 minutes , Cook time: 30 minutes , Serves 4

Ingredients:
3 Tbsp olive oil
3 Tbsp lemon juice
1 Tbsp fresh chopped mint
1 pound lamb chops
½ tsp sea salt
¼ tsp ground black pepper
1 zucchini, sliced thinly
3 cups baby spinach

Instructions
1. Preheat your air fryer to 400 degrees F and prepare your air fryer tray with a piece of foil.
2. In a large bowl, whisk together 2 Tbsp of the olive oil, lemon juice, and mint.
3. Add the lamb chops to the bowl and toss to coat. Cover the bowl and place in the fridge for two hours.
4. Add the remaining tablespoon of olive oil to a saute pan and heat over high. Sear the marinated lamb chops on each side for 3 minutes, just to brown.
5. Move the browned pork lamb to the prepared, foil lined tray and pour the remaining marinade from the bowl over the chops.
6. Add the zucchini and baby spinach, placing them over and around the lamb chops.
7. Place the tray in the preheated air fryer for 20 minutes. Serve hot.

Nutrition Facts Per Serving
Calories 233, Total Fat 8g, Saturated Fat 2g, Total Carbs 8g, Net Carbs 5g, Protein 25g, Sugar 4g, Fiber 3g, Sodium 397mg, Potassium 263g

Curry Brussels and Lamb Chops

Prep time: 20 minutes , Cook time: 30 minutes , Serves 4

Ingredients:
3 Tbsp olive oil
3 Tbsp lemon juice
3 Tbsp minced garlic
1 pound lamb chops
½ tsp sea salt
1 tsp curry powder
1 pound sliced Brussels sprouts
1 lemon, sliced thinly

Instructions
1. Preheat your air fryer to 400 degrees F and prepare your air fryer tray with a piece of foil.
2. In a large bowl, whisk together 2 Tbsp of the olive oil, curry powder, lemon juice, and garlic.
3. Add the lamb chops to the bowl and toss to coat. Cover the bowl and place in the fridge for two hours.
4. Add the remaining tablespoon of olive oil to a saute pan and heat over high. Sear the marinated lamb chops on each side for 3 minutes, just to brown.
5. Move the browned pork lamb to the prepared, foil lined tray and pour the remaining marinade from the bowl over the chops.
6. Add the Brussels and lemon slices, layering them over and around the lamb chops.
7. Place the tray in the preheated air fryer for 20 minutes. Serve hot.

Nutrition Facts Per Serving
Calories 206, Total Fat 7g, Saturated Fat 2g, Total Carbs 8g, Net Carbs 4g, Protein 25g, Sugar 3g, Fiber 4g, Sodium 397mg, Potassium 263g

Appendix 1: 28 Days Keto Meal Plan with Air Fryer

Day	Breakfast	Lunch	Dinner	Snack	Dessert	Total Carbs
1	Three Cheese Omelet	Tuna Stuffed Mushrooms	Crispy Salmon	Turkey Pepper Nachos	Peanut Butter Cookies	21
2	Hard Boiled Eggs	Cauliflower Soup	Spinach Maple Bacon Casserole	Cranberry Dark Chocolate Granola Bars	Cinnamon Cake	21
3	Chocolate Chip Muffins	Maple Brussels and Pork Chops	Cheesy Italian Meatloaf	Chicharrones	Chocolate Walnuts	21
4	Sausage and Cheese Omelet	Broccoli Parmesan Fritters	Extra Cheese Pizza	Bacon Muffin Bites	Chocolate Chip Cookies	24
5	Bacon Cheese Frittata	Crispy Flounder	Roasted Mushrooms and Grits	Blueberry Dark Chocolate Granola Bars	NY Keto Cheesecake	25
6	Blueberry Muffins	Cream of Asparagus Soup	Spicy Crunchy Salmon	Asian Style Brussels Sprout Chips	Peanut Butter Brownies	23
7	Spinach Parmesan Baked Eggs	Tuna Cakes	Bacon Lasagna	Spicy Garlic Bread Muffins	Butter Cookies	25
8	Zucchini and Sausage Bake	Chicken Nuggets	Creamy Tuscan Pork Chops	Herbed Parmesan Crackers	Caramel Cake	26
9	Bacon and Eggs for 1	Turkey Garlic Mushrooms	Prosciutto Parmesan Pizza	Spicy Hot Pepper Nachos	Peanut Butter Chocolate Chip Cookies	31
10	Almond Flour Pancake	Crunchy Garlic Salmon	Tomato Lasagna	Bacon Cheddar Crackers	Seedy Cookies	22
11	Raspberry Muffins	Egg Salad	Garlic Chicken and Spinach	Cauliflower Crunch	Mexican Chocolate Walnuts	20
12	Avocado Baked Eggs	Tuna Sticks	Bacon Mushroom Baked Zucchini	Double Dark Chocolate Granola Bars	Strawberry Cheesecake	21
13	Meat Lovers Omelet	BBQ Fried Chicken	Bacon Pizza	Spicy Chicharrones	Coconut Cookies	24

14	Bacon Kale Frittata	Maple Walnut Flounder	Creamy Tuscan Chicken	Cheddar Crackers	Chocolate Mint Brownies	28
15	Strawberry Muffins	Spicy Meatballs	Greek Garlic Pork Chops	Broccoli Crunch	Pumpkin Chocolate Chip Cookies	22
16	Zucchini and Bacon Egg Bread	Pesto Fried Chicken	Black Pepper Parmesan Salmon	Cayenne Brussels Sprout Chips	Double Chocolate Brownies	21
17	Raspberry Almond Pancake	Tuna Melt Cups	Maple Dijon Baked Chicken Breast	Parmesan Garlic Bread Muffins	Peanut Butter Jelly Cookies	23
18	French Herb Omelet	Bacon Broccoli Fritters	Indian Style Lamb Meatballs	Veggie Pepper Nachos	Raspberry Cheesecake	31
19	Coconut Chocolate Pancake	Maple Walnut Chicken with Spinach	Garlic Shrimp and Bacon Bake	Coconut Dark Chocolate Granola Bars	Keto Shortbread	21
20	Spicy Cheese Omelet	Salmon Cakes	Dijon Roasted Pork Chops	Cocoa Chicharrones	Caramel Fudge Brownies	20
21	Veggie Egg Bread	Bacon Stuffed Mushrooms	Creamy Baked Scallops	Super Seed Parmesan Crackers	Vanilla Raspberry Cake	30
22	Blueberry Almond Pancake	Spinach Artichoke Casserole	Buffalo Chicken Pizza	Lemon Pepper Broccoli Crunch	Cocoa Cookies	26
23	Roasted Garlic Eggs	Red Pepper Grits	Cajun Tuna Cakes	Zucchini Chips	Almond Shortbread	21
24	Indian Masala Omelet	Bacon Pizza	Creamy Brussels with Chicken and Garlic	Brussels Sprouts Chips	Cream Cheese Cookies	25
25	Kimchi Breakfast	Cod Fish Sticks	Chicken Garlic Patties	Cheesy Garlic Bread Muffins	Pumpkin Spice Cheesecake	27
26	Strawberry Pancake	Butternut Squash Soup	Spicy Pepper Lasagna	Seedy Chocolate Granola Bars	Fudge Brownies	27
27	Cheddar Jalapeno Eggs	Lemon Feta Garlic Chicken	Cauliflower Bacon Fritters	BBQ Muffin Bites	Chocolate Almonds	23
28	Za'atar Eggs	Jalapeno Tuna Melt Cups	Lemon Garlic Lamb Chops	Cheesy Chicharones	Vanilla Cake	23

Appendix 2: Recipes Index

A

Almond Brownies 77
Almond Cake 67
Almond Cookies 83
Almond Crusted Salmon 99
Almond Flour Pancake 11
Almond Shortbread 90
Asian Broccoli Salad 173
Asian Style Brussel Sprout Chips 42
Asian Style Crunchy Flounder 107
Asian Style Crunchy Salmon 95
Asian Style Meatballs 176
Asian Style Meatloaf 175
Asparagus and Bacon Casserole 191
Asparagus and Tomato Casserole 156
Asparagus Egg White Casserole 156
Avocado Baked Eggs 5
Avocado Egg Salad 171

B

Bacon and Brie Frittata 9
Bacon and Cheese Casserole 191
Bacon and Cheese Egg Salad 179
Bacon and Cheese Fritatta 4
Bacon and Cheese Stromboli 181
Bacon and Crab Stuffed Mushrooms 117
Bacon and Egg Stuffed Peppers 23
Bacon and Eggs for One 6
Bacon and Kale Fritatta 9
Bacon and Mushroom Baked Zucchini 178
Bacon and Mushroom Baked Zucchini 179
Bacon Brussel Sprout Chips 42
Bacon Brussels and Pork Chops 187
Bacon Cheddar Crackers 46
Bacon Chicken Stuffed Mushrooms 146
Bacon Chicken Thighs 126
Bacon Lasagna 181
Bacon Muffin Bites 39
Bacon Pizza 179
Bacon Scallops 110
Bacon Stuffed Mushrooms 178
Bacon Veggie Casserole 192
Bacon Wrapped Fish Sticks 102
Bacon Wrapped Meatballs 176
Baharat Lamb Meatballs 197
Balsamic Brussel Sprout Chips 42
BBQ Chicken Melt Cups 138
BBQ Chicken Patties 139
BBQ Fried Chicken 123
BBQ Muffin Snack 40
BBQ Pork Pizza 180
Beef Muffins Snack 39
Beef Stuffed Mushrooms 177
Black Pepper Almonds 58
Black Pepper Brussels Sprout Chips 41
Black Pepper Chicken Thighs 128
Black Pepper Flounder 118
Black Pepper Parmesan Crackers 46
Black Pepper Parmesan Salmon 94
Blackened Chicken Patties 144
Blueberry Breakfast Cake 26
Blueberry Cake 64
Blueberry Cheesecake 71
Blueberry Dark Chocolate Granola Bars 33
Blueberry Pancake 12
Broccoli and Bacon Fritters 192
Broccoli and Grits 165
Broccoli and Mushroom Fritters 162
Broccoli Cheese Fritters 161
Broccoli Cheese Soup 157
Broccoli Crunch 47
Broccoli Parmesan Fritters 162
Broccoli Red Pepper Fritters 163
Brussel Sprout Chips 41
Brussels and Garlic Chicken 125
Brussels and Pork Chops 186
Brussels and Roasted Pork Chops 189
Brussels Hash 24
Brussels Sprout Casserole 156
Brussels, Tomatoes and Pork Chops 188
Buffalo Chicken Melt Cups 138
Buffalo Chicken Pizza 121
Buffalo Fried Chicken 136
Butter Cookies 82
Butternut Squash Soup 154

C

Cajun Butter Shrimp 120
Cajun Cauliflower Crunch 51
Cajun Chicharrones 37
Cajun Roasted Chicken Thighs 142
Cajun Salmon Fish Sticks 102
Cajun Salmon 94
Cajun Seared Scallops 110
Cajun Shrimp Bacon Bake 104
Cajun Tuna Cakes 97
Cajun Tuna Melt Cups 106
Caramel Cake 65
Caramel Fudge Brownies 79
Carrot Cheese Fritters 161
Cauliflower and Bacon Fritters 193
Cauliflower Crunch 47
Cauliflower Soup 158
Cayenne Almonds 57
Cayenne Brussels Sprout Chips 41
Cayenne Zucchini Chips 50
Cheddar Chicken Melt Cups 137
Cheddar Crackers 44
Cheddar Jalapeno Muffins 20
Cheddar Tuna Melt Cups 106
Cheesecake Fudge Brownies 81
Cheesey Stromboli 171
Cheesy Bacon Fritters 193
Cheesy Bacon Pancake 28
Cheesy Bacon Rollups 194
Cheesy Brussels Sprout Salad 172
Cheesy Chicharrones 36
Cheesy Egg Casserole 157
Cheesy Garlic Bread Muffins 37
Cheesy Italian Meatloaf 174
Cheesy Pancake 29
Cheesy Zucchini Bake 10
Chicharrones 35
Chicken and Egg Salad 151
Chicken Melt Cups 136
Chicken Nuggets 124
Chicken Patties 139
Chicken Pepper Nachos 32
Chicken Stuffed Mushrooms 146
Chicken Zucchini Boats 145
Chili Lime Broccoli Crunch 50
Chipotle Cheddar Crackers 45
Chocolate Almonds 61
Chocolate Cake 68
Chocolate Chip Almond Cookies 83
Chocolate Chip Cake 66
Chocolate Chip Cheesecake 73
Chocolate Chip Cookies 81
Chocolate Chip Shortbread 91
Chocolate Coconut Brownies 78
Chocolate Keto Cheesecake 72
Chocolate Mint Brownies 78
Chocolate Muffins 19
Chocolate Pancake 13
Chocolate Peanut Butter Walnuts 62
Chocolate Shortbread 91
Chocolate Walnuts Brownies 77
Chocolate Walnuts 60
Cinnamon Almond Pancake 13
Cinnamon Cake 64
Cinnamon Cheesecake 72
Cinnamon Chocolate Chip Cookies 88
Classic Meatballs 175
Cocoa Chicharrones 36
Cocoa Cookies 86
Coconut Cheesecake 75
Coconut Chocolate Pancake 15
Coconut Cookies 82
Coconut Dark Chocolate Granola Bars 34
Coconut Pancake 14
Coconut Rum Pancake 14
Coconut Shortbread 92
Cod and Asparagus 111
Cod Fish Sticks 98
Crab and Spinach Mushrooms 117
Crab Stuffed Mushrooms 117
Cranberry Dark Chocolate Granola Bars 32
Cream Cheese and Asparagus Stuffed Chicken 135
Cream Cheese and Kale Stuffed Chicken 135
Cream Cheese and Spinach Stuffed Chicken 134
Cream Cheese Cookies 89
Cream of Asparagus Soup 152
Creamy Baked Scallops 110
Creamy Brussels and Garlic Chicken 126
Creamy Garlic Chicken Thighs 125
Creamy Garlic Ground Chicken 133

Creamy Garlic Ground Turkey 133
Creamy Garlic Pork Chops 185
Creamy Olive Chicken 134
Creamy Tomato Chicken 131
Creamy Tomato Chicken 132
Creamy Tomato Turkey 132
Creamy Tuscan Chicken 131
Creamy Tuscan Pork Chops 184
Crispy Flounder 96
Crispy Salmon 93
Crispy Scallops 110
Crispy Shrimp 112
Crunchy Garlic Salmon 93
Cucumber Chips 54
Curried Lamb Meatballs 197
Curried Omelet 15
Curry Brussels and Lamb Chops 198

D
Deviled Egg Salad 172
Dijon Baked Chicken Breast 122
Dijon Baked Pork Chops 183
Dijon Baked Salmon 109
Dijon Roasted Chicken Thighs 142
Dijon Roasted Pork Chops 189
Dill and Onion Cucumber Chips 55
Dilly Almonds 56
Double Chocolate Brownies 76
Double Chocolate Cookies 87
Double Dark Chocolate Granola Bars 33

E
Easy Baked Eggs 5
Egg Cobb Salad 177
Egg Salad 152
Egg Stuffed Peppers and Cheese 23
Eggplant Bacon Caprese Rollups 194
Eggplant Bacon Hummus Rollups 195
Eggplant Caprese Rollups 167
Eggplant Parmesan Rollups 167
Eggplant Tahini Rollups 168
Eggplant Zucchini Rollups 167
Espresso Brownies 79
Espresso Cake 67
Espresso Muffins 20
Extra Cheese Pizza 165
Extra Juicy Meatballs 196

F
Fajita Chicken 150
Fall Broccoli Salad 173
Fast Seared Scallops 108
French Herb Omelet 15
Fruit and Nut Keto Granola 21
Fudge Brownies 76

G
Garlic Almonds 57
Garlic Brussel Sprout Chips 43
Garlic Butter Shrimp 119
Garlic Chicken and Spinach 129
Garlic Chicken Bacon Bake 144
Garlic Chicken Bake 145
Garlic Chicken Patties 140
Garlic Dijon Baked Salmon 109
Garlic Meatloaf 175
Garlic Parmesan Chicken Thighs 128
Garlic Parmesan Cucumber Chips 55
Garlic Shrimp Bacon Bake 103
Garlic Shrimp Prosciutto Bake 104
Garlic Shrimp Tuna Bake 105
Garlic, Spinach and Artichoke Casserole 155
Garlicky Cauliflower Crunch 58
Garlicy and Crab Stuffed Mushrooms 118
Gingerbread Cheesecake 74
Greek Garlic Chicken 124
Greek Garlic Pork Chops 184
Green Power Soup 160
Gremolata Eggs 17
Gruyere Shrimp Bacon Bake 104

H
Ham and Cheese Omelet 30
Ham and Cheese Stromboli 182
Ham and Pepper Melt 26
Ham, Cheese and Mushroom Melt 25
Hard Boiled Eggs 4
Hazelnut Brownies 79
Hazelnut Cake 69
Hazelnut Chocolate Chip Cookies 85
Hazelnut Cookies 85
Herbed Butter Flounder 119
Herbed Chicharrones 36
Herbed Fried Chicken 123
Herbed Parmesan Crackers 43
Herbed Tuna Melt Cups 105
Herby Cheesy Muffins 38

I
Indian Masala Omelet 16
Indian Style Lamb Meatballs 197
Italian Fish Sticks 101
Italian Lunch Lasagna 181
Italian Seasoned Chicken Nuggets 130
Italian Style Flounder 115

J
Jalapeno Chicken Melt Cups 137
Jalapeno Tuna Melt Cups 105

K
Keto Blueberry Muffins 6
Keto Chocolate Chip Muffins 6
Keto Fried Chicken 121
Keto Pizza 164
Keto Shortbread 89
Keto Tuna Melt Cups 103
Kimchi Breakfast 19

L
Lamb Meatballs 196
Lemon Cheesecake 74
Lemon Dill Parchment Salmon 114
Lemon Dill Wrapped Cod 113
Lemon Eggplant Rollups 169
Lemon Feta Garlic Chicken 128
Lemon Garlic Chicken Thighs 125
Lemon Garlic Lamb Chops 197
Lemon Garlic Pork Chops 185
Lemon Parchment Chicken 148
Lemon Parchment Salmon 116
Lemon Pepper Broccoli Crunch 48
Lemon Pepper Chicken Patties 140
Lemon Pepper Fish Sticks 101
Lemon Pepper Pork Chops 186
Lemon Roasted Chicken Thighs 142
Lemon Scallops 108
Lemon Shortbread 90
Lemon Tuna Cakes 98
Lime Shortbread 90
Loaded Baked Zucchini 153
Loaded Veggie Pizza 159

M
Maple Bacon Chicken Thighs 127
Maple Broccoli Crunch 49
Maple Brussel Sprout Chips 43
Maple Brussels and Pork Chops 187
Maple Brussels Sprout Salad 171
Maple Chicken Thighs with Brussels 127
Maple Dijon Baked Chicken Breast 122
Maple Dijon Baked Pork Chops 183
Maple Dijon Baked Salmon 109
Maple Roasted Chicken Thighs 143
Maple Roasted Pork Chops and Veggies 189
Maple Sesame Chicken Breast 149
Maple Walnut Chicken Breast with Spinach 149
Maple Walnut Chicken Breast 148
Maple Walnut Flounder 100
Maple Walnut Salmon 99
Marinara Chicken 132
Mascarpone Cheesecake 75
Meat Lovers Omelet 8
Mediterranean Chicken 147
Mediterranean Flounder 115
Mediterranean Salmon 114
Mexican Chocolate Walnuts 61
Mexican Stuffed Mushrooms 177
Minty Lamb Chops 198
Mocha Muffins 20
Mug Lasagna 166
Mushroom and Bacon Fritters 193
Mushroom Lunch Lasagna 166
Mushroom Spinach Fritatta 3

N
Nut and Dark Chocolate Granola Bars 35
Nutty Granola 21
NY Keto Cheesecake 70

O
Onion Lasagna 170

P
Parmesan Butter Flounder 119
Parmesan Flounder and Asparagus 112
Parmesan Garlic Bread Muffins 38
Parmesan Salmon and Asparagus 112
Parmesan Salmon and Brussel Sprouts 113
Parmesan Shrimp 120
Parmesan Tuna and Brussel Sprouts 113
Peanut Butter and Jelly Cookies 60
Peanut Butter Brownies 77
Peanut Butter Cake 68
Peanut Butter Chocolate Chip Cookies 59
Peanut Butter Chocolate Chip Cookies 84

Peanut Butter Chocolate Cookies 87
Peanut Butter Cookies 59
Peanut Butter Cookies 84
Peanut Butter Flaxseed Cookies 59
Peanut Butter Shortbread 92
Pepper and Cheese Meatloaf 174
Pepper and Prosciutto Chicken 141
Pepper Pancake 29
Pepper Stuffed Mushrooms 158
Pepper Stuffed Spinach and Feta Eggs 23
Pepper Stuffed Spinach Parmesan Baked Eggs 22
Pepper Stuffed Spinach Parmesan Baked Eggs 24
Pepperoni Mozzarella Stromboli 182
Peppers and Eggs 24
Pesto Fried Chicken 151
Pesto Omelet 17
Pizza Crackers 45
Prosciutto and Lemon Chicken 144
Prosciutto and Parmesan Pizza 180
Prosciutto Omelet 18
Prosciutto Parmesan Omelet 19
Prosciutto Wrapped Ahi Ahi 116
Prosciutto Wrapped Chicken 140
Prosciutto Wrapped Cod 107
Prosciutto Wrapped Salmon 108
Prosciutto Wrapped Tuna Bites 116
Pumpkin Chocolate Chip Cookies 88
Pumpkin Pancake 13
Pumpkin Soup 160
Pumpkin Spice Cheesecake 73
Pumpkin Spice Cookies 88

R

Raspberry Almond Pancake 11
Raspberry Breakfast Cake 28
Raspberry Brownies 80
Raspberry Cheesecake 71
Raspberry Cookies 86
Raspberry Muffins 7
Red Hot Broccoli Crunch 48
Red Hot Tuna Cakes 97
Red Pepper Breakfast Cake 27
Red Pepper Meatballs 195
Roasted Broccoli Salad 173
Roasted Brussels Sprout Salad 170

Roasted Chicken Thighs and Brussels 143
Roasted Chicken Thighs 141
Roasted Garlic Eggs 18
Roasted Mushrooms and Grits 152
Roasted Pepper Grits 153
Roasted Squash Grits 165
Roasted Veggie Soup 159
Rotisserie Style Chicken Thighs 129

S

Salmon and Asparagus 111
Salmon Cakes 96
Salmon Egg Salad 120
Salmon Fish Sticks 102
Salt and Vinegar Zucchini Chips 51
Sausage and Cheese Omelet 7
Sausage and Spinach Omelet 8
Sausage Omelette 30
Scallops and Spinach 111
Sea Salt and Black Pepper Cucumber Chips 56
Seedy Breakfast Granola 22
Seedy Chocolate Granola Bars 34
Seedy Cookies 85
Sesame Tuna Melt Cups 106
Sesame Walnut Tuna 100
Smoked Zucchini Chips 51
Smokey Cucumber Chips 55
Smoky Muffins 40
Soft Cheesy Pretzels 54
Soft Cinnamon Pretzels 53
Soft Garlic Parmesan Pretzels 52
Soft Pecan Pretzels 53
Soft Pretzels 52
Spice Cake 65
Spicy Broccoli Cheese Fritters 162
Spicy Cauliflower Crunch 47
Spicy Cheesy Omelet 17
Spicy Chicharrones 35
Spicy Chicken Bacon Bake 145
Spicy Chicken Melt Cups 136
Spicy Chicken Nuggets 130
Spicy Chocolate Walnuts 60
Spicy Cod Fish Sticks 100
Spicy Crunchy Garlic Salmon 94
Spicy Crunchy Salmon 93
Spicy Egg Salad 169

Spicy Eggplant Rollups   168
Spicy Fried Chicken   122
Spicy Garlic Bread Muffins   38
Spicy Hot Pepper Nachos   31
Spicy Meatballs 176
Spicy Meatballs 196
Spicy Pepper Lasagna   170
Spicy Sriracha Egg Salad 172
Spinach and Artichoke Casserole 154
Spinach and Bacon Casserole   190
Spinach and Maple Bacon Casserole   191
Spinach and Sundried Tomato Casserole   155
Spinach Parmesan Baked Eggs   5
Spinach Parmesan Egg Casserole 154
Spinach Stuffed Mushrooms   158
Strawberry and Nut Cereal   21
Strawberry Arugula Pizza   160
Strawberry Breakfast Bread   27
Strawberry Cheesecake   70
Strawberry Feta Pancake 29
Strawberry Fudge Brownies   80
Strawberry Muffins   7
Strawberry Pancake   12
Strawberry Vanilla Cake 66
Super Seed Parmesan Crackers   44
Sweet and Salty Almonds   57
Sweet and Salty Chicken 150
Sweet and Spicy Chicken Nuggets   130
Sweet and Spicy Dijon Baked Chicken Breast   123
Sweet and Spicy Dijon Baked Pork Chops 183
Sweet and Spicy Walnuts 62
Sweet Broccoli Crunch   48
Sweet Candied Pecans   58
Sweet Veggies Roasted Pork Chops   190
Sweet Zucchini Chips   54

T

Taco Cucumber Chips   56
Teriyaki Chicken Melt Cups   138

Three Cheese Omelet   4
Tomato Lasagna 169
Tomato Parchment Chicken   149
Tomato Parchment Cod   115
Tuna Cakes   96
Tuna Sticks   98
Tuna Stuffed Mushrooms 95
Turkey Garlic Mushrooms   147
Turkey Pepper Nachos   31
Turkey Stuffed Mushrooms   147

V

Vanilla Cake   63
Vanilla Raspberry Cake   63
Vegetable Hash 25
Veggie Baked Zucchini Boats   163
Veggie Crunch   49
Veggie Egg Bread   11
Veggie Melt   26
Veggie Omelet   3
Veggie Pepper Nachos   31
Veggies Roasted Pork Chops   188

W

Walnut Cake   69
Walnut Cookies 82
Walnut Shortbread   92
Warmed Nuts and Grits   164

Y

Yellow Zucchini Chips   51

Z

Za'atar Eggs   16
Zucchini and Bacon Egg Bread   10
Zucchini and Sausage Bake   9
Zucchini Bacon Rollups 195
Zucchini Breakfast Cake 27
Zucchini Caprese Rollups   168
Zucchini Chips   50
Zucchini Hash   25

Made in the USA
Coppell, TX
27 January 2020